CREATIVE INTERIOR DESIGN

BCA

LONDON   NEW YORK   SYDNEY   TORONTO

© Ward Lock Limited, 1994
A Cassell Imprint
Villiers House, 41-47 Strand, London WC2N 5JE

This edition is published 1994 by BCA by arrangement with
Cassell.

Based on *Creating a Home*
© Eaglemoss Publications Limited, 1994

ISBN 0 7063 7275 1

Printed in Spain by Cronion S.A.

10 9 8 7 6 5 4 3 2 1

CONTENTS

INTRODUCTION

HAVE you ever leafed through the pages of a glossy magazine and despaired of giving your home that easy flair without a team of professional interior designers to guide you? If you have, help is at hand. *Creative Interior Design* contains a wealth of photographs to inspire you, while detailed analyses of what creates a particular effect provide the knowledge and confidence you need to achieve it for yourself. The book is divided into five chapters which lead you stage by stage through all the basics of interior design.

At the heart of all good interior decorating lies an understanding of colour and how to handle it, and the first two chapters of this book are devoted to this subject. The first chapter examines the basic principles of colour, explaining the intricacies of the colour wheel and how you can use it to decide which colours will tone, which ones will harmonise, which will clash and which ones will complement each other. You learn how to build up a sample board of colour swatches and fabrics for an at-a-glance reference to how your finished decorating scheme will look. There is also advice on how to achieve the cleverest designer trick of all, making your rooms lead visually from one to the next, so that your house looks a coherent whole. There's also guidance on using colours to make rooms seem larger, smaller, warmer or more airy, and the chapter ends with sections on understanding patterns and textures and combining these to achieve a particular feel.

Chapter 2 takes eleven colour groups in turn, from quiet naturals, beiges and creams to the richest of reds and the stark simplicity of black and white. Using samples of paints, papers, fabrics, carpets and accessories in each colour range, this chapter shows you how to use these colours in bedrooms, bathrooms, living rooms and kitchens. Every section ends with helpful hints on choosing and using accent colours.

Chapter 3 looks at a number of popular design styles – ranging from the charm of the country cottage to the restrained elegance of the grand townhouse, from the streamlined leather and chrome lines of the city to the clutter of the Victorian home. Each section outlines the various decorations, soft furnishings, furniture and accessories that create each style.

A practical chapter follows, aimed at people who want to know exactly how to make the soft furnishings to complete their chosen look. Here are full step-by-step instructions for making elegant curtains and cushions, luxurious pelmets, swags and tails, practical blinds, easy lampshades and loose covers for furniture.

The final chapter of the book is crammed with bright ideas for giving your home a special, personal feel. Arranging things attractively is an art in itself, and there are hints on hanging groups of pictures on the wall, displaying a cherished collection of china and glassware, creating special effects with lighting and making the best decorative use of plants and flowers. There are practical soft furnishing ideas for bedheads and bay windows, and a host of decorating tips for small projects like repainting old chairs as well as special paint finishes such as ragging and sponging.

Whether you prefer modern sophistication or old world charm, whether you are tackling a whole house or a single room, this book is the perfect source of inspiration and reference. Rich in ideas and practical know-how, *Creative Interior Design* contains in one volume all you need to know about making a beautiful, individual home.

CHAPTER I

CHOOSING A
COLOUR SCHEME

THREE WAYS TO COLOUR SCHEME

Does choosing a colour scheme pose problems? Here are three ways to help you get it right.

Colour is probably the most useful of all the tools at the decorator's disposal. Handled properly, it can make a small room seem larger, a dark room lighter, or bring about a complete change of atmosphere.

Whether you're creating a colour scheme from scratch or updating an existing one, it's important to plan it properly. Take your time, get ideas from other people's colour schemes – in homes, offices or even restaurants – and make a note of those colours that you find satisfying and pleasing.

Before you commit yourself to a particular colour, sit down and work out what kind of look you are aiming to achieve. Start by defining the mood you want to convey – it might be warm and cosy, cool and airy, bright and cheerful, restful, pretty or stylish. Then think of which colours convey that mood. For example, warm pinks and reds create a cosy atmosphere, while cool pastels and whites give an airy, spacious feel.

Choosing colours and putting them together is partly a matter of taste, although there are general guidelines that can prove helpful.

First of all, *colours look different in different types of light.* A red which has a distinctly blue tinge in a showroom under strip lights may lose its blueness and appear a warm clear red when seen in a sunny room. A rich blue used in a dark room will appear even richer, but that same blue used in a brightly lit room can lose much of its intensity. So it is important to try out a large sample of the colour in the room in which it will be used.

Secondly, *a colour affects the colours next to it.* You may adore a certain pink and a certain green, but together they might prove disastrous. On the other hand, you may find a grey or beige dull on its own, but exactly right partnered with a lively splash of bright pink or orange.

This leads directly to the third point: *how much there is of a colour affects how you see it.* An entire room of bright pink or orange may be hard to live with, but small concentrations of those colours can make an all-white room 'sing'.

If you find choosing colours and patterns a little confusing – and most of us do – on the following five pages you will find three approaches to colour scheming, each using a different starting point.

Match making
There may be furniture, carpets or curtains already in the room you want to decorate, so use them as a starting point. The decorative scheme shown on the next page is based on this carpet sample.

The 'theme' scheme

The room above has a predominantly blue scheme but there are other colours used, all derived from samples assembled around the blue theme.

Most of the wall-coverings and fabrics here are dappled or textured for added interest and to counteract the cold quality that flat blue paint sometimes has.

Note how lighting affects the colours – the spotlights in this room make the colours less bright than the samples seen in daylight conditions (opposite).

POINTS OF DEPARTURE

Few of us have the luxury of being able to create a room scheme from scratch. You may be stuck with a major investment that can't be changed easily – a carpet or sofa, say – around which you have to plan. This can be turned to advantage, though, because it gives you a starting point from which to work. Indeed, overcoming limitations can be a greater spur to creativity!

Collecting samples One way to avoid expensive mistakes is to try out your chosen colours and patterns by collecting samples – like those opposite – so that you can see how they work together. Start by finding a sample of the fixture you can't change (if you can't find an exact match for your own carpet, for example, look out for one that's close to it in colour and texture).

Now start collecting scraps of fabrics, wallpaper, coloured wools and so on, in the colours you want to combine with your 'permanent fixture'. (You will find that it helps if one or two of the samples incorporate a bit of the 'fixture' colour to help tie it all together.) The current trend for co-ordinated ranges of fabrics, papers and borders makes this all much easier and more successful. You'll also be able to see whether the amount of

pattern is appealing, or too busy.

Mix and match Don't restrict yourself only to one range of tones. A room with light apricot walls, mid-apricot furniture and a dark apricot carpet may match perfectly, but it is also in danger of looking dull and flat. With imagination, any colour can be interpreted in many different ways. Blue, for example, can be 'true blue', blue-green or blue-violet – it can also be light or dark, pale or intense.

Subtle patterns mix and match more easily than strong, large-scale ones. Here mini-pattern and Berber weave carpets meet the practical need for a carpet

pattern without being too dominant.

The texture of a sample is also important. The blue of a cotton weave may be exactly the same as that of a shiny ceramic vase, but both 'read' differently.

Collecting samples will help you get the feel of how to vary your theme colour in interesting ways. Get together a good range of samples, then start whittling down the choice to your final selection. Finally, you can experiment with small bits of contrasting or intense accent colour to see which adds the right 'zest' that brings the whole scheme to life.

Variations on a theme

When collecting samples, remember to look for different surface textures and aim to incorporate one or two accent colours, too. Here the blues and blue-greens work well with either the grey or beige carpet – but notice how touches of terracotta and the mellow maple of the picture frame bring it all to life.

TAKE AN EXISTING PATTERN

Professional fabric designers are expert at handling colour, so if there is a strong pattern on the carpet, walls, curtains or upholstery, follow the designer's example and use those colours as the basis for your scheme.

The colour scheme of this room (left) is based on the upholstery fabric of the sofa (right). The pale apricot background colour becomes the background colour for the walls and curtains. The cool grey-blue in the pattern is echoed in the carpet, cushions and tablecloth, while the warm terracotta is used as an accent colour in the lampshade, book bindings, table underskirt and cushion covers.

The off-white in the fabric pattern is repeated in the coffee table, shelves and panelling, to provide a welcome touch

of freshness and stop the scheme from looking too heavy.

A pattern can tell you which colours go well together, but it can also suggest in which proportions they work best.

Look again at the picture on the left and you can see how this works in practice. The largest colour area in the pattern – apricot – is also the largest in the room. The second most dominant area, the carpet, picks up the grey-blue. Likewise, the accents of white and terracotta are used sparingly to avoid overpowering the main colours. Proportion is an exercise in subtlety and colour patterns will give you the key to a successful scheme.

By choosing such a harmonious blend of colours and tones, the owner has created a room which is elegant, restful and easy on the eye.

◁ *The 'pattern' scheme*
Taking the sofa covering as a starting point, this room's colour scheme is derived purely from the fabric pattern – apricot, grey-blue, terracotta and white.

Notice, too, that the colours are used in similar proportions: the apricot is the main colour and the grey-blue the secondary one, while others act as accents (right).

BRIGHT IDEA

COLOUR CUES

Use patterned fabric as a guide when deciding where and how much of each colour to use in a room.

Work out roughly how much of each colour is used in the pattern – the largest areas of colour, right down to small accent colours. Now list the parts of the room to be 'coloured',

from the largest areas, walls and floor, to small accessories.

But don't stick too rigidly to the proportion idea. The dominant colours will depend on the room's size and available light: a dark colour on the walls may not be advisable in a small room, for instance.

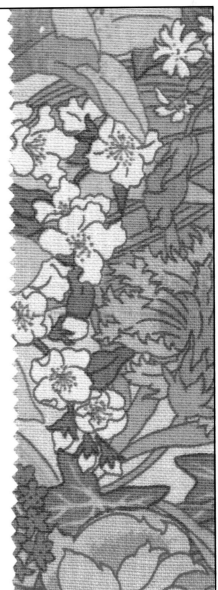

In the fabric, mid-green is the main colour; **carpet** is the largest area.

Pale green is the next main colour; **walls** are another main surface area.

The 'key' fabric used for the **curtains**, ties the scheme together.

Pale wooden **furniture** echoes the pale browns in the fabric.

Brightest colours in the fabric are used as accent colours in **lamps, vases** and **cushions**.

A pale, muted blue is used on the **bedspread**.

Finding inspiration

Cut out and collect pictures of rooms that you find appealing; this way, you can pinpoint which colours you feel comfortable with and use them as a basis for creating your own colour schemes.

The gold and apricot tones of the magazine photographs (left) were the inspiration for the bedroom scheme (above). Soft yellow walls, an apricot carpet and creamy lace curtains create a warm, mellow mood, enhanced by subtle accents of clear pink and off-white.

FIND YOUR PREFERRED COLOURS

You may subconsciously have a favourite colour or colour scheme but be unable to put it into words. Or perhaps you are confused by the vast choice of decorating colours.

To overcome this problem, borrow as many interior decorating books and magazines as possible. It doesn't matter if some are out of date, or don't feature many examples of the type of room you're planning to decorate, so long as they contain plenty of colour pictures.

Quickly thumb through them all, ignoring the style of the particular rooms, but marking the colour schemes of those that appeal to you. When you've finished, put the whole lot away and out of your mind.

Return to the books and magazines you selected a week later. You may be surprised to find that most of the pictures you selected have one or more colours in common and that frequently those colours are used in a similar way. By pinpointing your preferences, you can use this information to plan your ideal colour scheme.

Remember that colours you may like to wear are not necessarily colours you can live in!

THE LANGUAGE OF COLOUR

Understanding colour will give you the confidence to create successful colour schemes.

Different colour schemes can make the same room seem cosy or elegant, soothing, stimulating, dramatic, even playful — and can even appear to alter the room's proportions. But, perhaps because there are so many choices, it is often hard to know where to start.

The way professional designers talk about colour can make it sound very complicated. But once you understand the basic principles of colour theory, you'll be able to create colour schemes with confidence and achieve exactly the mood and effect you want.

THE COLOUR WHEEL
It is said that the human eye can distinguish over 10 million different colours. But every single one is based on the colours of the rainbow — red, yellow, orange, green, blue, indigo and violet — plus black and white.

To show how these basic colours relate to each other and how they combine to make all the other colours, scientists have come up with the colour wheel.

Primary colours The three key colours are pure red, pure yellow and pure blue. They are known as primaries, because you cannot mix them from other colours. All other pure colours can be mixed from primaries.

Secondary colours Orange, green and violet are mixed from equal amounts of two primaries. In between come any number of intermediate colours — dozens of different yellow-greens, blue-greens, blue-violets and so on — all mixed from their neighbour colours.

Contrast colours Colours that contrast most strongly are directly opposite each other on the wheel — red and green, yellow-orange and blue-violet, for example.

Harmonious colours These lie next to each other on the wheel. They share a common base colour — for example yellow-orange, orange and red-orange all have the colour orange in common.

Pastels, shades and mixtures The colour wheel is shown in pure colours (ie colours that are created from a mixture of only two neighbouring colours). But of course fabrics and paints and carpets also come paler (less intense) or lighter (with a mixture of white, known commonly as pastel). They come 'muted' or 'shaded' — with a mixture of grey or black. Or they come in subtle mixtures where a hint of colour from another part of the wheel is added — yellow-orange with a touch of blue, or a hint of red added to yellow-green.

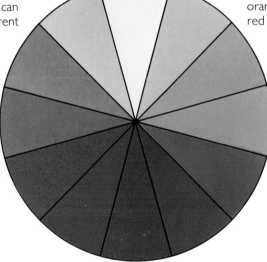

▷ **The colour wheel**
The wheel is a useful tool for understanding how colours relate to each other and how to combine them in colour schemes.

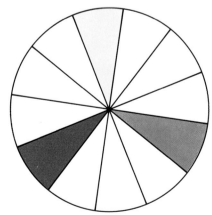

△ **Primary colours**
The colour wheel shows how primary colours — pure red, yellow and blue — divide the wheel into three equal parts.

▽ **Secondary colours**
Pure green is made from equal amounts of yellow and blue; violet from red and blue; and orange from red and yellow.

Warm colours

Reds, pinks, oranges, yellows – the colours associated with sunshine and firelight – create a cosy, welcoming atmosphere. Choose these warm colours – on the left-hand side of the colour wheel – to make a large room look smaller and friendlier, to brighten up a sunless room, or simply because you want a warm effect.

Warm peach walls, pink patterned curtains, rusty red tones in the carpet and a mass of cushions in pinks, reds and yellows set the scene in this cheerful living room. The touches of white and the cool green foliage of the plants help to balance the warm colours and prevent them from becoming overpowering.

When planning a warm scheme remember that the closer the colour is to a 'warm' primary (red or yellow), the stronger it is. Large amounts of such colours can be hard to live with, so it's often wiser to choose their softer cousins, such as pink, peach and primrose yellow, reserving the stronger colours for accents only.

Cool colours

The other half of the colour wheel is made up of greens, blue-greens and blues – the colours of cool water and shady forests, azure skies and dappled meadows. These are the colours to use if you want a room to have a cool, calm atmosphere.

The living room shown here has a distinctly tropical flavour: the various shades of cool blue used on the walls and seat coverings evoke the sea and the sky, and are perfectly complemented by the pale, sandy colours of the furniture and flooring, while the plants add accents of lush green.

Cool colours always appear further away than warm ones. That's why cool colours make a small room appear more spacious, by 'pushing back' the walls. Be careful, however, if the room faces away from the light – cool colours here could look too bleak. Rooms that benefit from a lot of natural light can take almost any of the cool colours without appearing cold.

Contrasting colours

You can brighten up a room by using a contrasting scheme which features colours opposite each other on the wheel – for example, red and green, or blue and orange. These pairs of colours are known as 'complementaries'. When placed close together, they intensify each other, and the result is lively and vibrant.

In this room scheme the colours have been chosen to create a cheerful, sunny effect. Contrasting colours – red and green, blue and yellow – appear in the wallpaper, paintwork and furnishings. The use of white is refreshing and accentuates the bright colours.

Contrasting colours used in equal amounts tend to produce an uneasy effect because they compete with each other, so make sure that one colour dominates. Here, the yellow sofa provides a focal point which pulls the whole room together. The green area of window is smaller, while red is only used in small touches.

Harmonious colours

If you pick two, three or four colours that lie next to each other on the colour wheel, you can be sure that they will combine comfortably because they are closely related.

Examples of harmonious groups of colours include pink, apricot, peach and gold – or clear blues, blue-green, aqua and green – or bluebell blue, mauve and heathery purple. They work together because nothing clashes or dominates and there is a common theme between one colour and the next.

The room scheme on the left dispels the myth that 'blue and green should never be seen'. Fresh minty greens, blue-greens and emerald greens are layered upon one another, with the colours of the room echoed in accessories such as the lamp and vases.

The reds and yellows in the sofa fabric provide a touch of warmth to offset the cool effect created by the greens and blues; a small accent of contrasting colour like this is a clever way to add pep to a harmonious scheme.

Pastel colours

Pure colours lightened with a lot of white are known as pastels. For example, red lightened with white becomes pink, pure green becomes apple green, orange becomes apricot.

These soft, gentle colours – sometimes called 'ice-cream' or 'sugared almond' hues – are always popular, since they look so fresh and pretty. They blend effortlessly with the lighter range of muted colours and with modern and traditional styles of furnishing. It is also interesting to note that any pastel colour will coordinate with another – even opposites on the colour wheel. This is because all the colours have a common element in that they contain a lot of white.

The light, airy and romantic style of this living room is achieved through the generous use of fabrics in pale blues, greens and mauves. Notice how several different patterns combine without clashing, because they're all pastels.

Subtle and muted colours

Pure colours which are darkened with black or grey are known as 'shades' or 'muted colours'. Then there are the more subtle colours which are a mixture of two or more pure colours – for example, orange with a bit of blue. But there is nothing dull about colours with such evocative names as russet brown, mustard yellow, sage green, petrol blue, or 'crushed berry' reds such as plum, mulberry and blackberry. Think, too, of the rich, exuberant lacquer colours inspired by the East – crimson, emerald green and gold.

Here muted colours create a cosy, autumnal feel. A variety of subtle and muted colours is used – warm pinks, browns and terracottas offset by cool greens and blues.

Since muted colours contain an element of black, they look particularly striking when teamed with black accents. However, you also need to introduce a sprinkling of brighter colours, to prevent the scheme from becoming too heavy.

Neutrals

In the home designer's terms, neutrals range from white, through to creams, beiges, tans and browns, and from the palest silver grey through to black. They are useful for combining with more definite colours and you can also use them to create all-neutral schemes.

Inspiration for neutral schemes can be found in the earth colours of nature. Think of the bleached white of sand, the soft browns and tans of earth and wood, and the yellowed white of ripening corn.

The group of neutral-coloured textiles shown here echoes the colours and textures of natural objects such as shells and pebbles, marble and wood. Textures and surfaces play an important part in any neutral scheme, since they add variety and interest.

Neutral colours are easy to live with, and provide a perfect foil for interesting furniture, pictures or plants.

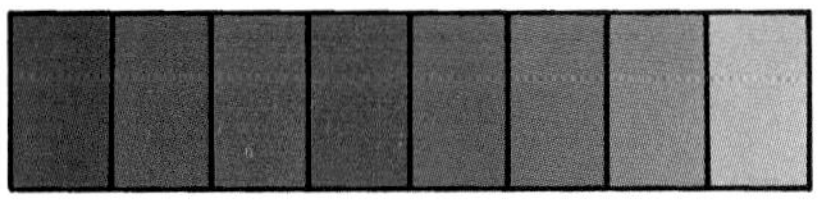

Tones

When you're decorating a room, it's important to think about the range of tones. Tone describes the lightness or darkness of a colour, as illustrated by these pink, red and maroon samples in light, medium and dark tones.

A room containing only light and dark tones can look disjointed and 'bitty' – so remember to include some mid-tones to link the lights and darks and give the scheme more flow. (In the group of samples, see how deeper pinks and muted reds link the very pale pinks and maroons).

To understand how tone works, think of a black and white photograph, where colours are converted into black, white and grey tones. Now imagine a room decorated entirely in light-toned colours. Boring and bland, it would photograph virtually as the same shade of grey. By using a range of tones – whatever the colours – a room scheme becomes more satisfying.

ACCENT COLOURS

It's amazing how small touches of bright and contrasting colour bring a room to life. Most colour schemes – particularly ones based on neutrals – benefit from the addition of an accent colour. Accents need to be handled carefully though: two or three patches, not a dozen. Otherwise the effect becomes spotty.

Contrast accents

A room that is predominantly one colour (monochromatic) needs a few accents to add pep and interest. The colour wheel provides a handy, at-a-glance guide to choosing appropriate contrast colours – simply pick one (in this case, blue) from the side opposite the dominant colour (yellow).

Sharp or bright accents

When the scheme is based on a pattern printed in several colours, it's usually effective to pick one colour, then go for touches of a brighter or more intense version of that colour. In this scheme, bright pink piping on the curtains and table mats gives style and zest.

WHOLE HOUSE COLOUR SCHEMES

When faced with four or five rooms to decorate and furnish at once, visual continuity is the secret of success.

Colour inspiration
This hallway is painted in three very pale colours which subtly introduce you to the rest of the house. First, the cream walls create a perfect foil to the stripped pine floorboards and oriental rug. The ceiling arches and radiators are picked out in palest green, the colour carried through into the rooms leading off the hall. The ceiling is palest lavender which again could be echoed in a neighbouring room. White cornices and wood tie the scheme together.

Professional interior designers consider visual unity very important. Experience enables them to see the whole of a house interior as one inter-related, complete decorating unit rather than a series of separate rooms. Viewing in this way helps avoid 'bittiness' and lack of continuity.

In smaller homes where space and light are usually at a premium, creating a light, neutral-coloured background using different shades of white, cream, beige and grey in walls, woodwork and flooring always work well. Any strong colour can then be added as accents with rugs and accessories. These items can easily be changed to give a neutral colour scheme a new look later on.

LINKING – WITH FLOORING

Visual continuity and a feeling of space can be achieved by using the same or similar colour floorings throughout a home. Your choice of floorcoverings do not all have to be exactly the same material or colour to produce an effect of continuity. For instance, a honey or tan miniprint carpet in the hall and on the stairs works well with, perhaps, slightly darker floor tiles in the kitchen and a toning plain caramel carpet for stripped floorboards in the living room.

Again, when it comes to floorcoverings for the whole house, neutral colours such as beige, grey and cream work very successfully because they allow a wide choice of decoration. Choosing a light shade for a floorcovering was once considered hopelessly impractical, but with some of today's new materials this no longer applies. Modern off-white and cream textured vinyls, for example, can be extremely hardwearing and perfect for brightening a dark hallway or kitchen.

A few well-chosen rugs in similar patterns and colours can also link different flooring areas throughout a home by leading the eye through. Oriental rugs in rich colours, dhurries in pastel shades, or strong geometric art deco design rugs in neutral colours can usefully echo and link colours in several room schemes.

▽ *Floor plan*
Each room on this plan echoes some of the colours in the adjacent room. Although the flooring is in different materials, these are linked by the same shade of grey. However, other colour links are more subtle.

FLOORING ALTERNATIVES

Carpet tiles are well worth considering. There are some most attractive neutral colour combinations such as grey/cream or beige/cream. Border effects can be created which also help to lead the eye through from one room to another. In common with other types of tile, damaged carpet tiles can also be easily taken up and replaced.

Some carpet tile ranges are also available with matching carpet. This is particularly useful in open-plan living/dining arrangements where you want the same flooring all the way through from the living room to the dining room. In this case, carpet tiles are a sensible choice in the dining area as floors here are especially vulnerable to spills and stains.

Patterned floorcoverings in neutral colours are a good compromise if you want to break up large expanses of floor and yet at the same time don't want anything too obtrusive. There is a lot of choice now in two-tone fleck, dogtooth checks, small geometric designs and stripes available in both hard and soft floorings.

Some of the newer carpet ranges have small all-over patterns in light or mid-tone colourways that suit smaller homes particularly well.

FLOORING THRESHOLDS

There is one unfortunate snag with the brass and aluminium carpet threshold plates that hold the carpet edges firmly in place in doorways: they can detract from the overall feeling of continuity. There are wooden threshold plates that suit some interior schemes and are also less obtrusive. These can be stained, polished, or painted to blend exactly with a floorcovering.

LINKING – WITH WALL COLOURS AND ACCENTS

The simplest way to handle all the different colours in rooms that lead off a hall or landing is to pick several different shades of the same colour. In this way they harmonize without appearing bland.

First, decide on the mood and whether you want it warm or cool. Magnolia, maize and deep egg-yolk yellow in rooms off a pale cream-painted hall or landing work well together and would give a warm effect. Pale blues, greys and lavender, on the other hand, would give a soft, cool feeling.

Accents in pictures, lighting and accessories also help to lead the eye through from one room to another. The eye will focus on any brilliant, primary coloured accents in an all-neutral scheme.

For instance, a slight touch of red in the framed print of the black and white living room opposite has been repeated in the framed prints in the hallway, red flowers on the dining room table and kitchen accessories. Small touches of red are also echoed in the red enamelled basin taps and striped blind.

▽ **Fabrics, wallpapers and carpet**
These fabrics and co-ordinating wallpapers sparked off the whole downstairs colour scheme. A mid grey carpet is a practical 'through' colour, while touches of bright red in accessories and pictures lead the eye through to the dining area and kitchen.

△ **Dramatic black and white**
Inspired by the wallcoverings and fabrics of the living room, the whole house has been planned from this black and white theme leading through to sunny yellows, creams and turquoise. A mid grey flooring is a good versatile colour that can take a wide range of accents.

△ Floor plan

This light and bright upstairs colour scheme has a soft atmosphere and a more feminine feeling. Walls have been covered with papers based on a range of co-ordinated patterns. Woodwork has been kept light throughout.

LINKING WALL PATTERNS

Today's top interior designers make great use of mixing different prints. It takes a little more care to manage two or more patterns, but with careful planning and attention to scale, proportion and colour matching, some truly original effects can be achieved. Well-chosen wallcovering and fabric patterns can also help to lead the eye through from one room to another. The trick is to think positively and make a bold statement.

Enormous choice now exists in patterned fabrics, wallcoverings and floor-ings. Practically any pattern is available, from spots and geometrics through to abstracts and florals. It is perfectly possible to mix all of them in, say, a complete upstairs or downstairs scheme – once the basic 'through' colours have been decided. And while you're in the mix-and-match game, don't forget that some textures also count as patterns. Painting techniques such as sponging, stippling, marbling and rag-rolling, whether you paint them yourself or use one of the look-alike wallpapers, also help to break up surfaces with pattern.

SCHEMING WITH PATTERNS

Patterns can make large rooms feel cosier but too many in a small room can be claustrophobic. An interesting border with complementary paper and fabric is more effective.

When colour scheming for adjoining rooms, first choose a pattern. In this case, the bathroom wallpaper and frieze inspired the whole upstairs colour scheme. It is a good idea to isolate the colours in the most dominant pattern and build your colour scheme on these. Work in natural daylight as it is difficult to achieve good results in artificial light.

The four rooms and landing in the floor plan opposite are all colour-schemed using a number of co-ordinating papers and borders. The apricot and blue in the bathroom frieze, for instance, are picked out in the spare bedroom's apricot and blue floral wall-papers and co-ordinating fabric. A muted green carpet emphasizes the greens in the frieze.

△ *Rosebud stripe*

This bathroom with co-ordinated wallpaper, frieze and tiles inspired the entire upstairs colour scheme. All the elements are shown in the sample board below.

COLOUR INSPIRATION

When visualizing a hall or landing colour scheme it helps to leave all the doors leading to the adjoining rooms open. You can then see how the hallway and landing walls act as a 'frame' for any rooms off. Instead of creamy-yellow and grey, grey walls and white woodwork in the hall below would look equally good and could lead into cooler neighbouring pale blue-grey and white rooms. For a warmer scheme the framed poster offers further inspiration: picking out the orange, for example, could successfully lead through to adjoining rooms painted in warmer peach and apricot.

Where woodwork is changing colour from one room to the next you are faced with painting the two sides of a door in different colours. Care needs to be taken in deciding exactly where one colour should end and the other begin. When the door is closed all is well, but when the door is open you'll see the edges as well. It works best to paint the opening edge of the door the same colour as the face which opens into the room and the hinged edge to match the other face. This way, when the door is left open, the colour of the visible edge and the face of the door are continuous from whichever room they are viewed.

▽ *Dramatic deco*
Black, cream and grey in this hall carpet and dramatic geometric deco rug team beautifully with cream walls, pale grey woodwork and natural ash furniture.

HANDLING SAMPLES SUCCESSFULLY

Samples – and a well-planned sample board – are the key to working out a colour scheme that turns out the way you want.

The prospect of putting a room scheme together – choosing colours for walls, curtains, floor and wall coverings – is exciting. But with so many possibilities to choose from it's hard to know where to start.

That's where samples come in. By collecting a variety of samples – a mixture of plains, patterns and textures, wallpapers, paint charts, carpets and fabrics – you can make sure the colour scheme is successful.

First you need a starting point of some kind. It could be a sofa, a carpet or some curtains you have already, or perhaps just an idea of the effect you want – warm and lively, for instance, or calm and harmonious. The colour wheel (see The Language of Colour, page 15) is a useful tool to help you identify the colours that work with your sofa or carpet, or that create the effect you're after.

Play with the samples in different groupings. Once you have decided what goes well together take it a step further and make up a sample board like interior designers do. This way, all the swatches of fabric, wallpaper, carpet and paint can be seen together in roughly the proportions they will be used. Then you can start to see in your mind's eye what the finished room will look like.

Finally, allow time for decisions. Impulse buys are usually the ones you regret later. Keep the sample board in the room for a few days to see how you feel about each element after the first flush of enthusiasm wears off.

◁ Patterns
There is an enormous choice available – floral and geometric, abstract and traditional. Small patterns may lose definition in a large room, while big patterns can overpower a small room.

◁ Plains
Plain paint, carpets, or fabrics such as cottons and velvets help to set off patterns and textures.

▷ Textures
Texture describes how a material appeals to the sense of touch – rough or smooth, ribbed or velvety. Fabrics and wallcoverings are also printed to look like textures – spattered, wood grain, watered silk and other tactile effects.

PLANNING AROUND A PATTERN

The starting point can be any existing pattern on a sofa, a carpet, curtains, wallpaper, even a cushion. This will provide the key to your colour scheme and your collection of samples.

Begin by identifying the different colours in the pattern and then select two or three to become the basis for the scheme.

Collect the samples in a variety of plains, patterns and textures, so you have plenty of choice. Plains do not always provide enough visual interest and patterns can sometimes be too much, so it's important to consider textures too.

Collecting the samples It is always better to choose from samples of the actual items – a square of carpet, for example, or a swatch of fabric – rather than from printed images in catalogues which may be different colours from the real thing. If you are designing a room around beiges, for instance, a carpet that turns out slightly pinker than the printed sample could spoil the whole scheme.

Handling patterns It is always difficult to imagine what a finished scheme will look like on the basis of tiny samples. So with large-patterned wallpaper or fabric, try to get a large sample.

Look at the photos in pattern books to help you imagine the overall effect and whether, in quantity, it will be pleasing or overbearing. If in doubt, it's better to buy one roll first rather than put up with long-term disappointment.

Handling paint In the same way, it is difficult to imagine what a whole room painted in a colour chosen from a paint chart will look like. You need to see the colour on its own, not as a tiny patch surrounded by other similar colours.

Once you've narrowed your choice down to one or two colours, it's a good idea to buy a small pot of each and try them out in the room – but remember that wet paint usually dries a shade or two darker. If you paint on to a large sheet of cardboard, you can see how the colour looks by different pieces of furniture, in the sun, or in a dark corner.

▽ **The starting point**
The sofa fabric makes a good base for the scheme because it contains so many colours.

▷ **Plains**
Identify the colours in the sofa fabric and collect samples of them – floor coverings and paint charts, fabrics and wallpapers.

▽ **Patterns**
The sofa fabric has a distinctive pattern, so choose other patterns that include the same colours. Check that pattern scales work together.

▽ **Textures**
Choose textured materials in similar colours for surface interest.

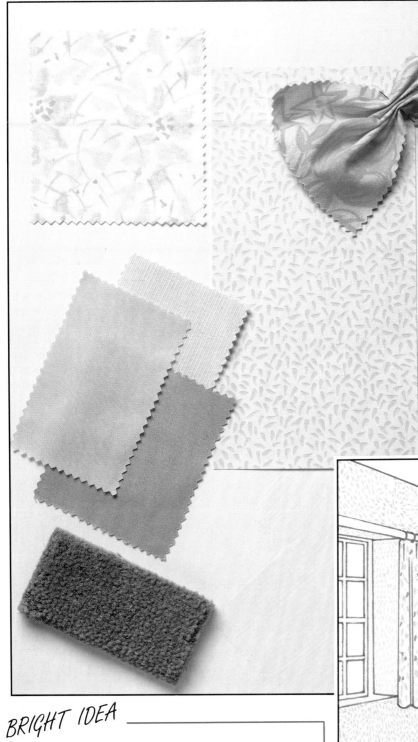

MAKING A SAMPLE BOARD

A sample board is one of the 'tricks of the trade' of professional interior designers. It helps you judge whether colours, patterns and textures work together, and gives a good idea how the scheme will look.

To make a sample board you need a piece of plain cardboard about 20cm × 30cm as a base (the grey/beige inside of a cornflakes packet will do, or a piece of white card, but keep the colour of the board neutral).

Usually about one sixth of the colour in a room comes from the floor, another sixth from curtains and upholstery, and the remaining two thirds from walls and ceiling. Try to aim for samples in these proportions so they virtually cover the board – if necessary, get two or three samples of the chosen carpet to make a large enough patch. If the floor is wood, see if you can find something to match.

Finally, try out bits of wool or paint chips to see which accents work best with the overall colour scheme.

Using the sample board
Left: the sample board. Below: how the room will eventually look.

BRIGHT IDEA

PATTERN HINTS

One problem in choosing a patterned wallpaper or fabric (particularly one with a large design) is imagining how it will look when it is hung. Some pattern books have photographs that show the overall effect in a room; and some shops provide a large 'viewing' mirror – an idea to copy at home.

If you stand well back and hold up the sample in front of the mirror the distance between you and the mirror is doubled, in the reflection, giving you a more objective view of how the sample will look. Some small patterns seem to 'disappear' or merge into a single colour when viewed at a distance.

To get an idea of the repeat effect, hold the sample at right angles close to the mirror: the pattern is reflected and appears twice as wide.

SHOPPING HINTS

It's worth exploring specialist furnishing shops to look at pattern books with well co-ordinated ranges of wallpapers and fabrics. Even if you don't buy them, they provide ideas for what colours go together and how to mix patterns and plains.

For a small fee, some shops will supply larger samples. Or, for a returnable deposit, they will loan a metre or more.

THE IMPORTANCE OF LIGHTING

When choosing paints and materials, it is essential to make your selection under the same lighting conditions as those in your home – another reason why collecting samples is a good idea. You should take the samples into the room to be decorated and look at them by both daylight, and by electric light at night. Consider when you use the room most. If it's during the daytime, then make sure you choose your scheme from the samples that look best in daylight. Think about the atmosphere you want to create, too – a warm, inviting living room or a fresh, sunny bedroom, for example.

It is easy to think that all electric lights are the same. In fact, the various types of artificial lighting affect certain colours in different ways. A normal tungsten light (the kind produced by standard light bulbs) makes pale blues slightly dull and grey, while reds appear more vivid. Under a warm white fluorescent strip, purples have distinctly pink overtones, but pinks appear dull.

Colours can vary in daylight conditions too. If you look around a room by day, you'll notice how the light on one wall is slightly different from that on the wall next to it – the intensity of light depends on the position of the windows and doors, the way the house faces and the time of day.

HOW COLOURS AFFECT EACH OTHER

The red used here is the same in every illustration. See how different it looks when it's placed next to other colours.

☐ White makes it look clear and intense, black makes it lighter.

☐ Grey makes the red darker, blue makes it brighter.

☐ Next to orange – a closely related colour – the red looks darker and less true; green – the colour directly opposite on the colour wheel – makes red appear very bright.

ONE PLAIN COLOUR – THREE DIFFERENT LOOKS

If you're starting with a plain colour – whether it's walls, carpet or upholstery – you have an almost limitless choice. So think about the kind of look you want to create – it could be elegant or cottagey, flowery or high-tech – and then choose with that in mind.

In the room schemes below the basic starting point is the toffee-coloured carpet. By mixing patterns and textures, and branching out with loosely co-ordinated colours and patterns, it is possible to create three schemes, each with a totally different feel.

The overall look of a room depends not just on colours, but also on the size and type of patterns – anything from large floral prints to small geometrical designs – and the textures of the materials used. So consider these different factors as you go about collecting samples.

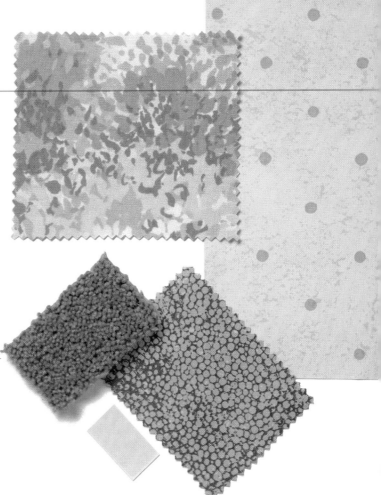

△ *Elegant and understated*
The subtle 'texture' patterns used in the fabric and wallpaper echo the carpet texture. The colours all relate to each other, and are colours found in nature, calm and subdued. The curtains and sofa are chosen for their understated, elegant lines, and the overall effect is one of lightness.

△ **Sophisticated fun**

Here pattern is combined with pattern, spots with stripes, stripes with florals for a spontaneous and freehand look. It works because the colours are slightly muted but still lively, the patterns abstract, the textures smooth. A touch of toffee in the fabrics is just enough to unify the scheme.

△ **Cottage effect**

Here, common denominator colours of sand, toffee and maroon make patterns of different scales and character work together. Sand-coloured cushions and piping break up the large area of maroon on the sofa, while the smooth wall surface offsets the woven cotton of the sofa fabric and the twist pile texture of the carpet.

SAME SAMPLES – TWO SCHEMES

Exactly the same materials can be used to create quite different effects, depending on how you use larger and smaller patterns, lighter and darker colours.

If you can find a picture of a room that looks roughly like the one to be decorated, it's worth tracing it on to plain paper and colouring in the different areas to match the samples. This gives an idea of how a large area of china blue on walls, for example, will look as opposed to a much smaller area of the same blue used for blinds or a cushion.

▷ *Light and airy*
The bold 'stencil-look' wallpaper pattern creates a fresh, airy look. Patterns with white backgrounds usually make rooms seem light and more spacious.

▷ *Rich and glowing*
For an all-over colour effect, the floral mini-print wallpaper is used. Note how the background blue predominates: coloured grounds tend to hold furnishings together, bring walls in.

HARMONIOUS COLOURS

Combine closely related colours to create harmonious schemes that are easy to live in.

Greens, blues and mauves work well together; pinks, peaches and apricots are a successful mixture, too. When you combine colours like these, which are closely related on the colour wheel, you can be certain of creating harmonious colour schemes.

The degree of harmony depends on how closely related the colours are. The colour wheel that appears on page 15 is divided into 12 sections but it could be divided into many more, with subtler differences in colour.

If you move around the colour wheel and choose any group of colours which lie near (but not necessarily adjacent to) each other, they will create a comfortable harmony. The most obvious way to divide colours is into warm and cool groups. Pinks, reds and yellows, for example, are all on the warm side; blues, greens and mauves are on the cool side. A warm harmony of colours creates an inviting atmosphere in a large or small room; and a careful combination of cool colours can create space.

TEMPERATES

You can also make successful harmonies by mixing colours which link the warm and the cool side of the colour wheel. These are called temperate colour combinations. Orange, yellow and green, for example, are a warm temperate harmony mixing warm colours (orange and yellow) with a touch of coolness (green). Red and pink with mauve are a warm temperate combination from the other end of the range.

Yellow used with green and blue, or blue and mauve with pink, are both cool temperate colour combinations in which cool colours are warmed up with a colour from the warm side of the wheel. So, if your starting point is blue – maybe in the carpet or on the walls – and you want an harmonious scheme you can move in either direction on the colour wheel, towards a sunny yellow or a warm pink.

Harmony is even easier to create using tints and shades of just one colour – think of the hundreds of shades there are of any single colour. However, this kind of scheme often lacks life, so additions of small accents of strong or more contrasting colours, and varying textures, help to make the overall scheme more interesting.

Natural harmony
Warm and cool harmonies are found in the subtle colours in nature – yellows, oranges, russets, ochres, reds and pinks; or soft blue, lilac, mauve, greens and purples.

WARM HARMONIES

Using a harmony of warm colours always makes a room appear inviting and comfortable. The warm range of colours stretches from scarlet through oranges, to yellow, and includes pinks, pale peaches, rich plums and ochres.

The closer a colour is to a primary such as red – the warmest and most vibrant of the warm range – the more intense the colour will be. These intense versions of warm colours are very lively and need to be carefully controlled, otherwise they can be very difficult to live with.

So, if you want to avoid a restless combination of colours, choose an harmonious scheme. Pick colours which are close together on the colour wheel, mixing pure colours with lighter and darker tones.

Remember that the strength of colours varies. The richness of autumn can be found in the darker versions of oranges and reds; the pastel equivalents are softer and fresher, and probably better suited to warming up a small cold room without being overbearing.

In this living room the apricot walls, scorched pink velvet upholstery and peach lampshade give it a warm, comfortable feel – with such a high ceiling it could easily have turned out cold and austere.

△ **Warm and welcoming**
The warm harmony of colours in this large living room are perfectly complemented by the rich gilt of the mirror frame and the natural wood of the table and the fireplace.

◁ **Oranges and lemons**
Yellow is a particularly useful temperate colour. It can be a warm sunny yellow with a hint of orange, or a cooler lemon, closer to green. It is also easily influenced by other colours.

The warm yellow in this room is tempered by the apricot and soft green in the floral print of the upholstery and the blinds.

◁ **Hot pinks, cool lilacs**
Pinks from the warm range of colours are cooled with a lilac-grey in this colour scheme. The warm coral pink is mixed with a vivid pink in the upholstery fabric and the blind. The lilac walls and the pale pink of the painted wicker chair blend with the lilac-grey carpet and the grey table.

COOL HARMONY

Blue sky and green grass – an harmonious colour scheme made in heaven. Almost any shade of blue goes with all the different greens – light blues with emerald, soft green with soft turquoise, mauve with deep green.

Interesting cool harmonies are simply created using differing amounts of several colours and by using different intensities of colour.

In the light airy bedroom above, for instance, a combination of blues with pale green creates a serene, restful atmosphere – refreshing to wake up to. The pale moss green and the lilac-grey of the carpet soften the cool crispness of the overall scheme.

In a colour scheme that is predominantly blue it seems quite natural to add a little green, a closely related cool colour, to lighten the effect.

COOL TEMPERATES

It is often a good idea to introduce a touch of warmth to the cools. In a scheme dominated by mauve, using deep pink, a warm colour close to mauve on the colour wheel, will maintain the harmonious effect and add warmth and interest.

Similarly, at the green end of the cool range, a warm colour such as a sandy beige, could be included – in cushion or curtain fabrics, perhaps – to warm up an otherwise cool scheme.

△ **Cool companions**
In this bedroom, which gets plenty of natural light and warmth, a combination of soft blue, mint green and lilac-grey creates a very fresh atmosphere.

◁ *Cool alternatives*
*Colours from the other end
of the cool range – blues and
greens – are combined here
with a soft, sandy yellow.
The coolness of the blues
and greens are equally
balanced; although the
green appears in smaller
areas it is more intense.
The element of warmth in
the yellowish beige softens
an otherwise cool scheme
and adds to the airiness of
the room.*

◁ *Greys and pinks*
*Here a cool harmony of
blue-grey lilac is combined
with deep pink.*

*The walls below the dado
rail are painted in a delicate
lilac; above the rail a soft pink
is sponged over white. The
matching curtain and
tablecloth fabric combines a
broad blue-grey stripe with
splashes of vivid pink,
repeated in the hydrangea
blooms outside.*

*White is used to bring
light and freshness into
the overall scheme.*

SINGLE HARMONY

Combining shades of just one colour is an alternative way of creating an harmonious colour scheme. Any colour you choose will have a wide range of tints and shades from the palest and freshest to the very darkest. A restful combination of greens, for instance, can include a pale jade and a deep green.

It's important to choose tones from all parts of the range so that the colour scheme works. Using a selection of shades from the dark and the light ends of the range tends to make the overall effect seem disjointed, because there are no mid-tones.

Once you've decided on the colour, it's quite straightforward to put together a single colour scheme, but it's also easy for these schemes to turn out to be monotonous. To avoid ending up with a dull lifeless room, add accents of colour in cushions or vases perhaps.

The accent colour need not be strong. However, they are most effective when they are contrast colours chosen from the opposite side of the colour wheel – red or orange with green, perhaps, or blue with yellow – but be careful not to break up the harmony by using too many.

△ *Cool and soothing*
A simple combination of shades of jade with white creates a restful – but monotonous – atmosphere in this sunny living room.

▽ *Strong accents*
Accents of a bright yellow – in the lampshade, cushions and vases – are just enough to add life to the scheme.

WORKING WITH ACCENT COLOURS

Learn how to use touches of colour – warm or cool, subtle or bright – to bring new life to your colour schemes.

Most colour schemes are improved by the addition of accents – the final touches of colour which can make a room come alive, or complement a colour scheme. They are usually provided by accessories, such as lampshades, cushions, picture frames, towels, soaps, tablecloths, candles, flowers or blinds. Using accents successfully is straightforward once you understand a few simple rules.

USING ACCENTS
The power of an accent colour depends on the background of colours it is combined with. If, for example, the colour scheme is dominated by a warm sandy yellow, the accent colour could come from the cool side of the colour wheel – blues or greens, perhaps – to introduce a lively contrast; a choice of red or pink accents – almost opposite yellow on the colour wheel – would be more striking.

Accents needn't be strong contrast colours to be successful. Adding accents which are closely related to the basic colour scheme has an harmonious and restful effect, and can be used to emphasize individual tones.

Don't be put off using accents if there is pattern in the room. A colour which is common to all the patterns can be picked out as an accent to provide a visual link between the various elements. A soft pastel floral wallpaper in pinks and greens combined with a plain striped sofa in a shade of green, for instance, would be perfectly complemented by a few accents in a more intense tone of the same green.

Try to avoid using the same accent colour in too many places, or too many accent colours in one room. In a living room, for example, limit the accents to three or four places, such as cushions, a lampshade or a picture frame which can be easily changed.

NEUTRAL COLOUR SCHEMES
Accents are particularly important in monochrome or neutral colour schemes which can sometimes look dull. Try covering up the shocking pink accents in the picture on this page and see how the well-balanced neutral colour scheme of grey and white loses its impact.

Neutral colour schemes can provide a background for a mixture of different accent colours. The combination can be harmonious or contrasting depending on the effect you want to create.

Colour power
This strong and plain neutral colour scheme needs splashes of a powerful colour, such as a bright vivid pink, to bring it alive.

CHOOSING YOUR ACCENTS

Look carefully at the contents of the room before deciding on accent colours. Upholstery fabric, paintings, posters or china are already part of the decoration scheme and often provide the inspiration. Accents are easy to change and a familiar colour scheme can be quickly given a fresh look with a new range of accents.

▷ **Quick change**
Changing a tablecloth is an easy way to bring fresh colours into a dining room. Here, the pink candles are used as accents to draw out the red of the checked tablecloth. Blue or white candles would make good alternatives.

▽ **Perfect link**
Checks, stripes and miniprints are combined in this living room. The strong yellow of the lampshade acts as an accent which links all the patterns together.

△ **Painted inspiration**
The accent colours used for the cushions in this living room are taken from the painting on the left hand wall. The cream walls and furniture provide a neutral background which can, therefore, take more accent colours than a coloured room. Here five different accents are used – pink, red, green, yellow, blue – any more and the effect would be spotty. The deep blue vase on the mantelpiece echoes the painting over the fireplace.

▷ **Blue and white**
In this bedroom, white was picked out of the painting on the wall and used as the accent colour for the wall lights, skirting board and traditional fireplace surround. It makes a strong, crisp contrast with the cool blue colour scheme.

Picking out the architectural features, such as the cornice, skirting board, ceiling rose, moulding on panelled doors or fireplace surround, is another way of bringing accents into a decorating scheme.

CONTRAST AND HARMONY

Contrasting accent colours can have a variety of effects on a colour scheme, from the strongest impact created by bringing together opposites on the colour wheel – a bright red used in a green room scheme, for instance – to subtle mixtures of pastel tones.

Harmonious accent colours are easier to use successfully. They should be close to the basic colour scheme on the colour wheel but they can be darker or lighter depending on the effect you want to create.

△ *Warm contrast*
The rich deep red in the floral curtain fabric has been picked out as a strong contrasting accent colour for the picture mounts, lampshade and cushion in this warm yellow living room.

▷ *Sharp accents*
Neutral colour schemes can take almost any colour as an accent. Dark grey and white provide an excellent background for strong primary yellow accents in this kitchen.

△ **Cool harmony**
You can add interest to an harmonious colour scheme – without destroying the harmonious effect – by using stronger or lighter versions of the same or closely-related colours. In this cool blue and green living room the lampshade in jade emphasizes the more delicate tones of the marbled wallcovering and the sofa fabric.

▷ **Country colours**
In this living room the colour scheme is based on the colours in the floral upholstery fabric – soft moss green, beige and pale blue. The coffee tables are painted in a deeper shade of blue to add interest without destroying the harmonious effect. A deep green would make a good alternative accent.

USING ACCENTS WITH NEUTRALS

Neutral colours include any shade of grey in the range of tones from white to black, as well as beiges, browns, cream and ochres. Neutral colour schemes can easily become dull and lifeless without accents; but almost any colour can be used as an accent and, to change the mood completely, simply change the accessories. In this beige scheme a variety of contrasting and harmonious accents have been added.

△ The fine black lines of the picture frames, the lamp bases and the trim on the bedcover and cushion work well as a strong neutral accent in this bland colour scheme.

△ A group of drawings in deep terracotta frames set against a cream marbled wall, with matching lampshades and piping on the cushions, add a warm touch.

△ A neutral colour scheme needs a range of textures and accents to add visual interest. Touches of a bright colour such as yellow liven up this scheme.

CONTRAST COLOUR SCHEMES

Room schemes made up from contrasting colours can be strong and eye-catching or gently coloured and restful.

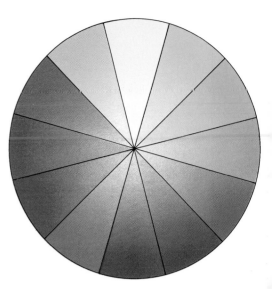

Contrast colour schemes, whether in bright or pastel tones, have one thing in common: their principal colours lie on opposite sides of the colour wheel.

They do not necessarily have to be direct opposites, but can be taken from anywhere on the opposing half of the colour wheel: with red as the parent colour, any colour from indigo to yellow ochre can be used as a contrast, or with leaf green as the parent, any shade from orange through red, pink, and violet can be used. Tonal values are important as the two main colours need to be fairly evenly balanced. The less intense the shades you choose, the easier the scheme will become: both pastel and muted shades, even when contrasting, in the end become harmonious.

Balance is important. Don't use two colours in equal quantities as they can 'intensify' each other. On the other hand, avoid the spotty effect created by just dotting the complementary colour around the scheme. At the same time, using just two colours can be sombre, so use others to act as background and accents to give the room a 'lift'. They can make the main colours more vibrant or tone them down.

△ **Graded colour wheel** shows all the hues, from deep tones to light pastels.

▽ **Confident contrast**
A colour scheme carried through with confidence. Strong, grass-green walls are countered by orangey-red blinds of equal weight. The beige, orange and green carpet provides perfect balance.

◁ *Clearly contrasting*
The parent colour – yellow – contrasts in classic fashion with clear sky blue. The yellow is present in two hues: soft daffodil painted on the table and skirting board, sharp buttercup as accent in the teapot, cup and saucer. The creamy-beige wall and blue-beige carpet tie the colours together

▽ *Contrast – or harmony?*
Pale pastel-yellow walls inset with cream panels act as the parent colour in this elegant room. A clear delft blue in the screen, tablecloths and cushions acts as a contrast. The creamy-grey carpet and upholstery form the neutral back-drop, with yellow piping and ribbons as accent. Light entering the room from the window makes the two sofas appear almost different in colour as it falls on them. The mix of pastels, while strictly complementary, is almost harmonious because they are so light in tone.

IMPORTANCE OF LIGHT

It's important to look at the colours in the room where they are to be used, as different light can affect colouring to a considerable degree.

If you want to use a strong colour for the walls, it is worthwhile buying a small pot of paint and painting a large sheet of card. Prop it against the wall for a few days to see the effect of different light conditions in your room. Strong colours tend to look even stronger on a large area and in a fairly small room the colour reflects from one wall to the other to intensify the effect.

Lay colour samples against each other while you consider them, not against white or a neutral, and don't put more than three intense colours to-gether. On the other hand, if you are using muted or pastel shades, you can mix any number of colours. Use pattern – in carpet, for example – to link the parent colour with complementaries.

▷ **Classic contrast**
Dark rooms with little light can take more intense colours in a contrast colour scheme because they become more muted. In this bedroom a very strong yellow – which might be overpowering in a lighter room – is used to good effect as the contrast colour against a mid-blue parent. The darker blue stencil designs on the wall and frills on the quilt, with white lampshade and frills on the canopy, act as accents. On the floor, the rug combines all the colours used and the coffee-coloured carpet acts as a neutral background.

▽ **Colour ranges**
A range of blue and yellow paint chips shows how well these two opposing colours work together in contrasting schemes.

△ Geometric contrast
Turquoise-painted walls and deeper-toned carpet form an all-enveloping parent colour contrasted by angular blocks of bandbox pink. A deeper-toned pink picks out the woodwork. Subtle indirect lighting hidden behind the bedhead causes interesting light-and-shadow effects on the wall above. Bed linen in the palest of pastel pinks forms the neutral relief colour.

◁ Three-way contrast
Three blocks of colour in almost equal weight make an exciting modern scheme in a café-style dining corner. While the yellow and turquoise are nearly the same tonal value, the deep red floor is altogether much darker. The same red, used with light navy blue, serves as accent colour in the painted border round the wall. The neutral shiny black table and chairs make the colours appear brighter.

CONTRAST COLOUR CHART

COLOUR	CONTRAST	ACCENTS	NEUTRALS
RED Scarlet Terracotta	Emerald — Dark ivy French navy — Bright blue	Tan/ Sand Naples yellow/ Dusky pink	Cream/ White Ivory/ Beige
GREEN Deep blue-green Citrus green	Peach — Deep dusty pink Royal blue	Light green/ Turquoise Purple/ Lilac	Oyster/ White Silver/ White
YELLOW	Mid-blue	Green	Yellowish white/ Green-greys
BLUE	Burnt orange	Scarlet	Blue-white/ Grey
PINK	Turquoise	Deep blue-green	Magnolia/ Blue-grey

BRIGHT IDEA

Work out a scheme You can work out an interesting contrasting colour scheme by using the standard colour wheel.

Trace over the diagram at right, then re-trace it on to card or thick paper. (Alternatively, use carbon paper to mark the diagram on to a sheet of paper underneath.) Cut out the shaded segments and pin the circle through the marked centre point on to the colour wheel printed on page 45.

The triangular segment represents the parent colour. Turn the circle round on the wheel, depending on which colour you are planning to use as the parent, and any of the colours showing through the semi-circular window can be used as a contrast.

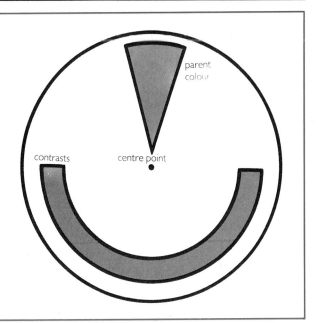

EXPERIMENT WITH COLOUR

If you're not totally colour confident, it's sometimes a good idea to experiment with colour scheming in a smaller room, or by using paints – which are inexpensive and easy to change if you are unhappy with the results.

A bathroom, shower room, or WC (all too often unexcitingly decorated) are good places to start. You may hit upon a colour scheme that pleases you, but if not, the walls can be quickly repainted. Try using lighter or more muted shades. Don't forget to include calming neutrals and one or two accent points to obtain the complete effect.

This sort of experimentation helps to build up your confidence and enables you to create a really exciting colour scheme in the future in one of the main rooms of your home.

△ **Holly inspiration**
The classic contrast of red and green, used here in mid-tones, gives this bathroom a cheerful aspect. Neutral white on the ceiling and painted beams add lightness and brightness.

▽ **Variations on a theme**
This bathroom with butterscotch walls contrasted by a lilac-coloured bath provides an interesting variation on a yellow-and-blue theme. The greyish-green hand-basin and tiles provide gentle accent colour, with white as the background neutral.

△ **Warming bathroom**
Rich terracotta walls give a warming glow, contrasted by the vibrant blue-painted bath exterior. Gleaming brass fittings act as accents and the neutral white ceiling lightens the whole room.

UNDERSTANDING TONE

If you can't put your finger on what is missing from a room scheme – it's often the tonal mix that is wrong.

Basically, 'tone' describes the lightness and darkness of a colour. Technically, the tone of a colour can be affected by two things: the *intensity* (amount) of the colour and *value* – the amount of black or white it contains. The combination of intensity and value produces the *tone*.

Whether you like muted or pastel shades, warm colours or bright contrasts, understanding tone really does help in making decisions about colours.

It also helps you to create a well-balanced scheme which is neither too bland and boring, nor too busy.

An all-over, one-colour scheme can be made visually interesting by using several different tones of that colour – from the palest pastel through to a really deep shade. Alternatively, a many-coloured, many patterned room – which might seem to be in danger of becoming a visual mess – can be saved if all the colours are closely related in tone. And when evaluating the overall tonal mix don't forget to take the tone of any woodwork into account.

To use tone successfully, it helps if you can recognise similar tones in different colours – something you are probably already doing subconsciously. Once you do understand tonal intensities and values, and how to combine them, you can create room schemes that are lively and interesting as well as satisfactorily balanced.

How tone works It is often hard to notice the tonal relationship of colours when looking at a coloured photograph, but in a black-and-white photograph or a film, where colours are converted into shades of grey, it is much more obvious. Good newspaper pictures and old 1940s films work because there's a good range of tonal contrast. The two photographs of the same room below – first in colour, then in black and white clearly show the different tonal values.

◁ *Balancing the tones*
The cheerful, multi-coloured patchwork blends harmoniously because many of the patches are of approximately the same tonal value; only the darker blue and white are different. Looking at the black and white photograph you'll notice how the darker blue tone ties in with the wood fireplace and that without the white patches the overall effect would be quite dull and lifeless.

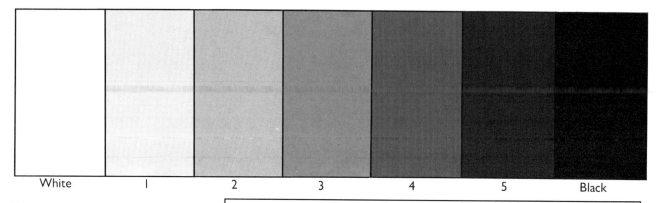

| White | 1 | 2 | 3 | 4 | 5 | Black |

TONE SCALE

The diagram above shows seven gradations of tone ranged between pure white and pure black. The tones range from very light through a semi-light, quite light, mid-tone, quite dark to very dark. This is a simplified tone scale, and is one that can be easily distinguished by the human eye. Your eye can quickly learn to give an approximate 1-5 rating to different colours.

Below is a range of shades in three colours progressing from the lightest shade to the darkest. Comparing the colours in a line across the page you'll notice that each shade has roughly the same tonal value or intensity.

HOW TO TEST FOR TONE

To consider the tones that are contained in a fabric design you are thinking of using, here is an experiment to try.

☐ First, match paint samples as closely as possible to the colours in the fabric.

☐ Next cut them out and then lay them out on an off-white background such as a grey or buff envelope.

☐ Then screw up your eyes and squint a little at the colours. Move them around if necessary, so that they lie next to other shades.

☐ Screw up your eyes again; if the colours seem to merge, then they are quite close together in tone. On the other hand, if they don't merge, then the colours are of quite different tones.

☐ Armed with this knowledge, you'll be able to make much more effective decisions when choosing the shades and tones of any accent colours you want to accompany your decorating scheme and enhance it to the maximum effect.

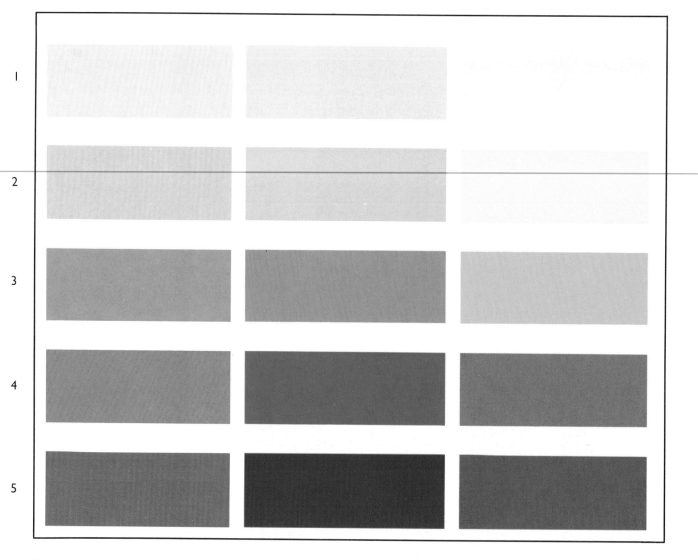

Working with fabrics

When learning to judge tonal ranges start with a flat printed pattern so you will not be distracted by light and shadow as in a complete room.

In the photograph on this page there is a fabric designed by William Morris with a well-defined, strong pattern that contains several colours and tones. Around it are grouped together samples of plain fabrics in the same dark tones and the same pale tones that correspond to the colours in the fabric. The two main colours – pink and green – are in the same tonal range.

The differences in tonal range show up well in the black-and-white photograph. Note how the extremities of the range – the very light and the very dark tones – are used sparingly, and act as accents.

FEW COLOURS/MANY TONES

Room schemes on a one-colour (mono-chrome) theme need not be dull. You can make them visually effective by working with a range of shades from very pale to very intense, running through the whole of the tonal range.

Shadows When evaluating the tonal range don't forget to take into account areas of permanent shadow, such as the folds of drapery or the shadow cast by a large wardrobe. These obviously darken the tone of any colour, adding an extra dimension to the tonal range.

▷ *One-colour schemes*
While basically one colour, this room works well because of its wide variety of tones. Here the intensely bright ribbon hanging down over the bed lifts the whole scheme and creates immediate visual interest. White lacy cushions on the bed and white paintwork mark the opposite end of the tonal range.

◁ *Sea-misty*
A wide range of sea-green tones come together to create a varied but restful mood.

▽ *The black-and-white photograph of the scene on the left clearly indicates the range of tones and how the areas of shadow created by the drapery add movement and variety to the overall scheme. The tone scale shows that every tone is included except black.*

MANY COLOURS/FEW TONES

A room scheme that combines too many colours can look busy and restless. However, if most of the colours are as close together as possible in the tone scale this will greatly help to calm and unify the whole scheme.

▷ *Multi-coloured schemes*
This bed-sitting room is decorated all over in rich, mid-to-dark colours – predominantly terracotta, blues and greens. There are two differently-patterned wallpapers and a paper border; and several fabric patterns. Even the ceramic lamp and paper shade have the same rich colours, as do the various cushions that are dotted round the room for accent.

The reason that this works as a cohesive and harmonious scheme – rather than just looking like a hotch-potch – is because, apart from the white accents outlining the paisley patterns, the colours themselves come from a narrow tonal range – as can be seen below from the black-and-white print of the lamp corner on the desk.

▷ *Warmth and light*
Although of quite a different colour, the mainly red lampshade blends harmoniously into the background of mainly green curtain fabric because – as can be seen from the black-and-white print – its tonal value is practically the same. In the evenings artificial light also plays a part in varying the tonal contrast, deepening shadows and highlighting the palest tones.

AVOIDING TONAL TRAPS

Sometimes it helps to see why schemes do *not* work, in order to understand how to avoid the obvious pitfalls. The left-hand column of drawings shows three common problems: the centre column shows the problem in black and white terms: and the right-hand column shows one way to put the tonal balance right. Now try to imagine what colours should be used to produce the tones illustrated in the third column.

Bear in mind the tonal range of wood too. Whether it is light ash, mid oak, dark mahogany or stained black will affect the overall tonal balance of a scheme, just as much as the more obvious colour differences.

Problem: spotty and stark
There are lots of intense red elements, with black and white.

Tonal analysis This scheme looks virtually all black and white, because intense colours are tonally very dark.

Solution Adding a mid-tone background – either on the walls or floors – helps to link extreme tones.

Problem: too garish
This scheme includes several pastels and several intense colours.

Tonal analysis As well as a variety of colours, there is a wide range of tones from very light to very dark.

Solution To maintain a colourful scheme, it's best to stick to a narrow band of tones for the colours.

Problem: bland and boring
All the colours are slavishly picked out from the blind fabric pattern.

Tonal analysis Everything – walls, woodwork, floor and fabrics – are in the same light tone.

Solution Make sure walls or floors are slightly lighter or darker, and introduce a little tonal contrast as an accent.

COLOUR AND PROPORTION

Learn how to use colours – warm or cool, light or dark – to change the shape and feel of a room.

The way you use colour on the six main areas of a room – the four walls, the floor and the ceiling – can dramatically or subtly alter the apparent proportions of the room. You can change how long a room looks, or how narrow or low it is, simply by the way you use colour and tone.

First, you need to give the room in question a long hard look. Does it basically have good proportions, or do they leave something to be desired? Is the ceiling a bit too high or too low? Does the hall feel like a long dark tunnel? Is the floor space rather small? Does the room feel too large for the amount of furniture in it? Are there awkward or untidy features – such as a sloping ceiling or a recess – which break up the space in the room and make it feel cramped?

A dark floor covering defines the edges of a large room, making the floor appear smaller than it really is.

If the room is well proportioned, you will want to make sure that you use colour and tone to enhance its good qualities. If the room needs help, the whole range of colours, from light to dark tones, are the home decorator's best friend.

CHARACTERISTICS OF COLOUR

A colour can make a surface appear closer or further away, and so look smaller or larger in comparison to another colour. Being aware of the visual effects of different colours and tones helps you to create the effect you want.

Cool colours, such as blue-green, blue or blue-lilac, tend to recede, pushing back the walls of a room and making it feel more spacious. Light colours recede too, and so using a pale cool colour creates the maximum illusion of space. Add a pale wall-to-wall carpet and you increase the sense of space even more, particularly if the skirting board is painted in a colour similar to the carpet.

In contrast, walls painted in warm or dark colours seem closer. Large rooms with high ceilings can often feel spacious and unwelcoming and so painting the walls and ceiling in warm restful tones helps create a cosier and more relaxing atmosphere.

◁ *Raising the roof*
This scheme is limited to beiges, browns and greys, in subtle tones which range from dark to light. It shows clearly how tone can affect the shape and feel of a room. A light ceiling and floor increase the height of the room, and a soft mid-tone draws in the walls slightly. A dark cornice gives added definition.

ALTERING SPACE WITH COLOUR

In high ceilinged rooms, corridors or narrow rooms, you can change the proportions of the space by contrasting dark floor and ceiling colours with light walls. This has the effect of appearing to lower the ceiling and increase the width of the room. In the same way, a long room appears shorter if the end wall is a warm rich colour.

A room with a low ceiling may feel oppressive, but if the ceiling is a much lighter colour than the walls, the room appears to be taller. Make sure that the walls are the same colour right up to the ceiling, not just to picture rail level, for maximum effect.

Sometimes rooms are squeezed into awkward spaces, particularly in flats converted from houses designed for more spacious living. Sloping ceilings, for example, can make a room feel cramped, but by blending the awkward shape in with the walls, you open up the space. Similarly, a recess can be drawn into a room by painting it in a warm or dark colour.

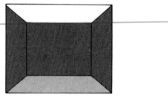

△ *Raising a ceiling*
To make a ceiling feel higher, paint it in a lighter colour than the walls. In this rather box-shaped dining room the ceiling has been painted in brilliant white, in stark contrast with dark green walls. The light ceiling makes the room feel taller than it really is, and the dark tone draws the walls inwards, creating an intimate atmosphere.

It is important that the colour of the walls is continuous, right up to the height of the ceiling. If, for example, details such as the picture rail were picked out in another colour, breaking up the wall, the effect would not be so successful.

▷ *Making space*
This is the same dining room as the one above, with the same furniture and carpet, but it looks completely different.

The walls and the ceiling are painted in soft pastel colours – a very light apricot and rose white. There is far less contrast between ceiling and walls than in the dark green dining room. Instead of appearing taller, the pale colours push the walls back and make the room feel larger and more light and airy. The cornice and picture rail are picked out in a slightly darker shade, to add definition.

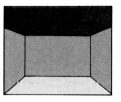

▷ *Lowering a ceiling*
Some rooms have ceilings which feel uncomfortably high for the size of the room. Painting the ceiling in a tone which is slightly darker than the walls makes it appear to be lower. The effect is increased if the ceiling colour is taken down to the level of the picture rail.

In this living room the problem is solved by painting the ceiling a dark ochre. Using the ceiling colour to outline the wall panels anchors the paler walls against the dark ceiling, at the same time balancing a colour scheme which could have been oppressive.

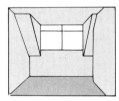

△ **Disguising awkward shapes**
Attic rooms such as this one feel poky because a sloping ceiling creates awkward spaces. When decorating it's hard to know where the walls end and the ceiling begins: the ceiling will seem very low if the wallcovering ends where the slope begins. The best approach is to paint or paper the walls and ceiling in the same colour to camouflage the awkward shape. In this room mini-print wallpaper covers all the wall surfaces.

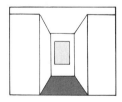

▷ **Widening a narrow room**
Corridors, galley kitchens, and small single bedrooms tend to be narrow, but if painted in very pale colours they appear more spacious.

The all-white fitted cupboards and appliances create an illusion of space in this narrow kitchen. The white venetian blind over the window blends the window into the wall when closed adding to this illusion. Bright red and white spotted tiles add interest to the white decoration.

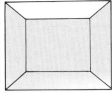

◁ **Making a room feel larger**
Pale colours reflect more light than dark colours, and cool colours recede. So a combination of the two is perfect for making a small room seem larger.

In this sunny little room, the walls, ceiling and floor are decorated in a range of cool pastels, creating a bright spacious airiness. Note that there are no great contrasts between colours to break up the overall effect. The woodwork of the window and the skirting boards are painted in pale aqua colours and the wooden floor is sanded and stained.

In a room that doesn't get any sun, temperate colours – such as pale lemon-yellow or pale lilac-grey – would be a better choice. A wall-to-wall carpet in a soft neutral colour is another way to add to the illusion of space, particularly if the skirting boards are painted in a similar colour. A neat window treatment, such as this roman blind, helps to keep the room uncluttered and spacious.

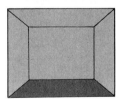

▷ **Making a large room cosier**
Spacious rooms can sometimes feel austere and unwelcoming, particularly if they get little sun. So, choose a tone from the warm side of the colour wheel – for both the ceiling and walls – to create a cheerful colour scheme which draws the walls inwards slightly and the ceiling downwards, making the room feel more inviting. The strength of the tone is as important as the colour itself, so use soft mid-tones for the best results. This large well-proportioned bedroom is painted in a soft rose pink to create a comfortable and restful atmosphere. The pink is warm enough to make the room feel cosier but not so strong that it becomes oppressive.

THE IMPORTANCE OF TONE

It's hard to notice the tonal relationships of colours when looking at coloured photographs of rooms. But it's the way in which light, medium or dark tones are used that affects the shape of a room, even more than the actual colours themselves.

These diagrams show at a glance how to achieve a range of different effects, highlighting points you like and disguising problems. If you make a tracing of this page you can colour in the drawings to see how a variety of different colours – and different tones – look.

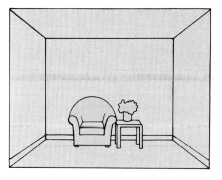

To make a room feel larger decorate in light colours. The lighter the colour the more light is reflected and the larger the room feels.

To make a large room feel smaller or cosier, use warm colours to bring the walls inwards and the ceiling downwards.

Dark colours and warm colours advance. A single wall painted in a dark colour will be drawn into the room.

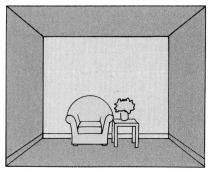

Cool colours recede. A wall painted in a light cool colour appears further away than it really is.

A dark floorcovering makes the floor seem smaller. It also defines the edges of the room and draws the eye downwards.

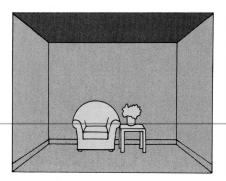

To lower a ceiling use a colour which is slightly darker than the walls but not so dark that it feels oppressive.

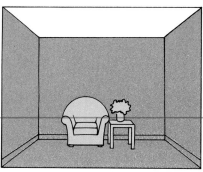

To raise a ceiling use a colour which is lighter than the walls. Increase the effect by painting the walls right up to the level of the ceiling.

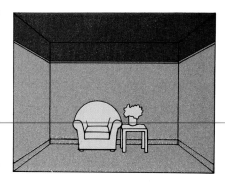

To lower a ceiling in a very large room paint the top section of the walls in the same dark colour as the ceiling.

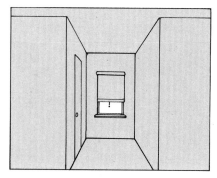

To widen a corridor use a very light colour on the walls, ceiling and floor. The reflected light will make the space seem less confined.

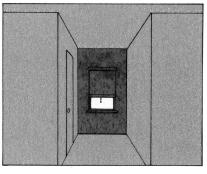

To shorten a corridor, or a long narrow room, paint the end wall in a dark or warm colour, to make it appear closer.

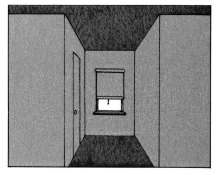

To change the proportions of a corridor, decorate the ceiling and floor in a darker colour than the walls. The space will appear wider and lower.

THE EFFECT OF LIGHT ON COLOUR

When planning a colour scheme, it's important to know how natural and artificial lighting affects furnishings.

Professional interior designers and colour consultants consider the direction a room faces. Whether it is north, south, east, or west, makes a great deal of difference to the choice of colour scheme. For instance, a bedroom that faces east and receives strong sunlight in the early morning will look very different when next seen late at night in artificial lighting. A west-facing room that has a warm glow in the evening can look dull in the mornings. Your choice of colour should take this into account.

Of course, an ideal aspect is not always possible for everyone. City flats may enjoy little naturally-available light and be overlooked on all sides. A north-facing room can expect less sun than a south- or west-facing one; but whatever the aspect, with clever lighting and colour scheming the interior can be made to feel welcoming and attractive.

The style of house you live in can also make a great deal of difference to the amount of available light in an interior. A country cottage may be in a superbly sunny location but have low ceilings and tiny windows which can make the interior feel dark and gloomy. Modern homes with spacious open-plan interiors and large picture windows will be even more affected by their aspect and seasonal changes. If there is a living room with a patio or conservatory attached which is used as an additional seating area during the summer but not in winter, the decor will have to be flexible enough to accommodate the changes.

For people in doubt over lighting and colour schemes some top interior designers suggest painting a room white before making a final colour choice. This is a good way to observe how changes in natural light affect an interior and helps you make the most of it when choosing a colour scheme. Interior designer David Hicks has recently incorporated every kind of domestic light fitting into his showroom so that clients can also see the effect of different kinds of artificial light on carpets, fabrics and wallpapers.

Diffused, even light
A room in typically diffused northern daylight: shadows are not too strong and the mainly pale neutral colour scheme with colourful accents makes the most of existing light conditions. However, at night under artificial light, colours may alter drastically.

MATCHING FURNISHINGS

The most usual way to colour match is to look at samples in the daylight. However, this doesn't enable you to judge the effect at home under artificial lighting conditions. Viewing samples under shop lights is also unsatisfactory as they mostly use colour-corrected fluorescent tubes resembling daylight. Neither type of light will give an idea of the average home's tungsten lighting with its distinctive yellow cast. Carpets and textured fabrics are particularly vulnerable to change from artificial lighting. Synthetic fabrics that match perfectly in daylight may no longer do so under artificial light.

Fabric The effect of artificial lighting on curtains is better seen if a sample metre of fabric is pleated and held upright; looking at lampshade fabrics lit from behind also gives a better idea.

Paint Window walls will appear darker as they only receive reflected light; ceilings always look darker than walls painted the same colour. If in doubt use a shade lighter than your first choice; once all the walls are painted they tend to appear darker than the paint sample on a card.

Carpets Put samples flat on the floor and move them around the room to see how different positions and lighting conditions can affect the colour.

△ ▷ *Lighting – day and night*
It's hard to believe that these two pictures are of the same living room. (Above) Natural daylight shows off the subtle, neutral colour scheme of white and bluish greys in this modern interior.

(Right) The same living room seen at night under artificial lighting. The yellow cast of tungsten lighting has turned the grey upholstery and carpet a yellow-beige and given the entire room a unifying, warm glow.

△ *Daylight*
Choosing colours by daylight can work well for rooms mainly in daytime use. But successful daytime colour combinations may not work well at night.

△ *Fluorescent*
Some colour-corrected fluorescents can give much the same effect as daylight. Other types of fluorescent have a cold, blue and harsh draining effect.

△ Tungsten
The lighting most commonly used in the home. This emphasizes the yellow-reds, so a coral and apricot colour scheme will look much more intense.

△ Tungsten-halogen
This has a much whiter light than pure tungsten and would benefit a neutral blue-grey colour scheme more as there is less colour distortion.

◁ **Peaches and corals for warmth**
North-facing rooms need to feel cosy. Although some primrose yellows may take on a greeny tinge and bright reds feel claustrophobic, soft, muted coral shades can work well in sponged, dragged or stippled paint techniques. Apricot or peach curtains at a window give a warm cast to white walls. A Chinese carpet with a coral background warms up the floor.

▽ **South-facing, cool neutrals**
A neutral colour scheme using cool blue-greys works well in this situation. White sheer curtains at the window diffuse and filter strong sunlight and protect upholstery and carpet from the sun's rays.

△ **Cool blue mood**
This room feels typically Mediterranean with its tiled floor and cool, blue colour scheme. Blue-lined curtains lend a cool cast to the walls.
In winter these curtains could be changed to a warm peachy print with peach linings; while loose covers in warm peaches and beige could transform this into a warm, cosy colour scheme.

▷ **North-facing using neutrals**
A semi-transparent blind cleverly provides privacy without blocking out too much daylight.
The light tan soft leather seating looks warm while the neutral beige carpet and touches of coral in an abstract rug and picture also help to warm up this scheme.

Adding light A white gloss-painted ceiling is a wonderful light reflector and in a dark room can act like a mirror and significantly increase the amount of available light. However, gloss-painted ceilings *must* be perfect – free from paint drips and unsightly cracks and bumps as a high sheen also emphasizes less-than-perfect surfaces!

△ *North-facing but warm*
Although green is generally considered a cool colour, the pale yellow-green on these walls combines successfully with a warm cream ceiling and the muted pink of the upholstery.

▽ *South-facing – using neutrals*
Browns appear less sombre in a south-facing room because the yellow emphasis of sunlight brings out the red which is the basis for browns.
White walls also take on a creamy look.

WORKING WITH PATTERN

Using pattern needs as much careful consideration as using colour to achieve successful results.

The number of patterns available in wallpapers, fabrics and floorcoverings nowadays is enormous, ranging from simple geometrics and colourful spatter designs to formal florals. How to choose patterns and how to use them can be an awe-inspiring prospect, but once you have learned about the characteristics of different patterns, creating the atmosphere or style you want becomes easier.

Pattern is an essential ingredient in any room scheme. It plays a part in creating the style and in enhancing the colour scheme, whether it is used in small areas – cushions, decorative paper borders or tiles, for example – or over much larger areas such as wallcoverings, ceilings and floors.

The strength of pattern should not be underestimated. Designs in a single bold colour appear to be more striking and imposing than a plain surface painted in the same colour. In the same way, a rather delicate pale colour is given more life on a patterned surface.

Scale is an important consideration, too. Large-scale designs can be wasted on the walls of small rooms, for instance, particularly if the wallpaper has a motif which is cut off in awkward places; and small bright designs tend to look busy.

On the next two pages patterned materials are divided up into eight different categories to provide a guide to the vast range of designs available.

Single colour
Mixing all sorts of patterns together seems like a risky business, but relating them to each other by choosing designs in the same colour is one way of making a successful combination.

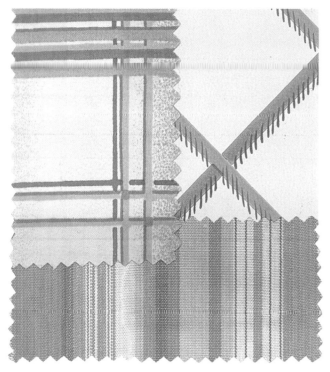

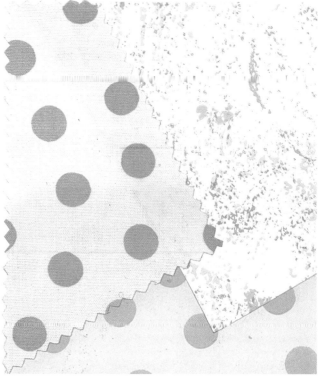

Checks, stripes and trellis

These patterns are some of the oldest and most striking designs. There are hundreds of variations in all colours, which can be traditional or modern in style – checks can be simple black and white squares, gingham or tartan, for example. A touch of one of these simple patterns makes a good accent in plain colour schemes.

Spots and spatters

These designs have a very modern feel to them. Spots can be regularly spaced or randomly printed, large or small. Spatter patterns imitate the effects of tiny droplets of paint splashed and dribbled across the wall. Strong colours can be mixed together to create lively and vibrant combinations.

Floral

Patterns range from large-scale oriental designs and traditional chintzes to splashy watercolour designs and very simple modern prints. The more dense florals need to be used in large rooms, but the softer colours and looser designs suit most rooms. They look good combined with plains which draw out the tones of the design.

Abstract

A collection of modern patterns used in wallpapers and fabrics. They have no recognizable motifs, such as flowers, plants or birds; instead, they are made up of random shapes – splodges, freehand zig-zags, torn paper shapes or combinations of crooked lines and gentle swirls of colour, for instance, in all sorts of colour combinations.

Geometric

The designs are made up of shapes such as triangles, chevrons, diamonds and key patterns. They come in all sizes and combinations of colours to create different effects – a crisp tailored look can be made by using geometrics for wallcoverings and window dressings, for instance. These designs often work well with mini-prints and florals.

Exotic

The designs are based on traditional patterns from all over the world – India, Asia, Africa, the Pacific and the Americas. Rich colours and textures are combined in bold patterns – stripes, geometric or floral designs, or simple images of people and animals. Chinese designs are in delicate colours; Indian and African patterns are dark and rich.

Mini-print

Wallpaper and fabrics are available in a wide variety of colours and patterns, including flower sprigs, florals and geometrical shapes. They can have a traditional cottagey feel to them and are especially suitable for small rooms where it would be easy for a larger patterned wallcovering to be overwhelming.

Textural

These designs are printed to imitate other materials, such as wood grain, and various paint effects including stippling, sponging, dragging, rag rolling or marbling, and fabrics, such as moiré silk. These patterns give large flat surfaces, particularly walls, more visual interest and a luxurious feel without being overpowering.

△ Daisy pink
A wallpaper and fabric design of Michaelmas daisies – a pattern created at the end of the 19th Century by the famous English designer William Morris – makes a cosy atmosphere in this living room without feeling overwhelming. A plain carpet provides a neutral background for the wealth of pattern and the deep pink cushions act as accents.

◁ Floral tradition
The small, rather old-fashioned floral design on the wallpaper and fabric looks light and airy in this pretty bedroom. The broderie anglaise trim adds to the traditional feel of the room.

ALL-OVER PATTERN

It is difficult to imagine what a pattern will look like over a large area when you are working from a sample. The main points to consider are the colours in the pattern, the type of design and its size.

Small designs, such as flower sprigs in pastel tones, can disappear on the walls of a large room – some even look like plains or textures from a distance. On the other hand, a small but boldly-coloured geometric makes a strong impact – this may be just the effect you want in a large and unwelcoming room, but it could be oppressive in a small room.

The type of design also affects the style of a room. If you are looking for a period atmosphere, go for traditional florals, Regency stripes, or paint effects, such as marbling, not brightly coloured geometrics, spots or checks.

◁ Blue all over
This simple colour scheme mixes mid-blue with the warm natural tones of wood and cane. The room is large and light enough to take the large-scale paisley pattern on the walls and ceiling without feeling dark or cramped.

△ Pastel patterns

The bed is the biggest piece of furniture in a bedroom, and so the bedcover is an important part of the decorating scheme, especially when using a single pattern throughout the room. The effect could easily be overpowering, if not carefully planned.

This large-scale check in soft pastels – blue, mauve, pink, orange and yellow – is used in matching fabrics and wallcovering. It is an unusual but refreshing colour scheme for a bedroom.

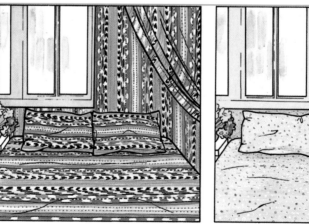

▷ Spots and stripes

The mini-print design (right) – in soft grey with spots of pastel tones – or the boldly coloured exotic stripe (left) – called ikat and based on the patterns created by American Indians – provide two very different bedroom colour schemes.

USING PATTERN WITH PLAIN

With just one pattern as the focal point in a room, there is a wide choice of ways to use plain colours open to you.

If you feel unsure about mixing and matching fabric and wallpaper patterns, then using one design with accompanying plain colours is the best way of building up an attractive and individual room scheme. Varying shades of one colour, or two or even three different colours picked from the chosen pattern can be used on walls and floor, upholstery and curtains. The many choices open to you for both paint colours and plain-coloured fabrics leave plenty of leeway to create different moods according to personal preference.

Textures, too, can be varied: a shiny chintz that reflects the light, or a rough, knobbly tweed that absorbs it, can create quite different effects even when they are the same colour.

If the pattern is in the upholstery, plain curtains edged with one other colour from the design look smart and sophisticated. Alternatively, if it is the curtains that are patterned, pick one of the colours in a self-patterned material for upholstery, with contrast piping and cushions in the curtain fabric.

Painted walls can be given added interest; the technique known as dragging adds a depth to the colour, while the techniques of ragging and sponging allow the introduction of two complementary colour shades that can be picked to tone with the fabric pattern.

Another possibility, of course, is that you have chosen a strongly-patterned wallpaper and wish to keep it as the main feature in your room. In this case, pick out two of the main colours for plain, tailored curtains or blinds.

Beige as background
Striking modern upholstery fabric makes a bold statement on its own. A nubbly natural tweed rug covers wood flooring and the walls are subtly dragged in pale blue on cream to echo the colouring of the upholstery. An unusual touch is the coffee table, which has been covered in pale beige chevron-design fabric to blend with the seating. Walls and table in all-over pale blue would create a much cooler feel in the room. The floral accents pick up the pink in the fabric but could equally well echo the blue.

PICKING OUT THE COLOURS

To help you decide which colours to pick for individual treatment, it's a good idea to match up some paint samples to the different colours in the pattern. Cut them out and look at them against a neutral background.

A multi-coloured fabric gives you a huge variety of colours to choose from: first, the shades that match precisely those contained in the pattern; second, a range of pastel tones in the same colours to soften the overall room scheme; and third, darker shades.

Those colours which are most pleasing to you – either because of their vibrancy or their soothing nature – are the ones to pick out for cushions, carpet, or walls.

△ *Colourful choice*
A really colourful curtain fabric offers a wide range of colour choice for other surfaces in the room. Here is a selection of some of the plain fabrics and paint colours that could successfully be used to accompany it.

▷ *Bright and cheerful*
Jazzy modern interpretation of a floral print draws the eye immediately to the window and the view beyond. Yellow walls keep up the cheerful feeling set by the bright curtains. Contrasting lavender-blue cushions pick up another of the colours within the pattern, while the grey carpet subtly reflects the mauvish tint.

△ *Summertime blues*
Focusing on the blues, a cooler scheme is created by putting very pale blue on the walls but a richer blue on the floor.

△ *Springtime freshness*
Picking out two different colours – palest pink walls and a mossy green carpet – brings a touch of spring to the room.

△ *Reversing the scheme*
The muted design on the wall is echoed in the cream curtains, grey carpet and reverse contrast-piped cushions.

▷ *The wallpaper and fabric samples used in the room above. A self-patterned cream weave adds an interesting texture.*

△ **Bright and light**
A deep blue background with a bright, multi-coloured floral design forms the basis for a unusual bedroom scheme. Echoing pastel tints on the sofa soften the overall effect. On the right are some of the shades that could be picked out of the pattern to use in a colour scheme. Different textures for upholstery and curtains or cushions result in a different effect.

WAYS WITH MINI PRINTS

Some of the most versatile patterns are the tiny, all-over designs that are not only pretty but also make good camouflage.

Mini prints were in vogue as soon as the first printed wallpapers and fabrics appeared in the 18th century. Their almost doll's house scale suited the contemporary Georgian homes and their elegant furniture. The Victorians, too, favoured tiny, all-over sprigged designs and frequently used them to great effect. Towards the end of the 19th century, however, mini print popularity declined in favour of larger, bolder patterns.

It wasn't until the 1970s that overall mini prints really came back into fashion. Firms such as Laura Ashley started to introduce them in ranges of closely colour co-ordinated wallpapers and furnishing fabrics that were largely inspired by both 18th century and Indian wood-block designs. They included sprigs of flowers, widely-spaced motifs and trellis patterns.

These small, pretty prints allowed people who had never before dared to mix patterns in a room to try their hand at it with success. Tile manufacturers then followed suit by matching their ranges to wallpapers and fabrics so schemes could be completely co-ordinated. Carpet manufacturers completed the mini pattern revolution by introducing tiny all-over designs.

HOW TO USE THEM

There is a practical aspect to decorating with mini prints. They are particularly successful at camouflaging unevenly plastered wall surfaces – small all-over patterns break up large areas by preventing the eye from concentrating on one spot and seeing the flaws. All-over mini patterned carpets are also excellent for rooms that get heavy wear, particularly hallways, as they tend not to show the dirt as easily as plain ones.

However, mini prints do need to be chosen with care. They can be overpowering if the colour contrast between background and pattern is too marked. Small patterns may also lose definition in a large room but can be more successful when used in combination with a larger scale print.

Muted background

The mini-printed paper here is highly reminiscent of 18th century style both in design and colouring. The muted beige background makes a gentle contrast in relation to the motif making the overall effect easy on the eye and a good backdrop for dark furniture.

△ **Traditional blue and white**
*Mini prints blend well with traditional
furnishings and suit older homes and
small rooms particularly well. Mixing
different designs together is easier if you
stick to matching colours.*

▷ **Mixing two together**
*The small-scale print on this dado area
combines most successfully with the
same pattern in a paler version on the
walls above. The effect given by the two
is surprisingly different.*

HOW TO CHOOSE

In a shop where all you have to choose
from is a sample book, it can sometimes
be difficult to imagine how large expanses of a small design will look on a
wall or hanging at your window. When-
ever possible, try to see a big piece of
the wallpaper or fabric. Stand away
from it, screwing up your eyes slightly to
get the effect. Some shops have made
choosing mini prints easier by covering
large display panels which can be
viewed at a distance.

On wide-spaced mini prints, that is
those with large areas of background
colour in between the motifs, the
spaces themselves start becoming more
important and even form their own
patterns within the design.

Geometric designs need to be considered very carefully. If your walls are
slightly askew, a mini-print of this kind
tends to emphasize it – especially if the
pattern contains stripes as well. A

pretty, overall floral design, on the
other hand, can help to disguise bumpy
walls.

Mini prints whose colours are closer
in tonal value tend to merge together,
whereas high colour contrasts look
busier and crisper. Spaced sprigs with
contrasting tones look even more widely spaced than ever. Generally speaking,
this type of design looks better in
smaller room schemes where there's
not too much furniture or clutter.

As a more modern alternative to
creating a romantic atmosphere with
pastel flower sprigs, look for more
geometric designs. Some of these
geometrics can perhaps be held within
stripes as they give a more formal look.
In common with sponging and stippling,
mini prints can soften dramatic expanses of wall and window colour by
giving a more muted, dappled impression. They can also be used to introduce
strong colour into a scheme.

TYPES OF MINI PRINT

Mini prints come in a variety of looks, styles and patterns. It's important to understand the different effects that can be created when the same pattern is viewed close to and from a distance of around two metres away.

△ *Dark and light*
A fabric or wallpaper with a predominantly red background brings walls and windows closer; white backgrounds make areas feel comparatively light.

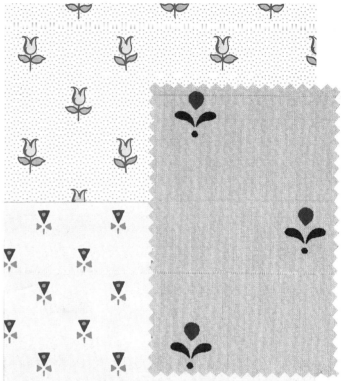

△ *Close together sprigs*
Over large areas, widely-spaced designs can sometimes give a restless, 'dotted' effect whereas 'close together' prints can make small rooms feel claustrophobic.

△ *Geometric*
These prints can usefully offset fussy all-over mini floral patterns, giving the eye a break and making a mini print scheme feel more restful.

△ *Contrast and close tones*
Motifs in colours that are similar in tone to their backgrounds simplify complex, busy patterns and give a pleasantly muted effect to large expanses of wall or curtain.

Prints here are two-thirds actual size

△ Traditional geometric
This Victorian-style mini print gives the impression of being light and lacy from a distance, but at close quarters it can be seen to be quite strong and dramatic.

▷ Cheerful open sprigs
A brightly contrasting striped print in red and white combined with a wide-spaced sprig pattern could be overpowering. However, the pale green leaves in the pattern bring relief by offsetting the sharp contrast. Adding a splash of deeper green plants makes the whole scheme feel more restful.

◁ △ **Patterned and plain**

This bedroom's deep blue-green wallpaper is broken up by the overall design of twining white flowers (see detail). A colourful patchwork tablecloth echoes the floral mini print design, while plain blinds and curtains offset any busy feeling.

▽ **Pattern for camouflage**

All-over prints can help to disguise odd corners, awkward angles and uneven surfaces often found in older homes. Co-ordinating fabrics on the bed and at the window help to give a unified feel.

TAKING THE ROUGH WITH THE SMOOTH

Learn how to use textures – rough or smooth, matt or shiny, hard or soft – to bring life to your colour schemes.

Texture describes how any material feels to the touch. Every surface has a texture. If you compare, for example, the surfaces of a telephone and a kettle you will find that although both appear to be smooth they have quite different textures. The plastic has a warm feel to it, and is slightly brittle, but the metal of the kettle is cold and hard.

Texture can be visual as well as something you can feel. Painting techniques such as stippling, sponging, dragging or rag rolling create interesting visual textures on a smooth surface.

Deciding on which textures to use is as important a part of decorating as choosing colours because texture has as much effect on the different elements in a room and the overall atmosphere. A haphazard collection of textures can be as unsuccessful as an unbalanced colour scheme, so think carefully about the materials you plan to use and the surfaces – walls, floor, ceiling, furnishings – you are going to cover.

CHOOSING TEXTURES

Textures are loosely divided into two groups – rough and smooth – which provoke quite different reactions. Rough textures, such as brick, wood, coir matting, wickerwork or suede, have a rustic homely feel about them. At the opposite extreme, the smoothness of glass, the hardness of chrome and the glossiness of plastic, for instance, bring a hard-edged look to a room.

You can create successful schemes using mixtures which are at neither one extreme nor the other. It's similar to mixing several different tones of one colour rather than just using dark or light ones.

Texture is also used in the same way as accents of colour. In a well-balanced but perhaps slightly boring colour scheme you can inject a little interest by adding a contrasting texture. Similarly, if a whole room is decorated using smooth textures, the addition of some rougher surfaces makes a lively contrast.

HOW TEXTURE AFFECTS COLOUR

Texture is linked closely to colour. The quality of a colour – its richness or brightness, for instance – varies depending on the texture of the surface.

Smooth surfaces reflect light and dull ones absorb it. So the colour painted in emulsion on a wall looks lighter than the same colour used in a heavy woven fabric. Compare for yourself two objects in the same colour which have different textures – a red towel and a red plastic soap dish, for example – and you will see how the colour is affected.

Combining textures
This living room combines textures of all kinds. The shiny, polished chrome contrasts dramatically with the heavy, rugged tweed cover on the sofa. Suede chair covers, cotton drapes and a berber carpet add less extreme textures.

WALLS

The walls of a room are the largest surface area to decorate and there are literally thousands of different ways of treating them. Wallpapers, paints, fabrics and tiles all provide a wide selection of different textures.

Wallpapers are available in all kinds of finishes which range from smooth and gleaming foils to rich flocks and include embossed papers, such as anaglypta or woodchip, and vinyls which imitate textures such as moiré or raw silk; and real fabrics, such as hessian, wool, silk, linen, or cork.

Paints come in several finishes, too – silk or matt emulsion for walls, and gloss or eggshell for woodwork. There are plenty of painting techniques which add visual texture to the surface of a wall but are less overpowering than a tangible texture such as hessian or anaglypta. Rag-rolling creates an effect like soft, crushed silk, stippling looks like the texture of orange peel, and sponging, using two or three colours, can produce a wide range of mottled effects.

WINDOWS

The texture of window dressings, whether they are curtains with swags and tails, or mirror venetian blinds, play an important part in creating the atmosphere of a room. Fabrics with a deep pile, such as velvet, suggest warmth; the sharp outline of a venetian blind has a cool businesslike quality to it; a neatly folding roman blind in cotton comes somewhere between the two.

The choice ranges from rich velvets to light, billowing sheers – and can include materials like muslin or felt.

The texture of window dressings is more pronounced because light not only shines on them but through them, too. The texture can be enhanced by the way the fabric is hung. Pleating or ruching, for example, creates a play of light and shadow on the surface of the fabric.

You don't have to limit yourself to one fabric at a window. Layers of different texture and pattern can be combined – a roller blind with curtains, two or three curtains of different weights, or draped fabric with blinds. The layers – say, lace, cotton and satin – are drawn back in stages to show off the different textures.

FLOORS

The floor is the surface we are in most contact with and so the texture of the floor surface – whether it feels rough or smooth, warm or cold, hard or soft – is as important as the choice of colour and any practical considerations.

Carpets can be smooth, knobbly, sculpted, or flocked to create visual texture; rugs, rush, coir or sisal matting, wood or cork flooring all have a warm feel to them; quarry tiles, ceramic tiles, marble and slate are hard cool surfaces.

The floor is frequently the starting point for a decorating scheme. Using several different materials, wall-to-wall carpet, coir matting, wood and quarry tiles, perhaps, would make the overall effect in a house more interesting than if the same material had been used throughout.

In houses where rooms have more than one function, a change in the texture of the flooring can indicate the different uses of the space. For example, a kitchen/dining room could be laid with quarry tiles, with a floor rug under the table and chairs to bring warmth to the area which does not need to be so functional.

OTHER SURFACES

Apart from the walls, floors and windows, there are many other surfaces to consider in a decorative scheme.

Furniture can combine all kinds of textures. Wood is a very versatile surface. Wooden furniture can be shiny and highly polished, or smooth with a matt finish, bleached, or pickled to bring out the grain, stained with a satin finish, or waxed to produce a subtle lustre or a hard glossy shine.

Wood laminates which are smooth and hardwearing are good for use in the kitchen. Other plastic laminates with a variety of surfaces – smooth, satin and matt stripes, marble effect, for example – are used for kitchen worktops, too.

Sofas and chairs can be covered in any number of furnishing fabrics ranging from nubbly tweeds, ribbed velvets, linen, glazed cottons, to leather and suede. Cane and rush seats are combined with wood or contrasted with chrome and cane furniture provides an alternative to wood.

Hard smooth surfaces such as glass and chrome create strong contrasts when combined with softer furnishing fabrics, but add to the smooth high-tech feel of leather, studded rubber or stainless steel.

NATURAL TEXTURES

The nubbly surface of a berber carpet, the roughness of unpolished wood or cork, the softness of woollen fabrics are just a few of the natural textures which help to create a warm homely atmosphere in a room.

In the inviting interior shown above a limited range of colours – beige, terracotta, cream and white – and the lack of any strong pattern, show off the variety of surface textures. The smooth finish to the nest of pale oak tables, the picture frames and the painted wood panelling, complement the rough surface of the coir matting, the wool weave cover on the sofa and the glazed cotton cushions.

Notice how there are no extreme contrasts between textures. The coir matting has a herringbone pattern which adds interest to a plain scheme without dominating it by being too strong. In the same way, the wood, although highly polished, does not have the cold hardness of metals such as brass or stainless steel.

The combination of real textures, some rougher than others, and visual textures – such as the grain of the wooden picture frames and the oak tables – is successful because it is well balanced, creating a comfortable feel to the room. Lighting is important here too. A soft light enhances the differences between surface textures.

△ **Rough and ready**
Pale cream wool weave, dark peach glazed cotton, coir matting and polished maple and oak make a comfortable mixture of real and visual textures.

SMOOTH SURFACES

Chrome, glass, marble, mirror, brass, ceramic and stainless steel are just some of the materials which have very hard, smooth surfaces. But not all very smooth surfaces are hard; materials, such as Perspex, vinyl, plastic laminates and leather, can have some flexibility in them, too.

Smooth textures can be shiny or matt: most shiny finishes, such as chrome, brass and mirror have a cold feel; in contrast, most matt surfaces, such as vinyl, stained wood or painted emulsion walls have some warmth in them.

A room which is made up entirely of smooth materials tends to have a hard-edged, even austere look to it. The dining room shown here is decorated with a variety of materials with smooth surfaces – chrome, perforated metal, vinyl, glass and stained wood – using a limited range of colours. The strong contrast between the colours – the black of the stained wood table and the white walls, for example – emphasizes the surface textures. The simple lines of the furniture bring this out, too. Look at the straight lines, sharp angles and geometric shapes, such as the glass and chrome side-tables shaped like cubes. The checked pattern of the vinyl floor makes an ideal background for this hard-edged linear scheme – although the effect is slightly softened by the use of grey rather than black with white.

△ **Going to extremes**
Polished chrome, glass, glazed china and vinyl combine matt and shiny finishes on smooth surfaces to give a hard-edged look.

△ Rough and smooth
Polished wood, a rag-rug, crisp lace and china with a pretty floral design combine with hard-wearing, smooth melamine and a shiny glazed tile.

FUNCTIONAL BUT COMFORTABLE

A combination of rough and smooth textures make a well-balanced room scheme. Practicality often plays a part. A deep pile carpet might seem perfect for a bathroom – warm and luxurious – but it's not very practical when there's a lot of water about. A lino or vinyl floor is a good alternative because it is waterproof, but a well-sealed cork floor would be better still, because it is both practical and warm to the touch.

A kitchen needs to be practical but it doesn't have to be high-tech. This kitchen achieves a balance between warm, homely textures – such as wood and cotton – and functional, hardwearing surfaces. The cupboards and work surfaces are finished in smooth white melamine with pale turquoise glazed wall tiles. The floor which looks fresh and is easy to clean, is painted in a matching blue with a white border and topped with a striped rug, which adds some warmth to the smooth floor without being impractical.

A simple cotton curtain hangs from a wooden pole above the stripped wood window frame. Notice that a roller blind in a contrasting fabric has been fitted as well. A rustic touch is added with the smooth stripped pine kitchen chairs and table covered with a finely woven white cloth with a pretty but simple lacy border.

MIX-AND-MATCH PATTERNS

Mixing several patterns together successfully in one room is now much simpler than it used to be.

Until recently, mixing patterns together in a room scheme needed an excellent eye for colour and self-confidence to carry through ideas. Co-ordinating a striped wallpaper with floral fabric and all the attendant accessories, meant trailing round the shops with cuttings, hoping that your purchase would be a faithful match to the original sample.

These days, more and more manufacturers are producing comprehensive mix-and-match ranges of fabric, wallpapers, borders – even trimmings.

These ranges allow for the creation of much more exciting room schemes without the risk of a disaster because they are intended to harmonize, even though the designs vary. They can include floral patterns, spots, stripes and plain colours – very often with a 'moiré' look or self-patterned weave in an upholstery weight fabric.

△ *Sample board*
Fabric and wallpaper samples used to build up the room scheme on the left.

◁ *Background link*
This warm beige background to the main pattern of apricot and blue flowers has a 'moiré-look' design. This is repeated on the wallpaper, which also echoes the apricot flowers. The table is covered with two cloths, both with a self-pattern. The top one is spotted and the bottom one has a moiré design to tie up with the overall theme.

△ Geometrics
Four different zig-zag designs of muted neutrals combine to make a strikingly modern bedroom scheme. The vertical saw-tooth pattern on the walls is echoed in the zig-zags of the bedlinen and adjoining wall, and the more intricate herringbone on the reverse of the duvet cover introduces a lighter element into the overall picture while maintaining the geometric theme.

◁ Trellis and flowers
A bright geometric trellis design forms a natural background to a floral pattern which employs the same colours. Although two quite different styles of design, this combination works successfully because of the association of flowers with trelliswork and because the two principal colours are an exact match, coming from the manufacturer's same range. The small repeat of the trellis in the wallpaper border breaks up the large expanse of wall.

PLANNING A SCHEME

When choosing a co-ordinated room scheme where all the design elements come from one range, first decide which pattern is likely to be needed in the largest amount. In most cases this is the wallpaper and the curtain fabric.

When considering the walls, there are further decisions to be made before your final choice. For example, will you need two wallpapers – above and below a chair rail, perhaps? Would you like to use a border – either to emphasise an architectural feature or to break up a featureless expanse?

With this settled you can then turn to the trimmings, details and finishing touches. If the curtains are long, would tiebacks enhance their appearance? If so, pick the same fabric or choose a blending one in a smaller design, and plan to repeat this in cushions or perhaps a tablecloth. If you want to dress the windows even more elaborately, consider adding a blind to match the tiebacks; there might, too, be a place for a window seat. Plain upholstery can be contrast-piped.

△ *Building up*
Lightly-patterned wallpaper of scattered leaves is topped by a more elaborate border – used again, but in reverse, above the picture rail. Colours in the curtain fabric are stronger, making them the dominating feature in the room.

Picking out the picture rail and coving in a paint that matches the colour of the wallpaper motif not only turns it into an interesting feature in its own right but is also a useful device for visually lowering the room height.

◁ *Eye-catching abstract*
Two vivid abstract designs can still harmonize because they contain the same colours and tones. Here, the pale straw background is repeated in the carpet, forming a soft, neutral contrast to the busy fabrics.

△ Mini prints
The common denominator here is the all-over wallpaper design of small sprigged flowers, which is repeated and then over-printed with larger, stronger-coloured flowers in the fabric used for both blind and window seat. This gives emphasis to the window so that it is separated from, yet blends well with, the walls.

▷ Checks and flowers
All-in-all, there are five different patterns, from geometrical checks and stripes to a large floral design and a leafy mini print, blending in to make this harmonious bedroom scheme. This scheme works because all the fabrics come from the same dye lot. The pastel tones impart a quiet air to what could have been a busy mixture of design and colour.

△ **Sample board**
Samples of the five linked designs in the room shown left.

△ **Sophisticated country**
Rich raspberry self-patterned chintz forms a perfect backdrop to old wood, while the flowery cushions echo the furniture's country feel. The designs are held together by rich pink, which appears throughout, and the three-berry motif on both wallpapers and floral cushion covers.

▷ **Simply elegant**
An elegant little breakfast corner has been created by keeping to two colours – blue and white – and two motifs – flower sprigs and tiny spots. The simple chairs and dresser are painted and the dresser doors covered in the wallpaper.

HOW TO BUILD UP A MIX-AND-MATCH SCHEME

Taking a window feature as an example, the illustrations show how an overall co-ordinated room scheme can be built up. Start with walls and drapes, then add festoons and a window seat, and finally the finishing touches of wallpaper border and cushions. Samples of the fabrics and papers used in the scheme are shown below.

△ **Stage 1** – Co-ordinating wallpaper and curtains are chosen hung and draped, with matching tiebacks.

△ **Stage 2** – A third co-ordinating design is added for festoon blinds and trimly-piped cushions placed in the window alcove.

△ **Stage 3** – Cushions introduce a fourth design, echoed in the border that neatly skirts the edge of the wallpaper.

CHAPTER 2

CREATIVE IDEAS WITH COLOUR

NATURALLY BEAUTIFUL

'Naturals' in interior design covers an enormous range of colours – from the palest of creams through all shades of beige to browns, greys and tans.

All greys and beiges contain colours that can be found in the earth, stone, rocks and grasses. These natural colours contain plenty of brown shades, though brown is not a colour in its own right but a mixture of reds and yellows. Most greys are a combination of blues and greens, although some of those found in nature often contain an amount of green and yellow as well.

Beige, for example, can either be creamy – which indicates it contains some yellow; pinkish – which indicates red; or slightly olive – indicating a mix of green and yellow.

Several natural colours and materials used together in a room scheme can combine to create their own restful, elegant atmosphere by making use of the natural harmony that exists even between different textures and tones of fabric and other materials such as wood.

On the other hand, naturals added to existing schemes can calm down the brightest of hues or have a unifying effect on a mixture of furnishings and colours. For example, a natural-coloured carpet throughout a brightly-furnished room softens the impact and makes it seem more spacious by not interrupting the eye's flow across the room.

Natural interest
Inspiration for a natural-based scheme can come from a shell, moss-covered twig or stone. They're full of unexpected colour.

▽ **Gentle harmony**
Natural-toned fabrics gently echo the wood chair and lamp and wicker-look pottery jug. The walls have been painted with drag technique to give subtle depth to the basic colour.

NATURALLY INSPIRED

One way that professional designers study colour is to work directly with samples from nature. Here, for example, a group of stones picked up at random from a beach, are carefully matched to colours from a paint chart, a section of which is shown at the top of the page.

Natural colours combined in this way are muted yet still full of character: they have an in-built harmony.

The corner of the sitting room shown on the right takes the harmonious shades of grey, beige, blue and brown contained in the pebbles to create a peaceful atmosphere.

100

Experimenting with samples To have the confidence to use naturals so that they are lively and interesting – and not merely safe – it is worth taking the time to educate your colour 'eye' as the professionals do.

Try this experiment: collect some samples of local stones, dried leaves, or bark, or sand and pebbles from a beach; you could even buy some dried grasses and flowers. Then, using paint shade cards, match the colours of the samples to the chart as closely as you can: you will find that it takes three or four – sometimes even more – paint shades to marry up all the colours contained in one sample. It's this subtle variety that is the key! It is remarkable how strong some of the colours are – and how many colours there are in just one pebble!

When you have matched your natural object up to the paint shades, use them to find the fabrics, carpets and accessories you need to create your own natural colour scheme.

USING NATURALS

Natural room schemes can be warm and welcoming or cool and elegant. Different textures in the same colour range can give quite different effects: for example, soft weaves in upholstery fabrics or shiny chintz cushion material.

In the same way, accent colours can dramatically alter the impression given by a neutral colour scheme: cool blues and greens add to an airy, sophisticated feeling, while the warmer side of the colour wheel – reds, apricots or honey – make a cheerful, friendly room.

To achieve an all-over colour effect, use accents sparingly – three patches are usually enough.

On the other hand, natural-coloured walls and carpeting provide a suitable background for striking colour, which might be in the form of curtains, sofa, or richly-patterned oriental rug.

Textures and paint finishes Texture is one way to recreate the subtlety, richness and variety of colours found in natural things. Think of a sleek, silky curtain with a rough linen upholstered sofa; they sit easily with a knobbly wool rug and stained wood table that shows off its grain.

Using paint in colour washes or sponging techniques is also effective, as both depth and subtle variations can be achieved by applying two or three different shades or colours so as to give a translucent or mottled colour. There is also a wide range of wallcoverings available that imitate these techniques and these can be a great boon if you are not too skilled with a paint brush.

△ *Plain and simple*
Clever combination of several natural colours all contribute to the quiet comfort of this elegant sitting room. The understated charm of simple scrubbed wooden tables and natural sisal flooring offset the sophisticated pearl grey walls and chair covers. Cane furniture covered with plump, feather-filled cushions, and accessories, such as the large urns filled with pampas grasses and the beautifully carved wooden ducks, carry on the natural theme.

△ **Blue accent**
This cool, sophisticated
dining room is enlivened by
touches of blue in the
tableware and on the walls.
The pale beech chairs, with
their unbleached fabric seats,
stand easily on the natural
dhurrie and highly polished
wood floor.

▷ **Warm welcome**
Stripped, unvarnished woods
with an unbleached linen-
look curtain and sisal flooring
combine naturally in this
hallway. Warm earthy-
coloured walls provide a
welcoming background that
continues the natural
colouring.

△ **Dappled shades**
Shades of blue and grey in gently
dappling designs introduce soft colours
and patterns reminiscent of driftwood
or shells found on a seashore. The
natural wool rug remains true to the
overall theme.

▷ **Natural ease**
Stone walls can provide a surprising
amount of colour variation. Here they
form an interesting background for sofa
and curtains made of blue and white
mattress ticking and bright red
embroidered cushions.

Wicker chairs and table, antique
wood furniture and a wooden curtain
pole are natural accessories.

BEIGE: BASIC BUT BEAUTIFUL

Beige is the most versatile of colours and also happens to be one of the easiest to live with.

Beige is usually seen as a neutral, a safe colour to use for the main and most expensive areas of a room. Thus beige is often used as the basis of a room's colour scheme for surfaces and materials which are too expensive to change frequently. These include fitted carpets and sheet flooring, storage units and other major pieces of furniture, tiles and upholstery.

Beige enjoys a reputation for 'going with everything', and it is indeed the most versatile of all decorating colours. But if it is not used with care and imagination, a beige colour scheme can feel dull and drab.

Generally speaking, beige is thought of as a pale brown. It usually contains a hint of another colour such as red, yellow, blue or green. These hints of colour can make the beige appear warm, rich and inviting or, on the other hand, cooler and more reserved.

Obviously, the amount of true colour in a beige is very small. This means that the quantity of black or white that a particular tint of beige contains play a significant role in determining its final shade. For instance, a red-orange beige with a small quantity of white and a slightly larger amount of black will create a sombre colour. One with a lot of white and a fraction of black added will have a distinct apricot tinge. Similarly, a beige which contains a hint of yellow-green can appear almost grey when the black predominates – or it can seem a great deal more sandy-coloured if it is the amount of white which is dominant.

KNOW YOUR BEIGE

Before you use beige in a colour scheme, it is important to work out what tint of beige will best suit your scheme. In common with other neutrals, beige has chameleon-like properties and is strongly affected by the colours it is seen against.

To see exactly what tint a beige is, place it against samples of the other colours you intend to use. A pinky beige will pick up any reds used in the room and can 'flood' a scheme with red. A beige containing yellow or grey, however, would provide relief and give a crisp edge. With yellow furnishings, consider a greeny-blue beige; with green, a yellow-beige and with blues a beige tinged with pink, apricot, or yellow.

◁ *Beige and white*
White painted woodwork and mouldings define the important outlines in this mainly beige room. Dark wood provides contrast.

△ **Beige and blue**
Beige looks restful teamed with natural pine furniture and cool blue furnishing fabrics. The beige background of the fabric calms down the blue and gives a softer, warmer effect than if a white background had been used.

▷ **Sample board**
The curtains and upholstery fabric, together with the wallpaper, used in the room shown above.

◁ **Striking statement**
Persimmon, jade and red above a base of cool beige ceramic tiles, make a striking colour combination that livens up a small bathroom.

WORKING WITH BEIGE

Beige appears as a 'natural' colour on many surfaces – light woods, wool, linen, raw silk – and so makes an excellent background colour.

While pale colour schemes were popular in the 1960s and 1970s, today's trend is moving towards more highly saturated colours. Try teaming beige with strong shades. Both red-beige and sandy beige look smart with black and white. Beige with smoky grey or navy is another sophisticated combination.

Ethnic designs, too, blend well with beige. Try introducing a dhurry with beige and a mid-toned colour such as terracotta or petrol blue in the pattern to pep up a mainly beige colour scheme. If the existing colour scheme is based on a pinky beige, then terracotta will liven it up. Similarly, smoky or petrol blue freshen a sandy beige colour scheme.

Beige and pastels If you are using beige with pastels choose the clearer, stronger shades such as primrose, sugar pink,

or lilac. Conversely, beige can tone down over-bright colour schemes to produce a quieter atmosphere without making a room seem cold. A warm beige can add a touch of softness to a room where unrelieved white is the dominant colour; it also gives quite a strong contrast effect, even though beige is not considered a strong colour.

Combining beiges As with any other colour, different shades and tones of beige can be used together. It is a subtle colour easily affected by the quality of light, so try to match samples away from strong colours and under good natural light.

A pale and dark tone of the same beige can be most effective, while contrasting shades create a harmonious and relaxed atmosphere. Many fabric designs, particularly florals, contain two contrasting beiges – if such a fabric is used for curtains, you can pick out colours from the fabric to add accents for cushions and other small objects. Echo the contrasting beiges on the walls

△ *Gently exotic*
A beige carpet and walls should be colour matched as accurately as possible as differences in shades of beige over two large areas can be disturbing. Here, the apricot-beige of the walls and carpet are matched to the beiges in the upholstery fabric and blend well with cool greens, warm peachy pinks and soft browns for a lively, exotic look.

and floors and in any upholstery fabrics the room demands.

Textures As with other neutrals, textures are important. An all-beige colour scheme will look more interesting if it involves plenty of contrasting textures. Combine rough, tweedy carpets and loosely-woven linen with smooth, matt leather, shiny satins and silks.

Beige walls and carpets also create a perfect foil for rich mahogany and pine furniture.

◁ **The warmer side of beige**
Indian dhurries offer great
inspiration for colour
schemes as seen with this
dhurrie woven in off-whites,
beiges, and pinky terracotta.
The terracotta has been
echoed in the curtains and
door paint.

▽ **Feminine looks**
Beige is a versatile colour
that can be interpreted as
masculine or feminine. Here,
soft pink-painted ceiling
covings and cushion details
accent a light creamy-
textured bedspread and the
greeny beiges of the room's
overall scheme.

USING ACCENTS WITH BEIGE

In common with other neutrals that may look dull on their own, beige benefits from brightly-coloured accents. Cheerful primary accessories can liven up sober beige schemes.

△ *Harmonious yellow*
Soft gold harmonizes with, and so emphasizes, the red and yellow tones in warm beiges.

△ *Bright blue*
Towels cool down the warm beige tiles of this bathroom. ·

△ *Sophisticated burgundy*
Rich wine-red brings out the pinky-brown tones in beige and adds a note of sophistication and warmth.

ADVENTURES WITH NEUTRALS

Infinitely versatile, neutrals are essential to the decorator's palette.

Neutrals play an important part in most decorating schemes providing a useful, unobtrusive background for displaying stronger colours.

In theory the only true neutrals are black, white and pure greys. But for the purposes of decorating, colours which are nearly neutral – whites and greys with a hint of colour (such as off-whites), beiges, greys with a hint of yellow or pink – are termed neutral.

True neutrals can be rather flat and dull and are not much used when decorating. This is especially true in northern Europe where – because of the cool, low light – the warmer greys, mid beiges and pale creams have tended to be more popular.

Neutrals abound in nature. Pebble beaches are exciting symphonies in greys and beige. Ravens' plumage, driftwood, slate and coal are natural variations on a neutral theme. On a more sophisticated level, offices have long enjoyed the practical virtues of neutral decor. Pale greys and white are light and spacious and provide the ideal setting for brightly coloured equipment, while deep grey carpets age well.

Anyone about to decorate a small house or bedsitter would be wise to consider the restful and versatile qualities of using a neutral colour scheme that can be pepped up with bright accent colours. Used with skill, whites, pale greys and beiges can also usefully tone down or bring into focus bright primary colours.

Versatile neutrals
These white kitchen units provide a neutral background that goes well with any other colour. A change of blind with a few well-chosen accessories are all that's needed for a new lease of life.

USING NEUTRALS WITH COLOUR

Look at most successful colour schemes and you'll find a neutral somewhere. Perhaps white paintwork to emphasize and give a crisp edge to a patterned wallpaper or to act as a link between the paper and flooring. Too much strong colour can be overwhelming and many patterns are on neutral grounds which provide relief from the areas of colour while bringing them into focus.

If you are the kind of person who likes to change things frequently consider a basically neutral scheme with a few strong colour accents such as bright cushions, throwovers, rugs and lampshades.

A NEUTRAL DECOR

Texture and tonal contrast become all-important to an all-neutral theme; using too many similar greys or beiges can too easily turn into a colour scheme that just looks dull and bland.

Contrasting brilliant white paintwork against black furniture as in very modern styles is one way of overcoming the problem. If you are set on a pale neutral scheme – an all cream or white, say – be sure to provide plenty of textural contrast: look out for nubbly weaves, textured carpets, lace, or shiny glazed cotton. Being light in colour, the textured surfaces will throw strong shadows and provide added interest.

△ *Neutrals as the link*
Creamy beige sculptured rug and grid pattern walls create a perfect backdrop for this seating arrangement. The two co-ordinating upholstery fabrics also share a neutral, off-white background which allows otherwise busy patterns space to 'breathe'.

▽ **Alternative accents**
Mid grey walls, flooring and furniture need colourful relief to avoid looking dull and cold. Here, cane panels on grey stained wood chairs appear yellow; bright flowers and table accessories also pep up this monochromatic scheme.

▷ **Light and airy**
Cream walls and carpet provide a spacious, calm backdrop that helps to emphasize the lines of traditional dark mahogany furniture. This kind of very plain, neutral colour scheme often benefits from a strong focal point: a boldly-patterned upholstery fabric, or some dramatic colour in a painting or flower arrangement.

KNOW YOUR NEUTRALS

Neutrals need to be chosen with care. The beige which looked just right in the shop may look quite different when placed next to your wallcovering and curtain fabric. If you look closely you will see that most of the different greys and beiges belong to a particular colour group which is either reddish, bluish or yellowish, or a mixture of these. Place a piece of red fabric next to a pinky-beige and it will pick up the red and appear very much warmer and pinker, whereas a greeny-beige will be obviously cooler. If you have a lot of light wood you might find a yellowish beige makes your scheme overwhelmingly yellow and that a bluish beige is a better answer.

△ *Neutrals for toning down*
Vibrant yellow curtains are a dominant feature of this room. White walls and woodwork with cream upholstery highlight the yellow but tone it down at the same time. Pale grey-blue would have the same calming effect.

△ Framing effect

The neutral white walls and a beige and white carpet in this living room have the effect of isolating objects and visually 'framing' them so they stand out more clearly. Fabric patterns and colours are also emphasized and allow the rich reds and complicated pattern variations in the cushions to show up more clearly.

▷ Cooler aspects

These provençal-style prints in blues and greens have similar patterns to the ones shown in the picture above and would also work well with a neutral colour scheme giving it a cooler emphasis.

◁ **Points to consider**

◁ **Points to consider**
First, know your neutral. Beiges and greys are available in many different colour groupings. When it comes to neutral colours in carpets it's important to pick one that complements both fabrics and wallcoverings. It is worth experimenting with several different neutral carpet samples and noting which one has a red, yellow or blue bias. Both fabrics and wallcoverings could then be made to feel warmer or cooler depending on your carpet choice. For instance the broken stripes in the fabric here are in yellowish and reddish greys while the square motif in the middle is a pale bluish grey. If a cool effect is wanted, choose a bluish grey carpet; for a warmer effect try a camel-colour carpet.

▷ **Neutral choices**
These two fabrics could go with any of the neutral paint colours here depending on the effect wanted. For a cooler neutral scheme, pick out pale blue-greys and green-beiges for walls and paintwork; for warmer schemes pinky-beige and ecru would work well.

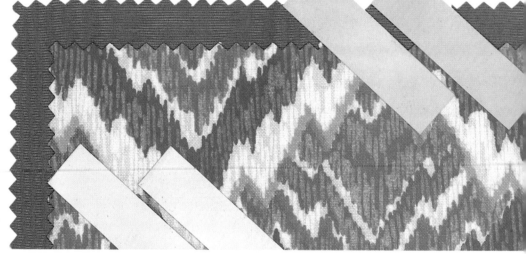

▷ **Playing the neutrals game**
This diagram using paint chip samples shows what kind of neutral creams, beiges and greys are needed to link the colours here. Starting with a mid blue paint chip in the centre, yellow, sage green, caramel and rust chips were then arranged around. Different shades of grey, cream and beige were then selected to act as a 'bridge' or linking device between each pair of strong colours.

116

CREAM – THE KIND COLOUR

Cream is good news for cold climate colour schemes as it creates space and light with a touch of warmth.

As a yellow with white added to it, cream ranges from delicate parchments and ecru through to deeper buttery shades of old ivory and clotted cream. When it comes to faded antique furnishings and old tapestries cream walls are kinder than stark white, and cream also has a softening effect on harshly bright modern furnishings.

Cream was a top colour with famous 18th-century architect, Robert Adam, who knew how cream could enhance rooms lit with diffused English light. By adding gold and white plasterwork he created the perfect backdrop for his rich mahogany furniture.

The Victorians used creamy lace to trim everything – from tablecloths to mantelpieces. After this era, cream suffered a decline and it took the 1920s and 30s to revive it as a major decorating colour. Cunard liners and Hollywood interiors were full of rich creams teamed with blonde bird's eye maple; pale primrose-creams teamed with pastels, white and gold furniture.

Today's all-cream interiors need dramatic handling if they're not to become bland and insipid. Roughly textured cream fabrics, sculptured carpets; sponged and rag-rolled paint effects help. Colour accents to use with cream include soft pinks, blues and black.

△ **Symphony in cream**
Cream has a soft, filtered, almost romantic quality that feels eternally sunny.

▽ **Touches of cream**
Use creamy lace, fringes and textured, woven and embroidered fabrics for definition.

△ **Light and informal**
Cream flatters both light and dark
woods and blends particularly well with
this plain ash Shaker-style furniture.
Painting walls cream rather than white
prevents the room looking stark and
helps to give an informal, almost
country cottage, atmosphere.

▷ **Raspberries and cream**
Romantic horizons are viewed through
this creamy lace austrian blind, the pink
bows look less strident than they would
with white lace. The mahogany vanity
unit helps to give a formal, classical air to
this delightful bedroom corner. The
whole colour scheme would work
equally well if soft turquoise was used
instead of raspberry.

WORKING WITH CREAM

Regard cream as a colour in its own right. Choose crisp white woodwork and fabrics to stop cream looking as though it is a white discoloured by age.

Cream is also essentially romantic: think of the rich creamy ivories of antique linens and lace – these were never harsh whites. It's a natural colour, easier to live with than stark white; cream conjures up visions of farmhouse dairies, raw silk, unbleached wool, linen and calico.

In all-cream colour schemes, textured carpets, wallcoverings and furnishing fabrics are important; lace and all kinds of slub weaves, embossed and anaglypta wallcoverings help to add interest. Cream floors reflect light: lay cut pile and sculptured carpets – or creamy tiles in polished marble or textured vinyls.

△ **Blue and cream**
Billowing curtains of creamy voile give a sunny-all-the-year-round feeling. Cream teamed with powder blue woodwork feels warm and luxurious. Modern dhurries use lots of cream. The striking patterns and colours of the one here echo the fabrics and wallpaper to perfection. Crisp white sheets and pillowcases make the cream bedding fabric seem almost pinky-beige.

△ **Country house cream**
While traditional, the choice of cream gives this room a modern airy feel. It's interesting to imagine how this room would look if typically Victorian wine velvet curtains and upholstery were substituted – most of the light would be lost. Today's cream furnishing fabrics look warm and luxurious and reflect the light; they can also be dry cleaned and pre-treated to repel stains.

◁ **Cream and grey**
Cream is a dramatic backdrop to dark blues and grey. Cream throwovers match the carpet and lighten dark sofas. Even the ceiling mouldings have been painted cream. A splash of dusky pink in the woodcarvings and flowering amaryllis off-set the sombre greys.

CREAM WITH THREE ACCENTS

Cream has chameleon qualities – it reflects surrounding colours and quietens down harsh tones.

▷ *Muted*
A chinese lacquer red has a muted effect on primrose-creams.

▷ *Cool and warm*
Turquoise cools down buttery cream walls while still retaining its warmth.

▷ *Dramatic*
Black brings out browns in cream making it look softer and more caramel.

A TOUCH OF YELLOW

Yellow – the colour of sunlight, sand and daffodils – brings warmth and light into your colour schemes.

Yellow in all its many shades is a warm and cheerful colour. Pure yellow is a primary colour, which is very bright and can be hard to handle; but there are many other shades – pale, delicate primrose, lemon, rich buttery tones and deep ochres, for example – which can be soft and mellow, or light and sunny, and are not nearly so daunting to use.

On the colour wheel, pure yellow is equidistant from red and blue – the other two primaries. The tones of yellow, such as lemon yellow, which move towards blue have a sharper, slightly astringent feel to them; the tones closer to red become warmer and warmer, gradually approaching apricot, peach and orange.

STYLES AND ACCENTS

Yellow suits any style of decoration. For a modern, bright and cheerful look mix pure yellow with other primaries and white; or for a soft and more traditional feel, reminiscent of the pastel shades used in the 18th century, mix primrose yellow with greys, apricot or pale blue.

Yellow makes a very refreshing accent colour, too. The sharpness of lemon adds zest to a neutral colour scheme of greys and white, or beiges, perhaps; a cool mixture of blues and greens can easily be warmed up with a few careful touches of sunny yellow.

NATURAL MIXTURES

A colour combination found in nature is a good starting point for planning a decorating scheme – cool sky blue and the pastel yellow of the summer sun, for example; or buttercup yellow and grass green, for a more powerful mixture.

Warm tones, such as apricot, orange or pink teamed with yellow, make successful harmonious schemes which are comfortable to live with. The colours in honeysuckle for instance – soft pink and creamy yellow – go together easily.

Like other warm colours, yellow used in wallcoverings makes a room look smaller. A strong daffodil yellow will turn a spacious but stark room into a welcoming space.

▷ Strong contrasts
One way of dealing with strong colours is to put them with other strong colours. Here a daffodil yellow colour scheme is anchored by the dark green carpet. Small touches of dark green – in the plants and on the sofa – and exotic patterns make a striking contrast.

▽ Clean lines
Two tones of yellow – on the walls and pinstriped upholstery fabric – make a dramatic contrast with accents of black in this very modern living room.

◁ *Finishing touch*
The small details of a room scheme need as much thought as the larger elements. Here pale yellow coloured kitchen cupboards are given added decoration by painting the moulding inside the panels a more intense tone of yellow.

▽ *Restful tones*
The warm golden yellow walls give this spacious dining room an inviting and restful atmosphere – with such a high ceiling it might have turned out cold and stark. A plain white ceiling and decorated cornice, and a cream carpet balance the rich yellow walls and set off the highly polished antique furniture. The floral fabric of the full-length curtains mixes white with touches of yellow.

▷ Bright and light
Pure yellow is a strong and vibrant colour and needs to be used carefully. The bold colour and broad stripes suit the clean modern lines of this dining room. Combined with white in crisp stripes and plains, it creates a warm sunny atmosphere without being overpowering. Notice how the fireplace has been picked out by reversing the stripes.

▽ Red, yellow and blue
Yellow works well with the other primary colours – red and blue. This small bedroom, with its sloping ceiling and walls painted in the same tone of deep yellow, has a cosy feel to it. The yellow provides a strong background colour for the blue of the bedcover and the red of the armchair cover. The combination of these three contrasting colours creates a lively effect.

△ **Pastel tones**
In this elegant living room, a restful atmosphere is created using pastel tones. A delicate primrose yellow is successfully mixed with two tones of grey. A variety of patterns – floral and stripes – are used in wallpaper, border and upholstery fabrics (samples below).

USING ACCENTS WITH YELLOW

A variety of visual textures and patterns – stripes, trellis and marbling – are combined to create interest in this soft yellow colour scheme. The addition of accent colours in a few areas can produce different effects.

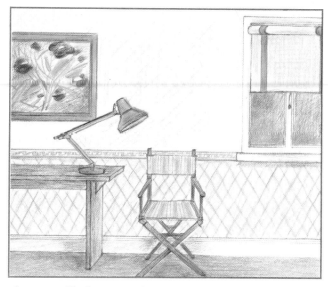

Accents of leaf green such as the angled work light and the wallpaper border add cool touches to the scheme.

Yellow and purple which are a mixture of the other two primary colours combine well to make a lively contrast.

A few charcoal-grey accents add a subtle but sophisticated touch to this simple colour scheme.

ALL ABOUT PEACH

A wide range of tones from fresh pastels to rich warm hues, make peach a versatile decorating colour.

Colours go in and out of fashion. In the early 18th century, soft pastel shades, such as pink, peach, apricot or pale blue were popular decorating colours. Wooden wall panelling was never left in its natural state, it was often painted in very delicate pastel shades.

Later, after the dark greens, ochres and browns popular in Victorian times, light colours became fashionable again. Rooms gradually became less cluttered with furniture, walls were no longer decorated with collections of pictures in dark frames and furnishing fabrics and wallcoverings became lighter. In the first ten years of this century white was internationally the most fashionable colour while peach was a particularly popular choice in the Art Nouveau interiors of the period, often combined with a light grey-green.

Peach is also one of today's most popular decorating colours. It is used on walls, ceilings and floors. Designs for furnishing fabrics, wallpapers and floor-coverings combine peach with all sorts of colours – greens or blues to make fresh lively mixtures; or pinks, apricots and yellows for warm harmonious effects.

SHADES OF PEACH

Peach comes from the warm side of the colour wheel, and is made up of yellow, red and white. It is a soft colour with a pinkish tinge which distinguishes it from the more orange-yellow shades of apricot. At its darkest, peach moves towards terracotta, but add more and more white to the basic mixture and you can create a range of the most delicate pastel tones.

Peach is a very versatile colour. It works equally well in all sorts of rooms large or small, traditional or modern. Add a pale peach to a mixture of subtle tones such as dusky-pinks or silver-greens, for a more traditional look; or bring a warm touch to the cool hard looks of high-tech colours such as slate-grey or jade. It brings out the tones of all kinds of woods, too, from the lightness of beech or white oak, to the rich dark tones of antique mahogany or walnut.

WORKING WITH PEACH

The subtle shades of peach create equally subtle changes in the atmosphere of a room according to the way in which the colour is used.

The blushing middle tones of peach create a warm welcoming atmosphere. It's an ideal tone for a hallway, for instance, where first impressions should be inviting. In a large room a deep peach draws the walls inwards making it feel cosier, but a light tone warms up a small room without making it feel any smaller.

Deep peach contrasted with light colours such as cream emphasizes how sensuous it can look – like peaches and cream. In contrast, a light peach looks fresh and bright combined with other pastel tones. Peach works well with colours it is found with in nature, too – a rich leafy green, or the deep raspberry and brown-gold of the peach stone.

Peach is a very successful accent in a scheme dominated by other colours. Touches of peach in lampshades or cushions, towels or bathmats, are enough to warm up a cool colour scheme of greens and blues.

▽ *Soft option*

In this modern bedroom, a very pinky shade of peach is successfully mixed with soft olive green and cream. All the furniture is painted in the same tone of peach, with a darker shade used in the curtains and cushion covers.

△ *Fresh peaches*

Pink and peach drag painted units with white handles create a pretty fresh atmosphere in this kitchen. Notice how the panels on the window shutters and the wall cupboards are picked out in a paler tone of peach.

▷ Warm and cool

Here, peach, pink and blue make a fresh and delicate mixture. The rosy pink of the floral chintz draws out the pinkish tinge in the peach on the wall behind, making it feel warmer. The peach works well with the pale blue of the lamp and china bowl and the crisp white of the tablecloth. The pink and blue theme is repeated in the floral prints on the wall behind.

▽ Traditional elegance

This colour scheme was designed around the painting over the mantelpiece. Peach and a pale grey-blue dominate and are mixed with other neutral tones to create an elegant feel in a traditional room. The soft peach of the walls is picked out in the trellis design of the floor rug, the cover on the sofa, the lampshades and ashtray.

▽ Peaches and cream

The colour scheme for this pretty bathroom was inspired by the pinks and peaches found inside the seashells used to make the mirror frame.

The neutral tone of cream used for the bathroom suite makes a good partner for a variety of shades of pink and peach. The walls are painted in two shades of peach above and below the cream dado rail. The deep pink of the drape over the window adds a strong accent to a delicately blended colour scheme.

△ Peach and grey
In this light and airy bedroom the pale shades of peach and grey-blue are a perfect choice to create a restful atmosphere. The fabric of the scatter cushions and tablecloth and the wallpaper border combine peach with the pale grey-blue of the painted cane furniture. The plain blue fabric has been added as a cool accent. The patterns and textures used in the room are shown close up in the samples (left).

COOL ALTERNATIVES

Tones of peach work well with a wide range of cool colours, either pastels or strong rich shades. A patterned fabric which mixes peach with a cool colour is a good starting point for planning a colour scheme.

Delicate pale peach used on the wall and floorcoverings provides a warm shell for cooler shades, such as sky blue, or pale jade, used in the furnishings – upholstery and curtains. The result is a well-balanced pastel colour scheme.

In predominantly cool colour schemes touches of peach take the edge off the coolness. A high-tech interior, which is dominated by dark greys and black, and hard smooth surfaces, is softened slightly with accents of a warm deep peach, for instance. Peach can work equally well as a fresh pale accent in a cool pastel scheme.

▷ Equal tones
Peach and a fresh pale green are equally balanced in this traditional bathroom. The minty green of the walls and woodwork is warmed up by the pretty peach design on the paper border, tiles and matching blind. Towels and flannels in matching colours make perfect finishing touches.

▽ Chilled peaches
Peach works well with the coolness of blue in either modern or traditional rooms. In this modern living room the walls are painted in two tones of peach. The covers on the sofas and the blind combine peach with pale blue in a floral and abstract design to cool down the overall effect.

PEACH WITH THREE ACCENTS

The feel of a room can be easily changed with the careful choice of different accent colours. In these three room schemes the same furnishing materials are used, in a range of peach tones. By adding different accent colours in a few small areas – the piping on the sofa, the cushion or the tiebacks for the curtains – quite different effects are created.

▷ *Natural mixtures*
Leaf green and peach is a combination found in nature. It is a lively mixture because green is almost opposite peach on the colour wheel.

▷ *Peach melba*
Combine the delicate shades of peach with touches of deep raspberry to make a rich and unusual mixture of colours.

▷ *Cool and calm*
Soft grey is a perfect partner for peach. Use it to bring subtle cool touches and a sophisticated feel to a warm colour scheme.

IN THE PINK

From softest pastel to the eye-catching bright, pink adds warmth to any scheme.

Pink, being a mixture of red and white with occasionally blue or yellow, comes from the warm side of the colour wheel. Often dismissed as a 'little-girl' colour, pink has hidden qualities. From rosebud to raspberry, through to fuchsia or Schiaparelli's 'shocking pink', it brings life to any colour scheme. A room with a cold aspect feels much warmer if pink is added as an accent or contrast colour. Inspiration can be found everywhere you look in nature – palest pink-tinted clouds against a blue sky or early blossom against leafless branches. Above all, pink sits well with green – whether the new leaf that backs pink-and-white apple blossom, or the greyish tint of the leaves of old-fashioned garden pinks.

Different shades of pink mingle gloriously with a host of other colours in traditional herbaceous borders. This mixture is echoed to perfection in the classic floral designs used for traditional-style room schemes.

In modern urban settings, startling bright pinks serve as emphatic accent colours against severe black-and-white decor, or can soften and warm a monochromatic scheme of greys or beiges.

PREDOMINANTLY PINK

If you choose pink as the predominant colour in a room scheme, it can be highly successful – but needs careful handling if you want to avoid an ice-cream pink impression. Subtle patterns in wallpapers, borders and fabrics, and a mixture of tones and textures in fabrics and flooring bring variety to one-colour schemes.

Pink in particular offers a wide choice of shades to mix and harmonize. Clear white accentuates the palest pastels while touches of cream soften strong vibrant hues.

◁ *Strong salmon pink*
Here the walls successfully emphasize the background pinks of curtains and upholstery. Acid green and yellow in the curtains would be more dominant if the walls were pale blue or green.

▽ *Dream of pink*
Palest pink walls make a soft backdrop for other, deeper shades – from brownish-pink picture mounts and a sharp pink lampshade to true rose pink in the flower arrangement. White paintwork forms a crisp, clear accent.

△ **Bathroom for relaxing**
Gentle shades of pastel pink and cream impart a truly restful air to this bathroom. The scheme is saved from monotony through lack of tonal variety by the austrian blind which features bold, almost coral, flowers. The green accents of plants echo the leaves in the design, which is picked up in the small pattern on the armchair.

▽ Samples of the three fabrics used in this room scheme.

ACCENTS TO USE WITH PINK

The very paleness of some pinks makes them the ideal foil for strong accent colours. As can be seen from these three illustrations, even quite small amounts of accent colour can create different effects within the same room scheme.

△ **Modern touch** *Using black as the accent brings a bold modern air to traditional-looking furnishings.*

△ **Role reversal** *Rich tones of naturally cool blue bring warmth and depth to a light pastel pink room scheme.*

△ **Natural mix** *Pink and green are natural neighbours, and a clear emerald adds life and verve to the delicate pink.*

MID-BLUE –
A COOL APPROACH

Use mid-blue to create fresh crisp colour schemes or to add a cool touch to a warm range of tones.

Mid-blue is a colour found in nature – the soft blue of summer skies, spring flowers or a sparkling sea – and some of the tones it works best with are partners in nature, too. Warm beiges with mid-blue conjure up visions of sea and sand; the natural combination of rich leaf-green and mid-blue looks good, despite the old saying that blue and green should never be seen.

Historically, this soft tone of blue was a popular decorating colour – in wallpapers, fabrics, tiles and porcelain. In early Victorian times when light tints such as lavender and pink were being used in bedrooms and living rooms, sober colours such as blue seemed more suitable for libraries and dining rooms, in formal flocks and stripes.

Mid-blue combined with white is a traditional mixture which is reminiscent of old Chinese porcelain, or Delft pottery, painted with pictures of animals and birds.

Nowadays, fabrics and wallpapers combine mid-blue with all sorts of colours to suit many different styles from the traditional looks of formal florals to the abstract designs used in modern interiors.

HARMONY AND CONTRAST

Mid-blue comes from the cool side of the colour wheel. It is a soft subtle tone between the richness of dark blue and the icy coolness of pale blue. Mixing mid-blue with its neighbours on the colour wheel – sage green, lilac or aquamarine, for instance – creates comfortable and harmonious schemes.

Mid-blue works equally well with delicate neutral shades and with warmer colours, such as reds, pinks and yellows. The colour which contrasts most strongly with mid-blue is orange, which is exactly opposite on the colour wheel. It makes a lively accent in a cool blue colour scheme.

USING MID-BLUE

This soft tone of blue need not be a cold decorating colour. Teamed with warmer tones to take away any chilly feeling, successful colour schemes can be easily created. It is, however, a colour best suited to light rooms; in sunless rooms mid-blue could be oppressive.

The striking combination of mid-blue and white makes an impact when used in a variety of patterns, such as stripes, bold florals, or abstract designs. You can mix and match all sorts of patterns and still be successful by using this simple combination of colours.

Mid-blue makes a good accent colour, either as an harmonious or contrast accent. In an all-white bathroom, for instance, touches of mid-blue make a sharp contrast and create a crisp and fresh look. It also has a subtle cooling effect in an harmonious scheme of warm colours, such as pinks and peaches, or yellow and beige.

▷ **Subtle shades**
Mid-blue, pale grey and touches of pink make an harmonious colour scheme in this light living room. The rag-rolled walls bring some visual texture into a room scheme with smooth finishes. The variety of pink tones in the cushions, lamp and curtain fabric act like accents.

△ **Natural partners**
A soft tone of mid-blue suits the clean, unfussy lines of this modern but relaxed living room. It goes well with the soft neutral shades of the wood floor, the wickerwork basket and the muslin drape over the window, adding a cool tone to the warm shades of beige. The rug combines all these tones in its simple design.

△ Flowery corner

A traditional-looking floral design is perfect for this corner window seat with leaded windows and a garden view. A vivid tone of mid-blue is teamed with rich shades of pink, green and beige in three different fabrics. The same tone of mid-blue is used for the simple rosebud sprig design on the wallpaper. The variety of patterns are held together because the same range of colours is used in each of them.

◁ Cool blues

Mid-blue and light blue mixed with white and gleaming chrome accessories give this traditional bathroom a crisp fresh feel. Notice how the moulding on the panels around the bath and the picture rail are picked out in pale grey.

▷ Warm and sunny

A simple mixture of sunny yellow and mid-blue create a warm restful feel in this elegant bedroom. The mid-blue of the mini-print designs on the patchwork quilt is picked out in the plain stripes in the curtain fabric and the carefully shaped pelmets.

△ Mostly mid-blue

Subtle patterns in wallcoverings and fabrics are useful for bringing a variety of textures to colour schemes which are dominated by a single colour and which tend to look flat and boring. In this mid-blue room, several textures have been added in the wallpaper and its border, the upholstery fabric and the trellis-patterned carpet. The fabric for the curtains combines the beige of the carpet with mid-blue in a simple floral design. Samples of the wallpaper and fabrics used in this room are shown left.

◁ *Blue and white*
A fresh shade of blue and brilliant white is a traditional combination which is always successful in fabrics and wallcoverings. This collection of cushions with two formal but contrasting patterns – stripes and a large paisley design – work well together using the same two basic colours.

▽ *Mixing patterns*
Mid-blue is the perfect choice for this comfortable modern living room. Simple floral and leaf designs which combine a subtle range of colours – dusky pink, soft jade green, for instance – with mid-blue, are mixed in fabrics and wallcoverings creating a cool temperate colour scheme.

USING ACCENTS WITH MID-BLUE

Mid-blue is a tone which works equally well in all sorts of colour schemes. Combine it with soft pinks and greens for a more traditional look, or with primary colours in a modern scheme. In this modern dining room the black lacquered wood furniture is mixed with mid-blue and a variety of accents to create different effects.

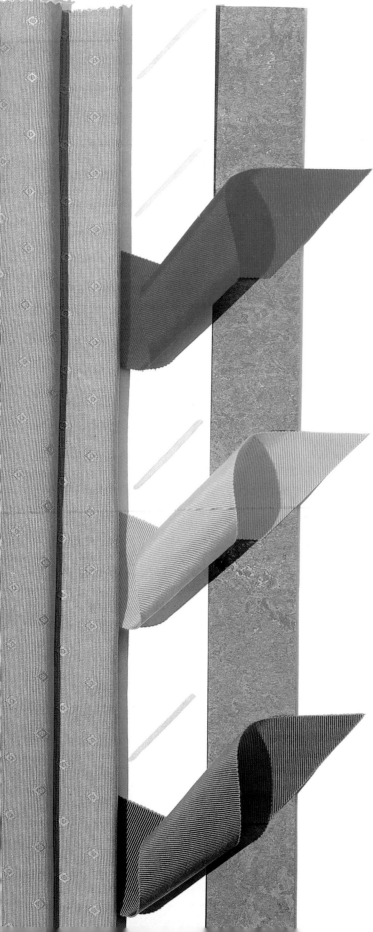

△ A few touches of shocking pink instantly add life to a simple mid-blue and white colour scheme.

△ Touches of yellow in a few areas are enough to bring the warmth of sunshine to a cool blue scheme.

△ Shades of mid-blue combined with a rich leaf green is an harmonious mixture found in nature.

RESTFUL SEA-GREEN

Green – especially blue-green – is the most restful on the eye of all the colours in the colour wheel.

Green is situated on the colour wheel between the two primary colours, yellow and blue, and can vary in colour from a very yellowish shade, through astringent lime green, lettuce and apple greens, to sage, peppermint and all the shades of the sea. Opposite it lie the hot oranges, pinks and reds that work so effectively as contrast colours.

Here the blue-green end of the spectrum is focused on, where the shades are softer, cooler and easier to handle in a colour scheme than the harder and more abrasive yellow-greens. This softness of tone means that the paler shades of blue-green can be used in some considerable quantity in a room scheme without becoming overwhelming in any way.

Although green is the colour most widely found in nature, it is surprisingly difficult to extract a natural dye. Dyes from nature tend to give rather pale, often muted shades. These are especially attractive when combined with other soft colours, as shown by work of the 19th century craftsman-artist William Morris whose designs are still popular.

STYLES AND ACCENTS

The soft blue-greens are ideally suited for cool, sophisticated colour schemes in smart town houses; and they create just the right atmosphere for shady rooms in hot climates. Deep sea-green can make a superb accent colour when used with pastels such as primrose yellow or pink.

Alternatively, pastel blue-green shades can form a harmonious background for many other colours: pinks – either pastel or a bright fuchsia – or yellows, while strong deep blues, such as cornflower, and reds, such as crimson, all make good accents.

Because they are so easy on the eye, pale duck-egg tints and other pastel hues make superb backdrops for naturals.

△ **Fresh and clean**
This light aquamarine colour is one you can use in quantity without it becoming overwhelming. Here it is used in two tones, with touches of white for freshness, coral-coloured shell stencils for warmth, and bright cornflower blue (in a bottle) for a surprising accent.

▷ **Colour partners**
Here the coral and turquoise chairs and straw-coloured mat all make happy partners with the blue-green walls. Daylight makes a subtle blue-green seem bluer, while electric tungsten light makes it seem greener: something to consider when devising a room scheme.

◁ *Deeper blue-greens*
Rich, deep blue-greens look good in conjunction with clear blue as well as apricot and shades of natural wood or brass. The glowing colours in this patterned chintz could easily dominate a colour scheme. However, a trellis-design wallpaper in pale sea-green and cream results in a pleasing and interesting harmony of patterns and colours.

▽ *A foil for wood*
Duck-egg colour walls make a superb background for every sort of wood and natural leather. They cool the warmth of the wood and, because the colour provides a complete contrast, enhance the sculptural outlines of furniture. Note how the cushions on the leather sofa pick up the blue-green theme in different textures and shades.

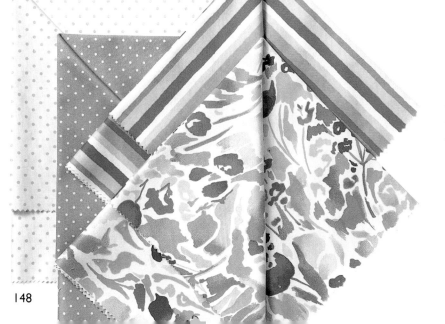

△ Traditionally pretty

Many plants with blue-green leaves, such as rosemary, have mauvish flowers. For a gentle, pretty scheme these colours – from the softest lilac, through warm, grapey blues, to pink – always combine successfully. The deep sea-green trim on the curtain valance provides a note of emphasis.

◁ You can pick out the colours more clearly in these samples.

▷ Coolly modern

Modern lines and blond wood are softened by using blue-greens all over the walls and stained floorboards. Note how ivory details – in lights, phone and flowers – look softer than white.

△ Richly sophisticated
Crimson red and black combined with rich blue-green produce a dramatic effect. By introducing beige in the sofa stripe, the designer prevents the scheme from becoming too sombre. Black painted furniture would look well in this setting too.

BRIGHT IDEA

Stencils in coral, cranberry or woody browns look good on aquamarine-painted surfaces. Incorporating a darker greeny-blue for stencilled foliage links the design to its background.

USING ACCENTS WITH BLUE-GREEN

Blue-green fits in with any style of decoration, whether modern or traditional, and makes a splendid foil for a wide range of accent colours, such as fuchsia or lilac, peach, coral or terracotta, and many shades of blue – such as cornflower or dark Oxford. In pastel tones it is especially suited to late 18th century and early 19th century styles, being reminiscent of the shades so popular for walls of the period. It also makes a soothing background for modern fabrics featuring strong colours.

△ **Strong accents**
Lilac picture frames, scatter cushions and tieback trim pick up one of the secondary colours in the curtains and contrast well with the marbled wallpaper and upholstery fabric.

△ **Dark and subtle**
With the same plain green carpet, self-patterned sofa and curtains quite a different mood is achieved using a more subtle deep red for the frames, lampshade and tieback trim.

THE RICHER SIDE OF RED

Reds and plums are very rich colours: used in the right way they can feel warm and luxurious all the year round.

True red is the strongest, most dominating of all the colours. It is a warm, powerful, advancing colour which, when used in any quantity, can draw in surroundings and make them feel claustrophobic. Used sparingly, red can make objects stand out and become focal points. Even functional objects such as pipework can be transformed into a decorative feature with a coat of glossy red. In the neutral-minded 1980s the orangey-reds have been played down in favour of the cooler, less insistent blue-reds. Combined with the cooler properties of blue, red is calmed down so that it becomes less eyecatching, varying from raspberry through the burgundies to deepest plum.

The softer, rich reds work particularly well in dining rooms that are mainly used in the evening for formal meals. Plum and raspberry are also wonderful welcoming colours for large hallways and landings, making these areas feel warmer and smaller because they seem to draw the walls closer together. In the same way, a chair upholstered in brilliant cherry red looks bigger and more important than one with deep blue upholstery.

Plums combine well with bright pinks, pale turquoise blues and minty greens. The darker plum shades are also practical colours that do not show the dirt easily. In hallways and landings, some of the small, all-over carpet designs with red backgrounds are a practical consideration. Sponging or rag-rolling walls with plummy reds gives a much needed warmth and softness that can benefit a room with a cold aspect. Contrast these reds with lots of crisp white-painted woodwork and a light creamy-beige floorcovering.

▷ **Pretty with pine**
Pink, blue and beige are a winning combination with plum. The same colours have also been picked out in the cushions, chair seat and co-ordinating wallpapers. A beige carpet and mellow pine furniture provide a neutral background for the busy wallpaper pattern.

▽ **Plum and white**
The use of white sets off the darker shades of plum and suits this Victorian bedroom to perfection. The patchwork quilt also cleverly echoes the plum and white colour theme. A picture rail and a built-in wardrobe all painted plum are attractive features to emphasize.

◁ *Border emphasis*
A simple red chequered border echoes the pattern in the rug and teams well with bluish-grey painted window mouldings. Touches of red in the flowers and accessories give an instant splash of colour to this predominately neutral cream and grey scheme.

▽ *Warm and inviting*
Red is an advancing colour that makes rooms look smaller and works well in areas where one doesn't spend much time. Red also absorbs light, so using a gloss paint for the brilliant red panelling helps reflect any available light.

WORKING WITH REDS AND PLUMS

A deep red Persian or Indian carpet is a good base from which to build a colour scheme. These carpets usually contain several muted reds, including plum shades and often one that is closer to orangey-red.

Try matching these carpet colours to the reds on paint shade cards – the paint samples can then be used to match up other reds in furnishing fabrics and wallpapers.

Shelving, an old table, or a trunk will look very handsome painted in a deep plum eggshell finish – this is easier on the eye than brilliant gloss paint.

A stencilled frieze in a brighter, more orangey-vermilion red on a plum-coloured background makes the plum appear browner and more muted. A pattern in a deep yellow also looks sophisticated. Other good combinations to put with the darker reds and plums are black-stained wood, natural pine or light oak furniture.

Natural wood floors and beige carpets also make a good foil for red walls. But avoid the use of too many boldly-patterned, contrasting red and white fabrics in any one room as these can be overpowering. A geometric mini print in dark red on a beige background is much easier to live with.

▷ **Crisp and modern**
A smart black and white geometric upholstery fabric sets off these softly sponged red walls and bookshelves to perfection. Striped curtain fabric containing the three colours helps link seating and wall colours together and creates a comfortable and modern reading corner.

▽ **Framing with red**
In this room the furnishing is fairly simple; interest is provided by the wallpaper and woodwork. One of the reds from this busy floral wallpaper has been chosen for the window frame and skirting to create a restful break for the eye while at the same time acting as a frame for the design.

LIGHTING

Because all reds absorb a lot of light, rooms with predominately red colour schemes need special care when it comes to lighting.

When buying red fabrics it is a good idea to take samples to view under the lighting conditions at home. Reds in fluorescent light can turn uncomfortably blue.

Avoid using translucent red silk lampshades as this not only reduces the amount of light but gives a theatrical pinkish glow which affects other colours in the room. For instance, blues will take on a mauve cast; yellows can turn orange and greens turn brown. If you do choose red lampshades, make sure they are lined in white, or pick cream colour shades which give a more neutral light.

Pepping up last year's scheme If you are tired of pastel and neutral schemes, try using reds in ethnic patterned fabrics such as ikat weaves, paisleys, batik prints and kelim rugs.

A beige carpet with sofa and chairs in a pastel floral print and plain beige curtains could be changed dramatically by replacing the upholstery and curtains with a daring ethnic print of plummy reds and adding an oriental rug.

Try and match ceramics and cushion fabrics to the reds in oriental rugs and the upholstery. Spray-painting wicker baskets a deep glossy red gives a bright, festive look.

△ **Exotic contrast**
Red makes objects look larger and
more important in a room scheme.
The red in the military chests here also
brings out the red in the richly
patterned curtains behind and prevents
them looking too heavy.

▽ **Sample board**
Traditional patterned fabrics with red
backgrounds look warm and inviting
and combine well with small, geometric
mini prints that are very close in tone.

USING RED AS AN ACCENT COLOUR

As red is such a strong predominating colour over large areas, it is often used as an accent colour to liven up quiet, cool, understated colour schemes.

Red paintwork and accessories – especially in a kitchen – can be replaced after a year or so if you find them overpowering. Try a cooler plum-red for a different effect.

Reds are especially good mixed with sombre neutrals, or the paler blues and greens.

▷ **Red with grey and black**
Neutral schemes using greys and black can benefit enormously from touches of brilliant colour seen in this red gloss painted window frame, red kitchen sink and accessories.

△ **Cheering up the blues**
Cool, receding pastels and mid-blues are brightened up considerably here with cheerful red accents.

△ **Pepping up the mints**
Greens lie in direct contrast to reds on the colour wheel; pastel and mint greens look livelier accented with red.

DRAMATIC BLACK AND WHITE

This striking colour combination needs sensitive handling if it is not to become stark and severe.

Disciples of ultra-modern minimalist and high tech styles of interior decoration adore black and white. It's a colour combination of dramatic simplicity: the ultimate in sophistication. The lines of 'designer' furniture, light fittings and accessories stand out in a room where no other colours distract the eye.

Black and white abounds in nature: dalmations spattered with inky spots, friesian cows and piebald horses are all natural examples of abstract patterns.

The present fashion for black and white started during the 1960s, when the op-art movement inspired a whole era of eye-teasing designs. Today, many of the most up-to-the-minute interiors are based on this combination.

In the 17th and 18th centuries, bedspreads and valances of blackwork embroidery (black thread on white cloth that resembled printed woodcut illustrations) depicting stylized fruit and flowers livened up many an oak four-poster. In both Italian renaissance palaces and the homes of Dutch burghers black and white tiled floors were equally favoured; the Georgians and Victorians, too, used them extensively in kitchens and bathrooms.

So 'no-colour' colour schemes made up largely of black and white needn't be ultra-modern: an eye for the right details in materials and accessories can bring warmth and tradition into this simplest of colour schemes.

△ **Smart and modern**
A black and white scheme highlights
detail. The lines of the furniture, the grid
of the tiles and even the blinds, provide
variety in this room.

▽ **Stark lines**
This simple colour scheme throws into
focus the shapes and lines used in a
symmetrical arrangement. Any severity
is softened by the wood table.

A GRAPHIC COMBINATION

A colour scheme based on black and white is a courageous choice and needs to be carried out with both consistency and conviction to be effective. Remember that black and white are natural delineators, and so make for a scheme with crisp, clear lines.

Purely black and white living rooms may look wonderfully chic in glossy magazines, but can be difficult to live with on a day-to-day basis. Black and white room schemes are unforgiving of chaos and require tidiness to look good. While too many extra colours can ruin the effect, one accent colour will provide a little visual relief.

The combination of black and white is especially appropriate in kitchens and bathrooms, where these colours enhance an atmosphere of efficiency, order and cleanliness.

Black and white schemes can also be very successful in short-stay rooms such as halls, dining rooms and cloakrooms. Take care, though, to avoid an abrupt colour change from a black and white hall into adjoining rooms; picking out black and white details in a wallpaper border, a rug, or black and white prints and using them in other rooms can lead the eye gently through the transition.

△ *A formal dining room*
Glossy black furniture combines happily with the fluid lines of a floral paper and more severe striped fabric.
See sample board at left.

▽ *Chequerboard chic*
A black and white chequerboard floor echoes the rectangular lines of this modern leather and tubular chrome seating.

USING BLACK AND WHITE

The use of pattern in black and white schemes demands careful thought: too many severe geometric designs could make the room look more like a zebra crossing than anything else. But different black and white patterns can easily be combined; thus floral prints can sit happily with more severe stripes, spots, or checks.

A black and white background makes a natural foil for the clean, sleek lines of modern furniture made of stained wood, plastic, chrome, or leather. As an alternative, try teaming them with the fine details and rich glow of antiques. Black and white ruthlessly draw attention to detail; so whatever furniture you choose, it must be well made and well designed.

Plain white or black floors look stunning, but soon become shabby without meticulous care; ceramic or vinyl tiles, or painted floorboards, make reasonably practical choices for plain floors, while chequerboard patterns add drama. If you prefer carpets, stick to a dark grey or mottled effect rather than plain black or white which will show every speck of dirt. Avoid creamy carpeting – it will look instantly grubby against true white. A timber floor adds welcome warmth to black and white schemes.

△ **Crisply framed**
Black-painted woodwork crisply frames door-hung storage against a mottled background. Attention to details such as the light switch and door furniture adds the perfect finishing touches.

▽ **A feel for the Thirties**
Lighting is important in black and white rooms. Here, wall-hung fittings provide a warm glow in a potentially severe bathroom. Clever detailing completes the sophisticated theme.

▷ **Pretty nostalgic**
A black and white colour scheme need not appear masculine. A mini-print wallpaper and demurely white bedlinen piled with lacy and frilly cushions soften the austere lines of a black iron bedstead trimmed with brass. The result is a romantic and feminine bedroom.

▽ **City sophistication**
In most black and white kitchens it is the white which predominates; here, though, black flooring and a wall of black tiles are combined with relatively small areas of pure white. However, the room is neither dark nor dreary – white grouting and pale wood-coloured units add lightness and freshness, and the glossy black wall and floor tiles reflect plenty of light.

RELIEVING THE STARKNESS

Although a colour scheme that's totally black and white can be stunning, the complete absence of anything else makes the eye work overtime searching for hints of colour. So it's usually a good idea to include at least one accent, perhaps on the floor, or in a painting or print. A neutral grey, bright primaries, or rich wood can all relieve the potential starkness of pure black and white. Whatever accent colour you choose, use enough to ensure that its impact isn't swallowed up by the drama of the overall theme.

△ **Fresh green accents**
Black and white is a very graphic, diagrammatic, combination. Touches of leafy green help to bring these rooms to life.

△ **A cheerful red** *picture frame, light fitting and tubular furniture brighten up a black and white scheme.*

△ **Primary yellow accents**
Add zest to white walls and woodwork and a black and white chequerboard floor by using contrasting bright citrus yellow as accent.

CHAPTER 3

INTERIOR DESIGN IDEAS

SOFT MODERN

Soft Modern is a style that is easy to like — and easy to live in. The kind of style that is wonderful to come home to after a tiring day.

Up-to-date and streamlined as it is, Soft Modern is the essence of comfort. It's a light airy look by day that is transformed by subdued lighting — lots of shaded table lamps and candles, no overhead lights — into a warm atmospheric look at night time. This is a style that suits almost any type of home, whether old or new. Architectural details are unimportant because you can use wallpaper borders in place of non-existent features — at dado or picture-rail height, for example.

Colours are predominantly pastels —

sometimes almost bleached out; at other times warmer but still subdued, like dusty pink. They are used with small amounts of earthy shades and stronger accents.

Patterns are mixed with patterns, but they are soft and blurred so that nothing clashes. Traditional motifs such as chevrons, checks and trellises, live happily side by side with abstract designs that imitate textures and small smudgy florals.

Subtle fabrics are used in profusion — on windows as well as for upholstery.

Tailored roman blinds look neat but generous. So do the simple curtains that hang straight or are held with tiebacks.

Walls are covered with papers of gently patterned designs. Or they are painted in soft shades using the popular techniques of ragging, dragging and sponging. Woodwork, too, is often subjected to this subtle treatment. Fireplaces are generally painted. Ceilings are invariably white to increase the feeling of space and light, while the floors are close-carpeted or of light-coloured wood.

Finishing touches are stylish too: ceramics with crackle glazes, rounded shapes or strangely angled; table lamps with big conical shades; vases of tall blooms; tailored cushions trimmed with piping; pale rag rugs.

Silent night

Comfortable and welcoming on a winter's night, this room is just as appealing in daytime when the curtains are drawn back — sunlight softens the strong pink of the chairs and makes the room seem light and fresh.

▷ **Kitchen – light and sure**
Gentle colour with wood is the very essence of the Soft Modern look. White appliances and glass-fronted cupboards emphasize the feeling of light and space, and accessories repeat the pink and wood theme.

▽ **Bathroom softly dappled**
Smudged blue and pale green tiles are divided by a dado rail, woodwork is drag-painted, the blind is splashed with gentle colour.

▽ **Bedroom – comfort and joy**
A bedroom designed for comfort and relaxation. The walls and furniture have been kept very plain – interest focuses on the patchwork quilt, while the white framed mirror behind the bed creates an illusion of space in a smallish room.

△ **Bathroom – luxury looks**
Although this elegant bathroom is large enough for a standard tub, using a corner bath means it feels more spacious – and looks luxurious. Classic floor tiles in soft and darker grey are a practical choice, and the introduction of pink in the floor-length curtains softens the overall effect.

△ **Bedroom – rhapsody in blue**
Masses of fabric around the windows and the bed in soft blue and white give a light, fresh look to this lovely bedroom. The patchwork quilt echoes the blue theme and adds a touch of pink. The long sweeping curtains are held back with ties for an almost theatrical effect – they give great style to what are, in reality, quite narrow windows.

The four-poster is a worthy centre-piece. You can build your own by boxing in a divan base and adding a frame of 5cm square posts. Position curtain tracks behind the frame at the top and hang with lightweight curtains, like these fine cotton striped ones.

◁ **Living room – pink and patterned**
The mixture of patterns in this stylish living room works because the colours are well co-ordinated and no one pattern is too dominant. The dark-stained occasional tables add interest, while the combination of long curtains and roman blinds shade the room from bright daylight.

ELEMENTS OF STYLE

This green and blue room is a perfect example of the Soft Modern style. It is simple and stunningly elegant.

Look at the features pointed out here and consider them when decorating in this style. Examine the photographs on the previous pages, too. Although each room is different, there is a very obvious common feel – the way the walls are treated, the kind of accessories, the type of furniture and fabrics, and most of all the use of colour and pattern.

It's a good idea to keep in mind how the room will look at night. Use subdued lighting – table lamps with big shades are good choices.

Window treatment
A roman blind is combined with a long draped curtain to elegant effect. The curtain is easy to make. Attach the curtain to the pole with Sew 'n' Stick Velcro (apply it using the method given on page 170). You may have to twist the fabric to the front so the right side is showing – the curtain will hang better if a lightweight fabric is used.

Walls
A soft, blurred wallpaper blends perfectly with the other patterns in the room. Co-ordination is an important feature of the Soft Modern style.

Picture rail
The picture rail is painted white with a wallpaper border below for added emphasis.

Accessories
Ceramics play a supporting role – choose rounded shapes, strangely angled ones and box shapes. They should be highly glazed, perhaps with a crackle finish.

Furniture
The sofa and the tables are streamlined – fussy curves and flourishes are inappropriate. The light wood used for the tables suits the other elements in the room – dark wood needs a warmer colour scheme.

Accents
Add interest with accents of stronger or contrasting colours. Here the green cushion and blue chair are very much in harmony with the rest of the scheme, the pink on the flower jug makes a pretty finishing touch.

Pastels and patterns

A mixture of patterns in soft pastel colours – such as pink, apricot and blue – in fabrics and wall coverings, combine with simple streamlined furniture and accessories to epitomize the Soft Modern look.

Here, patterns are mixed in fabrics with colours that blend perfectly; a small area of strong orange acts as an accent, in an otherwise pastel scheme.

A simple coffee table with a pale, wood laminate finish, round ceramic vases and table lamps, which cast a gentle light, are all finishing touches which contribute to the look.

DRAPED CURTAINS

This is a very easy method of making draped curtains. It is suitable for reversible fabrics such as plain or woven cottons, muslin and sheers.

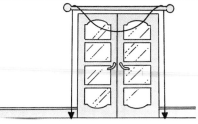

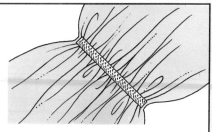

□ Fix the curtain pole in position above the window. Measure for the fabric using a length of string: from the floor, draped over the pole at each end and down to the floor on the opposite side. Adjust until you get an attractive drape. Add an allowance for two double 5cm hems.

□ The curtain is made from a single width, so choose a 122cm or wider fabric. You will also need a length of Sew 'n' Stick Velcro the width of the fabric. Stitch the hems at each end and press.

□ Hang the fabric over the pole and arrange the drapes into attractive folds. Mark positions for Velcro slightly behind where the fabric passes over the pole at each end.

□ Take down the fabric and, at both positions, sew two rows of gathering stitches across the fabric width and pull up evenly to half the fabric width. Fasten off. Stitch across gathers to hold in position. Cut the Velcro in half and stitch the 'sew' half over the gathering stitches on the wrong side.

□ Apply self-adhesive half of Velcro to the curtain pole at the correct positions. Hang curtains over the pole and press the Velcro together.

▽ *Touches of style*
Look out for accessories to complete this streamlined look. Elegant glasses, such as these champagne flutes, china in simple shapes and pastel colours with linear decoration, and stipple-patterned ceramic tiles for the bathroom, are perfect finishing touches.

CITY MODERN

Perfect for sleek city living, this look is uncluttered, functional and streamlined.

A look of stark contrasts, City Modern is based on monochromatic (single-colour) schemes. It is best suited to urban living.

A combination of streamlined styles from both past and present, the furniture and accessories for the City Modern look are primarily angular in shape. At the window, venetian blinds or tailored roman blinds are the most suitable. They still let light enter while maintaining privacy and allowing the window area to remain as plain as possible.

Colours too are functional, being predominantly black or grey, with chrome trimmings on the furniture.

Accent colour is kept to a minimum, often seen in simply-shaped vases that are carefully placed, or large abstract prints hung on the wall.

Furniture has clearly defined edges with minimal detailing. Cabinets are either glass-fronted to show off the contents – a few pieces of ceramic or chrome objects – or plain-fronted to hide away any clutter.

Dining tables are clean-looking, stained, often with metal legs. Tablecloths are abandoned in favour of showing the stained – often black – wood and clear lines of the table itself.

Upholstered furniture should be con-fined to sofas which are long, low-backed and covered in neutral colours such as grey or black. There are few armchairs: two or more sofas are pre-ferred, with the occasional tubular chrome and leather chair.

Lighting is an important aspect of this look as it must be both decorative and functional. Floor and table lamps have a 1930s feel, as do simple chrome standard lamps. Wall lights are used to create a softer atmosphere – which is essential when furniture and accessories are often so stark in outline.

Accessories are kept to a minimum: a ceramic vase holding tall flowers such as tulips or arum lilies, or a dramatic leafy plant. Chrome kitchenware ties in with tubular steel furniture.

Smart and sophisticated, this style is strongly defined and uncompromising. Its uncluttered lines are ideal for city flats, where space is so often at a premium.

▽ *Living room – city slick*
Classic chrome and leather chairs feature strongly, tying in with the tubular trolley. Lilies in a speckled vase fill the period fireplace, giving it a distinctly up-dated look.

▷ **Bedroom – cool and fresh**
The gentle curve of the grey bed frame, highly reminiscent of the 1930s, is echoed by the desk light. The plain white of storage units that hide all the clutter is relieved by simple grey handles. The lightly geometric-patterned wallpaper makes a suitable background for the contemporary prints that form a focal point in the room. Simple grey-edged yellow bedlinen adds a touch of freshness.

▽ **Living area – comfortably functional**
Pale grey is a slightly softer option for walls if white looks too clinical. Here the venetian blinds help to block out a dull view. Accent colour is provided by turquoise box files on the shelving unit, while shiny black vases – in or out of use – add an extra dimension. Tall flowers in a pale floor vase and a large leafy house plant help to soften this living area's otherwise strict functionalism.

▽ **Kitchen – sophisticated style**
Plain dove grey kitchen units are given added interest by the ridged door surfaces in this very stylish, compact kitchen. The stainless steel cooker hood, oven front, saucepans and swivel chair at the breakfast bar provide shiny accents. Marble-look floor tiles carry smooth city sophistication through the entire room,

◁ **Hallway – stunning entry**
This interesting interpretation of a period hallway has combined original features with the City Modern look. The 19th-century fireplace and mouldings have been retained and the area below the dado has been ragged. Rather than laying the standard chequerboard pattern, tiles have been used to form stripes. Thirties-inspired wall lights replace overhead pendants and a gallery of black and white photographs hangs along the wall, making a striking and thoroughly modern feature.

CITY SLICKER

This is a look that is surprisingly easy to create, featuring clear, simple lines in both furniture and accessories. Window treatments are also unfussy, with blinds or tailored curtains that can be used to block out an uninspiring view.

Lighting
Decorative as well as functional, atmosphere is all-important. Wall lights replace overhead pendants, while floor and freestanding lamps have shapes often reminiscent of the 30s.

Windows
Simplicity is the keynote here – blinds are roman, roller, or venetian, while curtains have a sophisticated tailored look, devoid of fussy detailing.

Furniture
Stained black ash features throughout the house. Detailing is kept to a minimum – coffee tables and dining furniture are often angular and have a streamlined look. Sofas and other upholstered furniture are covered in plain fabrics or leather.

Accessories
Choose cocktail glasses with a 30s feel, chrome kitchenware, speckled ceramics and elegantly-shaped tall vases. Accent colours are few. Yellow, dusky pink, cobalt blue, turquoise, bright green and red are all suitable, but use sparingly.

Walls
Wallpaper is light in tone with fine geometric patterns or stripes. As an alternative walls can be painted in white, cream or pale grey emulsion. Paintwork is also in neutral colours – and there should be no decorative dados or mouldings.

Flooring
Neutral colours predominate, and rugs with geometric designs provide interest to main rooms. Vinyl flooring suits this look if polished floorboards aren't an option.

△ Furniture

Furniture is black or grey. Stained ash tables, shelving and cupboards; simple but strong lines. Leather is the ideal upholstery material, not only for sofas but also for occasional and dining chairs. Combined with gleaming chrome, it typifies the City Modern look.

◁ Surfaces

Fabric designs are monochromatic and angular to tie in with the look.

Vinyl tiles – that can be laid in chequerboard or other patterns – and linoleum in speckled patterns cover areas where bare floorboards are unsuitable. Cream and grey can be used as alternative flooring colours to black and white. Plain walls suit this look and wallpaper should be used sparingly.

▷ **Accessories**

Small accessories are few in the City Modern flat as the look is essentially sleek, smart and uncluttered. Choose 30s inspired objects: black lacquer picture frames, shiny chrome kitchenware and stainless steel utensils. Ceramics should be highly glazed and smooth, in simple shapes and either black or white, or softly coloured for accent.

▽ **Essentials**

Large floor-vases in dramatic black, or vivid Mediterranean hues for bright accent colour, are essential accessories for any room. Speckled bowls and vases tie in with flooring and cushions. Floor-standing lamps also act as decorative objects, reflecting the influence of the 30s on this look. Venetian blinds, if used, should be fine and can provide another opportunity for colour. But keep principally to black and white for a successful City Modern look.

COUNTRY COMES TO TOWN

Bring a touch of country life into an urban setting and create relaxed but sophisticated interiors.

For city dwellers who choose the country look as the inspiration for decorating their homes, the country cottage model is not always a suitable choice. The scale of town houses often makes it difficult to recreate the cosiness of a small country retreat, particularly if the rooms lack any interesting features, and if the ceilings are high, or the windows are large, for instance.

This modern style captures some of the nostalgic atmosphere of the country cottage look, but it feels more sophisticated. It has touches of stripped pine in furniture and flooring, restrained colours in fabrics and wallcoverings, and collections of all sorts of china making a comfortable look which is easy and relaxing to live with.

COLOUR AND PATTERN

Country colours tend to be soft, and include not only the pretty pinks and fresh greens of the country cottage, but warm buttery yellows, cooled down with shades of blue. Matt or silk finish paints are the most suitable for walls and woodwork — such as tongued-and-grooved panelling — because they are close to the old finishes.

Patterned wallcoverings play a part in this look, too. Small geometrics are more suitable than tiny sprig designs which belong to the small scale of the country cottage style and would look lost on large walls. Stencilled borders — simple floral garlands, for example — or decorative paper borders add a touch of the countryside to a room scheme.

CHOOSING THE FURNITURE

Modern pine furniture with a plainer more streamlined outline mixes well with more traditional pieces; but don't go overboard with the stripped pine look, mix wooden with upholstered or painted furniture.

Cane and wicker furniture would be good choices too, either natural or painted to create a slightly more sophisticated look.

Dining room – simple elegance

A dining table with a mixture of different chairs does not suit this style. Here, the table, ladder-back chairs and corner cupboard are in a matching Victorian country style. The sprig wallpaper in a subtle mixture of colours has been carefully chosen to suit the scale of the room.

◁ **Bathroom – soft washes**
This traditional bathroom is painted in a sophisticated colour scheme of pinks and greys. Notice how the dado is blended into the overall wall colour rather than picked out in a different colour in the usual country style. A pinkish-grey carpet adds a luxurious finishing touch, topped with a dhurrie in deep pink, grey and jade stripes.

◁◁ **Elegant displays**
This Victorian-style pine cupboard, with attractive glass arched panels, makes an elegant alternative to the more familiar country dressers. A collection of glass is displayed inside and all sorts of jugs – some Victorian, some from the 1920s – are perched on top.

◁ *Living room – in the pink*
Deep pink is typical of the soft tones
which suit this town and country look.
Simple wooden furniture, a
comfortable modern sofa and a
Victorian-style tub chair create a
relaxed feel to the room. The collection
of watercolour landscapes and still life
paintings, and the stone jar filled with
flowers are perfect finishing touches.

▷ *Dining room – painted cane*
The natural materials of the country
look are combined in an unusual way in
this stylish kitchen/dining room. The
cane dining table and chairs have been
painted green to match the colour
scheme in the kitchen. The wall is
divided by a dado rail and the skirting
boards are stripped and varnished. The
polished wood floor gives a highly
finished look to the room.

▽ *Kitchen – a flowery touch*
Pretty floral curtains, matching cushion
covers and decorative border in
autumn colours set the tone of this
country-style kitchen. Delicate shades of
cream and blue are used for the walls
and also for the attractive tongued-and-
grooved panelled dado.

△ **Bedroom – well co-ordinated**
Mini-print wallpaper and matching
fabrics for the curtains and bedcover
are the perfect partners for the
traditional pine furniture in this
bedroom. The chest of drawers is
probably mid-Victorian with a little
decorative beading around the drawers
and glass knobs. A large jug and bowl
with a floral design, and a vase of fresh
flowers complete the rural look.

Notice how a painted dado rail has
been added to create a more rustic feel
to the room.

▷ **Window dressing**
A combination of café curtains, which
cover the lower half of the window, and
simple, short curtains gives these large
windows a country look. The lemon
yellow fabric with a tiny sprig design is
edged with a frill and tied back with a
matching ribbon.

TRADITIONAL ELEGANCE

This is a style that offers an elegant, refined and luxurious way of living suited to town or country.

Traditional Elegance harks back to the 18th century and the golden age of craftsmanship and design in Britain. During that period interiors were designed as frameworks for social events, and this style is still best suited to principal rooms. Proportions are important. If your home has large windows, high ceilings, and original features, this style is for you.

Often, the fireplace is the focal point of a room: a white marble Adam-type surround, with steel fender and grate, is still one of the most elegant styles to be found. A mirror or family portrait hangs above the fireplace, which can be filled with a flower arrangement.

Walls should be kept in pale background colours: blue, lemon, green or grey. Various painting techniques are well suited to this style, in particular ragging, dragging and marbling. Papers that echo these techniques are widely available. Alternatively, hang a paper with a discreet 'regency' stripe or tiny print, or one of the oriental-style designs known as 'chinoiserie'.

Windows are given a formal treatment: swags and tails or other elaborate headings, fringed or frilled curtains with heavy cord-and-tassel tiebacks.

Fabrics Large, often stylized florals or stripes are usual for curtains or loose covers; damasks or brocades serve for upholstery as well as curtains.

Floors can be polished wood with large, traditionally-patterned rugs. These days fitted carpets in discreet background colours are more common.

Lighting, too, is unobtrusive: wall lights, chandeliers in the main rooms, and ceramic table lamps with pleated silk or chintz lampshades all suit this style. On dining tables and sideboards silver candelabra lend atmosphere.

Traditional Elegance is exactly as it sounds – a sophisticated look which is perfectly suitable for town or country life.

Bedroom – pretty relaxing

Large floral-design frilled curtains have a single swag secured at either end with a bow. The mix of antiques and easy furniture makes this room ideal for relaxing as well as sleeping.

△ **Drawing room – muted elegance**
An elegant yet comfortably informal drawing room in pale, muted tones is lifted by the use of a vibrant blue. The large floral arrangement that fills the Adam-style fireplace when not in use and the symmetrically-hung pictures on either side are typical of this style. It is apparent, too, in the pretty window treatment with its interesting but unfussy pelmet and the choice of furniture that includes comfortable armchairs and sofas with antiques or good reproduction pieces.

▷ **Bathroom – formal and light**
The pale geometric-patterned wallpaper and roller-blind fabric, coupled with the very stylized window treatment, give this luxurious bathroom a rather formal air. The bath panels have been marblized to tie in with the real marble splash-back and surround. Edwardian taps and modern brass accessories work well with the pale marble, adding to the air of Traditional Elegance.

BRIGHT IDEA

Dress up a chair that needs re-upholstering by making a cushion from 5cm foam, cut to shape and boxed in a suitable fabric. Pipe the cushion with cord and make cord ties to secure the cushion to the chair back. Attach tassels to each cord end – four in all. Allow plenty of cord and large tassels.

△ *Hallway – discreetly striped*
This classic cream-and-gold treatment of hall and stairway shows how well the style adapts to a small town house. Discreet striped wallpaper is often associated with the Regency period and certainly suits this hall with its huge flower arrangement on the console and ornate gilt-framed mirror above. Careful attention has been paid to detail – the marble effect of the floor tiles has been extended to the skirting, with the colours repeated in the dado rail.

▷ *Sitting room – classical warmth*
The somewhat imposing proportions of this room are lessened by the use of warm apricot tones throughout. Brown and apricot-patterned curtains have a traditional swag-and-tail heading and the relief design on the painted fire surround is picked out in crisp white. A collection of family portraits is hung over the fireplace in classic style and prized ornaments displayed along the mantelpiece. Task lighting is provided by elegant table lamps. The furniture arrangement of comfortable sofa and armchairs forming two sides of a square and focusing on the fireplace makes the seating area the centrepiece of the room – ideal for easy conversation.

Accessories
Large carved and gilded mirrors hung over a mantelpiece or sideboard suit almost any room; prints and portraits also hang on the wall or stand on occasional tables. Choose a few pieces of china and silver and place a huge floral arrangement on its own. For the dining table go for good china and glass in classic 18th-century styling.

Walls
Painted or papered in pale classic background colours; discreet stripes or chinoiserie patterns to provide a backdrop for elegant furniture and accessories. Woodwork, cornices, and relief work should be contrasting.

DINING IN STYLE
The room most likely to be decorated in a traditional manner is the dining room, as furnishings and accessories here are often inherited pieces. It tends, too, to be the most formal room in the house, less used by children and more for evening entertaining, and therefore allowing the display of china and glass either on a sideboard or in display cabinets.

Furniture
Antique or good reproduction pieces in mahogany, rosewood or walnut veneer, especially in the style of Chippendale, Sheraton or Hepplewhite. Comfortable sofas and easy chairs where appropriate.

Flooring
Fitted carpets are often best for town houses. Alternatively, choose a large carpet to lay over polished floorboards. A big-scale design with a strong border, often in muted colours, is ideal.

Soft furnishings
Windows are often elaborately dressed with pelmets and tiebacks. Use rich damasks and stripes for upholstery and formal drapes; large floral designs for bedroom and living room curtains.

◁ *Accessories*
This is not a cluttered style. Choose pieces whose design harks back to the 18th century, the 'golden age' of fine craftsmanship in Britain. Jasperware by Wedgwood with its classical relief work, elegantly shaped china, and silver candelabra and tableware all suit this traditional style.

▽ *Furniture*
The 18th century is the one to follow for furniture that is both traditional and elegant. The dining chair with Prince of Wales' feathers is in Hepplewhite style, while the lower, square-backed chair is characteristic of Sheraton. Above all, furniture should be distinctive, as is this sofa-table with brass handles and ormolu mounts.

△ Essentials

Brass reproduction light fittings are most suitable, though they don't give the atmospheric light of real candles. For living rooms and bedrooms choose porcelain lamp bases in classical shapes and add a pleated silk shade. Plenty of cushions, in stripes or large floral designs, co-ordinate with other soft furnishings.

▽ Fabrics and wallcoverings

Use damask for upholstery and curtains, or a large-scale floral design – especially if you want to make the most of a large window area. Chinoiserie for both walls and fabrics has been popular since tea arrived in England, and striped 'regency' wallpaper and fabric is very suitable for the traditional elegance of this look.

CLASSIC ENGLISH FLORAL CHINTZ

It's flowers all the way with this style of fabric design that has become a recognizable look in itself.

Indian chintz caused a sensation when it first arrived in Europe around 300 years ago. Seventeenth century bedrooms boasted chintz spreads, curtains and even chintz floorcloths. The name 'chintz', derives from the Hindi word 'chints', meaning painted or printed fabrics and now describes any cotton furnishing fabric with a predominantly floral pattern and glazed finish.

Colours and patterns Early stylized floral chintz was much influenced by European embroideries brought out for Indian artists to copy.

Traditional English chintz usually means old-fashioned, very realistic, floral designs of full-blown roses, parrot tulips, peonies, lilies and wild flowers; often incorporating other motifs such as ribbons and birds. Today's chintz style favours larger, less defined blossoms and mixes several different patterns.

Choosing the furnishings Generous, full-length chintz curtains look best with frilled edges and pelmets. Roman or austrian blinds in plain or all-over prints in glazed cotton also add extra elegance. Sofas and armchairs are traditional and comfortable with chintz or complementary plain or printed linen loose covers.

Other furniture is mainly mahogany in traditional styles; for a more modern feel mellow antique pine works well. Round tables made from chipboard can be covered with floor-length cloths of patterned chintz or glazed cotton. Coolie lampshades covered in chintz or wall fittings with decorative sconces suit this look. Walls can be covered with flowery papers or emulsion-painted for a plainer look. Floors can be bare boards covered with oriental rugs, or pastel fitted carpets.

Living room – quiet elegance
This typically lush mid-Victorian glazed chintz mixes perfectly with modern mock-moiré glazed cotton in the austrian blind and tablecloth.

◁ *Seating – modern looks*
By the end of the 18th century industrial fabric printing had resulted in more natural-looking floral patterns and colours, mostly on light backgrounds. Today's chintzes come in paint-box fresh simple florals with a huge choice of background colours. Here, cushions and loose covers blend harmoniously with a striped, glazed cotton, roman blind.

▽ *Bedroom – plain and patterned*
Plain walls and a neutral carpet on the floor balance the Jacobean-looking print in these chintz curtains, covered bedhead and divan base. A quiet trellis-patterned glazed cotton quilt co-ordinates well with the busy patterned chintz without being too insistent. The wall lamps have plain brackets to emphasize this plainer chintz look.

▽ *Co-ordinating patterns*
For an all-over chintz look try mixing patterns. Here, floral patterns in similar colours link the curtains and upholstery. A plain glazed cotton tablecloth is less busy than a floral chintz would be for this style.

△ **Living room – cottage**
A plain white-painted dado provides relief to the busy floral walls and matching chintz curtains. Muted reds in the Indian rug and cushion covers here blend perfectly with the bright pinks and reds in the fabric and wallpaper. The trompe l'oeil painted vase of flowers and cat add witty touches.

▷ **Sitting room – warm and practical**
Warm apricots and cream are a practical choice with dark flooring and walls. The result is a less flowery look and a sunny all-the-year-round feel to this seating arrangement

STYLING WITH CHINTZ

Classic chintz is an essentially comfortable look and at home in both town and country settings. Walls can be plain painted, or papered in small-scale trellis, florals or stripes; floral borders also help to emphasize the flowery chintz feeling. Floorcoverings can be fitted carpets in neutral or pastel colours, or polished boards with oriental rugs. Lighting is atmospheric: table lamps with coolie shades of pleated chintz or silk shades in soft pastel colours. Wall lamps are either simple plaster candle bracket-and-shade fittings, or more ornate gilded sconces. Mix floral china in different patterns, fill china bowls with pot pourri to perfume the room. Plump, feather-filled cushions covered in different chintzes make essential accessories.

Lighting
For a traditional look choose silk shades in empire and panelled square shapes as decorative table lamps or wall lamps with candle holders and gilt sconces. Coolie shades covered in chintz with ginger jar bases give a more modern look.

Windows
Curtains should be generous and full, preferably with frilled pelmets and edges; grander windows can have decorative pelmets and tie-backs. Roman or austrian blinds can be in matching or co-ordinating chintzes — or plain glazed cottons.

Seating
Traditional-style comfortable sofas and armchairs, either upholstered or loose covered — often in serviceable linen union in a pattern that matches the chintz. Piping in a contrasting colour gives a tailored finish.

Furniture
A few good pieces of mahogany for chairs and tables, in 18th century and Victorian styles. Round chipboard tables can be covered with chintz or glazed cotton floor-length cloths and used to display family photos and fine china.

Flooring
Plain polished floorboards or fitted carpets in light and dark colours. Indian and Persian rugs in soft, muted colours go well with traditional chintz. Chinese cut-pile rugs with simple border patterns in pastel colours also look good.

Accessories
Pick traditional fine bone china in bright colours that emphasize the colours in the chintz. Choose plain ceramics and porcelain if you want to play down the floral effect.

▷ **Line and shape**
Wing-back chairs are normally upholstered in heavy, hard-wearing fabrics but the new, fresh chintzes give a softer, more feminine look that contrasts particularly well with dark wood side tables and comfortable upholstered stools.

▽ **Wallpapers and fabrics**
There is a lot of choice about in co-ordinating chintz-style wallpapers, borders and fabrics. To mix and match these successfully use patterns of different scales and contrast large exuberant rosy florals with trellis and small all-over prints.

△ Accessories
Pick Victorian bone china in bright colours and curvy shapes.
Have pretty chintzy table linens in the dining room and floral
boxes and bowls filled with pot pourri.

▽ Essentials
Chintz coolie shades have a modern feel; for traditional looks
pick silk empire shades. Mix different chintz cushions with the
occasional plain glazed cotton.

CONSERVATORY STYLE

With the right choice of furniture and accessories you can create a garden room even in a city-centre flat.

You can successfully achieve the conservatory 'look' anywhere in the house by making your rooms feel like an extension of the garden – or even a substitute for one. The overall effect should be light and airy and if you don't have a room with lots of natural light, you can still create a fresh, outdoor look with the right choice of colours, fabrics and furniture.

Colours are soft pastels, creams and white with a generous amount of green – from dark emerald to olive, through to the palest leafy greens. Patterns are busy, colourful floral designs to imitate herbaceous borders or sprays of flowers, or trellis designs – use anything that gives a garden feel.

Walls can be treated simply as background for plants – painted or papered in plain, pale shades – or as substitutes for plants and covered in rambling floral design wallpapers.

If you plan to fill the rooms with plants, then use flooring that won't be damaged by water spills – quarry or ceramic tiles or less expensive vinyl are suitable, as is natural-look sisal or coir matting which feels warmer underfoot. Add rag rugs for extra comfort and warmth. If you do choose carpet, keep to natural shades.

Furniture has a summery, outdoor feel: wicker, bamboo and cane are ideal. White-painted wrought iron, though attractive, can be uncomfortable. Upholstered seating is not really in keeping with this style, so try instead a mass of cushions in mixed sizes and flowery patterns or bright, glowing plains.

Window treatments depend on the size and shape of your windows as well as the other furnishings in the room. Try split cane or bamboo blinds with natural furniture, or floral design curtains or roller blinds with plumpy cushions.

For lighting, choose basketware shades or glass globe wall lights on wrought iron supports. Uplighters hidden among plants show off the foliage.

Of course you'll need plenty of containers to hold the profusion of plants that is central to this look – and plenty of fresh flowers for a summery feeling all year round.

Conservatory bay
Large windows give an unrestricted view of the garden beyond, and large potted plants thrive in the light. Furniture is simply-shaped cane and bamboo, with comfortable cushions in a floral print.

▷ **Dining room – olive green**
The fresh white and green colour
scheme gives a garden atmosphere that
is emphasized by bamboo chairs with
trellis-like framework. The chairs are
stained to match the olive green carpet
and seat cushions.

The darker green detailing on the
panelled door is echoed by the
trimming on the simple roman blinds.
Bistro wall lights look perfect in this
setting, while pale walls and tablecloth
complete the garden feel.

▽ **Living room – botanical corner**
A feeling of the outdoor prevails in this
beautiful sitting room. Furniture is
grouped next to the large french
windows. There are pots and vases
containing masses of greenery, botanical
prints hang over the table and wicker
chair – and even the chair cushions are
printed with pots of herbs.

△ **Bedroom – country-look**
Natural cane headboard and chair combine with softly-
patterned wallpaper and fabrics to pretty effect. The pine
dressing table has a stencilled design on each drawer.

△ **Dining room – flowery**
Busy, floral wallpaper
dominates this sunny dining
room where the pink on the
wall is picked out in the china
and cutlery. A bamboo blind
and plant holders match the
furniture and a thin louvre
door makes a feature of the
window.

◁ **Living room – all white**
Everything in this sunny
corner is painted white – the
walls and woodwork, the
cane furniture and plant
stand. The only colour and
decoration is in a delicate
floral border above the high
dado, and in the cushions and
accessories. Even the plants
in this peaceful garden-style
retreat are light and delicate.

GREEN AND PLEASANT

A major colour for this look is green – whether the clear green and white reminiscent of palm trees and foliage plants in a hot house/conservatory or the softer greens and gently-coloured blooms of an English country garden. If you can't have the real thing, then create your own indoor garden with colourful mixed floral-design wallpapers and fabrics.

Furniture and floorcoverings need to be kept as far as possible in natural materials and colours: cane or bamboo, for example. Trelliswork on the walls – either real or designed on wallpaper – adds to the garden room feeling and provides the perfect background for plants.

The finished overall effect is light and airy. Use as many pot plants and cut flowers as possible.

Plants
As many plants as possible, in terracotta, ceramic or basketware planters. You can vary their heights with jardinières or cane plant stands. Botanical prints or pictures with a summery feel are ideal, and vases of flowers and plain coloured cushions can be used to pick out accent colour from your floral fabrics.

Windows
Allow as much light in as possible. Louvred shutters give a dappled, summery effect. Bamboo, split cane or rice paper blinds are also suitable. For curtains, choose floral or trellis patterns.

Walls
Plain, pale walls reflect as much light as possible. Here they are off-white, but will work just as well in a pale green or peach. Wallpapers have flowery sprays or climbing roses, or trelliswork designs for a more formal look.

Fabrics
Florals are the best choice, in colours that are light and bright. A mixture of patterns imitates a summer herbaceous border. Plain cushions in bright, glowing colours act as accent points.

Flooring
Natural flooring looks best against wicker furniture. Sisal or coir matting is cheap and fairly hardwearing. Terracotta or ceramic tiles make your room look like a real conservatory but they can be cold underfoot; cover them with rugs. Carpet should be in natural shades.

Furniture
Has a garden or outdoor feel. Wicker, bamboo or cane are ideal, either left in their natural colour or painted in pastel colours. The glass top on the table in this picture makes it stable and thus ideal for serving drinks.

IN THE GEORGIAN MANNER

The restrained elegance of the 18th century can be adapted to suit 20th-century homes and lifestyles.

The Georgian era in the 18th century is considered by many to be one of the high points of British architecture and interior decoration. Inspired by the architecture of Greece and Rome, and fuelled by the growing prosperity of the age, this most English of styles developed in houses with large rooms, high ceilings and tall windows. The Georgian style can, however, be adapted to suit well-proportioned modern rooms, and Georgian elements can be included in more modest homes.

The restrained and graceful style favoured by the Georgians depended on their almost infallible eye for proportion. Symmetry and balance were all-important: what happened on one side of a room was balanced by what happened on the other. The fireplace – generally classical in shape and flanked by paired columns – represented the clear focal point of a room and the recesses beside the chimney breast were decorated identically. Furniture and ornaments were carefully arranged.

Architecturally, Georgian rooms were usually divided into three sections with a dado towards the bottom of the walls and a fairly wide frieze and cornice near the top.

Walls Wallpaper was expensive in the 18th century and was rarely stuck directly on walls. Fabric, or paper pasted on to canvas, was mounted on battens with beading covering the joins.

Timber panelling (known as wainscoting) was cheaper than either fabric or paper. Hardwood panelling was usually left in its natural colour but cheaper deal or pine panelling was always painted – stripped pine is definitely a late 20th-century fashion! Fitted furniture, however, is not a modern invention: cupboards were incorporated within the panelling, as were display niches on either side of the fireplace.

Early in the 18th century, panelling was often completely painted in a shade of grey, brown, olive green, or off-white. Later, though, a wider and brighter palette became available – yellow, red, or sky blue were not unusual – and in some homes white or coloured plaster mouldings (formerly used only for cornices and friezes) were teamed with contrasting panels of paint, paper, or fabric.

Windows in drawing rooms often extended almost from floor to ceiling. Twelve-pane sash windows (with six panes in each sash) were most typical. Fabric was expensive and was used fairly sparingly on windows. Elaborate swags and tails topped roman or austrian blinds or a single curtain was looped to one side.

Floors Flagstones or unpolished boards covered with rush or straw matting were most common. Carpets, which in previous centuries were hung on walls or draped over tables, made an appearance on the floors of grander houses and spread to less wealthy homes.

Drawing room – classical
This room abounds in classical features – a pedimented mirror, symmetrical alcoves flanking the fireplace, an elaborate cornice, and wall lights above a selection of miniatures.

FURNITURE AND FURNISHINGS

Mahogany furniture, chandeliers and candlesticks, and patterned fabrics characterize Georgian interior decor.

Furniture Georgian rooms were comparatively sparsely furnished with tables and chairs ranged around the walls; the dado (or chair) rail was there to protect the wallcovering.

The designs of the famous furniture-makers – Sheraton, Hepplewhite and Chippendale – typify Georgian taste in furniture. Although walnut was still used, the most popular wood was mahogany. Padded wing chairs with cabriole or straight legs were usual; armless, straight-backed upholstered chairs or stools made ideal seats for ladies wearing fashionably wide, hooped skirts. Coffee tables did not exist in the 18th century; their role was filled by drop-ended sofa tables and drop-sided Pembroke tables.

Lighting was provided entirely by candles or rush lights which, not surprisingly, were a major expense in the domestic budget! Chandeliers and decorative lanterns containing several candles became fashionable. Wall sconces were often backed with mirror for decoration and to reflect more light.

Fabrics and wallpapers Velvets and silk damasks were used in grand houses. Cottons, at first in simple block-printed designs, monochrome pastoral scenes (also used on walls) and, as techniques improved, colourful floral designs, were less expensive. Papers were plain, flocked, or decorated with flower and bird motifs in imitation of imported Chinese designs. There were also cheaper 'domino' prints with small geometric designs. Borders did not necessarily co-ordinate with the paper.

△ **Living room – the right mood**
Although this room lacks the architectural features of the Georgian era, it nevertheless has the correct feel. An evenly-matched arrangement of pieces of upholstered furniture is combined with a muted colour scheme.

▽ **Drawing room – symmetrical**
The symmetry which epitomizes the period is evidenced by the pair of windows, each of which is a mirror image of the other. The elaborate pelmet and simple treatment below are characteristic.

△ *Fireplace – uncluttered*
Choosing a wallpaper of the correct period helps set the mood in a Georgian room. The original fragment of this reproduction 'domino' print dates from around 1800 and was unearthed from below at least a dozen layers in a London house. Borders were commonly used to cover the edges where the paper was fixed to battens – this design dates from around 1780.

△ *Dining room – formal*
The Georgian look is particularly suitable for formal dining rooms. Deep blue wallpaper and fabric, together with Chippendale-style upholstered ladder-back chairs and lots of rich mahogany set off shiny silver candlesticks and crystal goblets to perfection.

◁ *Hallway – in character*
In a long and narrow entrance hall, Georgian simplicity of decor enhances the size of the space. Although the actual pieces of furniture themselves are not strictly typical of the period, the positioning of a pair of chairs flanking a mahogany bureau is typically Georgian. Note how the gilded mirror and two gilt-framed paintings echo the arrangement of the furniture.

ADAPTING THE STYLE

Creating a Georgian-style room need not be impossibly expensive, despite the fact that authentic Georgian furniture is costly and few people live in homes built during the period. Although large rooms are not essential, the style works best in spacious, high-ceilinged rooms. In less imposing homes, it's important to retain the Georgian sense of proportions – for instance, by not overloading a small room with the full complement of dado rail, cornice and frieze. Happily, many fabrics and papers of the period are made today. Keep elaborate or grand designs for large rooms and use small patterns elsewhere.

Coffee tables, so essential to modern life, did not exist in the 18th century. Instead, choose occasional furniture such as Pembroke or sofa tables. Large round library drum tables, with leather tops and alternate real and dummy drawers round the edge, were widely used; small modern adaptations of these tables make attractive side tables, and low versions can serve as coffee tables.

Walls
Plain, painted walls suit this style in either muted shades or the bright colours which became fashionable later in the century. Recreate the panelled look with painted or papered panels enclosed by plaster or wood mouldings or wallpaper borders.

Lighting
Lacking either electricity or gas, the Georgians relied on candles for domestic lighting. Ceiling-hung, candelabra-style fittings are suitable. Silver or brass candlesticks add a touch of authenticity.

Windows
Large windows, ideally reaching almost from floor to ceiling, are characteristic of Georgian architecture. Keep window coverings relatively simple – fabric was expensive in the 18th century!

Architectural details
A dado, frieze and cornice are essential ingredients of classic Georgian rooms. If your ceiling is not high enough for all three elements to work well, it is better to leave out one element. Perhaps a low dado and simple cornice, or a frieze and cornice but no dado.

Floors
Choose polished floorboards, wood-block or parquet flooring, or carpet the floor with sisal matting or a plain carpet in an unobtrusive colour. Add real oriental rugs, or modern copies, over any of these floorcoverings.

Furniture
Authentic Georgian antiques are expensive; instead look for Victorian or Edwardian copies or modern reproductions. Choose Hepplewhite, Chippendale and Sheraton styles for chairs and cabinet furniture, and upholstered wing chairs.

Fireplace
Reproduction Georgian fireplaces are widely available. Keep the style you choose in scale with your room. A large, ornate fireplace will be too dominant in a smallish room; instead choose a more modest and restrained design.

◁ **Essentials**
Although it is impractical to rely only on candlelight, as the Georgians did, choose electric fittings which look as if they were designed to be used with candles.

Traditional brass and glass chandeliers and pendant lanterns suit Georgian rooms. Look for modern versions of wall-hung lamps (sconces) with mirrored backs. Wall-mounted brass picture lights also have the right feeling for the period.

As well as real candles, choose table lamps with tall bases like candlesticks or classical columns.

▽ **Line and shape**
A fireplace with classically simple lines sets the style in a Georgian room. Choose substantial mahogany furniture and chairs with straight legs and ladder- or shield-backs; upholstered wing chairs also have the right period feel.

▷ Accessories

Look for copies of original Georgian silver: this teapot was made in the 1930s and the wine coaster is even newer. While tableware was earthenware or porcelain, modern floral china is acceptable. The white jug and dish are copies of Georgian designs.

▽ Surfaces

Fabrics and wallpapers range from simple block-printed patterns to multi-coloured, stylized designs and flowery prints. Narrow wallpaper borders in architectural patterns and gilt fillets (edging strips) give papered walls a panelled feel. Traditional plaster mouldings are still being made today.

VICTORIAN VALUES

Ornate furnishings in distinctive colours and patterns are hallmarks of this style.

The Victorian era – the period between 1837 and 1901 – was a time of massive industrial development and this was reflected in people's homes. Factories started to mass produce items which previously only the wealthy could afford. Ornate furniture could be factory-made faster and at a lower cost than simple handmade pieces. With improved printing and weaving methods, patterned wallpapers and fabrics were used instead of paint and hand woven furnishing fabrics.

Colours and patterns of this style are distinctive. The Victorians were very keen on nature and this was reflected indoors. Floral patterns are used a lot, often in strong rich colours as well as prettier pastels.

The Orient was a strong influence, too – this was the height of the British Empire – and traditional designs from the East are used in rugs laid on polished boards or over carpet.

Windows are covered with heavy drapes, held back with tasselled tie-backs and often combined with decorative pelmets and floor-length lace panels.

Furniture ranges from the highly ornate to the more bulky and solid, preferably in dark woods. The original furniture is quite expensive but good reproductions are available.

There should be plenty of knick-knacks and pictures framed in dark wood and photographs in silver frames, patterned china and leather-bound books. And, of course, plants. No Victorian home would have been complete without at least one aspidistra.

Living room – old and new
A clever mix of furniture, fabrics and objects, centred by a pretty fireplace, gives this room an authentic air. The furnishings and the many ornaments provide the typical cluttered look.

△ **Bedroom – height of luxury**
Strongly patterned wallpaper and fabric
are hallmarks of the Victorian style.
In this bedroom the curtains are long
and generous to match the canopy over
the bed, and there are frilled cushions,
pictures and colourful knick-knacks in
silver and porcelain. The circular
bedside tables are covered with long
patterned cloths and glazed chintz over-
cloths. The screen, an item often seen in
19th century homes, is painted and
decorated with cards and some
interesting dolls' straw hats.

▷ **Kitchen – modern and traditional**
These days, a real Victorian kitchen,
with a large range and cook's pantry,
would not be very practical. But if you
incorporate modern technology into a
Victorian-style kitchen you can get the
best of both worlds. Here, new units
provide the necessary storage space
while the original fireplace, with a
selection of prints on the chimney
breast above, gives the room its period
character. The stained-glass window
and chequered floor tiles add an
authentic air.

204

◁ **Bathroom – typically tiled**
Original Victorian tiles are the focal
point of this tiny bathroom. Recurring
colours of rust, green and cream allow
the different patterns to work together.
A similar look can easily be created with
the wide range of reproduction tiles
available today. And it is still possible to
find old bathroom fittings with their
brass taps in working order.

△ **Living room – pattern**
The rich colours of sage
green, cream and brown in
the living room above were
frequently used in Victorian
homes. Plain coloured velvet
upholstery is the perfect foil
to the patterned wallpaper.
The original cast-iron
fireplace has been painted.
Plants complete the effect.

▷ **Dining room – in bloom**
In this dining room the pretty
floral wallpaper and matching
curtains provide a charming
contrast to the heavy
wooden furniture and create
a definite air of Victoriana.
The circular table can be
draped with a cloth and
covered with lace when not
being used.

ELEMENTS OF STYLE

This pretty bedroom combines many elements so typical of the Victorian period. The style is ornate but cosy and surfaces are covered with china, framed family photographs, leather-bound books, ornaments and other decorative accessories. China washing bowls and jugs on a mahogany washstand are typical.

In bedrooms dark woods are contrasted with attractive floral prints or stronger patterns. Curtains and bed linen are flounced and frilled with matching or contrasting material. Pattern and colour combine well when mixed, and bedlinen, curtains and tablecloths are often trimmed with lace.

Wall-mounted lights which give a warm and atmospheric tone are used in preference to central pendants. And note the abundance of pictures on the walls and the variety of different shaped frames. All this adds to the look.

Wallcovering
Highly patterned wallpaper in pretty floral colours as well as richer reds and blues for living rooms. For contrast a plain paper is often used below the dado or above the picture rail. Notice how the bed head, the valance and the quilt match the wallpaper.

Finishing touches
Accessories are vital for a period look. Cover walls with paintings, needlepoint and photographs in frames of differing shapes and sizes, and other surfaces with bric-a-brac. China water jugs and washing basins are typically Victorian as are richly-coloured tapestry bags.

Furniture
This is usually made of dark polished wood, preferably mahogany, although light wood furniture can be stained in imitation. Look for reproduction pieces and second-hand shop finds. Chairs and sofas are often button-backed and deeply upholstered.

Window treatments
Curtains should be heavily draped, in flowered chintz for bedrooms and tasselled velvet for living rooms. Curtains are held back with matching tie-backs during the day, and undercurtains are made of lace.

Soft furnishings
More often than not these are decoratively patterned, although plain fabric is frequently used for upholstery and cushions – velvet and velour are popular choices and Dralon is a good modern alternative.

Floors
Boards are usually stripped and stained or possibly covered with plain carpet. Patterned rugs with an Oriental or Persian feel are then laid on top. Shades of reds, blues and greens are always popular.

Fireplaces
Fireplaces are made of marble or slate in grand rooms and cast iron and painted wood in bedrooms and less important rooms. In Victorian times fires were the main form of heating and cast a soft flickering light which added atmosphere.

▷ **Line and shape**
Furniture is a mixture of the
elegant and the heavy. Dark
polished woods prevail with
plain coloured upholstery.
Chairs are balloon back for
dining and button back
'Victoria and Albert' for living
rooms. Rugs have an Eastern
feel.

▽ **Richly patterned**
Fabrics and wallpapers are patterned in regal colours
and fresh florals as well. Wallpaper borders can be
used at cornice, picture rail and dado height to
emphasize or replace architectural details. Curtains,
upholstery and tablecloths are trimmed with braids,
tassels and lace.

▷ **Accessories**
Choose carved, dark woods for fruit platters, posy holders and trays, patterned china for plant holders and tea sets, brass or china for door handles. Plants should be large with heavy green leaves or fine and feathery.

▽ **Soft and light**
Cushions are fat, fringed and frilled. They feature tapestry designs, patterned chintz, or plain velvet. Reproduction oil lamps and gas wall brackets are more in keeping than central pendants – however, if pendants are used they should be ornate with two or more shades on brass or gilt stems. Pictures depicting rural scenes and botanical prints are typical of the era.

THE EDWARDIAN PERIOD

The turn of the century moved from Victorian richness to simpler lines and lighter, airier rooms.

From the 1880s onwards there was a reaction against the heavy, dark and over-furnished interiors of the previous decades. Younger Victorians – the Edwardians – started to favour a simpler, lighter look for their homes. Paler woods such as oak, walnut, birch or sycamore were popular. Paintwork, too, was lighter – cream or white, green, pink or pale yellow.

A key influence on Edwardian design was William Morris, whose Arts and Crafts movement inspired a revolt against the mass-produced machine-made furniture of the earlier Victorian era. Everything from furniture to ceramics was produced by hand and so had a more individual quality.

Other influences were Ambrose Heal, whose pioneering furniture designs favoured a simple construction that allowed the natural beauty of the wood to show, and Liberty, whose famous Art Nouveau prints became one of the most distinctive hallmarks of this period.

Furniture featured curving lines and rounded fronts. Distinctive details include slim, high verticals on chairs and bedheads; hollow hand-holes on drawers instead of metal handles; and plenty of decorative carving on wood.

Wallpaper and fabric designs were inspired by the country and the garden. Roses rambled everywhere, while stylized elongated tulips and irises echoed the lines of the furniture.

Floors were still mostly stained wooden boards with Oriental or Persian-look rugs. Hallways were often tiled, either in chequerboard black and white patterns, or in blues, browns and beiges for more complex designs. In many Edwardian houses tiling beginning on the path outside and continuing along the hallway inside can still be seen. Stained glass provided pattern for the front of the house, and windows and glass doors.

Accessories Plates, bowls and vases were made from embossed pewter or copper. Decorative enamels and new, experimental glazes on pottery provided a wealth of detail and interest.

Bathroom – mellow comfort
Edwardian bathrooms were often full of books, plants, pictures – even chairs. This modern copy features an etched glass screen, brass fittings and mahogany fittings for a true period air.

△ **Dining room – clever mix**
This attractive room emulates a typical
Edwardian mix of shapes and styles,
with dark wood cabinets and airier,
mock-bamboo, rush-seated chairs.

Interesting details are the loop-over
curtain heading and the use of a
papered interior to lighten the dark
wood china cabinet. The rise-and-fall
lamp is also very much of the period.

◁ **Edwardian elegance**
The wooden back of this delicate sofa is
carved in elongated lines (including a
couple of hearts) until there is more air
than wood. Creamy wallpaper covered
in pink roses and lacy cushions add a
feminine touch.

◁ *Sitting room – authentic feel*
This is a good example of how antique and reproduction elements can work together to create an authentic atmosphere. Fabric and wallpaper are adapted from an original William Morris design and all the woods – from the fireplace surround to accessories – are picked for their soft, mellow tones

▽ *Bathroom – a lighter look*
Light greens were very popular (this was the time when the term 'greenery-yallery' came into vogue). Festooned lace, bracket lights with glass shades, solid, dark wood furniture, and a warm Persian-style rug on the floor are all in keeping with the period mixture of the late Victorian love of mahogany and the Edwardian trend towards a lighter look.

LUXURIANT LIVING

Romantic is undoubtedly the word to describe this pretty, lace-filled bedroom. The Edwardians loved the light, delicate look of lace and used it for everything from window panels to tablecloths, as well as to trim bed linen and covers, cushions and lampshades.

Whereas in downstairs rooms practicality – and a lack of modern cleaning methods – called for heavier and darker fabrics, bedrooms and bathrooms lent themselves to a more self-indulgent approach, inviting pleasure-lovers to relax in easy comfort.

Simpler lines for furniture and lighter floral designs in fabrics gave the Edwardian home an altogether airier, less cluttered feel than its immediate Victorian predecessor. Dark wood furniture was backed by paler walls.

Walls
The overall look is less cluttered than the Victorian mixture of patterns with dozens of pictures. Walls can be papered or painted with the possible addition of a dado rail. Downstairs colours are richer – moss, rust and creamy-beige. Upstairs, pinks, pale greens and white predominate. Patterns are mainly derived from nature with flower or leaf designs.

Windows
As a general rule downstairs fabrics are heavier in weight and warmer in colour. Velvets, brocades, or linen unions are used for curtains, with lace panels stretched over the window. These days lace can be used as curtains or made into ruched blinds.

Lighting
Brass wall brackets, rise-and-fall ceiling pendants, table lamps and standard lamps are all in keeping. Shades are glass, with shapes varying from plain coloured conical to wavy-edged designs and elaborate stained and leaded Tiffany-style.

Accessories
Photographs and prints in silver, walnut or birds-eye maple frames; flowered china, often with unusual glazes as part of the pattern; vases and scent bottles with filigree silver overlays; pewter and copper for plates, tankards and decorative pieces; and enamelware.

Furniture
The Victorian legacy is still seen in mahogany and other dark woods, but wood is usually lighter, with oak being the most common. Furniture shapes are less elaborate. Small circular tables covered with floor-length cloths are still popular for bedrooms and carved wooden bedheads replace cast-iron frames.

Floors
Generally, stained wooden board covered – almost entirely – by rich rugs. Patterned tile floors feature largely in halls, kitchens and bathrooms. Fitted carpets are a more comfortable modern alternative, but add Eastern-style rugs for an authentic feel.

▷ Line and shape
Furniture features simple flowing lines and straight, square legs with minimal detailing. Darker woods become simpler in line. More light woods such as oak, birch and sycamore begin to appear. Upholstery becomes less stuffed and buttoned, more slim and elegant.

Distinctive details are elongated uprights on chairs, extending above curved crest rails, and cut-out motifs, such as hearts on chair backs and cabinet fronts.

◁ Authentic fittings
Shades for pendant lights, table lamps and wall lights are often glass, either etched, stained or left plain. Light fittings sometimes echo stylized floral shapes. Painted wooden dado rails are an important feature and brass figures largely for light fitments and door furniture.

△ Accessories

Flower symbols appear in all sizes and colours. Elongated shapes for items such as candlesticks and cutlery echo the lines of furniture. Lace is everywhere from curtains to table linen.

▷ Colour and pattern

Green, cream and rich red or golds are popular colours for tiles, fabrics and wallcoverings. Rich floral patterns are balanced with plain colours. Dado rails divide plain walls and embossed designs, such as this original Edwardian one in Lincrusta, are still available. Fringing and tassels add interest to plain fabrics, but only in moderation.

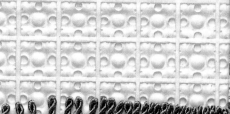

A FEEL FOR THE THIRTIES

The streamlined forms and geometric motifs of Hollywood and Art Deco furnishings complement modern interiors.

Suburban homes were the first to feel the full force of 1930s streamlined car, boat and train design. Living rooms and bedrooms were filled with large, rounded ocean liner-style furniture in blond woods trimmed with chrome.

But perhaps the most famous 30s design influence was Art Deco. The name derives from the 1925 Paris exhibition of Decorative and Industrial Arts where exhibits had to represent contemporary lifestyles. Out went the flowing lines and muted pastel colours of Art Nouveau. In came bright oranges, mauves, lime greens and angular lines inspired by the contemporary *Ballet Russe* sets and costumes. Other design influences owed more to the discovery of Tutankhamen's tomb: Egyptian ornament was popular. The stepped 'ziggurat' terraces of Aztec temples were also to be seen everywhere.

Walls were marbled or ragged in cream and beige while simple friezes were much in evidence. Floorcoverings were good-quality parquet, linoleum and rugs. Improved plywood moulding techniques also affected furniture design and shape, with rounded corners an important feature. Chrome, glass, leather and black lacquer were popular combined with pale sycamore, bird's eye maple, walnut and light oak and other, dark woods.

Windows had wooden pelmets, painted or covered with fabric with jagged motifs picked out in paint or tape. Venetian blinds in metal or wood were alternatives to curtains. Typical light fittings were opal glass bowl lamps, bronze and chrome lady bases.

Dining area – black and chrome
A modern sophisticated interpretation of 1930s style, with black-stained oak furniture and a pale grey, apricot and tan colour scheme.

△ **Living room – tiled fireplace**
Ceramic 30s-look tiles and ornaments make a focal point of
this decorative fireplace. The fireplace opening has been filled
in with a board covered in mirror tiles.

△ *Classic trolley*
This chrome and glass trolley has 30s
Hollywood appeal yet still fits in well
with modern interiors. It is one of the
many copies of original 1930s designs
which are still widely available.

▷ *Bedroom – liner looks*
Luxury looks redolent of the Queen
Mary are seen with these built-in
bedside fittings of blond and black
wood combined with generous panels
of mirror. Scalloped edging on the bed
linen softens the severe streamlined
look of the bed and its built-in sofa.
Strip lamps concealed behind coving
mouldings provide softly-diffused
atmospheric background lighting.

◁ *Bedroom – decorative*
An original maple bedroom suite with
the typically rounded corners seen on
furniture of the period. Accessories are
an important part of creating the 30s
mood. Face wall plaques and vases are
still readily found in antique markets and
large circular mirrors are available in
DIY outlets.

BRIGHT IDEA

ADDING A MOTIF

Stepped Aztec-inspired 'ziggurat' designs and Egyptian sunrise motifs were seen everywhere during the 1930s and were used to decorate furniture and windows.

You can apply an Art Deco-style motif to plain flush-fronted modern storage units using self-adhesive rigid plastic edging strip. The strip is available from larger DIY shops and is approximately 12mm wide; it comes in a wide range of colours, including pastel shades and bright primaries. Use a sharp trimming knife or sharp household scissors to cut the strips and arrange them into different shapes to decorate a plain surface.

Arranging storage units to create a stepped outline also helps to emphasize the 30s feeling to great effect.

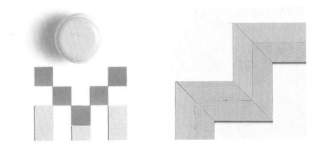

PUTTING ON THE RITZ

Take from the style as much or as little as you like: a rounded, chrome and glass occasional table or rugs with geometric motifs, perhaps. Choose venetian blinds or curtains in Art Deco geometric prints and match up motifs with a stencilled border on sponged walls. Pick seating with smooth, curved backs and sides with fat rectangular cushions. Show

wood can be of lacquered wood, pale ash or light oak. Upholstery can be leather or figured moquette in soft orangey golds or pinks and greys.

Art Deco sunrise and geometric rug patterns have recently been reproduced to fit in with modern colour schemes. These blend happily with some genuine period pieces. There are still real bargains to be had in 1930s

dining furniture, sideboards, wardrobes and dressing tables. Painted cream or black they can look very modern. Look out for Art Deco pottery vases and jugs in primary colours and fill them with fake blooms. Decorative cut-glass dressing table sets in pastel colours and items of *pate de verre* (opaque) glass, bakelite plastic clocks, mirrors and photo frames are inexpensive.

Accessories
Statuettes, particularly female figures; pottery decorated in bright orange, yellow and green geometric and stylized flower designs. Have a set of cocktail glasses and a chrome shaker.

Lighting
The overall effect is soft and atmospheric. A marbled glass bowl pendant hanging on chains, stylized figure table lamp, wall and freestanding uplighters are all typical of the 1930s.

Walls
Plain painted, sponged, stippled or papered with an all-over geometric or stylized floral print. Creams and beige were favourite colours. Borders were used at picture rail or ceiling height and also to divide a wall into framed panels.

Furniture
Look out for sideboards, dressing tables, wardrobes, dining tables and chairs with rounded corners and in pale woods and exotic veneers such as bird's eye maple, sycamore, walnut and light oak. Chrome and glass tables and trolleys are useful extras.

Seating
Thirties upholstery was made to last; leather was popular but more usually, three-pieces suites were covered in moquette – either cut to give a velvety pile or uncut, to give a looped effect. Seating frames were often of bent plywood or chrome.

Flooring
Lino in beige, brown, creams and green was popular in hallways, kitchens and bathrooms. Polished parquet or woodblock floors with rugs featuring geometric motifs were used in living rooms.

Stencilled motifs
A geometric 30s-style stencil creates a more modern effect by combining it with a simple painted stripe running along the top of the wall and about a third of the way down at each corner.

▷ Essential lighting

Appropriate lighting is a vital ingredient when re-creating the 30s style. This selection of reproduction fittings is representative of the period and can all be purchased at various specialist lighting shops.

▽ Line and shape

Sleek, streamlined forms and geometric shapes as reflected in a 'ziggurat'-top mirror, set the scene. The curve of the sides of the chair is broken by the square shape of the seat. The curve is repeated on the sunrise-shaped lamp and horseshoe-foot table.

△ **Accessories**
Authentic objects from the 1930s give the finishing
touches if you want to achieve this look. Fortunately,
bric-a-brac, clocks, pottery and glass can still be found
inexpensively on market stalls and in junk shops.

▽ **Fabrics and paper**
Add a wallpaper border with a geometric motif to a
plain wall. Look for shagreen (imitation sharkskin)
papers and fabrics and figured chenille upholstery
fabrics.

CHAPTER 4
CURTAINS & SOFT FURNISHINGS

SIMPLE UNLINED CURTAINS

Unlined curtains involve a minimum of
sewing and are simple to make up.
Detachable linings are easily
added to unlined curtains.

Unlined curtains are ideal for use in kitchens, bathrooms and playrooms, or on any window where insulation and light exclusion are less important than easy laundering and versatility. Use sheer fabrics to filter harsh sunlight, or try decorative lace over a simple practical blind that can be pulled down for warmth and privacy.

Detachable linings added to cotton curtains will shut out more light and provide better insulation. They can also be washed separately from the main curtain.

The technique for making unlined curtains is basic to making any curtain. Curtain tape attached to the top has slits for the hooks from which the curtain hangs on a track or pole.

Measuring up Before measuring for curtains, it is essential to fix the track or pole in place so that the exact height and width can be taken. The track or pole is fixed in the window recess or outside the recess and just above the frame. If it is outside the recess it should extend, if possible, at least 15cm/6in on each side of the frame so that the curtains can be fully drawn back from the glass for maximum daylight. The height of the pole will depend on the curtain length you choose.

What length curtains? Curtain lengths fall into three categories: sill length, just below sill length (clearing the top of a radiator, for example), and floor length. The length you choose depends on the size and shape of the window, your style of furnishings and the visual effect you want.

Choosing heading tape The type of heading tape you choose will influence the 'look' of your curtains, and determine the width of fabric needed. Standard heading tape is economical on fabric and gives a softly gathered, even fullness suitable for lightweight, unlined curtains.

Smart stripes
A simple unlined curtain with softly gathered pencil pleating is a good choice for this neat bathroom. It is quick to make and easy to wash.

Heading tapes for more tailored pencil or pinch pleats require more fabric. A special heading tape is available for detachable linings, and can be used with any decorative curtain heading.

Use synthetic fibre tape for sheer and synthetic fabrics, cotton tape for natural fabrics.

Choosing fabric Lightweight and sheer furnishing fabrics are ideal for unlined curtains. Cottons, either plain or printed offer the widest colour range. There is also a wide range of semi-transparent fabrics, usually in synthetic fibres, from fine net and voile to heavier lace designs and open weaves.

If possible buy fabric that is wide enough to make up a curtain without having to make seams. To work out how much fabric you need, see overleaf.

Pattern repeats Plain fabrics and small prints are the best choice for a beginner; avoid large patterns and horizontal stripes which need extra care in cutting and matching up. Pattern matching is covered in detail on page 229.

Sewing thread The sewing thread should match the fibre content of your fabric. Polyester thread is best for synthetics, cotton for natural fabrics.

HOW MUCH FABRIC DO YOU NEED?

Use this method of calculating the total amount of fabric needed for all curtains, lined and unlined. A pocket calculator may be helpful.

To get the width, measure the length of the track or pole and multiply by at least 1½-2 times for standard heading tape (by up to 3 times for other heading tapes – check manufacturer's instructions).

Add 2.5cm for each side hem allowance (5cm for sheers).

Add 10-15cm to each curtain width if the curtains are to overlap on a cross-over arm at the centre.

Divide the total figure by the width of your fabric to give the number of fabric widths needed. Round up to the next full width if necessary.

To get the length, measure from curtain track or pole to the desired length (sill, radiator or floor). Add 4cm for top hem (for standard heading tape) and 15cm for bottom hem. Double the hem allowances for sheer fabrics.

To get the total amount multiply this figure by the number of fabric widths. This quantity of fabric is then divided between the number of curtains required.

☐ If the fabric has a pattern repeat, add one full pattern repeat per fabric width.

☐ If washable fabric is likely to shrink, buy an extra 10cm per metre. Either wash the fabric before cutting out or make up with all the excess in the bottom hem. The curtain can then be let down after the first wash.

1 **Cut out the fabric**
Lay the fabric flat on a large table if you have one, or clear an area of floor space to work on.

Curtains will not hang properly unless you start with a straight cut across the width. If the fabric has a straight thread pattern across the width, pull out a thread as a guide for a straight cutting line. Otherwise cut at a right angle to the selvedges. Line up the pattern repeat, if necessary, before cutting subsequent widths.

2 **Join fabric widths △**
If the fabric is narrower than the curtain width, make up the required width by adding a strip of fabric to the outside edge.

3 **Stitch the seams ▷**
Using a simple flat seam, pin the two pieces of fabric together with right sides facing and edges and pattern matching. Tack and stitch 1.5cm from edges. Remove tacking and press seam open. To prevent puckering, clip into the seam allowance (particularly if it is a selvedge) every 10cm along the edges.

4 **Stitch side hems ▷**
Turn 5mm of the allowance to the wrong side and press. Fold remaining 2cm of hem allowance to the wrong side and tack. Then machine or slipstitch through all the layers.

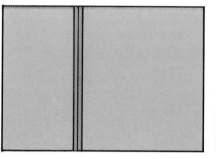

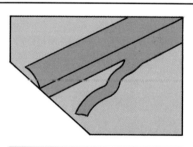

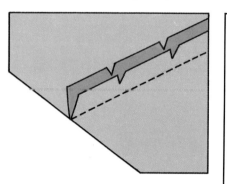

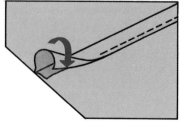

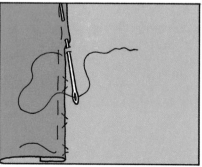

DELICATE FABRICS
If the fabric is likely to fray or you want a neater finish, turn this flat seam into a flat fell seam. Trim off half one seam allowance, then fold the other seam allowance over it to enclose the raw edges. Tack and topstitch through all the layers. This stitching line will show through on the right side of the fabric.

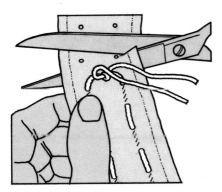

5 Prepare the heading tape △
Cut a length of heading tape to the finished width of the curtain plus 8cm (for neatening the ends). At the end where the curtains will meet or overlap, pull 4cm of each cord free on the wrong side of the tape and knot securely.

Trim off surplus tape 1.5cm away from the knot; press this surplus to the wrong side. At the other end of the tape, ease out 4cm of each cord on the right side. Turn surplus tape to wrong side and press.

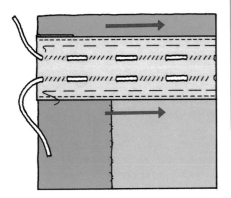

6 Attach heading tape △
At the top of the curtain turn 4cm to the wrong side and press. Position tape on the wrong side of the curtain to cover raw hem edge, with top edge of tape no more than 2.5cm below the top and the loose tape cords on the outer edge of the curtain. Tack the tape in place. Machine stitch both long edges of tape in the same direction to prevent puckering; stitch across the short knotted end of tape. Remove tacking.

7 Gather curtain heading ▷
Holding the loose cords together, gather the fabric until fully pleated, easing out evenly until the right width. Tie the cords together, and tuck out of sight; don't cut them as they are needed to release the curtain fullness for cleaning. Insert hooks at about 8cm intervals all along the tape.

TIPS FOR SEWING SHEER FABRICS

Seams, particularly in fine nets, tend to be very obvious against the light of a window so avoid making joins if possible. If one fabric width is too narrow for your window, make up separate curtains to hang side by side – or simply hang widths without sewing – allowing the fullness of the curtain to hide the overlapping edges. If you do join widths, a flat fell seam (see opposite) or french seam makes a neat finish. Very fine lacy sheers should be overlapped to match the shape of the design and seamed by hand.

Finish sheer fabrics with machined

Cool, white and light
Full-length sheer curtains with a delicate pattern are teamed with white painted shutters which are closed for privacy at night.

double hems to look neat and prevent raw edges from showing through – use a special translucent synthetic fibre tape made specifically for sheers and nets. A double hem at the top will mask the outline of heading tape. Take care when turning hems on open weave fabrics to match up the weave and ensure a maximum of solid pattern area to sew through.

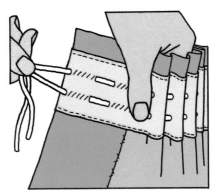

8 Turn up bottom hem
At bottom edge, turn 1cm to the wrong side and press. Turn balance of hem allowance to wrong side, pin and tack. Press complete curtain and hang on the track or pole for several days as fabric usually 'drops' slightly. Then adjust the hem if necessary and slipstitch into place.

Fabrics can be weighted to improve the way they hang by putting special lead weight tape in the hems.

DETACHABLE LININGS ADDED TO SIMPLE CURTAINS

Unless curtains are sheer, or specifically intended to filter light, it is usually best to line them. This protects the curtain fabric from the damaging effects of strong sunlight, and to some extent from outside dirt, as well as cutting out bright light and draughts from the windows.

A detachable lining is the simplest of all to make up and can easily be added to existing unlined curtains. Separate curtain linings are especially useful if curtain and lining have different laundering requirements – if one fabric is dry-cleanable only and the other washable, for example. The linings can be removed easily for frequent cleaning, and you can take them down during the warm summer months to create a lighter, airier atmosphere and to filter the sunlight.

Another plus for detachable linings is that they generally use less fabric than sewn-in linings since, whichever type of heading is on the curtain, you need only 1½ times the track width of fabric.

Lining fabric is generally cotton although, for a little extra cost, you can buy thermal curtain-lining fabric which provides better insulation. It is available in three colours, cream, black and silver.

Special heading tape for detachable linings is designed to be used with the hooks which are attached to the heading tape on the curtain. Some curtain track runners have a curtain hook combined with an additional ring for hooking on a lining.

1 Make up the lining
Measure up and cut out the lining fabric using the same method as for standard unlined curtain. Bear in mind, though, that the lining must be 2.5cm shorter than the curtain so that it will not show when the curtain is hung.

Join fabric widths as necessary and stitch side hems.

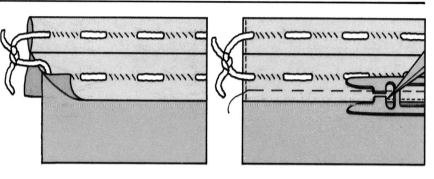

2 Prepare the tape
Lining heading tape is made up of two 'skirts', which fit over the top of the lining fabric like an envelope. The right side of the tape is the corded side.

Cut a length of heading tape to the width of the lining, plus at least 8cm for neatening the ends. At one end of the tape, pull the two cords free and secure with a knot. Trim off surplus tape up to the knot.

3 Attach the tape △
Ease the two skirts apart and slip the top of the lining between the skirts, with the corded side on the right side of the lining and the knotted end at the centre edge of the lining, overhanging by 1cm. Fold this short tape edge to form a 5mm double hem on the wrong side of the lining and stitch in place.

4 Stitch the tape △
At outer edge of the lining, pull 4cm of each cord free and trim surplus tape so that it overhangs lining by 1cm. Neaten the tape edge with a 5mm double hem on wrong side of lining, leaving the loose cords free for gathering up. Tack and machine tape in place, close to the bottom edge, stitching through both skirts of the tape and the curtain. Machine down both short sides, taking care not to stitch over the loose cords. Remove tacking.

5 Gather the heading
Pull the loose cords gently, pushing up the fabric and tape at the same time, until the fabric is the required fullness and width. Then knot the cords and tuck them out of sight.

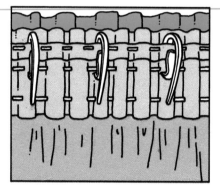

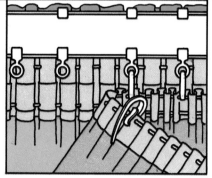

BRIGHT IDEA

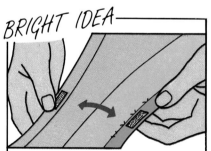

SECURE THE LINING
To hold a detachable lining in place and improve the hang of the curtains, stitch short strips of narrow Velcro to the side hems of linings and curtains at about 30cm intervals.

6 Hang the curtains and linings △
Insert hooks every 8cm along the top of the lining tape. With wrong side of lining and wrong side of curtain facing, fit the hooks through the slits on the curtain heading tape, so that both lining and curtain hang from the same hooks.

Combined hooks and runners △
If the curtain track has runners with combined hooks and rings, slot the hooks on the lining tape through the rings under the main curtain hooks.

CURTAINS WITH SEWN-IN LININGS

The sewn-in method of lining is suitable for most curtains and gives them a neat finish and a good hang.

A curtain lining acts as a barrier between the curtain and window and fulfils several functions. It cuts down light penetration, provides extra insulation, and protects the curtain fabric from the damaging effects of sunlight, and to some extent from dirt and dust. A lining also weighs down the curtain, giving it more body and a better hang.

There are several ways of lining curtains: the method you choose largely depends on the size and weight of the curtain – see below. This chapter covers making sewn-in linings. It also covers matching patterned fabrics, and adding a pleated frill to the edges of the curtain.

CHOOSING THE LINING METHOD

The method you choose depends on size of curtain, weight of fabric and, of course, personal preference.

A sewn-in lining is one of the easiest methods of lining curtains, and is ideal as long as the curtain fabric and lining can be laundered together. The lining is attached to the curtain across the top and sides, but left free at the hem for the best possible hang.

A locked-in lining is suitable for curtains that are very wide, or long and heavy or when an interlining is used. In addition to being attached across top and sides, the lining is invisibly lock-stitched to the curtain fabric at regular intervals over the whole curtain.

A detachable lining is ideal if curtain and lining fabrics have different laundering requirements, or if you want to add a lining to an existing unlined curtain – see opposite.

LINING FABRIC

Lining fabric is generally 100 per cent cotton, with a close weave to cut out light and draughts, and is available in a wide range of colours. Thermal curtain-lining fabric, with a special coating on one side, is a little more expensive but provides extra insulation. It is available in cream, black and silver.

Estimating fabric Calculate the amount of fabric needed for each curtain using the same method as for unlined curtains – see page 224.

Then work out what the curtains will measure when made up. The lining fabric should be the same length as the finished curtain, but 1cm less than the finished width of the curtain.

A neat finish

These full-length curtains benefit greatly from being lined. As well as cutting out bright light and draughts, a lining gives curtains more body so they hang better and it makes them look tidier from the outside of the window.

SEWN-IN LININGS

A sewn-in lining is the most common way to line curtains. With this method, curtain and lining are attached by being sewn together down the side hems and across the top while the hem of the lining is left hanging loose.

Before making up sewn-in linings, see Simple Unlined Curtains for basic curtain-making techniques.

1 Join fabric widths

Cut out curtain and lining fabric. If necessary, join fabric widths together to make up each curtain and lining, using 1.5cm flat seams as described for unlined curtains.

Flat fell seams or french seams are not necessary as the edges of the seam will be hidden between the lining and the curtain.

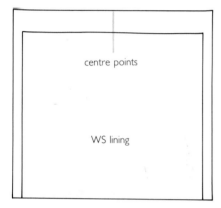

2 Mark centre point on fabric △

Mark the centre point on the wrong side of both the curtain fabric and the lining fabric with tailor's chalk.

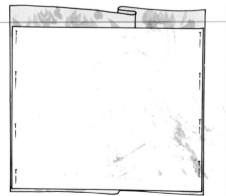

3 Pin lining and curtain fabric △

Position the lining on top of the curtain fabric, with right sides together and the top of the lining 4cm (if using standard curtain heading tape) below the top of the curtain fabric.

Match raw edges together down both sides, pin and tack. You will find that the curtain fabric is a little wider than the lining, so allow the curtain to form a few folds in order to match raw edges exactly.

4 Mark the curtain length △

Measuring from the top edge of the lining fabric (this will also be the top edge of the finished curtain, see Step 6), mark the curtain length required on to both lining and curtain fabric with tailor's chalk. Then mark the position of the hem sewing line for the curtain, allowing for a 7.5cm double hem.

Taking 1cm seams, stitch down both sides from the top of lining to within 10cm of the chalked hem sewing line.

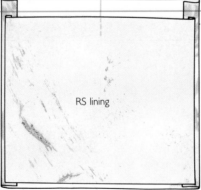

5 Press curtain and lining △

Press the side seams open. Then turn the curtain and lining fabric through to the right side.

Carefully press the complete curtain, making sure that the chalk-marked centre points on the lining and curtain fabric (see Step 2) match up exactly, so that there is a 1.5cm margin of curtain fabric showing on each side of the lining.

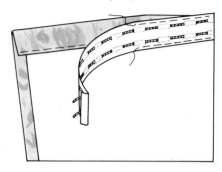

6 Attach heading tape △

Fold top of curtain fabric to wrong side over top edge of lining, turning the corners in at a slight angle if necessary. Press and tack. Position heading tape over raw edge of curtain fabric, tack and stitch in place.

7 Hem curtain and lining △

Turn curtain and lining through to the wrong side. Turn up a double hem 7.5cm deep along the bottom of the curtain fabric, with mock mitres at corners (opposite). Pin and tack.

Turn up a double hem to wrong side of lining fabric, so that lining hangs about 2cm above bottom edge of curtain. Make the lining hem the same as, or just less than, the depth of the curtain hem, trimming off surplus fabric if necessary. Pin and tack in place.

8 Pull up heading tape

Turn curtain right side out again and press. Pull up heading tape to make the curtain the right width for the window, and hang in place for several days to give the fabric time to 'drop'. Then adjust hems if necessary, and slipstitch in place. If the hang of the curtain needs to be improved, enclose curtain weights in the hem of the curtain before stitching it down.

Finish by slipstitching the lower side edges of lining to the curtain.

MOCK MITRES

Mitring is the neatest way of finishing corners of hems. A true mitre should be at a 45° angle. On curtains, however, the bottom hem is deeper than the side hems and a 'mock' mitre is the simplest method. To make a mock mitred corner, only one side of the corner (the bottom hem) is mitred, and not at a 45° angle.

With sewn-in linings, the lining and curtain fabric are sewn together to within 10cm of the curtain's hem sewing line – see Step 4.

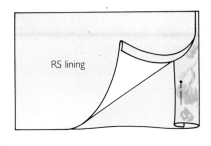

RS lining

☐ Turn in and press the remaining side seam allowance along each side of curtain.

☐ Turn up and press a double 7.5cm deep hem along the bottom of the curtain fabric.

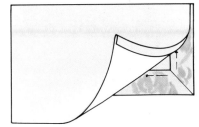

☐ Fold corner of hem in at an angle until top of diagonal touches top of side hem.

MATCHING PATTERNS

Unless windows are very narrow, a curtain will probably be made up of more than one width of fabric. If you are using fabric with a bold pattern, the pattern must match horizontally at seams and at the leading edges (where a pair of curtains join when closed). To do this, you must allow extra fabric so that 'pattern repeats' can be adjusted to match up.

Pattern repeats The pattern repeat is often quoted on fabric details. If not, measure the depth of the pattern repeat along the selvedge edge of the fabric between the top of one pattern and the top of the next pattern down. Then add one pattern repeat for each fabric width required.

BRIGHT IDEA

COLOURED LINING

Use pastel-coloured lining to alter the tone of light that comes through pale curtains – soft pink or peach can dramatically warm up cold winter light. Make sure that the lining colour complements that of the curtain by holding the fabrics up to the light together.

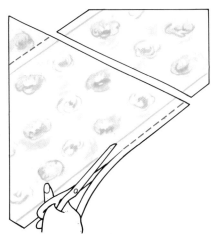

1 Position the pattern △
Before cutting out the fabric, plan how the pattern repeat should be arranged on the curtain – for best effect, you need to show a representative proportion of the pattern along top and bottom edges.

With floor-to-ceiling curtains (left), it's generally best to position the pattern repeat so that it starts near the top turning of the curtain.

With short sill-length curtains (right), the lower edge is nearest eye level and it's best to position the pattern repeat so that it ends near the bottom hemline. You'll find that a half pattern at the top of the curtain is more easily absorbed in the heading.

2 Start cutting out fabric
Cut the first piece of fabric to the required length (drop of curtain plus top and bottom hem allowances).

Make sure you cut perfectly straight across the width. If the fabric has a straight thread pattern, pull out a thread which runs across the width and cut along the gap. Otherwise, mark a straight cutting line at right angles to the selvedges with tailor's chalk and a straight edge.

3 Match the pattern △
Lay the first piece of fabric out flat, right side up. Then lay the rest of the fabric out alongside, right side up, and match the pattern horizontally with the first cut piece.

Cut the second piece of fabric so it starts and ends at exactly the same point of the pattern as the first piece. Continue in this way until you have cut all the required number of fabric widths.

4 Join fabric widths
Mark with a pin the centre of each pattern repeat along the side edges of the two fabric widths that are to be joined. Using a flat seam, lay the two pieces of fabric together with right sides facing, and the edges and pins matching. Then pin along the seamline 1.5cm from the edges.

Turn the fabric to the right side, check that the pattern is matching exactly along the seam, and make adjustments if necessary. Tack along the seamline, remove pins and stitch seam. Remove tacking and press seam open.

◁ **Pleated perfection**

A pleated curtain frill along bottom and closing edges gives a smart professional finish to curtains used in any room.

Here, a pleated frill in a plain toning colour is emphasised with a piped trim in the deep blue of the curtain fabric.

ADDING A PLEATED FRILL

A pleated frill along bottom and leading (or closing) edges of a curtain looks crisp and smart. For a neat trim at seams between frill and curtain, use piping cord covered with a toning coloured fabric.

Measuring up Cut curtain lining to the same size as curtain fabric, and join fabric widths as necessary to make up each curtain and lining.

To calculate the amount of fabric needed for a double-sided pleated frill, double the finished frill width (say, 6cm) and add a 3cm allowance (to give a total width of 15cm). If you have a ruffler attachment for your sewing machine, you can use this to make single-sided pleats quickly; in this case, neaten the lower long edge of frill with a double 10mm hem.

For the length of the frill, measure leading and bottom edges of curtain. Multiply this measurement by three and add a 3cm seam allowance, plus additional seam allowances if joining strips of fabric to make up the length. Then allow for an extra pleat to help ease the frill round the bottom corner. To do this, decide on the pleat width (the part visible when the pleat is stitched in place – usually between 12mm and 3cm wide), and multiply by three.

1 Fold fabric in half
If necessary, join strips of fabric together with flat seams pressed open. Fold the frill fabric in half along its length with right sides together, and stitch across each end with 1.5cm seams. Then turn fabric to the right side – wrong sides together, raw edges matching – and press.

2 Make up pleats
To get the number of pleats, divide the length of the edge to be frilled by the pleat width. Then add on one pleat (the extra allowed for the corner).

Lay the frill fabric flat, and use tailor's chalk to mark the width of the pleat (A-B, B-C and so on) along the fabric at right angles to the frill edge. Then fold and pin A to C, and repeat until you reach the end of the frill. Tack along top and bottom of the pleats to hold them in place and press.

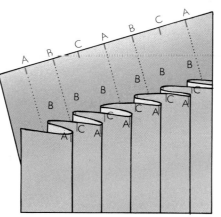

3 △ Sew piping to curtain
Make up the piping. Then use tailor's chalk to mark a 1.5cm seam allowance on the right side of curtain along closing and bottom edges. Pin and tack piping along this chalk line: at the bottom corner, snip into the piping fabric up to the stitching and ease it round in a slight curve.

To finish, trim the piping cord level with what will be the edge of the finished curtain. Trim the fabric covering the cord to within 1cm of edge and tuck inside to neaten.

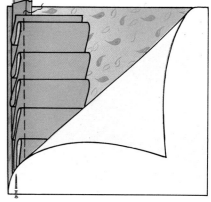

4 Sew frill to curtain fabric △
Place the frill over the piping on the right side of the curtain, with raw edges matching; pin and tack in place.

Then lay the lining fabric on top of the curtain fabric (so that the frill and piping are sandwiched in between at bottom and closing edges), with right sides facing and raw edges matching. Pin, tack and stitch in place. Trim, then press seams and turn curtain through to the right side.

5 Complete the curtain
Pin the top edges of the lining and the curtain fabric together. Fold the top of the curtain and lining fabric to the wrong side, press and tack in place. Position heading tape to cover the raw edge of the curtain fabric. Pin, tack and stitch in place leaving the frill and piping free. Then press the complete curtain.

Finally, pull up the heading tape so that the curtain fits the window, tie the cords together and tuck them out of sight. Insert hooks and hang the curtain.

LACE AND SHEER CURTAINS

Net curtains can be merely functional, affording a measure of privacy, or they can add an extra decorative touch.

Sheer curtains are traditionally hung at windows to give privacy to a room which is overlooked, or to screen an unsightly view. Since they become transparent at night, when the light is on in the room, it is also necessary to hang additional curtains – or fit blinds – for privacy at night. However, in some situations, sheer or lace curtains are hung purely for decorative effect, adding a feminine touch to a room. In such situations it may not be necessary to hang any extra curtains, although they are often a practical addition, helping to cut down on heat loss at night. Roman, austrian, festoon or roller blinds may provide alternative screening at night.

NET EFFECTS

The simplest effect with sheer curtains is a plain, translucent drop of white or off-white cotton or synthetic fabric. Such curtains are usually hung from a lightweight track, using a slightly transparent heading tape specially designed for use with sheer fabrics. You can also hang the curtains from an expanding curtain wire or lightweight rod (such as a café rod), slotted through a casing in the top of the curtain.

There are innumerable other effects you can achieve: there are specially designed ready-made net curtains in crossover or jardinière styles, for example. You can also create tiered effects with café curtains, tied-back curtains and valances all in net fabrics. Or if you only want to do a minimum of sewing you can simply drape panels of lace or voile over a wooden curtain pole.

If the sheer curtains are to be fitted to a pivot window or a glazed door, you can stop the fabric from flapping and getting trapped in the window or door by making a casing at both the top and the bottom of the curtain and slotting both casings on to wires or rods.

BUYING FABRIC FOR SHEERS

There is a wide range of sheer fabrics to choose from if you are planning to make net curtains.

Many manufacturers produce sheer plain or patterned fabric by the metre, in the same standard widths as ordinary curtain fabric, as well as wider widths for larger windows. You can also buy panels of lace in various sizes ready to make up into curtains. These panels usually have a pattern designed to suit the size of the panel, often with scalloped edges. They sometimes have slots or eyelets at the top, so that you don't need to do any sewing at all. You just thread them straight on to a curtain rod.

Another alternative is to buy special sheer curtain fabric which is made with a casing along one edge and a scalloped or hemmed finish along the opposite edge. This type of fabric is used sideways, so that the width of the fabric you buy becomes the drop of the curtain. When you buy it by the metre, the length should be about one and a half times the finished width of the curtain. All you have to do is hem the ends to form the sides of the curtain. If you are buying this type of sheer curtain it is advisable to check on the different widths available before you fit the curtain rod.

Layered look

A single café curtain screens the lower half of this window, while a pair of curtains with a matching heading add a decorative touch. Both tiers are hung from rings on substantial brass poles set inside the recess.

SPECIAL SEWING TECHNIQUES

Because of the nature of sheer fabrics, there are one or two points to bear in mind when working with them.

Seams are unsightly in sheer fabric. Where possible, avoid them altogether: simply make up two or three curtains to fit the window, and arrange them so that the gathers hide the edges of the fabric. If you do have to join widths of fabric (when making a long frill to edge a curtain, for example) use french seams, which are stitched so that the raw edges are neatly tucked inside the structure of the seam.

Hems should be double (1cm double hems down side edges, 4cm double hems across lower edges of curtains). It is essential that raw edges are cut straight and even, as you will be able to see them inside the hems.

If the fabric is synthetic, you will have to take extra care when pressing it: use a very cool iron. After washing sheer synthetic curtains, it is advisable to hang them *in situ* to dry, so that the creases fall out as much as possible to save unnecessary pressing.

Always use a sharp, fine needle and a fairly long, loose stitch. Choose a fine thread, and use polyester thread for synthetic fabrics and cotton for cotton sheers.

FRENCH SEAMS

Avoid seams in sheer fabrics where possible. If necessary, use french seams to join widths of fabric. Allow 2cm seam allowance for seams made by this method.

1 *Join the widths* ▷
The first step is to join the two widths of fabric, wrong sides facing and raw edges matching, taking a 1cm seam. Trim a couple of millimetres from the raw edges for a neat edge.

2 *Turn and neaten* ▷
The second row of stitching forms the actual seamline, and encloses the raw edges at the same time: turn the fabric back on itself so that the right sides are facing and the seam allowance is enclosed between the layers of fabric. With right sides facing, pin, tack and stitch, positioning the seamline 1cm in from the previous row of stitching. When you look at the seam from the right side of the fabric, there are no obvious stitching lines.

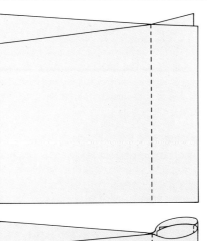

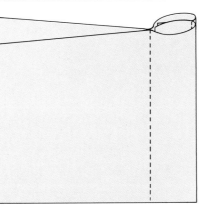

CHECK YOUR NEEDS

☐ Appropriate hardware – curtain track, rod, pole, or expanding curtain wire – with hooks, runners or rings as necessary
☐ Lace or sheer fabric
☐ Sharp cutting-out scissors
☐ Tape measure
☐ Heading tape (unless made up with a casing)
☐ Pins, needles, and thread
☐ Sewing machine
☐ Contrast fabric for trimming (fine cotton or lace – optional)

CURTAINS WITH HEADING

Lace or plain sheer curtains with a heading formed by a specially-designed tape are made in the same way as unlined curtains. You have to take extra care to ensure the stitching is straight and even, since the transparent nature of the fabric means that any faults on the wrong side will show on the right side.

Measure up
1 Fit the curtain track or pole in place at the top of the window, or half-way up for café curtains. Measure the length of the pole and the drop of the curtains. In most cases, you will make a single curtain to screen the whole window, unless you want to be able to draw the curtains back for any reason.

2 *Calculate fabric quantities*
The length of fabric required is equal to the length of the finished curtain, plus 3cm for the heading and 8cm for the hem. The width is 1½-2 times the width of the finished curtain (the length of the curtain track). If you need to join widths of fabric, check whether you need to include an allowance for pattern matching.

3 *Prepare the fabric*
Check that the fabric has been cut squarely across the lower edge. (You can use the edge of a rectangular table to check this: lay the fabric out so the sides are parallel to the sides of the table, and check that the ends run parallel to the ends of the table.)

4 *Side hems* ▷
Turn under a 1cm double hem down each side edge, and pin, tack and stitch in place. If the selvedge is not too tightly woven, take a single, 1cm hem.

5 *Lower hem* ▷
Turn under 4cm across the lower edge, and then a further 4cm. Pin, tack and stitch in place, using a machine straight stitch. (On heavier, patterned cotton lace you may prefer to use a hand slipstitch.)

Cut the heading tape to the same width as the curtain, plus 4cm. Turn under 2cm at each end of the tape, pull out the cords and knot them together.

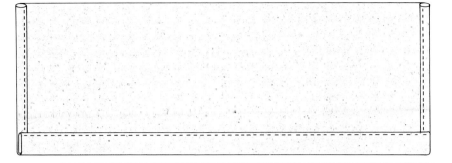

6 *Heading* ▷
Turn under 3cm across the top of the curtain, turn under the corners and press. Pin the tape to the wrong side of the top of the curtain, a couple of millimetres below the fold line so that the raw edge is covered. Tack and stitch in place a couple of millimetres in from the edge of the tape. Draw up the fullness so the curtain is the same width as the track and hang in place.

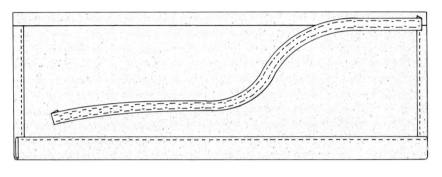

FRILLED CURTAINS

These curtains are made up in plain Terylene sheer fabric, with a cased heading. A 6cm-deep frill in a fine (non-sheer) patterned fabric stands out around each curtain. In the instructions given here the edge of the frill has been hemmed. Alternatively, you could bind the edges, or neaten them with a closed-up satin stitch (in which case you can omit the hem allowance along one edge of the frill).

The curtains are made up as a pair; for extra effect you could arrange them so that they overlap, joining them together at the top before adding the casing.

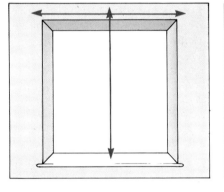

1 *Measure up* △
Decide on the position of the curtain rod: for this style it is better to fit the rod on the outside of the recess. If it is fitted inside the recess it should be 6cm down from the top of the reveal, to allow room for the frill to stand at the

top of the curtains. (If the rod is inside the recess you should also allow 6cm for the frill on either side.) Measure the length of the rod and the finished overall drop of the curtains (including the frills all round).

2 *Calculate sheer fabric*
Divide the length of the curtain rod by two. For the plain part of each curtain you need a panel of fabric 1½-2 times this measurement, depending on the fullness required. The panel should

be the length of the finished curtain, less a total of 10cm to allow for the frill and a 1cm turning top and bottom. You will also need a strip of fabric 4cm wide to form a casing across the back of the curtain.

3 *Calculate fabric for frill*
The length of the frill for each curtain is 1½ times the total perimeter of the panel calculated in Step 2 (2 × length + 2 × width). The depth is 6cm plus 3cm hem and seam allowance.

4 *Make up the frill* ▷
Join lengths of fabric to form a frill 1½ times the perimeter of the plain panel. Join the ends of the frill to form a complete ring. Use french seams for a neat finish. Turn under and stitch a 1cm double hem along the long, outer edge of the frill. Pin, tack and stitch in place, then press. Alternatively, omit seam allowance and bind edge of frill or use a closed up zigzag stitch for a neat finish.

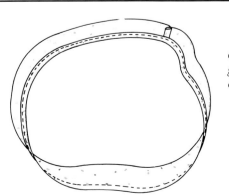

5 *Gather the frill*
Divide and mark the frill into four equal sections. Make two rows of gathering stitch along the unfinished edge, 1cm from the raw edge.

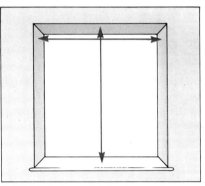

6 Attach the frill ▷
Mark the centre of each edge of the panel. Draw up frill so that it is the same length as the perimeter of the panel. Pin the frill to the panel right sides facing and raw edges matching. Distribute the fullness evenly, and match the marks on the frill to the marks on the panel, allowing a little extra fullness at corners. Tack in place. With the right side of the curtain facing you, stitch through both layers of fabric, taking 1cm seams. Remove gathering and tacking stitches and neaten raw edges together with zigzag stitch. Carefully press the seam allowances towards the frill.

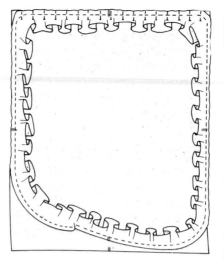

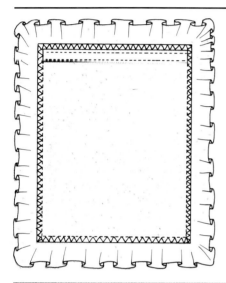

9 Attach casing ◁
Lay the frilled panel out, wrong side up. Pin the casing to the panel so that the top of the casing matches the seamline. (Note that the casing should match the plain panel, and not overlap the frill.) If the curtains are hung in a recess, you should make the strip for the casing slightly shorter than half the width of the curtain rod. Tack the casing in place along upper and lower edges. Stitch the casing to the curtain 2mm from each long folded edge of the casing. Make up the second curtain in exactly the same way. Slot the curtains on to the rod. If they tend to pull apart, stitch the corners together.

7 Prepare strip for casing △
Cut a 4cm-wide strip of fabric half the length of the rod. Turn under and tack a 1cm hem down each long edge.

8 Gather heading
Run two lines of gathering stitch across the top of the panel, one line just inside the seamline, and the other 17mm below that. Draw up gathering threads so that the width of each curtain is approximately the same length as the prepared casing.

BRIGHT IDEA

ADDING A TRIM
If you do not like the designs of lace-trimmed sheer fabrics that are available ready-made, you can add your own trim. Buy a piece of plain sheer fabric 1½-2 times the width of the window and slightly longer than the finished length you require. Buy a strip of trimming the same width as the sheer fabric. Lay the lace over the lower edge of the curtain, wrong side of trim facing right side of curtain, so that the lower edge of the trim is level with the unfinished edge of the curtain. Pin and tack in place. Zigzag stitch the lace to the sheer fabric, about 1cm from the top edge of the trim, following the shape of the trim if appropriate. Turn over and trim away the raw edge of the sheer fabric close to the zigzag stitching before making up.

◁ **Frilled to perfection**
Panels of plain sheer Terylene fabric have been finished with frills to match the bed linen in this teenage bedroom. The heading is a simple casing, which slips on to a curtain rod fitted across the top of the recess.

CAFE CURTAINS

Traditionally used in French cafés to screen the lower half of the window, these curtains are economical to make.

Café curtains are a practical alternative to net curtains, to screen part of the window during the day where you want to maintain privacy without blocking out all the light, or where you want to hide an unsightly view. They hang from a pole, rod, or curtain wire fixed halfway up the window, and are not usually as tightly gathered as normal curtains. There is usually only a single curtain at each window, rather than a pair. They can be left unlined, both to let in as much light as possible and for economy.

CHOOSE YOUR FABRICS

Café curtains look particularly good in crisp cotton furnishing fabrics. Choose fabrics which are fast dyed, as they are likely to be exposed to sunlight for a fair proportion of the day.

Another point to bear in mind is that the curtains will be seen from outside the window. Colour-woven patterns, such as gingham, might be an appropriate choice if you are worried about how the curtains look from outside.

Otherwise, you can line the curtains in much the same way as standard curtains using plain lining or self fabric (see Curtains with Sewn-in-Linings.)

STYLES OF HEADING

There is a wide choice of different headings suitable for café curtains.

Casings A simple casing can be made at the top of the curtain by making two parallel rows of stitching and slipping the curtain on to a curtain rod (or expanding curtain wire).

Curtain tapes You can use any of the light- or medium-weight curtain heading tapes, and then hang the curtains from rings on a rod or pole. Special café rods are available for this purpose.

Simple scalloped heading One of the most traditional styles for these curtains is to cut semi-circular scoops out of the top of the curtain, neatening them with binding or a facing, and stitching a ring between each of the scallops. The ring then slips on to a purpose-designed 'café rod' (usually brass), or a lightweight wooden curtain pole.

Looped and scalloped heading Another alternative is to hang the curtain from a pole by loops made by cutting deep scallops out of the top of the curtain. The strips between the scallops are extended so that they can be stitched to the back of the curtain to form the loops which are slotted on to the pole. Alternatively, cut out deep rectangles, rather than scallops, for a castellated effect at the heading.

Scallops and pleats A more sophisticated variation of this is to combine scallops with hand-made triple pleats. Cut scallops as before, but leave a wider strip between them so that you can make pleats by hand, and hang the curtain by rings from a pole. For a neat finish, the curtains should be lined, or the scalloped shapes faced with matching fabric.

FINISHING TOUCHES

Frills in either matching or contrasting fabric are an appropriate optional extra for café curtains.

You should also think about how to dress the rest of the window. Instead of ordinary curtains or a blind to draw at night, you could add a pair of short curtains, made in the same way as the café curtain. Hang them from a rod at the top of the window, so that they close above the café curtains.

A valance at the top, made to match the curtain, helps to frame the window if you don't want to screen it completely at night. Another idea is to make simple swags and tails to give the window a dressier look.

MEASURING UP

Measure the window where the café curtain is to hang: usually the track is positioned halfway down the window, but you may want to adjust this slightly to suit the window.

Once you have fixed the rod in place, measure the finished width and length of the curtain. For a plain scalloped heading you will need a piece of fabric slightly wider than the window; for a pleated scalloped heading you will need a piece of fabric nearly twice the width of the window, and for a cased heading you will need enough fabric to make up a panel one and a half times the finished width. Add an allowance for side hems, headings and hems.

Country style
Bring a breath of fresh air to a kitchen or bathroom – here a scalloped heading has been made, and fitted on a white, fluted café pole.

CHECK YOUR NEEDS

☐ Curtain fabric
☐ Interfacing (optional, for scalloped headings)
☐ Lining (optional)
☐ Curtain pole or rod
☐ Curtain rings (for scalloped headings)
☐ Sewing thread
☐ Needles and pins
☐ Sewing machine
☐ Paper for pattern (for scalloped headings)

PLAIN, SCALLOPED CURTAIN

The simplest scalloped curtains have curtain rings stitched or clipped to the strip between each scallop. They are unpleated, and should be made slightly wider than the window. To ensure a neat finish, the top is faced. The instructions here include interfacing for a crisp look.

1 Measure up
Start by fitting the pole across the window at an appropriate height. Measure the distance from the pole to the sill, and the width of the window.

2 Calculate fabric amounts
The width of the curtain is equal to the width of the window, plus 3cm seam allowance, and an extra allowance of about 10cm to allow the curtain to hang in very gentle folds. The length is equal to the measured length, plus 10cm to make a turned-under facing. The top of the curtain will hang about 1cm beneath the pole, so taking this into account, you need allow only 3cm for a 2cm double hem along the lower edge.

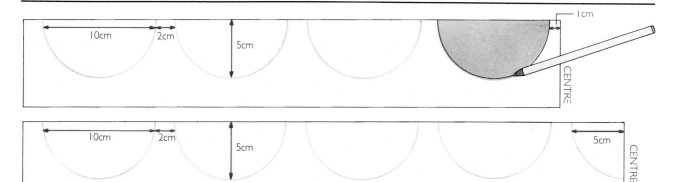

3 Make a pattern △
Use a strip of paper 9cm deep and half the width of the finished curtain to make a pattern to ensure the scallops are evenly shaped and spaced. One end of the paper will be positioned at the centre of the curtain, and the other at the outer edge.

Semi-circular scallops create a pleasing effect, so use compasses or a suitable saucer to draw them. Good dimensions for the scallops are about 5cm deep, 10cm wide and 2cm apart. They will be easier to draw if you first cut out a card template. Position the scallops so that either one is in the

centre of the curtain, or there is a space between the scallops at the centre (in this case, allow 1cm, as the pattern is placed on a fold). Adjust the size and spacings of the scallops and the width of the curtain until they fit neatly across the width. Cut out the scallop shapes.

4 Cut out fabric
Adjust the calculations made in step 2 to accommodate an exact number of scallops if necessary, including the appropriate turning allowance down each side. Cut out the fabric to this measurement. Turn under and press

10cm along the top edge. Cut a strip of iron-on interfacing 9cm deep, and the same width as the finished curtain, to interface the top edge of the curtain.

5 Interface the top edge
Position the interfacing on the wrong side of the curtain, 1.5cm in from each side edge and 1cm from the top edge, so that the lower edge of the interfacing matches the fold line at the top of the curtain.

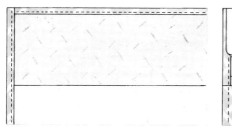

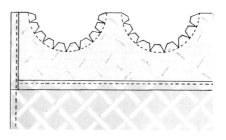

6 Neaten edges △
Turn under and stitch 1cm along top edge of curtain, over interfacing. Turn under 5mm and then a further 1cm down each side edge.

7 Mark scallops △
Turn the interfaced section over to the right side, turning back along fold line and pin in place. Mark the centre of the curtain. Position centre edge of pattern on centre mark and pin in place. Draw round the curves of the scallops. Remove the pattern and repeat for opposite half of curtain.

8 Cut out and stitch △
Cut out the scallop shapes along the top folded edge, cutting 1cm outside marked lines to allow for a seam. Machine stitch along each of the marked lines to create a series of scallops. Notch seam allowances. Trim and layer seam allowances. Press, turn right side out and press again.

9 Finish edges and attach rings
Slipstitch neatened edges of curtain and facing together at each end of the heading.

10 Turn up hem
Turn up and stitch a 2cm double hem by hand or machine, mitring corners neatly.

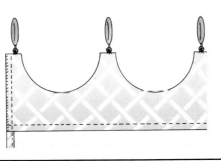

11 Attach rings ◁
Stitch a curtain ring to the top of each scallop by hand, and thread the curtain on to the pole.

TRIPLE-PLEATED, SCALLOPS

Adding pleats to the curtain heading creates a fuller, more sophisticated effect. They are made in much the same way as unpleated café curtains, but you have to allow an extra 12cm between the scallops, so that you can create a set of three 1.5cm deep pleats.

1 Make a pattern
Start by making a pattern the finished width of the curtain, as for the plain scalloped heading opposite. Cut down halfway between each scallop. Space the scallops an extra 12cm apart, so there is a 14cm space between scallops. Pin them on to another strip of paper and draw round them, to create a wider pattern. You will now have a pattern for half the curtain.

2 Calculate fabric amounts
The width of fabric is twice the width of the pattern, plus 5cm seam allowance at the sides. The depth is the same as the distance from the pole to the sill. No seam allowance is needed at the top, since the top of the curtain hangs about a centimetre below the pole. Add 5cm hem allowance. The lining should be the same depth but 2cm narrower.

3 Make up curtain △
Place lining on fabric, right sides together and raw edges matching across top and bottom. Pin together down side edges, raw edges matching. Stitch down sides, taking 1.5cm seam.

4 Make scalloped heading ▷
Press lightly so that lining is central to curtain (with a 1cm border down each side). Trim seam allowances and press open. Pin lining to curtain across top. Position pattern across top of curtain, 1cm from top edge. Mark curves on to lining, first on one half, then on the other.

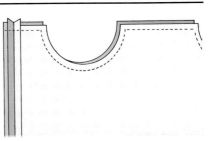

5 Interface heading
Cut a strip of iron-on interfacing the same width as the finished curtain, and 10cm deep. Position on wrong side of curtain, level with top edge. Iron in place.

6 Cut out and stitch scallops ▷
Cut out marked scallops through both layers of fabric and interfacing leaving a 1cm seam allowance. Pin, tack and stitch along upper edge of curtain, between and around scallops, taking a 1cm seam allowance. Notch curves. Turn right side out and press.

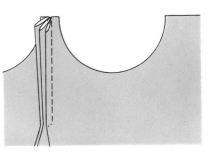

7 Make pinch pleats ▷
For each pinch pleat, fold the section to be pleated in half, wrong sides facing. Make a line of stitching by hand or machine 4.5cm from fold line (i.e. 1cm from the edge of the scallop). The stitching should extend 10cm down the curtain from the top edge. Open out fabric and lay it so that the stitched fold sticks up and the stitching is flat against the surface. With one finger on either side of the pleat, open the pleat out, pinch the centre fold, and push it down towards the line of stitching to form a triple pleat. Grip the pleats in place and smooth them so that the folds are even. Pin in place.

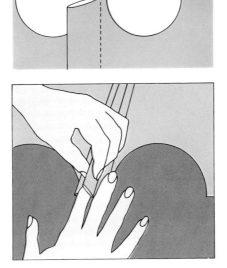

8 Stitch the pleats △
With the inner folds firmly pinned so they are as close to the vertical line of stitching as possible, stitch across the pleat, level with the bottom of the vertical line of stitching, using a fine stab stitch. At the top of the pleat, catch the inner folds in place.

9 **Turn up hems**
Turn up hems on curtain and lining and stitch by hand.

10 **Attach fixing hooks**
Attach special pinch pleat hooks (with spikes) to each pleat, ready to hook on to the curtain rings.

CASED HEADING AND FRILL

Two lines of stitching across the top of the curtain make a casing with a crisp, upright stand at the top. It is a quick and easy method of heading a curtain, economical on both time and fabric. A frill along the lower edge softens the effect.

1 **Measure up**
To find the finished size of the single café curtain, measure from the top of the café rod or pole to the sill, and measure the length of the track (the width of the window).

2 **Calculate fabric amounts**
The length of the fabric panel for the curtain is equal to the measurement from the top of the pole to the sill, less 7cm (for an 8.5cm deep frill), plus 8cm to make the cased heading and allow a little extra fabric so the curtain will slot

on to the pole easily. The width should be about one and a half times the length of the curtain pole. You also need a strip of fabric 11.5cm wide and three times the length of the curtain track to make the frill across the lower edge.

3 **Cut out fabric**
Cut out pieces of fabric to make up the panel for the curtain and the strip for the frill. Remember to allow 1.5cm for seams if you need to join widths of fabric. Join fabric widths if necessary.

4 **Make up frill**
Turn under 5mm and then a further 1cm along the lower edge and ends of the strip for the frill. Run two rows of gathering stitches along the upper edge.

5 **Attach frill**
Draw up gathering threads so that frill is 3cm shorter than the lower edge of curtain. Pin and tack in place, right sides together and raw edges matching. Stitch, taking 1.5cm seams. To neaten raw edges, trim and zigzag stitch raw edges together and press seam upwards.

6 **Neaten raw edges**
Turn under 5mm and then a further 1cm down each side edge of the curtain. Pin, tack and stitch in place.

7 **Make casing along top edge** ▷
Turn under 1.5cm and then a further 6cm along top edge of curtain. Make two lines of stitching 1cm from each folded edge, to make a casing 4cm wide (to fit a pole up to 25mm diameter).

8 **Fit the curtain**
Slot the curtain on to the café rod, sliding it along the pole so that the fullness is evenly distributed.

▷ **Frilled finish**
A crisp, unlined café curtain on a brass pole hides an unsightly view without cutting out too much light. A simple frill along the lower edge adds extra interest.

238

TRADITIONAL FABRIC PELMETS

A fabric pelmet is quite simple to make, and adds a decorative and distinctive finish to a window.

A pelmet is mainly used to add a decorative finish to the top of curtains, but it also conceals the curtain track and heading and helps to balance the proportions of a window. It can, for example, be fixed higher than the curtain track to make a window appear taller, or be extended at the sides to make it appear wider. Pelmets are also an effective link between curtains on adjoining sets of windows.

A traditional fabric pelmet is made of stiffened fabric that is attached to a pelmet board fitted across the top of the window. The board is a semi-permanent fixture once screwed into place, but the pelmet itself should be easy to remove for cleaning and is best attached with a touch-and-close fastener such as Velcro. Stiffened fabric is not washable, but it can easily be brushed and sponged with weak detergent or spray-on, brush-off dry cleaner.

The simplest pelmet is a straight rectangular one, or the bottom edge of the pelmet can be shaped for added interest. It can be made from the same fabric as the curtains, or from a contrasting or co-ordinating fabric.

Choosing fabric Almost any furnishing fabric, except very open weaves and sheers, can be used to cover a pelmet.

Before calculating how much fabric you need, fix the curtain track and pelmet board so that exact measurements can be taken – see overleaf.

CHOOSING A STYLE

Pelmets can be pretty and decorative, classic and elegant, or plain and simple. The style and shape that you choose depends on the style and size of the window and curtains, and the overall decor of the room. It also depends on the fabric being used for the curtains and pelmet, as certain fabric designs suit particular pelmet shapes better than others – stripes and geometrics, for example, go best with castellations, while florals combine well with pretty scalloped edges.

Draw up your own design, perhaps following one of the shapes illustrated here, or use a self-adhesive stiffening material that has various pelmet shapes printed on the backing paper.

Decorative shapes

△ *Good shapes for pelmets include soft scallops, castellations and zigzags.*

◁ *This attractive step-shaped pelmet, covered in a pretty floral chintz to match the curtains, adds interest to a rather plain window.*

TYPES OF FABRIC STIFFENER

The material traditionally used to stiffen fabric pelmets is buckram. More modern self-adhesive stiffener costs a little more, but is easy to use and ideal if you want to use a ready-printed design for the pelmet edge. Both can be bought from furnishing fabric departments.

Buckram is an open weave fabric that has been treated to make it stiff. Iron-on buckram is also available.

Making a pelmet with buckram involves quite a lot of hand sewing which takes time but gives a very professional finish. The pelmet fabric covering the buckram also needs to be backed with bump interlining or iron-on interfacing for a smooth finish.

Self-adhesive stiffeners have a peel-off backing paper printed with several pelmet styles, as well as a grid to simplify drawing your own design.

There are two main types of self-adhesive stiffener – single-sided and double-sided. With the single-sided type, the front is self-adhesive and the back is coated in a velour-style finish that makes lining unnecessary. Double-sided stiffener – with adhesive on both sides – does need lining but gives a neater finish. Both come in 30cm and 40cm widths; double-sided is also available in a 60cm width.

CHECK YOUR NEEDS
For the pelmet board:
- ☐ Plywood, 12mm thick
- ☐ Steel rule
- ☐ Saw
- ☐ Nails
- ☐ Hammer
- ☐ Brackets
- ☐ Drill and bit
- ☐ Screws
- ☐ Screwdriver

For the pelmet:
- ☐ Fabric
- ☐ Buckram or self-adhesive fabric stiffener
- ☐ Lining material (unless using single-sided self-adhesive stiffener)
- ☐ Interlining or iron-on interfacing (if using buckram)
- ☐ Tape measure
- ☐ Paper to make a template
- ☐ Scissors
- ☐ Sewing thread
- ☐ Pins, needles
- ☐ Sewing machine
- ☐ Iron and ironing board
- ☐ Velcro fastening
- ☐ Decorative braid plus fabric adhesive (optional)

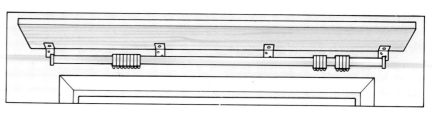

A pelmet shelf ▽

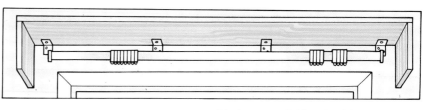

A pelmet box ▽

FITTING THE PELMET BOARD

The pelmet board may be constructed in various ways, depending on the shape and size of the window. It is made from 12mm thick plywood.

For most windows, a pelmet shelf (above, top) is adequate. This should be about 10cm deep to leave sufficient clearance for the bulk of the curtains when pulled back, and the same length as the curtain track plus about 12cm to give 6cm clearance on either side.

If the pelmet is particularly wide or deep, a pelmet box (above, bottom) with rectangular end pieces gives the fabric extra rigidity. In this case, nail a 10cm square piece of plywood at right angles to each end of the pelmet shelf.

To fix a shelf or box, position it centrally just above the curtain track and/or window frame, at the height where you want the top of the pelmet to come. Then fix it to the wall with small brackets spaced evenly along the board at approximately 20cm intervals. If there isn't sufficient space above the window for the fixings, you may be able to fit the board by screwing the brackets to the outer side edges of the window frame.

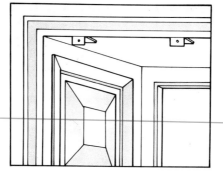

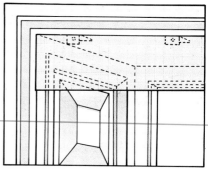

Recessed windows △
On deeply recessed windows (above, left and right), the pelmet board can be cut to the exact width of the recess and fitted across the front of the window area, flush with the recess, with the fixing brackets screwed to the upper surface of the recess.

HANGING THE PELMET

The simplest method of hanging a pelmet so that it can be removed easily – for cleaning, say – is to glue the hooked half of a strip of Velcro to the edges of the pelmet board. (The other half of the Velcro is stitched to the wrong side of the pelmet when making it up.) Alternatively, you can sew small brass rings to the back of the pelmet, and hook these over nails or screws fixed to the edge of the pelmet board.

A third method is to tack the pelmet to the board with upholstery tacks and cover the tacks with braid glued in place with fabric adhesive, but this has to be dismantled every time you take the pelmet down for cleaning.

MEASURING UP

Measure along the front of the pelmet board, and round the short side ends if you're using a pelmet box. This gives the finished length of the pelmet.

Having chosen a suitable shape for the pelmet edge, the depth of the pelmet depends largely on the size of the curtains, but 15-30cm is about average.

MAKING A TEMPLATE

If you're making a pelmet to your own design, you need to make a template from which to cut the pelmet shape. (If you're using self-adhesive stiffener, you can of course draw the shape directly on to the backing paper grid.)

1 *Draw the shaped edge*
Cut a strip of paper slightly longer than the finished length of the pelmet and slightly wider than the deepest section of the planned shape. Fold the paper in half widthways, and mark the position of the side edges, if any, with a crease. Then draw half of the pelmet shape you want on to the folded paper – working from centre out to edges.

2 *Cut out the shape*
Cut out the shape from the folded paper, and trim the top edge if necessary to make the template fit the pelmet board exactly. Unfold the paper and check its proportions against the window before cutting out the fabric.

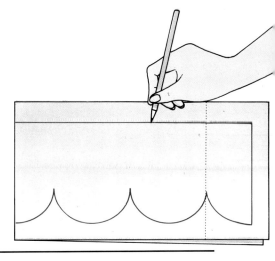

CUTTING OUT

To make up the pelmet, you need to cut out the following:

☐ *Fabric stiffener* Cut a piece of buckram or self-adhesive stiffener to the finished shape and size of pelmet.

Both types of stiffener are available in narrow widths, so the length can be cut from one piece without much wastage. Joins are best avoided as they have a tendency to create ridges and can reduce the stiffness of the pelmet.

☐ *Main pelmet fabric* Cut a piece of fabric 2.5cm larger than the pelmet template all round.

Plain fabrics can sometimes be cut along the length to avoid joins. If the fabric has a one-way design or a definite nap, however, you may need to join widths to make up a strip that is long enough for the pelmet. Join extra fabric to either side of a central fabric width using flat seams, and press seams open.

☐ *Lining* If using buckram or double-sided self-adhesive stiffener, cut a piece of lining material 1cm larger than the pelmet template all round.

☐ *Interlining* For a buckram pelmet, you also need a piece of bump or iron-on interfacing in the same shape and size as the template. If necessary, butt edges together and use herringbone stitch to join widths and make up pelmet length.

MAKING A PELMET WITH BUCKRAM

Buckram is quite stiff to handle, so make sure you use a strong, sharp needle when stitching by hand. You may also want to use a thimble.

1 *Attach interlining* ▷
Place interlining centrally on wrong side of pelmet fabric. Pin. Press iron-on interfacing into place. If using bump, lock stitch interlining to fabric.

Lock stitch Fold back the interlining 30cm from right hand edge, and lock stitch it to the pelmet fabric. Working from top to bottom edge of interlining, pick up a single thread from each layer of fabric. Place stitches about 10cm apart, and keep the thread fairly slack so that it doesn't pull the fabric. Fold interlining back over fabric, and work further lines of lock stitch 30cm apart along the length of the pelmet.

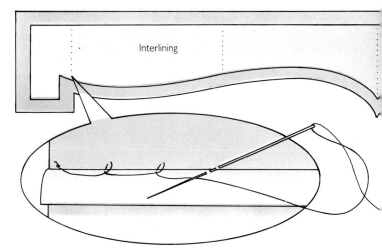

2 *Attach buckram* ▷
Place buckram centrally on top of interlining: pin, then tack through all the layers of fabric. Clip into the fabric seam allowance around curves and at corners, and trim away excess where necessary so that you can turn the border of fabric over the buckram.

If using iron-on buckram, dampen the edges and iron the fabric turnings in place. With ordinary buckram, pin and slipstitch the turned fabric to the buckram.

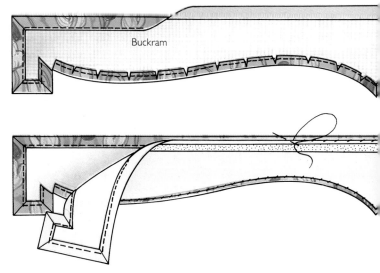

3 *Sew lining to main fabric* ▷
Turn in a 1.5cm seam allowance on lining fabric to make it 5mm smaller all round than the pelmet, clipping and trimming as necessary; tack and press. If you intend to hang the pelmet with Velcro (opposite), stitch the soft half of a strip of Velcro along top edge of right side of lining at this stage.

Then place lining, right side up, on top of buckram. Pin, tack and slipstitch all round, catching lining to the seam allowance of the main pelmet fabric.

MAKING A PELMET WITH DOUBLE-SIDED SELF-ADHESIVE STIFFENER

First cut out the stiffener, then cut fabric and lining – previous page.

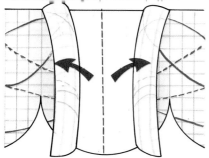

1 *Remove backing paper △*
Ease backing paper from centre of stiffener, cut it across the width and peel back a little on each side. Place wrong side of pelmet fabric centrally on top of exposed adhesive, and press down. Continue peeling away paper while smoothing down fabric, working from the centre outwards.

Clip into fabric seam allowance around curves and into corners, and fold to wrong side of pelmet. Peel backing off other side of stiffener and press down fabric turnings to stick.

2 *Prepare lining material ▽*
If hanging pelmet with Velcro, sew the soft half of Velcro to right side of lining 2.5cm from top edge. Press a 1.5cm turning to wrong side all round.

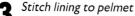

3 *Stitch lining to pelmet*
With wrong side of lining to wrong side of pelmet, smooth the lining down on to the adhesive surface, working from the centre outwards. Then slipstitch it to the main fabric all round.

For a neat finish, you can glue or slipstitch a decorative braid trim to the top and/or bottom of the pelmet, folding the braid into neat mitres at corners. Then hang the pelmet.

Smart stripes ▷
A simple classic pelmet shape complements a striped fabric. Here, the row of green braid along the bottom edge of the pelmet gives the shape definition without making it look heavy.

BRIGHT IDEA

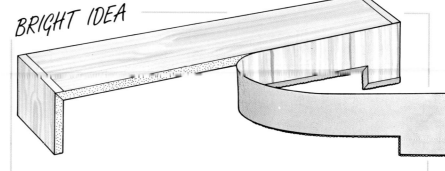

USE SINGLE-SIDED STIFFENER

The simplest and quickest way to make a pelmet is to use single-sided self-adhesive stiffener as it can be put together without any sewing, and does not require lining.

This type of pelmet is also very easy to hang, as you need attach only the coarser hooked side of a strip of Velcro to the pelmet board. The velour backing on single-sided stiffener clings to this and acts as the other half.

To make the pelmet Start by cutting the fabric 2cm larger all round than the pelmet. Cut the stiffener to shape: the backing is marked with a grid to make it easy to mark out a pattern. Then simply peel the printed backing paper off the strip of stiffener, and place the wrong side of the pelmet fabric on top – see Step 1, Making a pelmet with double-sided stiffener.

Press fabric down and smooth into place. Then use sharp scissors to trim the fabric edges flush to the pelmet shape. For a neat finish, stick a decorative braid or fringe over the cut edges of the pelmet with fabric adhesive.

MAKING CURTAIN VALANCES

Elegant and formal, or frilly and charming, a curtain valance adds a decorative feature to your window.

Curtain valances are often confused with pelmets, but a pelmet is a rigid fitting, either in wood or stiffened fabric, whereas a valance is a strip of fabric, gathered by hand or with heading tape. Like pelmets, valances are used to disguise the tops of curtains and the curtain track, or to enhance the proportions of a window, as well as for their decorative effect.

The valances discussed in this chapter can be hung above a curtain on tracks, wooden curtain poles, rods or a simple shelf-style fitting.

The style depends on the fabric the curtains are made from and the way the room is furnished. A simple gathered valance made from a printed cotton gives a country look, while a valance of regular or grouped pleats provides a more formal touch for heavier fabrics.

Proportion The depth of the valance depends on the proportions of the window as well as personal taste. For example, a deep valance tends to lower a tall, narrow window, and helps to obscure an unsightly view, while a shorter valance allows light in through a small or shaded window.

There are no hard and fast rules on the depth of valance, but bear in mind that, unless it is on a pole, it must cover the fitting or track on which it is hanging and the heading of the curtains. Start with the valance being one sixth of the curtain drop; this gives a point from which to work.

The right lines
This window has been fitted with a gathered, pencil pleated valance. It gives the window a smart finish, hiding the roller blind fitting as well as the curtain heading and track.

VALANCE FITTINGS

Rod or wire fitting (top left) If the valance is to hang within a recess, it can be made with a cased heading and threaded on to a rod or curtain wire that is drawn very taut.

Wooden curtain pole fitting (top right) A valance can be hung from rings on a decorative wooden curtain pole. The pole should be at least 12cm longer than the curtain track and project far enough to clear the curtains.

Shelf fittings An alternative is to fix a shelf supported by angle irons or wooden brackets above the curtain track. It should be 12cm longer than the curtain track (unless in a recess) and protrude from the wall by 4cm more than the track. The valance can be hung with curtain hooks fitted to screw eyes round the edge of the valance shelf (centre left), or it can be tacked to the side and front edges, and the tacks covered with braid, glued in place to hide the tack heads (centre right).

Valance track fittings (below right) Some manufacturers produce special valance tracks which are fitted to the curtain track with extended brackets to clear the curtains. The valance is then fitted to the track like a curtain, using curtain tape and hooks. It is not practical to fix valance track above decorative curtain poles.

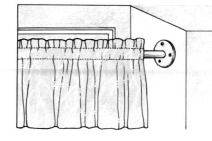

Rod fitting

Wooden pole fitting

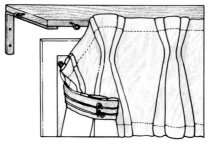

Shelf fitting with hooks

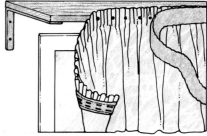

Shelf fitting with tacks

MEASURING UP

Cut a paper template to represent the valance, one sixth of the length of the curtain drop, pinning it in place over the top of the curtains. Then trim or lengthen the pattern to give the effect you want. Add a 2cm hem allowance. The top seam allowance depends on the heading, as does the width of fabric required.

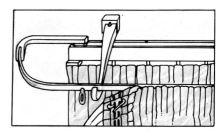

Valance track fitting

A CASED HEADING

This is the easiest valance to make and hang as the supporting rod, tube or wire is simply threaded through the cased heading.

How much fabric? To calculate the length of fabric required, decide on the depth of the pelmet as described earlier, adding a 6cm top seam allowance to make a casing for a rod up to 2cm in diameter.

To get the correct width of fabric allow for one and a half to two times the length of the rod, tube or wire.

1 *Cut out the fabric*
Cut out strips of fabric to the depth of the finished valance plus hem and heading allowances. Join strips to make one long valance, one-and-a-half to two times the length of the paper pattern. Use flat seams, neatening raw edges.

2 *Hem side and lower edges*
Turn a double hem (5mm, and then another 1cm) to the wrong side down each side edge of the valance, and machine stitch.

Turn a double 1cm hem (1cm, and then another 1cm) along the lower edge of the valance and stitch. Alternatively, you can trim off the lower seam allowance and bind the cut edge with a contrasting binding.

3 *Make a casing* ▽
Along the top edge, turn under the raw edge by 1cm and tack. Turn under a further 5cm seam allowance to the wrong side of the fabric, then stitch 5mm from the first fold. Then make another row of stitching 4cm above this one to form a casing for the rod.

Press well and add trimmings before threading the valance on to the rod.

CHECK YOUR NEEDS
☐ Fabric
☐ Lining (optional)
☐ Iron-on interfacing (optional)
☐ Curtain heading tape (optional)
☐ Hooks or tacks (optional)
☐ Paper for pattern (optional)
plus:
☐ Steel tape
☐ Tape measure
☐ Tailor's chalk
☐ Scissors
☐ Pins
☐ Needles
☐ Sewing thread
☐ Sewing machine
☐ Iron
☐ Ironing board

A simple gathered heading
This method can be adapted for a simple gathered heading attached around a shelf fitting. Instead of adding a second row of stitching along the top edge, make two rows of gathering stitches and pull up to fit the shelf.

Nail in place round edge of shelf and cover the nail heads with braid, or bias binding. Glue in place with fabric adhesive, turning under ends to neaten.

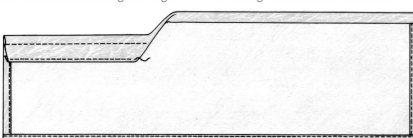

VALANCES WITH HEADING TAPE

This style of valance is made up in the same way as a short curtain – with either a gathered, pencil-pleated or triple-pleated heading, depending on the curtain heading tape you use.

It can be made like an unlined curtain or it can be given more body with iron-on interfacing, in which case it should be lined for a neat finish.

How much fabric? The depth of fabric required is as described before plus a top seam allowance of 4cm.

The width of fabric depends on the manufacturer's recommendation for the type of heading tape used. Standard heading tape requires at least one-and-a-half times the length of the track; others require more.

AN UNLINED VALANCE

This type of valance is straightforward to make, and gives an easy, informal look to a window. Use a standard heading tape to emphasize the effect.

1 Cut fabric
Cut out the fabric to the required measurements, and join widths if necessary with 1.5cm flat seams. Cut heading tape to right length

2 Attach heading tape
Neaten the side and lower edges of the valance as for a cased heading (see Step 2). At the top of the valance, turn 4cm to the wrong side and press. Pin heading tape in place on wrong side of valance to cover the raw hem edge.

Turn in the raw ends of the tape – but not the pulling up cords – and tack, then stitch in place.

3 Hang the valance ▽
Pull up the cords until the valance is the right width and tie the ends to secure. Even-out the gathers, insert curtain hooks and hang the valance as if it were a curtain.

For a shelf fitment, line up the curtain tape with the edges of the shelf and attach with upholstery tacks. Cover tack heads with braid.

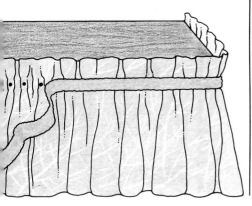

AN INTERFACED VALANCE

An iron-on interfacing can be used to give the valance more body and a much crisper look. The finish is more suited to formal styles – pencil or pinch pleated headings. There are several weights of interfacing – so select the weight that, together with your fabric, gives the desired thickness.

A lining gives your curtain valance a much tidier looking finish when viewed from outside, and also helps to protect it from sunlight. Choose lining to match curtain lining.

1 Cut out the fabric
Cut out the main valance fabric to the required length and width plus seam allowances in exactly the same way as for an unlined valance. Then cut the lining and interlining to the exact finished measurements, this time without seam allowances. If necessary, join the fabric widths and lining widths with 1.5cm flat seams.

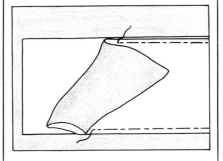

2 Attach interfacing and lining △
Position the interfacing on the wrong side of the valance fabric so that it lies within the seam allowances. Dry iron in place, following the manufacturer's instructions for heat setting. Tack the lining in place, matching the edges of the lining to the edges of the interfacing.

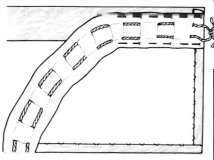

3 Attach heading tape △
Turn under double hems along the side and lower edges of the valance, as for the cased valance (see Step 2), so the hems overlap the lining. Pin and slipstitch down to the lining. Finally turn down the same allowance along the top edge and pin, tack and stitch the heading tape in place.

A VALANCE WITH A HAND-PLEATED HEADING

A hand-pleated valance should be interfaced and lined, as with the interfaced valance with heading tape.

How much fabric? To get the length of fabric, measure the depth of the valance and add 2cm for the lower seam allowance plus 4cm for the top seam.

For the width measure the length of the rod or pole. Then use a strip of paper to work out the size and type of pleat that will suit your valance and fit evenly into its length. Three times the finished width, plus seam allowances is needed for continuous pleats.

1 Cut fabric
Cut fabric to required measurements. Then cut lining and interfacing to exact finished measurements (without seam allowances). Make up the valance in the same way as the lined version with heading tape but, after folding over top, do not add heading tape.

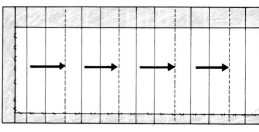

2 Mark out the pleats △
Following the pleat size from your experimental paper strip, mark out the valance into even divisions using tailor's chalk on wrong side of fabric.

Fold and press the pleats, one by one, and pin and tack in position.

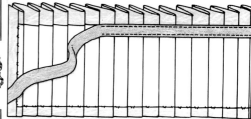

3 Attach tape △
Pin a length of plain tape, about 2.5cm wide, over the raw hem edge at the top on the wrong side of the valance, and stitch in place. You can hand sew the tape if you don't want the stitching lines to show on the right side, but be sure to stitch through all but the front layer of fabric in order to secure the pleats. If necessary neatly catchstitch the top edges of the pleats together on the right side to ensure a crisp finish.

Sew rings or hooks to the tape to attach the valance to its support.

FINISHES FOR STRAIGHT VALANCES

However the valance is made, and whatever method of fixing you choose, you can add decorative trims to add extra interest at the top of the window, and to create a definite division between the valance and the curtains.

Adding a frill A frill can be added for a feminine, country finish. Once the valance has been made up, cut a strip one-and-a-half times the length of the flat valance, and about 7cm deep. Join lengths with flat seams, neatening seam

▽ *Triple pleats*

This valance has been triple pleated, using a heading tape. The valance is interfaced, and the hem left unpressed to soften the effect.

allowances. Turn under a 1cm double hem along lower and side edges. Run two lines of gathering stitches along frill, about 1cm from top. Draw up gathers to fit, then, right sides facing, pin, tack and stitch 4cm from lower edge of valance, stitching along gathering, distributing fullness evenly.

Bound edges Once you have made up your valance, you can bind it with bias binding or a broader strip of bias or straight cut contrasting fabric.

Fringes and tassels You can also buy ready-made decorative fringes which can be used down the length of curtains as well as along the lower edge of the valance. For a tailored effect, stitch the fringe to the valance so that the lower edge of the fringing is level with the lower edge of the valance.

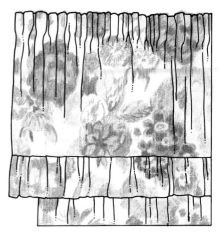

△ *Valance with frill*

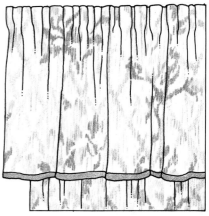

△ *Valance with bias binding*

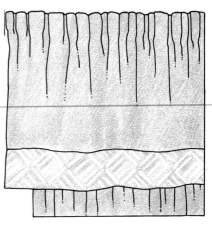

△ *Valance with contrasting fabric*

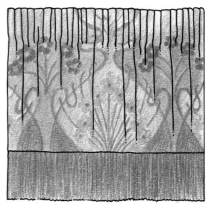

△ *Valance with fringed edging*

SOFTER SHAPES FOR VALANCES

For luxurious effects, go to town with clever shapes and flounces to frame your windows.

In formally-furnished or cottage-style rooms, you can set the style with an extravagant curved valance to top off your windows. The effects and details are almost limitless: tight gathers, formal pleats, piping, frills, contrast lining, or neat boxed headings.

CHOOSE YOUR FABRICS

In most cases the valances look best if they match the curtains: choose cotton sateen and glazed cottons, plain repps and slub weaves or damasks. Velvet pile fabrics are not so suitable for these elaborate effects. A fabric with a sheen to it will show off the gathers better, and look more luxurious. If you are adding frills and piping, these often look best in a contrasting colour – so look out for suitable fabrics of a similar weight for trims. Bear in mind that, with

several layers of fabric to stitch in some of the seams, you should avoid very thick fabrics which will give unmanageable bulk.

Most of the effects described here look best lined. Curtain lining fabric comes in a wide range of colours, with the darker shades giving a richer look. Paler ones are more suitable if you are trying to achieve a fresh, cottage style. However, you are not restricted to using lining fabric: since the 'wrong' side is often on view almost as much as the 'right' side, if your budget allows, line valances with the same fabric that you choose for trims such as frills and piping.

Co-ordinating the effect To enhance the effect, choose fabrics to co-ordinate with other furnishings in the room: for example, in the bedroom shown here, a striped fabric has been used to line and

trim a flowery valance. The curtains are in the same floral fabric, with the tiebacks in the striped fabric, matching the blind. Elsewhere in the room, it would be a good idea to have furnishings in the same, matching fabrics. For example, combine pink and white candy-striped bedlinen, with a floral quilted bedspread, or a bedroom chair upholstered in stripes, with floral, frilled cushions, piped with the pink striped fabric.

MEASURING UP

As with pelmets and gathered valances, the finished length of the valance is the length round the pelmet shelf, or across the front of the alcove of a recessed window. Once you have decided where the valance is to hang, put up the necessary fixings. Often, the simplest solution is a pelmet shelf, fitted on angle irons above the window, with the valance fitted to screw eyes round the shelf and the curtains fitted to tracks under the shelf.

As with plain valances, there are no rules as to the depth of the valance, or the shape. Normally, you don't want a valance to hang more than a sixth of the way down the window. However, it could be curved to hang a third or half-way down at the sides of the window.

To finalize the shape of the valance, it is necessary to sketch out some designs, copying them from pictures if you see exactly what you want. Then, the easiest way to transfer the sketch to the fabric for cutting out is to make a pattern for a pelmet, and 'spread' it to give you the necessary allowance for gathering the heading. 'Spreading' involves measuring the pattern at even intervals, and marking the measurements on to a second pattern, spacing them farther apart.

Before you can finalize the amount of fabric, you must decide on the heading of the valance: an easy way to make a neat heading is to use pencil-pleated curtain heading tape. For a luxurious effect, make the valance three times the length round the pelmet shelf. An alternative finish, described in detail here, is to gather the valance and fit it to a box heading. One advantage of this finish is that you can use Velcro tape to hold up the valance – this saves on curtains hooks and screw eyes, and prevents the valance sagging.

All dressed up

An ordinary window becomes special with a frilled valance tumbling down to frame the window and dressing table. Note how the valance is lined with the same fabric used to make up the frill.

DESIGNING A SHAPED VALANCE

To finalize the shape of the valance and check that the planned depth is suitable, it is best to make a paper pattern first.

1 *Sketch out a shape* ▷
Sketch out your ideas for a shaped valance, copying and adapting from favourite pictures or from ideas you have seen in showrooms. Mark in accurate measurements of your window, and approximate measurements for the valance. Choose the fabrics you want, and get hold of small samples if possible to check colour and effect.

2 *Draw out the pattern* ▷
Using a piece of wall lining paper, sketch out the approximate shape and actual size you want the valance to be making use of a flexible curve (a wire-reinforced rubber ruler). At this stage, do not include any allowance for gathers or frills. These are added later.

3 *Cut out the pattern*
Hold up your sketch in position at the top of the window. It will be easier to judge the finished effect if the pelmet shelf is in place and the curtains are already hung. If you think your sketch looks promising, fold the paper in half down the middle and cut through both thicknesses together to ensure the pattern is symmetrical.

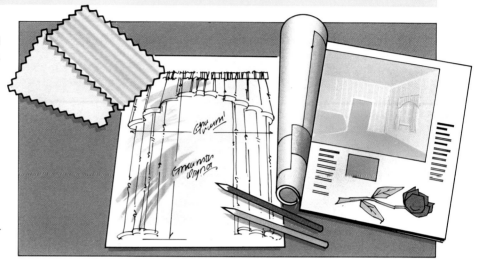

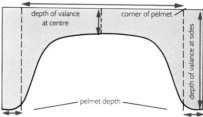

4 *Check the effect* ▷
Use masking tape to hold the pattern up to check the effect again. If you are happy, use this pattern, otherwise trim it as necessary, or trace it out again adding depth and shaping where needed. If you are going to add frills, these hang down below the main fabric of the valance, so bear this in mind when finalizing your design.

CUTTING OUT THE FABRIC

1 *Calculate the amount of fabric*
From your pattern, work out the overall dimensions of the fabric needed for the valance. This will be three times the width of the valance pattern, plus 3cm for turnings, by the depth of the valance, plus 3cm for turnings. For a double thickness frill, 6cm wide, you will need a strip of fabric 15cm wide by six times the measurement of the long, shaped edge of the pattern.

2 *Prepare the fabric*
Using flat seams, join up sufficient widths of fabric and lining to make panels the overall size of the valance, plus a 1.5cm seam allowance all round.

3 *Spread the pattern* ▷
Cut another piece of lining paper one-and-a-half times the length of the first, plus 1.5cm seam allowance at one end. Fold the first pattern in half down the centre. Measure the depth of the pattern at each end, and at 5cm intervals across its width. Add 3cm allowance to these depths. Mark the depths on the second pattern. Position the mark for deepest measurement, 1.5cm from the end of the second pattern, and the centre mark at the other end. Space the intervening marks 15cm apart rather than the 5cm that they were on the first pattern. Now draw a gentle curve through the marks, to give you the cutting line.

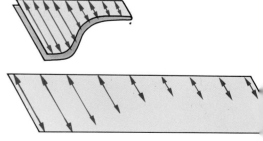

4 *Cut out the fabric*
Lay the second pattern on the folded fabric, with the short end of the pattern on the fold line. Pin in place, then tack the layers of fabric together and cut out. Repeat for the lining. Cut out sufficient 15cm-wide strips of fabric to make up the frill.

MAKING UP A FRILLED VALANCE

These instructions are for a deeply shaped valance, with one double-thickness frill set into the lower edge.

1 *Prepare the frill* ▷
Join up the strips of fabric for the frill, using flat seams; press open. Fold the frill in half along its length, right sides facing, and stitch across ends, 1.5cm from raw edges. Trim seam allowance, clip across corner to help the end of the frill to lie flat and turn right side out. Press to make a frill 7.5cm wide with a folded edge.

2 *Gather the frill*
Run two lines of gathering stitches along the long, unfinished edge of the frill, through both layers of fabric, within 1.5cm of the edge. Draw up frill to match curved edge of valance, leaving free 1.5cm at each end of the valance for seams.

3 *Make up the valance* △
Lay the valance fabric on a flat surface, right side up. Position the frill along the shaped edge, raw edges matching, ensuring the ends of the frill are clear of the seam allowance at the ends of the valance. Pin and tack in place, distributing fullness evenly. Lay the lining fabric on top of the valance fabric, right sides facing and raw edges matching, sandwiching the frill in place. Pin and tack in place all round, taking care not to catch side edges of frill in the seam.

4 *Stitch the seam*
Stitch all round the valance, leaving a 20cm opening in the top edge. Trim seam allowance, particularly along the frill. Clip seam allowance at corners. Turn right side out. Turn in and press seam allowance along opening.

There is no reason why you shouldn't adapt the design, adding a second, deeper frill, or binding the edges of the valance. Bear in mind that with bound edges you do not need the 1.5cm seam allowance which has been included. With the fabric cut out, making up the valance is straightforward.

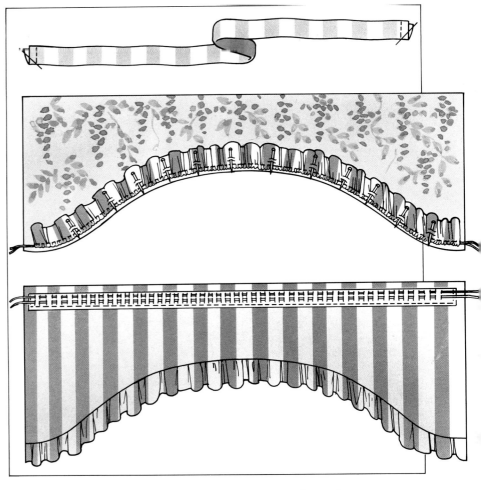

5 *Attach heading tape* △
Cut the heading tape so that it is about 4cm longer than the width of the valance. Turn under 2cm at each end. Pin in place, positioning the top of the tape 5mm from the top of the valance. Ease the cords out from the ends of the tape where it is turned under. Tack, then stitch, leaving ends of cord free.

6 *Draw up the cords*
Draw up the cords until the valance is drawn up to a third of its width, and matches the length of the pelmet shelf. Knot the cords, and carry the ends to one side, pinning or tacking them in place so they don't dangle below the valance.

BRIGHT IDEA

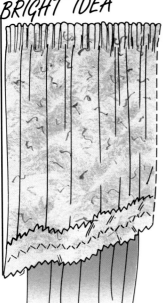
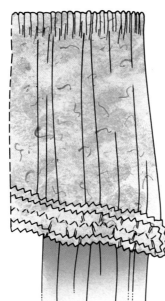

Quick frills Frills with pinked edges are a quick alternative to a double frill. Make up the valance as described above, without the frill sandwiched in the curved seam. Cut strips of fabric, 6cm wide, with pinking shears. Make a single line of gathering stitches along the centre of the frill, draw it up slightly (it need not be as much as twice the fullness of the valance) and pin it to the lower edge of the valance. Tack, then stitch in place with a zigzag stitch.

You can use the same technique to add a double frill, cutting an 8cm-wide strip in contrast fabric and a 6cm-wide strip in fabric to match the valance. Lay the narrower strip on top of the wider one, then gather and stitch them to the valance as though they were a single strip.

Alternatively, cut a 5cm wide frill. Pink one long edge, gather the other edge and set into the valance.

SHAPED VALANCE WITH BOXED HEADING

Rather than making a heading with curtain tape, and attaching the valance to screw eyes, you can gather the valance on to a boxed heading and attach it to the pelmet shelf with Velcro. The boxed section is interlined for a soft finish, and the lower edge bound with contrast fabric as an alternative to a frilled edge. Piping round the edge of the boxed heading makes a neat finish.

1 *Prepare the pattern*
Draw up a pelmet pattern, as for a shaped pelmet (see page 248). Cut 10cm off the top of the pattern.

2 *Calculating fabric*
For the gathered section of the valance, you need a panel of fabric three times the length of the pattern, plus 3cm seam allowance, by the depth of the pattern plus 1.5cm seam allowance along the top edge. You also need a strip of fabric for the boxed section, the same length as the paper pattern, plus 3cm seam allowance, by 13cm (for a 10cm deep box). You need enough piping cord and 3.5cm wide bias-cut piping to go all round the box. For binding the lower edge you need a 7cm wide bias-cut strip, the same length as the curved lower edge of the valance (see page 253 for details of cutting bias strips).

3 *Cut out the fabric*
Join up panels of fabric and lining to make a strip three times the length of your paper pattern, by its trimmed depth plus 1.5cm seam allowance along the top edge. Fold the pelmet pattern in half and 'spread' it to allow for gathers as described on page 248, adding 1.5cm seam allowance. Place the valance pattern on folded fabric and cut out as before. Cut out strips of fabric and lining for the box section, joining widths if necessary. Cut out bias-cut piping to fit all round the boxed section, and binding strips to fit along the lower edge of the valance. Join up strips as necessary, and prepare piping.

4 *Make up gathered section*
Lay valance fabric on top of lining, right sides together and raw edges matching. Stitch together down side edges. Turn right side out and press. Tack fabric to lining along lower edge, then bind it, taking 1.5cm seams and slipstitching the binding in place on the back of the valance. Neaten ends of binding by slipstitching in place. Run two lines of gathering stitches along top edge.

5 *Interline the box section*
Cut a piece of interlining the same size as the finished box section. If you need to join strips of interlining fabric, make as flat a seam as possible by overlapping the selvedges by about 7mm; then pin, tack and zig zag stitch through both layers. Lay the interlining on the wrong side of the panel of fabric for the box section, leaving a 1.5cm seam allowance all round. Hold in place with herringbone stitch.

6 *Add the piping*
Lay out the fabric, right side up, and position piping round panel, raw edges matching. Clip into seam allowance of piping at corners. Pin, tack and stitch in place. Lay the lining on top of the piped panel, right sides facing and raw edges matching. Pin, tack and stitch lining to fabric, enclosing piping, round side and upper edges. Trim seam allowances, clip corners and turn right side out. Press under seam allowances along lower edge.

7 *Set in the gathered valance*
Draw up gathering stitches so that the top edge of the gathered section matches the lower edge of the boxed section. With right sides of fabric facing and raw edges matching, pin the gathered section to the box section, sandwiching the piping. Distribute gathers evenly, then tack and stitch in place. Stitch folded edge of lining to seamline by hand.

8 *Add the Velcro*
Pin the furry half of the Velcro to the back of the boxed section, positioning the top edge of it level with the top of the lining. Stitch the Velcro in place by hand, just catching the front of the fabric so that the valance cannot roll down and show the lining, or sag away from the pelmet shelf when fixed in place. Staple the hooked half of the Velcro round the edge of the pelmet shelf, using a staple gun.

◁ **All boxed up**
This gently-shaped valance has a boxed heading, which is piped all round for a neat finish. Interlining the boxed section adds a touch of luxury, and broad binding along the lower, curved edge adds to the crisp, tailored look of the valance.

TAILORED SHAPED CURTAIN TIEBACKS

Tiebacks are an easy way to dress up curtains. They are also pretty and practical.

Curtain tiebacks can be made up in a variety of shapes and styles, with different trims to suit your personal taste. They are easy and inexpensive to make yourself and can give a new lease of life to dull or old curtains.

If you are making tiebacks to add to existing curtains, don't worry if you have not got any of the original fabric. In fact, even if you have a remnant of fabric which matches, the chances are that the curtains will have faded, so the remnant will no longer match. You only need a remnant of fabric to achieve some dramatic effects — if you cannot match it to the curtains exactly, create added interest with contrasting fabric.

You can make perfectly plain straight tiebacks, but they work more effectively and look better if you shape them to give a more tailored finish. For a distinctive finish, pipe or bind the edges or add a frill all along the lower edge of the tieback.

CHOOSING FABRICS
Most light- or medium-weight, closely woven furnishing fabrics are suitable. Don't try to use heavy brocades or velvet as they are too bulky and won't make up successfully. Both sides of the tieback can be of furnishing fabric, or you can use lining fabric for the backing if you haven't got enough, or if the fabric is too bulky or rather expensive.

MEASURING UP
To calculate where to place the tieback and how long and how wide it should be, loop a tape measure around the curtain about two-thirds of the way down from the top and create the folds or the draped effect you want to achieve. Note the measurement on the tape measure as this will be the length of the finished tieback.

While the tape measure is still in place, make a small pencil mark on the wall or window surround to indicate the position for the fixing hook.

For sill-length curtains, the depth of the tieback should be no more than 10cm, but for longer curtains it may be enlarged proportionally. Instructions given here are for 10cm deep tiebacks. Seams throughout are 1.5cm unless otherwise stated.

Tidy lines
A perfect solution for a graceful, arched window: the curtains are fitted to the top of the window frame, and rather than opening on a track they are held open by the tiebacks. In this case, the chair rail has been used as a fixing point for the tiebacks, almost exactly a third of the way up the window. The bound edges emphasize the shape of the tiebacks.

MAKING A STRAIGHT-EDGED TIEBACK

1 Cut out a pattern
Start by drawing a rectangle on a sheet of paper: the length should be the same as the length you measured with the tape measure, and the depth should be 10cm. Cut out.

2 Cut out the fabrics
For each tieback, pin the pattern to a double thickness of fabric and cut out, (or cut out once in fabric and once in lining), allowing an extra 1.5cm all round for seams.

Pin the pattern to a single thickness of interfacing and cut out without any seam allowance.

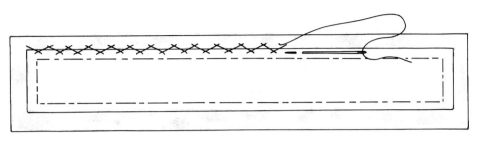

3 Attach the interfacing △
Lay the interfacing centrally on the wrong side of one piece of fabric. Tack in place. Herringbone stitch all round the edges of the interfacing to catch to fabric. Work the herringbone stitch from left to right, first taking a small stitch horizontally in the tieback fabric and then diagonally lower down on the interfacing. The stitches should not show on the right side of the tieback fabric.

MAKING SHAPED TIEBACKS

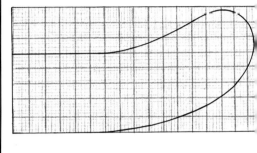

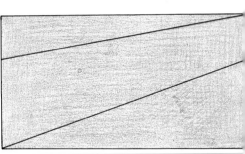

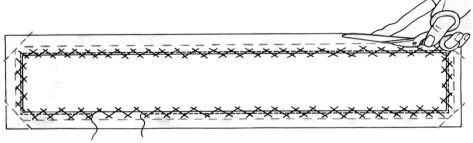

4 Make up the tieback △
Place the two tieback pieces right sides facing and tack together all round, leaving a 10cm gap for turning through to the right side. Machine with the interfacing uppermost, being careful to sew close to, but not over, the edge of the interfacing.

Trim the seams and clip diagonally across the corners. Remove tacking. Turn through to right side and slipstitch the open edges together to close. Press.

Make up a second tieback to match in the same way.

1 Draw up the design △
Measure the length of the tieback as before. Cut a piece of graph paper printed with 1cm squares the length of the tieback by at least 15cm deep and fold in half widthways. Either follow one of the charts here for a simply-shaped tieback, or draw out your own design. Cut out the pattern, open flat and hold in place to check that the shape is effective.

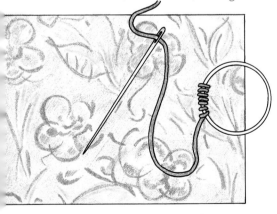

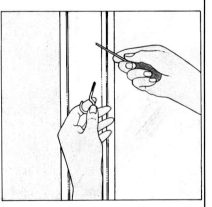

5 Attach the rings △
Sew a curtain ring to the middle of each short edge. Working on the wrong side of the fabric, overcast the ring just inside the edge so that enough of the ring protrudes to fit neatly over the hook which will be fixed to the wall.

6 Fix hooks to hold tiebacks △
Fix a hook to hold the tiebacks in place where the mark is. If the window surround is wood, you can simply use a cup hook, making a small pilot hole with a bradawl first.

If there is a plaster finish at the point where the tieback is to be fixed, you will have to drill and fit a wallplug.

2 Cut out the fabrics
Cut out twice in fabric (or once in fabric and once in lining) with a seam allowance and once in interfacing without seam allowance for each tieback.

3 Make up the tiebacks
Make up the tiebacks and attach rings and hooks as for straight-edged tiebacks, following the instructions in step 6.

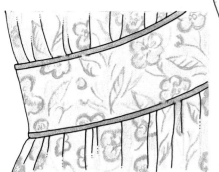

Piped edges Piping in the seam line emphasizes shape and can at the same time provide a contrast colour. Either cover the piping cord with bias strips cut from the same fabric as the tieback or use purchased bias binding, 2.5cm wide. Cover the cord and apply to the right side of one piece of the tieback, raw edges together. Continue making up the tieback as before, sandwiching the piping between the two layers of fabric. Use a zipper foot to sew the seam, stitching as close to the piping as possible. (For more information about working the piping, see Making Cushions, page 286.)

Bound edges Binding all round the edges gives the chance to introduce a contrast colour, or to pick up a plain colour from a patterned fabric. Again, you can use bias strips cut from the fabric or purchased bias binding. Cut out the fabric and interfacing to shape you require, without any seam allowance.

With wrong sides facing, sandwich the interfacing between the two pieces of fabric, and tack together around the edges. Round off any corners slightly to make it easier to apply the binding. Attach bias strips or bias binding, slipstitching in place on the wrong side (see below).

Frilled edges Measure along the bottom edge of the tieback and cut a 7.5cm wide strip of fabric twice this measurement. Turn under double hem along one long edge and two short edges of the frill. Sew two lines of gathering threads along the remaining raw edge. Place the frill on one tieback piece, right sides facing and with raw edge of frill matching lower raw edge of tieback. Pin each end of the frill 1.5cm in from the side edges of the tieback, and pull up the gathering threads until the frill fits along the edge of the tieback. Tack in place. Continue to make up the tieback as for the straight version.

USING BIAS BINDING

Using bias strips means that you can ease the binding round gently curved shapes, such as tailored tiebacks, because fabric that is cut diagonally will stretch and give slightly.

Most commercially-available bias binding is made from a 3.5cm strip of fabric, folded in half down its length, with 5mm turnings pressed under along each long raw edge.

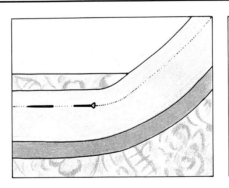

1 *Stitch to right side* △
Open out the bias strip; and with right sides facing, pin, tack and stitch along the fold line of the binding.

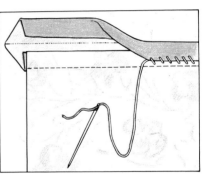

2 *Slipstitch in place* △
Turn binding over the edge of the fabric. Slipstitch the folded edge to wrong side, just inside row of stitches.

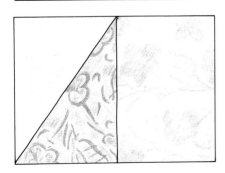

CUTTING YOUR OWN BIAS STRIPS
1 *Mark the diagonal* △
Choose fabric to match or contrast with the tieback or item you are sewing. Find the bias or cross of the fabric by laying the fabric flat, and folding one corner at a 45° angle. Press.

2 *Cut the strips* △
Mark a series of lines parallel to this fold line, at least 3.5cm apart, depending on the finished effect you want. Cut along marked lines.

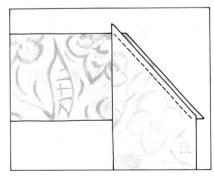

3 *Joining strips* △
If you need to join bias strips, place the two strips to be joined at right angles to each other, with right sides facing. Sew with a narrow (5mm) flat seam. Press seam open.

MAKING A SCALLOPED TIEBACK

1 Draw up the basic shape
Draw up a pattern for the basic shape of tieback you require, following the instructions for shaped tiebacks on the previous page. Use a folded sheet of graph paper at least 20cm wide marked with 1cm squares.

3 Cut out the pattern and fabric
Cut out the paper pattern and open out flat. For each tieback, cut out twice in fabric or once in fabric and once in lining with an additional 1.5cm all round for the seam allowance. Cut out in interfacing.

4 Make up the tiebacks
Continue to make up the tiebacks as before, sewing carefully around the scallop shapes. Snip into seam allowance on curves and turn to right side.

2 Mark in the scallops ▽
Using a suitable size curve – an egg cup or the rim of a small wine glass – draw a series of even-sized scallop shapes along the lower edge of the paper pattern. Start with a full scallop at the fold and, when you reach the end,

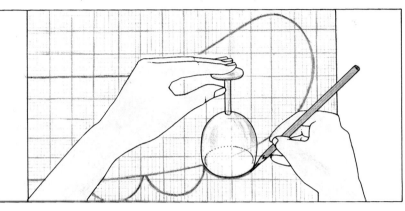

adjust to finish with either a half or a complete scallop, or draw a shallower scallop to fill the space if you prefer. Adjust the scallops until you are happy with the effect. You can make progressively shallower scallops if you prefer a tapered look.

QUICK SCALLOPED TIEBACKS

1 Draw the template
Draw the template up on graph paper using an egg cup or wine glass to make the scalloped shapes as before.

2 Cut out the fabric
Cut out twice in fabric, allowing a 1cm seam allowance all round, and once in interfacing.

3 Attach the interfacing
Attach the interfacing to the wrong side of one piece of fabric as before, then, with wrong sides facing, pin, tack and stitch the fabric pieces together, sandwiching the interfacing, stitching close to the edge of the interfacing.

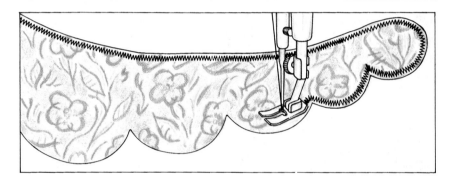

4 Finish the edges △
Set your machine to a closed-up zigzag stitch or satin stitch. Zigzag stitch round the edge of the tieback following the seam line. As an alternative, you can zigzag the edges of the scallops with a contrasting coloured sewing thread.

5 Trim the edges
Use a small pair of sewing scissors to trim the seam allowance close to the stitching, making sure you do not cut any of the stitches. Repeat for the second tieback and add rings.

BRIGHT IDEA

RIBBON DEVELOPMENT ◁
If you haven't the time to make your own tiebacks, improvise by using a broad, good quality satin or velvet ribbon. Trim the edges diagonally or into a deep V shape to prevent fraying, and add a ring at the centre of the ribbon to hang it on a hook.

LACY DAYS ▷
Another trick is to use a length of broderie anglaise. It will look especially pretty on fresh cotton print curtains, and will add a touch of femininity to otherwise ordinary curtains. Use pre-gathered broderie anglaise to save extra sewing. To introduce some colour, use double-edged, ungathered broderie anglaise with eyelets and thread the eyelets with a thin piece of ribbon to match the curtains.

DRAPED SWAGS AND TAILS

For a dramatic effect at your windows dress them up with swags and tails – fabric draped around the top and sides.

Swags and tails have had their place in grand country houses for centuries, but there is no reason why you should not adapt the style to dress up windows on a smaller scale. However, they are extravagant in their use of fabric, and can be difficult to drape effectively, so it is not a project for someone who is inexperienced at home sewing.

Choosing fabrics The fabrics you use will depend on the finished effect you are aiming for: traditional curtain fabrics create a formal atmosphere, but you could use finer fabrics or even muslin or sheer curtain fabric for a fantasy effect. Avoid using heavy fabrics such as linen unions or velvets.

Formal swags and tails should be lined to add to the luxurious effect and help them to hang properly. Also, bear in mind that the back of the swags are visible where they fold back on themselves, so a contrast lining and bound edge can produce an effective finish.

Suitable windows This type of finish is best suited to larger windows, since not only is it a particularly grand style, it also cuts down on the amount of light coming through the window. As well as the swags across the top of the window and tails down the side, you will probably want some other form of screening at the window: traditionally the choice is lined curtains with a pencil-pleated heading (see Simple Unlined Curtains and Curtains with Sewn-in Linings, pages 223-231) and tiebacks to hold the curtains in place (see pages 251-254). For a more up-to-the-minute look, you could install blinds or sheer curtains, or leave the windows uncurtained if you have a pleasant outlook and are not overlooked.

Proportions To ensure you don't end up with skimpy tails, they should fall about two-thirds of the way down the window. However, the swag should not drape more than a sixth of the way down the window, to avoid cutting out daylight. But there are no hard and fast rules: you will have to make a pattern from a spare piece of fabric and be prepared to tack it up more than once until you are satisfied with the effect.

FITTING AND MEASURING

The swags and tails are fitted to a pelmet shelf above the window – if you don't have one already, then the first thing to do is to fit one – see Traditional Fabric Pelmets. The swags and tails are held to the top of the pelmet shelf with Velcro – or they may be stapled in place if you are not going to want to take them down regularly to clean them.

Start by looking at plenty of pictures to get an idea of the different styles and shapes you can create: the line drawings overleaf give you a selection of ideas.

Once you have decided on the effect you want, measure up carefully: each swag and each tail is made up as a separate piece, but the aim is to create an illusion that the whole thing is made from one piece of fabric.

Sunny and elegant
Triple swags and softly-pleated tails in crisp cream cotton help to create a sunny feeling in this drawing room. Note that the tails have dark blue linings for extra definition.

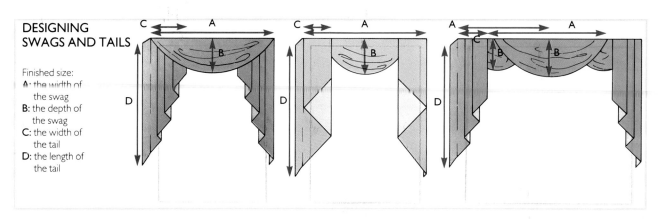

DESIGNING SWAGS AND TAILS

Finished size:
A: the width of the swag
B: the depth of the swag
C: the width of the tail
D: the length of the tail

CHECK YOUR NEEDS
- ☐ Pencil and paper
- ☐ Tape measure
- ☐ Lengths of lining, muslin or old sheets for making pattern
- ☐ Staple gun
- ☐ Fabric for swags and tails
- ☐ Fabric for lining/binding
- ☐ Velcro fastening
- ☐ Pins and needles
- ☐ Sewing machine
- ☐ Sewing thread
- ☐ Dressmaker's chalk

CALCULATING FABRIC AMOUNTS
Measure up and draw a plan of your window, then sketch in the effect you want before calculating how much fabric you need.

1 Finished size of the swags
First decide on the total length you want the swags to cover, ensuring the ends will be tucked well under the tails, or hidden over the top of the pelmet shelf. At the same time, decide how far down the window you want the swags to hang. The diagrams above give some idea of the different shapes to go for.

2 Amount of fabric for the swags
Calculate approximately how much fabric you will need, so you can make a pattern. The length of fabric for the swags is equal to the finished length of the swags, plus 3cm seam allowance and 5–10cm to allow the fabric to drape at the centre of the window. The width of fabric needed is 1½ times the finished depth of the swag, plus 3cm seam allowance and a 5cm allowance to go over the top of the pelmet shelf. You will need the same amount of fabric for lining. The ends will eventually be cut at an angle (see steps 5 and 6).

3 Finished size of the tails
Decide on the style and finished size of the tails: how far you want them to hang down the window, how many pleats you want, and what width you want them to be. In the example here, there are four folds, creating two pleats,

but you can make up your own variations. The secret of getting well-balanced folds is to cut the lower edge of the fabric on the bias. (This can be a bit wasteful, so try to find a use for the triangle you have to cut off.)

The pelmet shelf usually protrudes

from the wall, and the tails should wrap round the ends of the shelf (the return) to butt up against the wall. This gives a neat finish when you see the window from one side. Measure the depth of the pelmet shelf, so you can allow for the return.

4 Amount of fabric for the tails
For each tail you will need a length of fabric equal to the finished length of the tail, plus an allowance equal to the depth of the pelmet shelf at the top to allow for fixing, and a 3cm allowance for

seams. The width is three times the width of the pleated section of the tail, plus the width of any unpleated section. Add an allowance for the return down the outer edge of the swag if needed and a 3cm seam allowance.

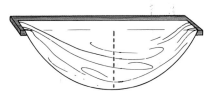

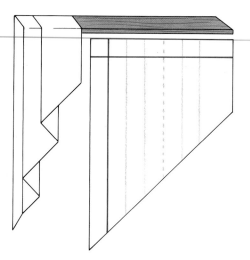

5 Make pattern for the swag △
To guarantee that your swags and tails will drape well, use some lining fabric, muslin, or even an old sheet to make a pattern. This is essential if you want to make a series of swags across the top of the window. Use the calculations in steps 1 and 2 to work out the approximate dimensions and cut a piece of fabric for the pattern, omitting the seam allowances along the top and bottom edges, but allowing an extra 5–10cm at each end. Mark the centre of

the swag on the piece of fabric for the pattern. Drape the fabric across the top of the window where the swag is to go, and gather or pleat the ends in place. You will find that you need to make the lines of gathering stitching at a slight angle, as shown in the diagram (above). When you are happy with the shape, trim the ends of the swag 1.5cm outside the lines of gathering stitches. Open out the pattern and mark the lines of gathering stitch with dressmaker's chalk.

6 Make pattern for the tails △
Cut a piece of fabric for each tail, omitting seam allowances, and cutting the lower edge of the bias. Hang them in place and adjust the folds, then staple the pattern to the top of the pelmet, so you can check the effect. Mark the pleat lines (shown in blue), the fold for the return and the line of the top of the pelmet shelf (shown here in red).

7 *Make adjustments to calculations*
Use the fabric patterns to check exactly how much fabric you need. Make sure you have included an allowance of 1.5cm for seams all round and include an allowance for matching patterns if this is necessary.

MAKING THE SWAGS

Use the pattern you made from lining fabric as a guide when making up the swags. Unpick the gathering stitches at one end, so you can use the pattern as a guide to both cutting and gathering the fabric for the swag.

1 *Cut out fabric and lining*
Using your pattern as a guide, and adding 1.5cm seam allowance all round, cut out the swag in both fabric and lining fabric (or contrast fabric).

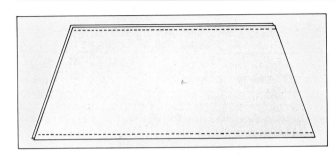

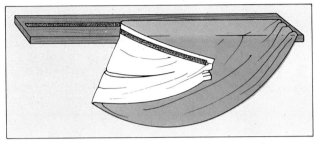

2 *Make up the swag △*
Lay the two pieces of fabric on top of each other with right sides together. Pin, tack and stitch together along top and bottom edges, leaving the ends open. Press and trim seam allowances. Turn right side out and press.

3 *Gather the ends*
Gather or pleat the ends of the swags to match the pattern you made. Temporarily staple the fabric to the top of the pelmet shelf to check the effect. Take down the swag, and, if you are happy with the gathers, trim the raw edges and bind along the gathered edge to give a neat finish.

4 *Fit the Velcro △*
Stitch the hooked half of a strip of Velcro to the top edge of the swag, and staple the other half to the top of the pelmet shelf. (If you do not want to take down the swag for cleaning, you can staple or tack it directly in place along the top edge.)

MAKING THE TAILS

The tails are made up using the pattern you have already cut, like the swags. Start with the pattern piece opened out flat, with the fold lines and pelmet positions marked on it, as shown in step 6 on the opposite page.

1 *Check the pattern pieces*
Check that the patterns for the tails are exact mirror images, and adjust slightly if necessary. Cut out a pair of tails in fabric and lining, including a 1.5cm seam allowance all round. Transfer the fold lines and the line marking the corner of the pelmet shelf (where appropriate) to the tails.

2 *Make up the tails*
Position the panels of fabric for each tail on top of each other, right sides facing, and stitch together down sides and across lower edge, leaving top edge open. Press, trim seam allowances and clip corners and turn right side out. Press.

BRIGHT IDEA

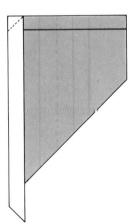

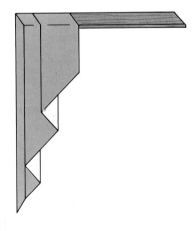

3 *Make pleats △*
If the tails are to go around the return of the pelmet shelf, fold the tail back on itself, right sides together, along the marked corner line. Make a diagonal row of stitching through both layers of fabric (like a dart) from the outer corner of the pelmet shelf to the top corner of the tail. This will give you a neat box shape at the top of the tail. Pleat the fabric along the marked lines and tack together across the top.

4 *Finish top edge △*
Check the fit by hanging in place. Press. Trim the top edge if necessary, and bind or oversew raw edges.

5 *Attach Velcro*
Stitch one half of the Velcro to the underside of the top of the tails, and attach the other half to the top of the shelf. Hang in place, then add extra tabs of Velcro if necessary where the swags and tails overlap, to hold them together.

Swathed in lace For instant effect with a minimum of sewing, you can simply drape a length of lace over a wooden pole above the window. Just measure the length from the floor to the top of the pole, double it, and add an allowance for a generous sweep of fabric. Velcro can be used to anchor the drape in place

COUNTRY-STYLE SWAG

For cottage-style windows, you can make swags and tails on a simpler scale from a single length of fabric, fixed at each end to a batten above the window. If the curtains are fitted in a recess, a 50 × 12.5mm batten is sufficient. If the curtains have to be hung outside the recess, fit a 50 × 32mm batten, and fit the curtain track to the underside of the batten.

1 *Measure up the window ▷*
Measure the batten above the window and decide how far down you want the swag to fall, and how long the tails should be. The easiest way to measure is to loop a tape measure where the swag is to be hung. Alternatively, hold a piece of string or strip of fabric in place, check the effect and then measure that to see how much fabric you will need for the swag.

2 *Calculate amount of fabric ▷ ▷*
For a neat effect, it is best to shape the ends, and make the gathering stitches at an angle. You can use lining fabric or old sheeting to made a pattern, marking the lines of gathering with dressmaker's chalk. The length is the length calculated in step 1. The width should be about 1 ½ times the depth of the swag. Include an allowance for neatening the edges of the drape (see below).

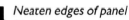

3 *Cut out the fabric*
Use the pattern to cut out fabric for the swag. The edges may be bound, in which case you will not need to add an allowance for neatening, or you can turn under a 1cm double hem all round the edge of the panel. A third alternative is to line the panel, in which case you should include a 1.5cm seam allowance, and cut a matching panel in lining fabric or some other toning fabric to the same measurements.

4 *Neaten edges of panel*
Bind or hem raw edges, or line the panel by stitching the lining to the panel, right sides facing, stitching all round the edge, leaving a 10cm gap: turn to right side and close opening.

5 *Gather corners*
Fold the panel in half, right sides together. Mark the points where the swag is to be gathered, to match the fixing points at the ends of the batten above the window. Make two lines of gathering stitches at each point. Draw up the gathers. Stitch the gathers to a piece of tape at the back of the swag.

6 *Neaten the front △*
Use lengths of ribbon or a rosette or bow made from matching fabric to cover the lines of gathering stitches. A neat tab gives a more tailored effect.

7 *Hang the swag*
Hang the swag at the window, either by screwing small cup hooks to the batten, and curtain rings to the back of the gathers, or with a length of Velcro fixed to the top of the swag and the batten.

▷ *Simple swag*
This small window has been dressed with unlined curtains, with standard headings. A simple swag across the top covers the curtain track and adds a country feeling in a teenage bedroom.

CHOOSING CURTAINS

An appealing window treatment immediately attracts attention and transforms and enhances any room.

This chapter covers simple curtain treatments to help you choose the right style to suit your furnishings. Later chapters cover curtain tracks and poles and various types of blinds so that you can plan your window treatments.

The style of the curtains should complement the decor as well as the shape of the window. Do you want the curtains to look informal or rather 'dressy', tailored or romantic, modern or of a particular period? Decide whether you want the curtains to stand out or blend with the furnishings. If there is a spectacular view, keep the curtains simple. If the view is unattractive you can disguise it with a permanent curtain made from a sheer fabric or, if daylight is not important, choose curtains that are fixed at the top and held back at the sides.

Lined or unlined? As a rule, lining makes a curtain look and hang better, as well as adding insulation and protecting the curtain fabric from fading. Thermal linings and interlinings both help insulate against cold.

Unlined curtains, however, do have a place. Lightweight fabrics, laces and sheers filter the light attractively, and can be teamed with a blind for night-time privacy.

Fabrics for curtains It is usually better to be generous with a cheaper fabric than mean with an expensive one. Buy a short length of your chosen fabric to take home so you can check how it drapes and see how it looks with the rest of your furnishings, and in different lights. (You can use it to make tiebacks or a cushion cover later on.)

HOW LONG?

Sill-length curtains work well in cottagey rooms or with horizontal windows in modern homes. Curtains should barely touch the sill.

Below-sill length can look untidy when drawn back but if you have a radiator under the window you can finish the curtains just above it.

Floor-length curtains work best with sash windows, in bays and bows and, of course, french and picture windows. The curtains should almost touch the floor with no visible gap.

Café curtains give privacy at the lower half of a window while letting in light at the top.

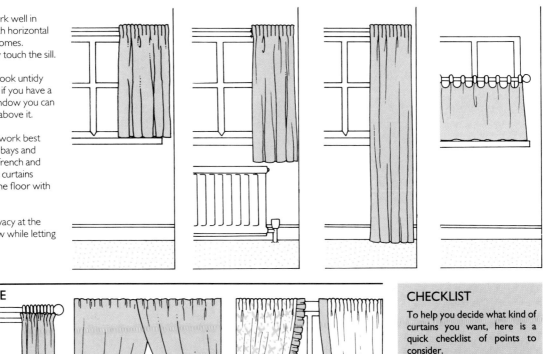

CURTAIN STYLE

STRAIGHT CURTAINS
Style Suitable for long or short curtains in modern and most traditional rooms.
In use Hang from a track or pole, with or without pelmet or valance.

TIEBACKS
Style Used to hold curtains back in an elegant curve to give a softer, fuller look.
In use Curtains can be left touching at the centre and looped back, or half drawn and looped back, depending on light.
Watchpoints Don't pull curtains into a straight line, but ease them into a curve. Not recommended for velvet.

CURTAIN TRIMMINGS
Style A decorative edge gives a curtain a lot of extra style. A narrow frill looks pretty; a plain co-ordinated border is more tailored.

CHECKLIST
To help you decide what kind of curtains you want, here is a quick checklist of points to consider.

- ☐ What shape and size is the window?
- ☐ What look do you want to achieve?
- ☐ How long do you want the curtains to be?
- ☐ What heading?
- ☐ Lined or unlined?
- ☐ Hung from a pole or track?
- ☐ With or without a pelmet or valance?
- ☐ To hang straight, to curve with tiebacks?
- ☐ Combined with a sheer/net curtain or blind?
- ☐ What is the main function – privacy, insulation, light exclusion?
- ☐ Will frequent cleaning be necessary?

TYPES OF HEADINGS

A ready-made curtain heading tape is the easiest way of creating a decorative effect for both curtains and valances.

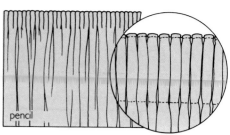
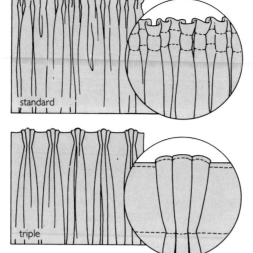
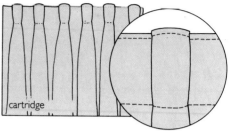

STANDARD HEADING

Style Suitable for sheers and informal, lightweight, sill-length curtains.

In use Gives an evenly gathered, narrow heading. A synthetic tape is available for sheers and nets.

Watchpoint Curtains can look unfinished without a pelmet or valance when drawn back.

PENCIL PLEATING

Style This neat, unobtrusive heading suits most furnishing styles, particularly rooms with a modern look.

In use Tape comes in two widths: narrow for short curtains, deep for longer ones. The tape forms neat pleats, and is suitable for lined and unlined curtains in a medium-weight fabric. The curtain can be hung from rings or hooked to stand up in front of the track and so does not need a pelmet or valance.

TRIPLE PLEATING

Style This heading looks well on long curtains and suits more traditional styles of furnishing. The regular, full folds look good in velvet.

In use The tape forms spaced pleats which can be straight or fanned out. It is suitable for medium- to heavyweight fabrics and can be hung from rings or to cover the track.

Watchpoint Position the tape so that the pleats fall evenly across the curtains with equal space at each end.

CARTRIDGE PLEATING

Style A formal heading, especially suitable for heavier, floor-length curtains in an elegant setting. Again, good for velvet.

Watchpoint Position the tape so that the single pleats fall evenly across the curtain.

PELMETS AND VALANCES

straight pelmet

valance

shaped pelmet

frilled valance

A pelmet or valance hides the curtain track and heading and adds a decorative touch to a window.

STRAIGHT PELMET

Style The simple clean lines suit a formal or modern setting. The depth and width can alter the proportions of the window.

In use You can paint or paper the pelmet to match the walls.

Watchpoint Make sure the pelmet projects sufficiently to clear the curtains.

SHAPED PELMET

Style Choose a decorative edge – scalloped, curved, castellated, etc – to suit a more elaborate style of furnishing.

In use The stiffened pelmet backing is pre-printed with a variety of shapes: simply remove the adhesive backing and cover with the fabric of your choice.

Watchpoint Fabric-covered pelmets are difficult to clean, so do not use them in rooms such as kitchens and bathrooms.

VALANCE

Style The depth of a valance varies according to the size of the window and style of curtain. Short curtains need a minimum of 75mm/3in; long curtains can take a valance as deep as 30cm/12in. Simple valances look best in informal, cottagey rooms.

In use Valances fix to a pelmet shelf or hang from a valance track. Use a heading tape that matches the curtains below.

FRILLED VALANCE

Style For a more decorative look the bottom edge of a valance can have a frill added. It can also be ruched like a festoon blind, swagged or curved so that it is deeper at the sides.

Watchpoint The depth of the curve must be in proportion to the length of the curtain.

MORE CURTAIN IDEAS

These simple ideas for windows are mainly suitable for sheer or lightweight fabrics and do not use any complicated curtain-making techniques.

Cross-over curtains made from lace or voile look pretty and romantic. A length of bordered cotton lace is draped over a pole and looped back at the sides by rosette brackets. Sew hems at each end to neaten and team with a roller blind for privacy.

A draped fabric curtain made from a length of lightweight furnishing fabric adds an elegant finish to a more formal room. One end of the fabric is wrapped around the pole (staple or use Velcro to hold it if necessary), and the fabric is then arranged in a deep swag across the window and down one side. An elegant roman blind will complement this style as well as giving privacy at night.

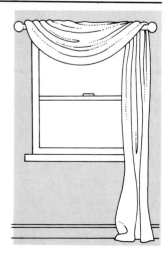

CHOOSING FABRIC FOR CURTAINS

Whatever curtains you want, there is a fabric for the job – finding it is just a matter of knowing what to look for.

There's more to shopping for curtain fabric than seeking out the perfect print or the weave that complements the colour scheme to perfection. Furnishing fabrics are not all suitable for every situation. With the wide range of weaves and weights of cloth available, make sure the one you buy will do the job you have in mind.

The two most important factors to bear in mind when looking for curtain fabric are resistance to fading and the weight of the fabric.

Light resistance Curtains, being so close to windows, take a lot of punishment from sunlight. Make sure to choose fabrics that are resistant to fading and rotting by the sun's rays, particularly for rooms which get the sun throughout most of the day. If the fabric you choose is subject to fading – a dupion for instance – line it with curtain lining fabric or add some form of sunscreen such as sheer curtains or plain roller blinds.

Fabric weights Look at the weight and quality of the fabric. In general, all but the lightest curtains are worth lining, and even some of the thinner softer cloths which drape well look very limp unless they are lined. It is worth taking trouble to line or interline an expensive fabric – this will enhance the appearance of the fabric and also help to insulate your room.

Heavyweight curtain fabrics are best made up into, full-length curtains, as they can look stiff and bulky when made up into sill-length curtains.

Making the right choice When you have decided what curtain fabric you want, it is worth investing in a metre to bring home. This way you can check colour and pattern against the existing furnishings and see how the fabric reacts both to the natural and the artificial light in the room. The extra expense is worthwhile to make sure you have made the right choice, and to avoid making an expensive mistake. The odd length of fabric can always be made into covers for scatter cushions.

Before the fabric is cut for you in the shop, check that there are no flaws in the weave. If it is a print, make sure that the pattern is printed square on the fabric – if you are joining widths to make up the curtain and the pattern is printed off the grain by more than a couple of centimetres, you will not be able to match the pattern without distorting the fall of the cloth.

FABRIC FIBRES		
Acetate	A synthetic silky-looking fibre often combined with cotton or linen in brocades and open weave effects. Usually washable and non-shrinking.	
Acrylic	A synthetic fibre used for lightweight but strong and crease-resistant fabrics and also for velvets and satins. Does not fade and is washable, but on no account should it be boiled as this harms the fibre.	
Cotton	A strong and hardwearing natural fibre which becomes stronger when it is wet, so it can be rubbed, scrubbed and boiled during washing. It is very absorbent and so takes dyes and printing well. Cotton is inclined to shrink when first washed unless it has been pre-shrunk by the manufacturer. So before making up, shrink cotton materials by damping or immersing them in water. All types of cotton are suitable for curtains.	
Fibreglass	A synthetic flame-resistant fibre which makes full drapes. Dry clean.	
Hessian	A natural fibre made from jute or hemp, available in a wide range of colours. Prone to fading. Dry clean.	
Linen	A natural fibre made from flax; stronger than cotton. Used to make a variety of fabrics from strong linen cloth to fine lawn.	

Milium	A synthetic fibre used for aluminium-backed curtain linings with good insulation properties. Dry clean.	
Nylon	A synthetic fibre used for fabrics of all weights and types. Varieties include nylon velvet and nets. Shrink-resistant, washable, but can fade.	
Polyester	A very strong synthetic fibre often blended with natural fibres. Does not shrink or fade. Popular for its sheer and opaque qualities.	
Rayon	A synthetic fibre originally known as artificial silk. Includes taffeta, linen types and velvet. Tends to fray. Follow manufacturer's instructions.	
Silk	A natural fibre produced by the silkworm. It has always been a luxury furnishing fabric and traditionally, all velvets, taffetas, moirés and damasks were made of it. Pure silk curtains always need to be lined and interlined to give the weight and substance required. It will fade and rot in sunlight, but shouldn't shrink if washed with care. Dry clean or hand wash according to manufacturer's instructions.	
Wool	A natural fibre which is crease and soil-resistant and dyes well. If not pre-shrunk, fabric will shrink. Follow manufacturer's instructions.	

Most manufacturers disclaim responsibility for faults once the fabric has been cut, so it is important to make sure that there are no faults in the fabric before picking up your scissors.

Fabric care The after-care of made-up curtains also needs some thought when choosing fabric. Unless a fabric is labelled and sold as pre-shrunk or fixed-finished, a shrinkage of between five and six per cent is considered normal,

and even after pre-shrinking, a fabric can still shrink by up to three per cent.

It is always recommended that lined curtains should be dry cleaned. This is because the various components, the fabric, the lining and the thread, as well as the cord and tape, do not necessarily shrink at the same rate.

If curtains are going to need regular washing it is sensible either to pre-wash the fabric, lining and tape, or to make

curtains with detachable linings.

Full-length curtains, where the shrinkage potential will be more noticeable, should have generous hems, loosely stitched in case they need to be let down later on. (It is advisable to undo the stitching before washing for the first time.)

Remember the 'true' length of a curtain should be the drop it has to cover plus allowances for hem and heading.

FABRIC WEAVES AND FINISHES

The characteristics of the fibres in a fabric determine how well the fabric hangs, washes and wears.

△ BROCADE

This is a woven fabric with a raised floral design that looks like embroidery. It can be made from silk, linen or cotton, or from synthetic yarn.

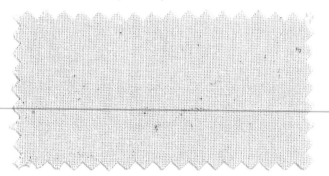

△ CALICO

This is an unbleached plain woven cotton of medium weight in a matt finish, available in natural off-white. It is relatively cheap and must be used lavishly to look effective. It looks good draped into dramatic window treatments. It is a strong firmly woven fabric, which washes well although it tends to crease and shrink, so wash with care.

COTTON SATIN

This is a less expensive and more practical alternative to satin (which was traditionally made from pure silk). It is a hard wearing, very close weave with a distinctive sheen. A heavy-quality version makes luxuriously soft and natural curtains that drape extremely well. It adds a sophisticated finish to curtains in the more formal rooms of your home.

Cotton satin is often used as the base cloth for printing, but is also popular as a plain self-coloured weave. Sometimes a minor design, such as a spot or small diamond, is introduced as surface decoration.

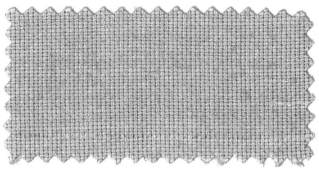

△ COTTON LINEN OR LINEN UNION

This is a blend of cotton and linen to which small quantities of nylon are added for strength. When made up into heavy full lengths it drapes reasonably well, but is really too stiff for short curtains.

Wash at a maximum of 40 °C; the two fibres do not shrink evenly at higher temperatures.

△ DAMASK

This was originally made in silk but now comes in cotton and various natural/synthetic blends. Its weave produces patterns which appear matt against a shiny, satin-like background.

△ DUPION

This fabric mimics silk, but is much cheaper. Sometimes it is heavily slubbed (woven with alternate thick and thin threads) to resemble raw silk. It is usually woven in synthetic fibres, often on an acetate warp (lengthwise threads.) There are a few washable versions available in viscose/cotton or acrylic/linen blends, but it usually has to be dry cleaned. Dupion is a lightweight cloth that needs lining and preferably inter-lining, but it drapes well and can be made up successfully into short and full-length curtains.

As with pure silk, problems can arise with fading, especially with stronger and brighter colourways.

EASYCARE COTTON

This is a cotton which has been treated to a polished finish which gives a soft and silky touch to the surface of the cloth. The easy-care finish means the fabric drapes and washes beautifully.

GINGHAM

A lightweight cotton fabric or poly/cotton with a checked pattern woven in using two coloured yarns.

△ GLAZED COTTON OR CHINTZ

This has an attractive shiny finish which suits prints intended for curtains in more formal rooms, although it is available in plains as well as prints. The glazing can be light, giving a soft sheen, or high for a bright, crisp effect; it is applied only to 100 per cent cotton. The cloth is usually lightweight but tightly woven, so it accepts dyes and glaze well.

Glazed cotton is often called chintz after the early Indian-inspired chintz prints which were finished in this way.

It can be dry cleaned or hand washed. The fabric should not be rubbed and should be kept as flat as possible in the water. Iron while damp.

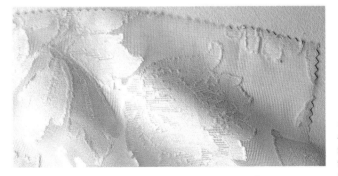

△ LACE AND MADRAS

These are attractive alternatives to voiles and sheers. Lace was originally made from linen and the fine open work patterns were hand-made. These days most laces are machine-made from cotton, nylon or viscose. Although quality and care depend on whether natural or synthetic yarns are used, cotton lace and fine madras can be washed with care and starched for a crisp finish.

△ MUSLIN

A fine, loosely-woven cotton, ideal for sheer curtains.

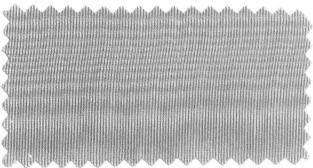

△ MOIRÉ

Also known as watered silk, this is now usually made from synthetic fibres. The distinctive, light-reflecting, wavy pattern is applied by machine to a plain, lightly ribbed cloth. To preserve the pattern, fabric should be dry cleaned. It makes elegant curtains, suited to formal rooms. Moiré fabrics are available in plain colours and in stripes, and occasionally over-printed with a traditional design.

Moiré can react to changes of temperature and humidity in a room. It absorbs and releases moisture, shrinking and expanding like wood, so it should be sewn with as loose a tension as possible to allow for this potential movement in the cloth.

△ POLYESTER COTTON

As its name implies, this is a blend of cotton and the synthetic fibre, polyester. Although usually associated with bedlinen, some curtain prints are made in this fabric. Many printed polyester cotton bed sheets can also be made up into light and inexpensive curtains, which wash well and withstand strong sunlight with only minimal fading.

It is an easy-care fabric – strong and durable, reasonably crease-resistant and keeps its shape. When putting fabrics of blended fibres such as polyester cotton in a washing machine, programme the machine according to the most delicate fibre in the blend.

△ PRINTED COTTON

This offers the widest choice of patterns and designs in a large variety of colours. It makes up well and the dyes are generally colourfast. Price variation reflects the quality of the base cloth, the exclusiveness of the design and the number of colours used.

SATEEN

A lightweight fabric, used mainly for curtain linings, although heavier weights may be used for curtains. Similar to satin, it is generally made of cotton.

△ SEERSUCKER

The characteristic appearance – puckered and flat stripy effect – is achieved by a heat process in manufacture or by grouping the lengthwise threads alternatively tight and loose when weaving. It is ideal for light, airy, unlined curtains, is usually made of cotton and is washable.

△ VELVETS

With the exception of silk, which is very expensive, cotton velour is the best quality velvet to use. It drapes softly even though the fabric is heavy and makes up into good short as well as long curtains. Dyes are generally good and shouldn't fade. Velvets can be crushed for effect or cut to form patterns.

Acrylic velvet, often called Dralon, (the brand name of the major manufacturer of acrylic fibre) is an upholstery cloth, but the lighter qualities can be made into curtains. However, they do not have the good

draping qualities of cotton velour and do not make good short curtains.

The pile can lie either up or down but make sure that the same direction is maintained throughout. If the pile runs upwards the colour is usually richer than when it runs downwards. Take care not to crush the pile when making-up; any pressure marks should steam out. Once curtains have been hanging for a few weeks any marks made while making up should disappear.

△ VOILES AND SHEERS

These are usually made from synthetic fibres such as nylon and polyester and can be hand or machine washed with virtually no shrinkage. They are made from closely woven yarns, which give a flimsy, fluid effect.

Some voiles co-ordinate with printed cottons so that the same outline or motif is repeated on both fabrics. They are also available in a plain weave.

Voiles and sheers are often used to give privacy to rooms which are overlooked and also help to filter strong sunlight and protect furnishings and curtains from fading.

CHOOSING FABRICS FOR BLINDS

Here are some guidelines to help you make the right choice when it comes to selecting fabrics suitable for blind making.

Roller blinds Fabric needs to be flexible enough to roll around a wooden dowel. All medium-weight fabrics can be used, but look for tightly woven cottons for really reliable results. Fabric should be treated with a stiffener, but allow for slight shrinkage from this process. Use flame resistant and wipe-down fabrics for kitchen or bathroom blinds.

Roman blinds give a tailored yet elegant look. Use cotton prints or any closely woven fabric of medium weight. Do not treat fabric with a stiffening agent as this stops it falling into natural folds.

Austrian blinds are made from light or medium weight fabrics which hang well and look good when gathered into swags. For best results they should be lined. They can be trimmed with a ruffle or length of lace or madras. A lining fabric might also be necessary.

Festoon blinds use much more fabric than austrian blinds. Soft, lightweight and delicate fabrics which allow the light to filter through are most suited to the permanent ruched swags.

CURTAIN TRACKS AND POLES

The choice between hanging your curtains on a track or a pole depends to a certain extent on the look you wish to achieve.

Poles are usually chosen for the more traditional style of furnishing or where the curtains feature as a focal point in a room. They are particularly suitable for long straight runs and heavy floor-length curtains, and look better than tracks for curtains without valances or pelmets. Wooden poles can be mitred at corners to fit bow windows, but they cannot be used on curved bays.

Pole kits are sold complete with brackets, rings and pole ends. It is also possible to buy these items separately, so you can make up a set to suit your particular requirements or add brackets or rings to a kit.

Tracks have a streamlined look suitable for most modern furnishing styles and are generally cheaper than poles. The curtains are hooked on to runners designed to glide smoothly along the track. Lightweight plastic and aluminium tracks can be bent to fit bow and bay windows and steel tracks are available for the heaviest of curtains.

Tracks are sold with fittings to fix them to the wall or ceiling and with or without runners, end stops or cross-over arms (see over). Runners are made from plastic or brass and vary in style to fit a particular track. If the track doesn't have a cord pulley, an end stop needs to be fixed at each end to prevent the runners from falling off.

Cording Although some poles and tracks have integral cording, cording sets can be added to most types so that the curtains can be drawn without handling the fabric.

Wire and rods are the simplest supports for lightweight curtains. Thread them through a casing and use them in small windows or across a recess.

POSITIONING THE POLE OR TRACK

A pole or track can be fixed within the window recess if it is a deep one, or if a bay or bow, on the window frame itself or outside and above it.

The placing of the pole or track can make the window look larger or smaller. For example, the pole can be extended well beyond the frame (right), so that the curtain can be pulled clear of the window, letting in the maximum amount of light and making a small window seem wider.

A pair of curtains fixed together across the top of a window and held back at the sides (far right) will reduce the height of a very tall window.

A concealed track placed along the top of the window makes an unobtrusive curtain fitment which can be painted or papered to match the paintwork or wallpaper.

WOODEN POLES
Style Plain varnished poles fit a traditional or country setting while painted poles suit a modern or informal style. The pole ends can be simple or elaborately turned to suit the furnishing style.
In use Cording sets can be added to the wider diameter poles.
Watchpoint Allow sufficient diameter poles and brackets to support the weight of curtain and width of the window.

BRASS POLES
Style Brass or brass-finished metal poles suit a more formal style of furnishing. The pole finish can be reeded with elaborate pole ends for elegant curtains or plain with simple ends for a modern setting.
In use Some poles have internal cording sets to draw curtains on concealed runners instead of rings. Ring-based cording sets can be added to wider diameter poles. Some poles adjust telescopically.

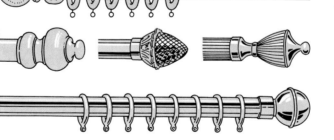

CONCEALED TRACK POLE
Style Available in both brass and wood finishes to suit most traditional furnishing styles. The fake finish looks best seen at a distance, so use the poles over tall windows or at ceiling height.
In use The semicircular pole conceals the track system which is combined with a cording set.

Watchpoint The track is less rigid than a solid wood or brass pole so several mountings may be needed to support it, according to the width of the window.

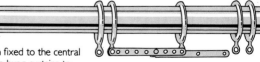

Cross-over arm fixed to the central rings allows pole-hung curtains to overlap at the centre.

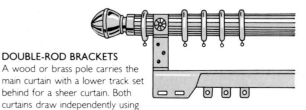

DOUBLE-ROD BRACKETS
A wood or brass pole carries the main curtain with a lower track set behind for a sheer curtain. Both curtains draw independently using cording sets.

CURTAIN TRACKS

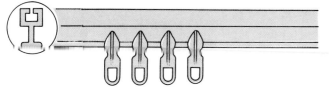  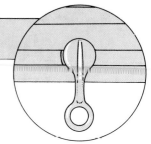

BASIC TRACK
Style Lightweight plastic or aluminium track, with or without a cross-over arm, is suitable for light- to medium-weight fabrics and sheers.

In use Can be fitted within a recess, on the frame, or above it if frame is flush to the wall. It comes in different lengths and is cut to fit. Is best used under a pelmet or valance.

RAIL WITH CONCEALED TRACK
Style Suitable for light- to medium-weight fabrics. Track can be left plain or papered to match wall. It is also available with a reeded gold trim.
In use Available with or without internal cording and cross-over arms and fixed at intervals, depending on the weight of the curtains. Comes in different lengths and is cut to fit. The plastic track can be bent by hand to fit round bays or bow windows. Aluminium track is bent professionally when ordered.

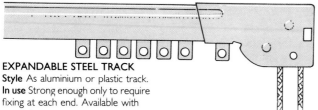

EXPANDABLE STEEL TRACK
Style As aluminium or plastic track.
In use Strong enough only to require fixing at each end. Available with integral cording set and cross-over arms.

CEILING MOUNTED TRACK
Style Available in two styles. A narrow, neat plastic track that can be fitted to the underside of a window or recessed into plaster; it is suitable for lightweight curtains and is ideal for small windows. Or a wider track with a pulley housing at one end for the cording, suitable for medium-weight fabrics.
In use The simpler types of heading tape are best.

TRACK WITH DOUBLE HOOKS
Style Made from plastic or aluminium and can be bent to fit into the most awkward of bay windows.
In use The double hooks are detachable and simply clip on to the face of the track; they are designed to carry curtains with separate linings. Cording sets are available for straight runs.

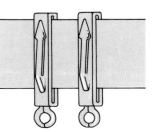

COMBINED TRACK AND VALANCE RAIL
Style The plastic track/rail can be bent by hand; the aluminium track needs to be bent professionally.
In use The curtain hangs from the track and draws in the normal way, while the valance hooks simply clip over the rail.
Watchpoint Match the valance and curtain heading tapes.

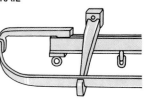

Watchpoint The track needs to be well fixed to the ceiling.

CURTAIN WIRE AND RODS

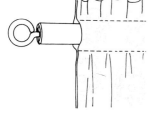 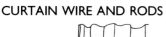 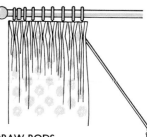

PLASTIC-COVERED EXPANDABLE WIRE
Hooks on each end of the wire clip into fixed screw eyes. Use with lightweight or sheer fabrics with a casing at the top or at both top and bottom.

ADJUSTABLE RODS
These have a telescopic spring fixing which grips inside a reveal or window recess. Sizes range from 40-185cm. Use for light- to medium-weight fabrics with a cased heading or with rings for a shower curtain.

DOWEL RODS AND METAL TUBES
They fit into metal sockets screwed into a reveal or recess and make a strong, more permanent rail. Suitable for heavier curtains.

SWIVEL RODS
Fixed to a bracket at one end, these are ideal for curtains that need to be swung back out of the way, such as at dormer windows.

DRAW RODS
These are attached to the leading ring at the centre front of pole-hung curtains, making them easy to draw – repeated drawing by hand marks the curtains and drags at the pole and rings. When not in use the rods hang at the back, hidden by the folds.

SUPPORTING LONG POLES AND TRACKS

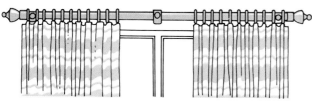 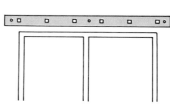 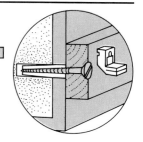

Choose the wider diameter poles for long runs over wide picture windows and for floor-length curtains in heavy fabrics. Prevent sagging by adding one or two extra brackets (position them so they won't affect the drawing of the curtains).

Tracks need brackets along their length to support any but the lightest fabrics.

Many windows have a concrete lintel above the frame, so to avoid drilling for several mountings, it is better to screw a batten into the lintel and mount the brackets on this. The batten can be either painted or papered to match the wall covering.

DEALING WITH PROBLEM WINDOWS
Oddly shaped, very small or very large windows can be difficult to fit with curtains.

△ *Three-way bay*
Roller blinds are a simple, effective way to cover a bay made up of three large windows.

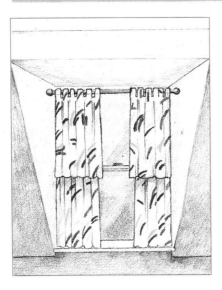

△ **Deep dormers**
Two layers of café curtains are a good way to treat deep dormers – and to adapt curtains which are too short for other use.

ATTIC IDEAS
<u>Problem</u> Sloping roof lights and attic windows set into a deep dormer can be difficult to curtain without cutting off natural light.

<u>Solution</u> If you are fitting new sloping rooflights, look for the type with a blind sandwiched between two layers of glass. Special venetian blinds are available for existing windows. They don't drop forward and can be adjusted to any angle to restrict or admit light. Sheer curtains or lace panels can be held at the top and bottom of the frame with a brass or wooden rod.

Deep dormer windows let in less light than sloping windows. If the window is not overlooked, fit a simple café curtain. If it is, fit a second set of short curtains fitted at the top (see above). This is a good way to make use of curtains which are too short or narrow for other windows in the house. Simply cut them in half, hem the bottom of the top pieces and add a heading to the bottom pieces.

Another way to treat this sort of window is to fit just one sheer curtain on a pole.

COPING WITH ARCHES
<u>Problem</u> Hanging a conventional curtain track at arched windows spoils the shape of the arch and the proportions of the windows.

<u>Solution</u> Try to choose a treatment to flatter the shape of the windows. You can suspend a lace panel across the window just before it begins to curve, or fit curtains which clear the sides and the top of the arch when they are open. To do this, fit a curtain track about 10cm (4in) above the arch of the window and about 7.5cm (3in) wider than the window at each side.

For a classic look, fit shutters the same length as the window (measured from the centre of the arch to the bottom). The shutters can be kept open during the day and closed at night.

It is possible to fit a track, pelmet and curtains to follow the shape of the arch (see below) but this is a job for a professional curtain maker and fitter as the track must be specially bent and the fabric cut on a curve.

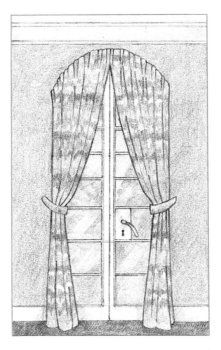

△ *Professional treatment*
This sort of treatment makes the most of an arched window but needs the skills of a professional to make and fit curtains.

THREE WINDOW BAYS
<u>Problem</u> In many homes, the main window at the front of the house is a bay made up of three large windows, sometimes with a space between each one.

<u>Solution</u> Curtains for bay windows should clear the window during the day, not divide it up. Hang the curtains on a track which bends so that the curtains follow the shape of the bay. A corded track is best – wide, heavy curtains are difficult to pull by hand. If the bay is overlooked, hang sheer blinds for daytime use. The curtains and blinds can be combined with a matching pelmet.

If you want a simple, unfussy treatment, hang roller, roman, venetian, slatted wood or straw blinds at each window, (see above).

LEADED LIGHT CASEMENTS
<u>Problem</u> Small, leaded light (diamond or square pane) casements are difficult to curtain without cutting off nearly all the natural light.

<u>Solution</u> Keep the curtains short on leaded light windows. Mount them on a pole, or add a crispy pleated valance. Position the track about 7.5cm (3in) above the frame and make it about 7.5cm (3in) longer at each side so that the curtains clear the window during the day and let in the maximum amount of natural light. Tiebacks can be used to hold the curtains away from the window when they are drawn back.

It is important to consider the size of the pattern on the curtain fabric in relation to the size of the window. Small casements look best hung with mini-print florals, small ginghams, candy stripes or plain fabric in a pale or subtle shade. Use a simple heading, such as triple pinch pleats. Don't use a bold design – it tends to look silly if only part of the pattern repeat covers the window or if the fabric has to be cut part of the way through a repeat.

△ **Top treatment**
An elaborately draped or swagged top makes tall, narrow windows seem much shorter and wider.

TREATMENTS FOR TALL WINDOWS
<u>Problem</u> A row of tall narrow windows look even longer and thinner when fitted with curtains hung from a conventional heading and track.
<u>Solution</u> Tall, narrow windows are usually sash type and are often in a row of two or three. The best way to make them look less long and thin is to fit an 'important' top treatment, such as a large, elaborate pelmet with 'tails' coming down over the curtains, a swathe of fabric wrapped around a pole (see above) or a pinch pleated or ruffled valance with floor-length curtains.

Alternatively, use a fabric with a strong horizontal pattern or with a deep border in a strong colour. Venetian blinds with shaded slats, starting with a light colour at the top, deepening to a dark tone at the bottom of the blind are a less fussy way to lower height.

ROOMS WITHOUT A VIEW
<u>Problem</u> An ugly or depressing view (such as a blank wall) can spoil the atmosphere of a room, but hiding it cuts out light as well as the scene outside.
<u>Solution</u> If the window is small (on a landing, for instance) and light isn't too important, hide the view with glass shelves filled with plants or a collection of coloured glass. Light from above to make a stunning display point. Where light is needed, fit a lace or sheer blind, or net café curtains over the bottom.

If the window looks out on to a blank wall, it may be possible to improve things by painting the wall white and training a climbing plant up it, or, if you are artistic, use vinyl emulsion to paint a pretty scene over the brickwork.

BATHROOM PRIVACY
<u>Problem</u> In many older houses, the bathroom is fitted into what was once a living area and has large, sash style windows fitted with clear glass.
<u>Solution</u> The obvious solution is to replace the panes with frosted glass but this does not look attractive from either inside or out. You can fit mirror glass so that you can see out but those outside can't see in – but this is expensive and available only from specialist glaziers. A lace blind is another simple solution, or a voile, lace or net café curtain can be fitted across the bottom half of the window.

Half shutters, either louvred and stained or painted or with the centre panel decorated to match the walls, are more inspiring (see below). They can be hinged, or fitted to a track so that they lift out for cleaning.

△ **Bathroom shutters**
Simple shutters are an unusual and attractive way to screen the bottom half of a big bathroom window.

AWKWARD WINDOWS
<u>Problem</u> When windows are positioned close to a fireplace, chimney breast, door or other obstruction, it is difficult to use two curtains.
<u>Solution</u> Austrian, roller or roman blinds solve the problem as they are pulled down from the top rather than from the sides. Use the same fabric as other curtains in the room, or choose a complementary plain colour. Plain blinds can be edged with a patterned fabric to match other curtains.

If you prefer curtains to blinds, hang just one curtain (see above right). The curtain should be one-and-a-half times as wide as the window so that it gathers at the top but still stretches from side to side. Hold the curtain back with a matching tieback or a piece of plaited fabric during the day. In a room where natural light is in short supply, the curtain can be made from a sheer fabric or from net.

△ **The single solution**
Where hanging two curtains is impossible, hang one extra wide curtain tied back at one side.

DEALING WITH PATIO DOORS
<u>Problem</u> Many homes have patio doors or french windows, often flanked by two smaller windows, which need a more interesting scheme than long curtains.
<u>Solution</u> Simple roller, roman or austrian blinds fitted to each window allow light in during the day and give privacy at night. If you want a more elaborate and decorative scheme, combine lace or voile blinds with long floor-to-ceiling curtains which can be pulled right across. During the day, the curtains can easily be held neatly in place against the side walls with matching or complementary tiebacks.

Where privacy during the day is important (if, for instance, the garden is overlooked) fit voile curtains to all three sections. They can be held at the top and bottom with a brass rod. In a high-tech room, slimline venetian or vertical blinds in grey or a cool pastel shade are a good choice.

THROUGH ROOMS
<u>Problem</u> 'Through' living rooms where two rooms have been joined often have a mixture of bay windows at one end and patio doors at the other.
<u>Solution</u> The first rule is to use the same style of curtains at each end of the room. As this type of room often looks long and narrow, try to use a bold, horizontal pattern on curtains at each end of the room. Make the curtains from floor to ceiling and preferably from wall to wall.

As an alternative, the patio doors can be fitted with roller blinds in a plain colour to complement or match curtain fabric. If the room has other small windows, fit them with plain blinds.

AUSTRIAN BLINDS

Austrian blinds – softly swagged and gathered – look impressively complicated but are easy to make.

These soft gathered blinds look good on their own, or can be used in addition to normal curtains or even simple roller blinds.

An austrian blind has a gathered or pencil-pleated curtain heading, and looks like an unlined curtain when completely lowered. The deep swags are made by pulling the fabric up by cords that are threaded through vertical rows of tape stitched to the back of the blind at regular intervals.

You can leave the blind plain, or add a frill to the bottom and side edges for an even softer effect.

Measuring up The blind is hung from a curtain track fixed to a wooden batten or from an austrian blind track. Fix the support temporarily in place so that exact measurements can be taken.

On a recessed window, fit the batten or track to the ceiling of the recess. If there is no recess, extend the batten or track 15cm beyond the edges of a plain window or flush with the outer edges of a moulded window frame.

Choosing fabric Choose a light fabric that drapes well so it gathers evenly across the blind. Suitable fabrics include moire, silk and voile, slubbed satin and soft cotton.

Types of tape For the vertical tape on the back of the blind, you can use a lightweight, narrow curtain heading tape with regular pockets so that rings can be attached for threading the cords.

Alternatively, use special austrian blind tape which has loops for holding the cords instead of rings.

To work out how much fabric and blind tape you need, see overleaf.

Ruffled charm
Austrian blinds work well in light fabrics that drape well. Here, peach-coloured seersucker is frilled and ruched into luxurious flounces.

CHECK YOUR NEEDS

To make the blind:
- ☐ Fabric
- ☐ Standard or pencil-pleat curtain heading tape to fit total fabric width
- ☐ Austrian blind tape or small plastic or metal curtain rings (split rings) and narrow heading tape with regular pockets to hold them
- ☐ Non-stretch cord
- ☐ Curtain hooks
- ☐ Cleat to tie the cords when blind is raised

- ☐ Sewing thread
- ☐ Tape measure
- ☐ Tailor's chalk
- ☐ Scissors
- ☐ Pins
- ☐ Needles
- ☐ Sewing machine
- ☐ Iron and ironing board

Note: Austrian blind kits can be bought from most department stores and include everything required for making a blind, apart from fabric and basic equipment listed above.

To mount the blind:
- ☐ Austrian blind track
OR
- ☐ Wooden batten – 2.5cm thick, 5cm deep, and the same width as the window recess. If there's no recess, it should extend beyond the window
- ☐ Screw eyes to thread the cords through – you will need one screw eye for each vertical length of blind tape
- ☐ Curtain track of same width as the batten
- ☐ 2 angle irons (optional)

CALCULATING QUANTITIES

To calculate fabric needed, first fix the batten or track temporarily in place .

To get the width multiply the length of the battening or track by 2 times for standard gathered heading tape (by up to 2½ times for pencil-pleat tape – check manufacturer's instructions).

Divide this figure by the width of the fabric to give the number of fabric widths needed. Round up if necessary.

To get the length, measure from the top of the batten or track to the sill and add 15cm so that the lower edge of the blind is prettily swagged even when fully covering the window.

To get the total amount, multiply this figure by the number of fabric widths.
- ☐ If the fabric has a pattern repeat, add one full repeat per fabric width.
- ☐ To work out how much fabric you need for a frill, see page 272.

To get the amount of tape needed for the back of the blind, divide the total width of fabric into sections that are 20-40cm wide (see Step 3). You need sufficient tape to run from top to bottom of the blind along each vertical division and down both sides of the blind.

Cord for pulling up the blind – you need about double the amount of tape required (see Step 8).

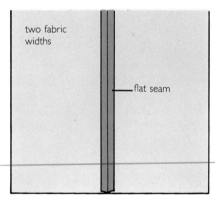

two fabric widths

— flat seam

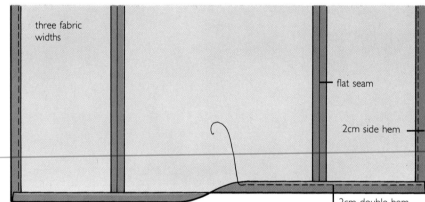

three fabric widths

— flat seam

2cm side hem —

2cm double hem

1 **Join fabric widths △**
For most windows you need to join at least two pieces of fabric to make up the width of the blind.

Use a simple flat seam and pin the widths together with right sides facing and any pattern matching. Tack and stitch 1.5cm from edges, then trim the seam allowance to 5mm. Remove tacking and press seam open.

Cut any surplus fabric evenly from both widths.

For three fabric widths If you need to join three fabric widths to make up the width of the blind, position a complete width in the centre and add two equal pieces of fabric to the sides.

2 **Hem the fabric △**
Down each side edge of the blind, turn a 2cm hem; pin and tack in place. Do not make this hem if you're adding side frills.

For a plain bottom edge, turn a double 2cm hem; pin, tack and stitch in place. Remove tacking and press.

Adding a frill If you're adding a frill to bottom and/or side edges, do not hem fabric. Instead, make up frill and sew it in place (see page 56).

3 **Mark positions of vertical tape**
Lay fabric, wrong side up, on the floor. Use tailor's chalk to mark vertical lines at regular intervals across the blind for the tape.

Mark the positions so that tapes cover the side hems and any joining seams in the fabric. Then mark vertical lines in between, spacing them evenly 20-40cm apart.

The size of the swag when fully drawn up will be about half the distance allowed between the tapes.

BRIGHT IDEA

Vertical guidelines
To make it easier to mark vertical lines across the blind, fold the fabric lengthways like a concertina every 20-40cm and press.

Open the fabric out again and you will have straight guidelines for positioning and attaching rows of tape.

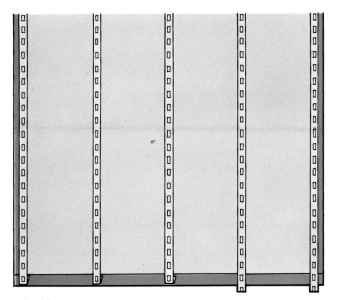

4 *Attach vertical blind tapes* ◁
Cut lengths of tape equal to the length of the blind plus 1cm. Make sure that you cut the tape at exactly the same points so that the pockets (or loops) will line up across the width of the blind.

At one end of each tape, turn 1cm to the wrong side and tack in place. Position the tapes – with pockets or loops facing upwards, and the folded end of tape to the bottom edge of the blind – along the chalked lines and down each side hem. Pin and tack the tapes in place, then stitch down the long edges.

5 *Prepare and attach curtain heading tape*
Cut a length of heading tape equal to finished width of blind plus 8cm for neatening ends. Then prepare tape cords as for a curtain – see Simple Unlined Curtains.

At the top of the blind turn 4cm to the wrong side and press. Then sew the heading tape to the top edge of the blind, as for a curtain, but do not gather up yet.

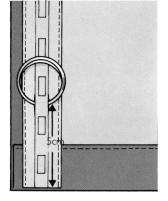

6 *Slot in rings* ◁
If you're using tape with pockets, start at the bottom left-hand corner and slot a ring through a pocket on the first length of tape, 5cm up from the bottom edge of blind. Attach rings all the way up tape, about 20cm apart.

Repeat for the other tapes, making sure that rings align horizontally.

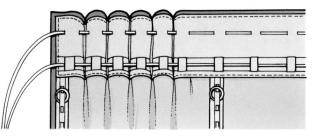

7 *Gather heading tape* △
When all the rings are in place, pull up the cords in the heading tape at the top of the blind and gather the fabric until it fits the window.

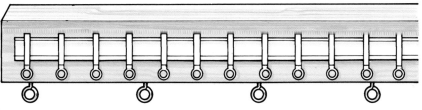

9 *Mount curtain track on batten* △
Lay the batten on the floor and screw the curtain track to the front of the batten, close to the top edge. Insert curtain hooks in the blind and fit on to the curtain track.

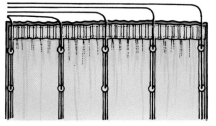

8 *Thread the cords* △
Lay the blind, wrong side up, flat on the floor. Cut lengths of cord to equal the length of the blind plus the top width, plus one metre. You will need one cord for each vertical tape.

Starting in the left-hand corner, tie the end of a cord to the bottom ring (or loop) on the first length of tape. Then thread it up through all the rings/loops on that tape. Repeat with each length of tape. If you are using austrian blind track, follow the manufacturer's instructions for threading, mounting and hanging the blind.

10 *Fix screw eyes to batten* △
With wrong side of blind facing up, pencil in the positions of each vertical tape on bottom edge of batten. Remove blind from track and fix a screw eye on each pencil mark. Fix the batten to the window frame.

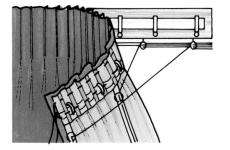

11 *Hang the blind* ◁
Hang the blind on the curtain track. Thread the left-hand cord through the screw eye directly above it and then to the right through all the screw eyes. Repeat for the other cords.

Mount the cleat on the wall or window frame to the right of the blind, about half-way down the window.

12 *Check the blind*
Pull cords evenly together so that the blind gathers into soft swags.

Then lower the blind so that it's flat. Knot cords together, near the top screw eye and about 2.5cm from the outside edge of blind; trim ends to make a neat bunch. Pull the blind up again and secure cords round cleat.

ADDING A GATHERED FRILL

A simple frill along the bottom edge emphasizes the softly gathered swags of an austrian blind. Frills can also be added to the side edges for extra decorative effect.

Make the frill from fabric that matches or co-ordinates with the main blind fabric. For a smart finish, insert piping at the seam between the frill and the blind.

Measuring up Allow a depth of 10-16cm for the frill, including turnings.

To calculate the length of a frill for the bottom edge, double the finished width of the blind; for each side frill, allow double the finished length of the blind. Add on a 2cm hem allowance (plus 1cm for any joins necessary to make up the length).

Team work ▷

Austrian blinds often look best when only partly drawn and they combine well with curtains. These blinds and light cotton curtains can be drawn separately or used together for added warmth and privacy.

Lace makes a pretty frilled edging for plain coloured blinds.

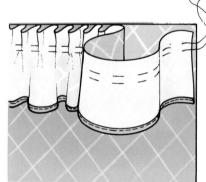

1 Cut out the fabric
Cut a strip of fabric to the calculated depth by about 2 times the length of the edge to which the frill is to be attached.

If necessary, stitch short edges of strips together with flat fell seams to make up the length.

BRIGHT IDEA

Pleat it
A pleated frill looks crisp and smart. You will need a strip of fabric 3 times the length of the edge to be frilled, plus hem and seam allowances. The depth of the frill and the width of the pleats will depend on the size of the curtain.

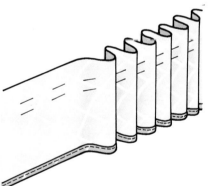

2 Gather the fabric △
Turn a double 5mm hem at each short end and along the lower edge of the frill. Pin, tack and stitch.

On the remaining long edge, sew two lines of gathering stitches 1cm and 1.5cm from the edge; then draw up the frill to fit the bottom (or side edge) of the blind.

For long frills, divide the frill and the blind into three or four equal sections; work rows of gathering stitches in each section and draw up to fit corresponding section of blind.

3 Attach the frill △
Pin the frill to the blind, with right sides facing and raw edges matching. Tack along the 1cm gathering thread, remove pins and stitch the frill in place.

If you want a piped trim, insert the piping in the seam between the frill and the blind at this stage – see page 230 for details.

Remove tacking, and finish raw edges with machine zigzag or overcast by hand. Press seam towards the ungathered fabric.

MAKING A ROLLER BLIND

Roller blinds are an attractive alternative to curtains, and need only a fraction of the amount of fabric.

Blinds really come into their own where space is limited and curtains at the window would either block out too much light or simply get in the way. They're also relatively inexpensive to make.

The simplest and most economical types of blind are roller blinds which are rolled round a wooden roller at the top of the window and pulled down to hang flat against the window. They are an excellent choice for kitchens and bathrooms, but they also combine well with curtains for a softer effect.

Roller blinds work best on small to medium-size windows: on wide windows, you run into problems with joining fabric widths and it's best to hang two or three narrow blinds together. They are easy to make from a kit, or you could use the roller from an old blind with new fabric. The lower edge of the blind can be left plain, or it can be trimmed or shaped into a decorative feature – see page 276.

Roller blind kits A basic kit comes with a wooden roller with a winding mechanism at one end, and a detachable cap and pin at the other. There are also brackets for hanging the blind; a wooden batten that is inserted in a casing at, or near, the bottom of the blind to make it hang straight; tacks for attaching fabric to the roller; a cord holder and cord.

MEASURING UP

To work out the blind kit size, first decide whether the blind is to hang

inside or outside the window recess – generally, blinds are fitted inside a deep recess if there is one.

On a recessed window, measure from one side of the recess to the other – the store should make the necessary allowance for brackets. On a window without a recess, allow an overlap of at least 3cm on either side of the window to prevent light showing round.

Kits come in a range of sizes. If the width you need is not a standard size, buy the next size up and cut the roller to fit after fixing the brackets.

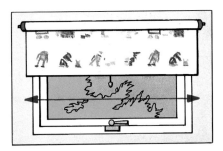

CHOOSING THE FABRIC

Roller blinds should be made of medium-weight, closely-woven fabric – if the fabric is too thin or flimsy, it creases when rolled up; too thick and it won't roll up evenly.

Pre-stiffened blind fabric is one of the easiest options as it is treated to make it stiff and fray-resistant; in some cases, it can be sponged down and is fade-resistant too. Most are reversible.

Pre-stiffened fabric comes in wide widths up to about 2m. If it is plain, or has a small random pattern, you may be able to cut the blind length from the fabric width which can save on fabric.

PVC does not need stiffening, and is ideal for kitchens and bathrooms as it is waterproof and can be sponged down.

Furnishing fabrics provide the widest choice of designs, but do require stiffening (see below). A densely-woven cotton is best.

Stiffening the fabric Many fabrics shrink slightly when stiffened, so treat the fabric before cutting it to size. Stiffener is available in liquid or aerosol form. With a liquid, the fabric is either dipped or painted on both sides, while an aerosol is sprayed on to both sides of the fabric. Follow manufacturer's instructions, and always test a sample piece of fabric first to see if it is colour fast and can be stiffened.

Blind options
Roller blinds have neat lines that look good in any setting. In this child's room, a cheerful roller blind allows a small window to remain uncluttered – the painted window frame, echoing the red in the blind, looks effective too.

HOW MUCH FABRIC DO YOU NEED?

Before calculating the fabric, work out the roller size and mark the fixing position of brackets on the wall, so that you can take accurate measurements.

The width of fabric should measure the full length of the roller (excluding the protruding pins), but allow a little extra for squaring off the blind (see Step 1). Side hem allowances are not required as stiffened fabric should not normally fray at the edges when you cut it.

Make the blind from one fabric width if possible. If you must join two, cut one width down the middle, stitch one half to either side of a full width with flat seams and bond seam allowances to the blind with iron-on hem webbing.

To get the length, measure from the position of roller to the windowsill and add at least 30cm to allow for the batten casing, and for the roller to be covered when the blind is pulled down.

Allow extra fabric:

☐ If furnishing fabric is likely to shrink with stiffening.

☐ For centring a design, so that the pattern repeats cover the blind evenly.

☐ For pattern matching, if joining fabric widths or making two or more blinds that are to hang close together.

☐ For adding a decorative edging (see page 276).

CHECK YOUR NEEDS
☐ Roller blind kit
☐ Fabric
☐ Stiffener (optional)
plus:
☐ Steel measuring tape
☐ Pencil
☐ Bradawl or drill and bit
☐ Screws and screwdriver
☐ Junior hacksaw
☐ Hammer
☐ Set square or try square
☐ Ruler
☐ Tailor's chalk
☐ Scissors
☐ Iron-on hem webbing
☐ Adhesive tape
☐ Sewing machine and thread
   OR fabric glue

FIX THE BRACKETS ▷

Screw brackets in place before cutting a roller to size. If fixing into a recess, place brackets as close to the sides as possible, but 3cm below the top of the recess to allow for the rolled-up blind. If fixing outside a recess, place them 5cm above window and 3cm to either side to stop light showing around edges.

Check kit instructions for positioning brackets. Normally, a slotted bracket (for the square pin on the roller) goes on the left side, and one with a hole (for the round pin) goes on the right, so that the blind goes up behind the roller and rolls round it. However, if you're using non-reversible fabric and don't want the wrong side to show on the roller, fit the slotted bracket on the right – so the blind hangs from the front of the roller and hides it.

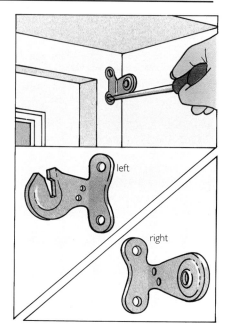

left

right

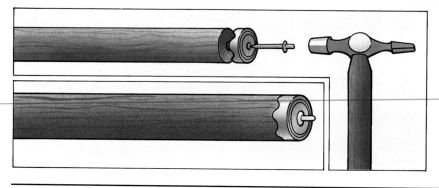

CUT THE ROLLER TO SIZE ◁

Most kits come with the end cap and pin left unattached so that the roller can be cut to size if necessary.

Measure the distance between the brackets on the window with a steel tape, then saw the bare end of the roller to fit between them. Cover the cut end with the cap, fit the pin into the hole and gently hammer it home. The roller is now ready to take the fabric.

MAKING UP THE BLIND

The steps below cover using a kit to make a basic roller blind with a plain bottom edge.

1 Cut out the fabric ▷
Clear a large working area and lay the fabric flat to prevent creasing.

Stiffened fabric can be cut to the exact measurements of the roller. To

ensure that the blind hangs straight and rolls up evenly, each corner must be a perfect right angle. Use a set square or carpenter's try square to mark accurate 90° angles, and a sharp knife or scalpel along a ruler, or something similar, to cut straight lines.

If the fabric has a design on it, make sure that the pattern is centred on the blind before cutting out.

2 Neaten the edges
Stiffened fabric should be fray-resistant and edges should not need neatening. However, if it does have a tendency to fray, machine zigzag stitch the edges. Don't make side hems as this will give you an uneven thickness of fabric on the roller.

3 Make the batten casing
Trim the wooden batten to 1cm less than the blind width. Then make a stitched or glued casing for the batten along the bottom of the blind.

A stitched casing (see diagram opposite). With wrong side up,

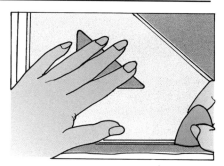

turn a single fold along the bottom edge that is deep enough to take the batten. Finger press the fold and hold in place with short strips of sticky tape. Stitch close to the raw edge, then overstitch with zigzag to neaten. Slip batten into casing and sew up both short ends with tiny overcast stitches.

A glued casing (far right) Lay the fabric wrong side up. Spread fabric glue on one side of the batten and position the glued side carefully along the bottom edge of the blind. Spread glue on the other side of the batten, turn up the batten so that it's enclosed in fabric, and weigh down – with kitchen weights set out along a ruler, for example – until the glue has dried.

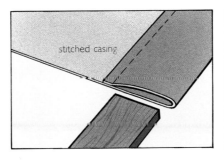

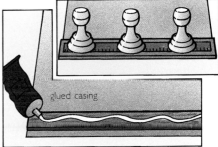

4 *Attach cord pull* ◁
Make up the cord pull by pushing one end of cord through the hole in the cord holder, and make a knot behind it to secure. Thread the other end of cord through the acorn and knot. Then screw the cord holder to the centre of the batten – this can be fixed to the front of the blind, or you can screw it to the back to hide it from view.

5 *Mark the roller*
The roller may already be marked with a line along its length where the top edge of the blind fabric should be tacked in place. If the roller doesn't have a guide-line, clamp the roller in a carpenter's vice, or get someone to hold it very still for you, while you draw a straight line along its length with a pencil and ruler.

6 *Position roller on fabric* ▷
With fabric right side up, place the roller along the top edge with the spring mechanism on the left. (If you're using non-reversible fabric and do not want the wrong side to be displayed on the roller, lay fabric wrong side up with spring mechanism on the right so the blind hangs over the front of the roller.) Lift the edge of the fabric up on to the roller and fix it along the marked line with sticky tape.

7 *Fix fabric to roller* ◁
Some rollers are fitted with a self-adhesive strip to take the fabric, others come with fixing tacks.
If using tacks, space them evenly all along the roller at about 2cm intervals. Position the first tack in the centre and work out to both sides. Then peel off the sticky tape. If you own or can borrow a staple gun, you'll probably find that stapling the fabric to the roller is easier.

8 *Hang the blind*
Carefully roll the blind up round the roller by hand and fit it into the brackets. Pull the blind down to cover the window, and check that the tension of the spring is correct – the blind should roll up when you give the cord a gentle tug. Don't let go of the acorn.
If the tension is wrong, the blind will be sluggish and jerky as it rolls up, or it may not roll up at all. Try again – lift the extended blind out of the brackets, rewind it by hand and test as before. Repeat until you get the correct tension, but be careful not to make the tension of the blind too tight as the spring may break.

Wave shape ▷
Roller blinds can be finished with a decorative edge to soften their rather austere lines. Here, a shallow-waved edging trimmed with white braid adds interest to a prettily-sprigged fabric roller blind.
The blind also combines well with the louvred shutters, picked out in stripes of green and white.

DECORATIVE EDGINGS

The simplest way of decorating a roller blind is to stick or sew braid or rows of ribbon, for example, along a straight bottom edge. Alternatively, if the batten that holds the blind straight is inserted higher up the blind, the bottom edge can be shaped into scallops, waves, zigzags, or whatever.

A shaped edge Calculate fabric as for a plain blind, and add 5cm to the length. You'll also need paper, iron-on interfacing and fabric for a facing that measures the width by 13cm deep.

To make up the blind, follow Steps 1 and 2 on page 274. Then make a tucked or topstitched batten casing – see below.

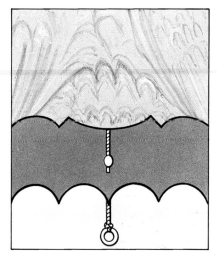

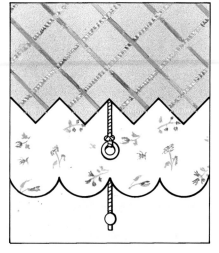

Making a tucked casing ▽

This is only suitable for plain or small all-over patterned fabrics. Measure 13cm up from bottom edge of blind and mark each side edge; measure a further 9cm and mark again. With right sides facing, fold fabric across width to bring the two sets of marks together. Finger press the fold, and stitch a 4.5cm tuck on the wrong side of blind to form a casing. Stitch one short end of tuck, leaving the other end open to insert batten.

Making a topstitched casing ▽

A topstitched casing is used when fabric has a large pattern that a tucked casing would interrupt.

Cut a strip about 5.5cm deep from bottom edge of blind fabric, and zigzag the edges. With blind fabric wrong side up, position the strip, right side up, across the blind width and 13cm up from the bottom edge. Hold in place with sticky tape, and topstitch down long edges and across one short edge.

Facing the bottom edge ▽

Facing is necessary to give the fabric extra body for a shaped bottom edge, and to prevent it from fraying.

With wrong sides together, place the strip of fabric facing to the bottom edge of the blind just below the batten casing, with a strip of iron-on interfacing sandwiched in between. Iron the fabric to fix, then cut out the shaped edge using a paper pattern or a pelmet stiffener template (see below).

MAKING A PAPER PATTERN

For a repeated cut-out shape, first make a paper pattern so that you can transfer the design to the blind fabric. Alternatively, pelmet stiffener has a variety of shapes printed on it which can be used as a template for cutting out.

2 *Make a paper pattern ▷*
Cut a strip of paper 13cm deep by the width of the blind. Then fold it, concertina fashion, into equal sections measuring the width of the scallop (or whatever shape you have chosen). On the top fold, make a mark 6cm up from the bottom and draw the required shape from this point. Then cut out through all the layers of paper.

3 *Cut out the design*
Open out the pattern and lay it on the wrong side of the blind below the batten casing. Use short strips of sticky tape to hold it in place, and carefully draw round the shaped edge with a sharp piece of tailor's chalk.

Zigzag stitch around the shaping, following the chalk line, then carefully cut out the shaping with sharp scissors.

1 *Calculate the pattern*
Any regular, repeated shape must be calculated so that an exact number fits across the bottom of the blind.

To calculate the number of scallops, say, that you need, decide the width of the scallop and divide the blind width by

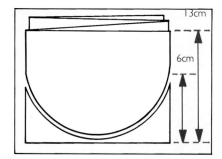

4 *Complete the blind*
Insert the batten into the casing and stitch the open edge closed. Attach the cord pull to the batten on the back of the blind. Then complete the blind, following Steps 5-8 on previous page.

this measurement. If you want scallops about 14cm wide and the blind is 132cm wide, divide 132 by 14. This gives 9.4. As a part scallop looks wrong, take the nearest whole number – 9 – and divide the blind width by this to give the exact scallop width – 14.7cm.

BRIGHT IDEA

WAVE SHAPES
These differ from repeated shapes, such as scallops, as one shape covers half the blind width and is reversed to cover the other half.

Cut a strip of paper 13cm deep by the blind width and fold in half, short ends together. For a deep wave shape, draw a line across the width of the folded paper 6cm up from the bottom edge; for a shallow shape, draw the line 4cm up. Draw two or three evenly-spaced vertical lines and use these and the horizontal line as a guide for drawing the required shape.

SMARTLY PLEATED ROMAN BLINDS

Roman blinds, falling in pleats, are a smart and economical way to dress your windows.

Blinds are an increasingly popular way to dress windows: and roman blinds are smart, unfussy and relatively economical on fabric. Unlike roller blinds, they can be lined for extra warmth and good looks. They are drawn up the window in concertina pleats by means of cords and rings fitted behind the blinds (rather like austrian blinds). At the top they are fitted to a batten which is in turn fitted to the top of the window recess.

For a really crisp finish, the blinds are fitted with a dowel or batten at each fold to hold them taut across the window.

They are relatively simple to make, the most important point being to ensure that lines of stitching are absolutely straight. Crooked stitching, or stitching running at an angle, will distort the shape of the blind so that it does not pull up neatly.

There are several different techniques for making roman blinds. The instructions here are for lined blinds, with a series of dowels stitched into the blind to keep it neatly pleated.

CHOOSE YOUR FABRICS

You can use almost any smoothly-woven furnishing fabric which is sold as being sutiable for curtains – plain or printed furnishing cottons, glazed cotton or cotton sateen, for example. Roman blinds are rather severe in style, so plainer fabrics and geometric prints are a better choice than heavy floral patterns. You can trim the blinds with bands of contrasting fabric or braid.

For the method described here it is essential to line the fabric. Normal curtain lining is perfect for the job. The lining prevents too much light penetrating the blind, gives it extra body and helps the blind to wear better (direct sunlight has a detrimental effect on furnishing fabric).

Calculating fabric amounts These blinds look best if they fit neatly into a window recess. Measure up the window and decide on the finished dimensions of the blind (see Making a Roller Blind). For each blind you need a piece of fabric the size of the finished blind, plus an allowance of up to 3cm down each side for turnings. You also need to allow 5cm at the top of the blind, and 16cm at the lower edge. For the lining, you need a piece of fabric the same dimensions as the finished blind.

Focus of interest
Roman blinds can play an important role in a room's decoration. Against plain white walls, the blinds in this informal dining room have been made from a fabric with a lacy design to provide – together with the painting around the clock – decorative interest.

CHECK YOUR NEEDS

For measuring and planning:
☐ Tape measure
☐ Pencil and paper

For making up the blind
☐ Fabric
☐ Lining
☐ Wooden dowels
☐ Small curtain rings
☐ Nylon cord

For fixing the blind:
☐ Batten, 50mm × 25mm
☐ Screw eyes
☐ Angle irons (optional)
☐ Cleat

For trimming the blind:
☐ Braid or contrast fabric

TOOLS AND EQUIPMENT

As well as the usual sewing equipment, you will need some other items which you might not normally expect to use when making up blinds.

Dowel Lengths of dowel about 6-9mm in diameter are needed to fit in casings stitched across the blind at 30cm intervals up its length. These dowels help to stop the blinds sagging, and are essential in larger windows.

You will also need a stout (25 × 50mm) batten to fit the blind to the top of the window. If you cannot screw directly into the top of the window surround, you may need angle irons to support the batten.

Rings The blind is pulled up by cords, running through small (1.5cm) plastic or metal curtain rings stitched to the back of the blind. For the method described here, the rings are stitched to the back of the casings. The rings should be spaced about 60cm apart: work out how many rings will fit across your blind at this spacing, positioning one 1.5cm in from each side with the rest evenly spaced between. For some methods of making roman blinds, the rings are stitched to tapes running vertically down the back of the blind.

The rings should be sewn to each casing channel, so work out how many rings you will need up the length of the blind and multiply by the number of rings across the blind to give the total number needed.

Cords and cleat You will need sufficient medium-weight nylon cord, available from curtain accessory departments, to run up each line of rings, across the top of the blind and down one side. You will also need a cleat to fix the cords when the blind is pulled up.

MAKING A LINED ROMAN BLIND

These instructions are for a lined blind with a length of dowel positioned at each pleat, set into a casing. The casing is formed by stitching through both the blind fabric and the lining, across the width of the blind.

1 *Cut out fabrics*
Cut a piece of fabric for the blind, the size of the blind plus 3cm down each side edge and 19cm at lower edge. Also add 5cm at top to allow for fixing to the batten. Cut a piece of lining the same size as the finished blind plus 5cm at the top.

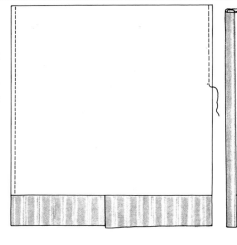

2 *Join fabric and lining △*
Lay the lining on top of the fabric, with right sides facing, positioning the lining so that the top edges are level and lower edge is 19cm up from the lower edge of the main blind fabric. Make a gentle pleat in the blind fabric so that the side edges of blind and lining match. Stitch the side seams taking 1.5cm seams. Trim slightly, then press seams open.

3 *Press the blind △*
Turn right sides out and press so that lining is centred on main fabric. Press under the side turning allowance down the remainder of the main fabric.

4 *Stitch casing at lower edge*
Turn up 1cm across lower edge of blind, and then a further 18cm. Stitch two rows, 1.5cm apart, positioning the bottom row 16cm from the lower edge of the blind.

---

5 *Stitch casings up blind ▷*
Mark off the top 5cm and tack the two layers of fabric along this line. Mark positions for casings up the blind, approximately 30cm apart. The distance between the casings should not be more than twice the distance from the lowest casing to the lower edge of the blind. The distance from the top casing to the tacking should equal the spacing between the casings. Stitch the casings with two rows of stitches 1.5cm apart. For a neat finish, zigzag top edge.

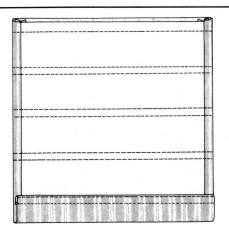

6 *Fit dowels*
Unpick a couple of stitches in the seam where it crosses each casing down one side of the blind. Cut lengths of dowel 5mm shorter than the width of the finished blind. Slip dowel into the opening, then stitch up the seam again. At the lower edge, slip the dowel into the casing and slipstitch the ends to hold it in.

7 Stitch rings in place ▽
Stitch the rings to the casing channels with one row down each side as shown and one or more rows down centre.

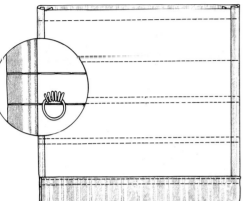

8 Cut up lengths of cord ▷
Decide which side of the blind you want the pull-up cord to hang. Lay the blind out flat, with the lining facing you. If you want the cords to hang down the left of the blind when it is hung, then with the wrong side of the blind facing you the cords should hang to the right of the blind (remember it is reversed). Cut the cord into appropriate lengths to run up the blind, across the top and down one side, allowing a little extra for knotting the cords.

Tie one end of each cord to a ring at the lower edge of the blind. Thread the cords up through the line of rings.

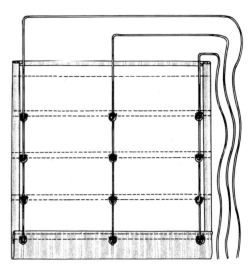

9 Prepare top batten
The batten is fitted with one narrow edge towards the window. Either drill holes in top batten to take suitable screws to fix the batten straight into the top of the window recess or attach angle irons to the underside of the batten so that it can be fitted to the wall or surround above the window.

Staple or tack the fabric to the batten so that the 5cm allowance lies over the top of the batten. Make sure the blind is absolutely straight.

10 Fit screw eyes ▷
Fit a screw eye into the batten at the top of each line of rings. Thread cords through the screw eyes, running them all to one side of the blind. Finish neatly by plaiting the ends of the cords and tie into an acorn.

11 Hang of blind
Either screw the batten straight into the top of the window recess, or fit angle irons above the window. Fix the cleat at one side to anchor cords.

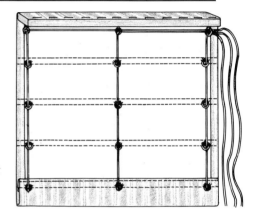

BRIGHT IDEA

NET EFFECTS

There's no reason why you shouldn't make roman blinds out of sheer fabric, to replace net curtains. Here, two layers of net have been used, with casings stitched to hold dowels as for lined blinds.

The two pieces of fabric should be cut 1.5cm larger down the sides and across the lower edge than the measurement of the finished blind, with an allowance of 5cm across the top as before. Join the two layers of fabric down the sides and across the lower edge, taking 1.5cm seams. Trim seam allowance and clip across corners. Turn right side out, and make up as for the lined blind, positioning the first casing about 10cm from lower edge. Space the casings about 20cm apart up the blind. Unpick the seam at one end of each casing. Slip dowels into the casings and then slipstitch the open end to hold the dowels in place. Note that only two rows of rings have been used, positioned close to the sides of the blind, so as to avoid clumsy cords running up the back of the blind.

TRIMS FOR ROMAN BLINDS

Because of the geometric styling of the blind a simple trim in plain braid or contrasting fabric is most effective.

1 *Braid trim across lower edge*
The simplest way to trim a roman ·
blind is to add a length of braid across the lower edge. This looks particularly effective if it is attached close to the bottom of the blind so that it shows when the blind is pulled up. Allow a little extra fabric for turning at the bottom of the blind if you are using a wide braid, so that the bottom section of the blind hangs below the pleated section and the braid shows when the blind is pulled up. Stitch or glue the braid in place before inserting the lengths of dowel.

2 *Braid trim all round blind* ▷
Braid can be stitched in place down the side and across the lower edge of the blind, positioned a couple of centimetres in from the edge, with neatly mitred corners. Stitch the braid to the fabric before you start making up the blind: this will be easier if you use dressmaker's chalk to mark the finished edge 3cm from each side edge and 19cm from the lower edge of the fabric after cutting out. Decide on a suitable distance to space the braid from the edge of the blind (half to twice the width of the braid gives a good spacing, depending on that width). Then pin, tack and stitch the braid in place before joining the lining fabric and stitching the channels

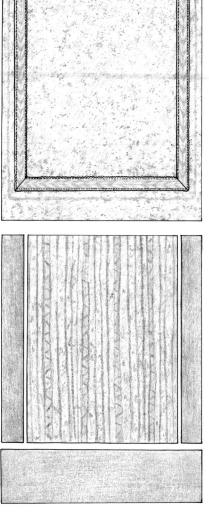

3 *Fabric border* △
An alternative finish is to add a fabric border to the edges of the blind To make a 5cm border round the blind, cut the main fabric so that it is 3.5cm smaller down the sides and across the lower edge than the finished blind. Include a 5cm allowance at the top of the blind as before. Cut strips of fabric 9.5cm wide to run down the side edges, the same length as the piece of fabric for the blind. To go across the lower edge, cut a strip of fabric 25.5cm wide by the width of the finished blind plus 3cm at each side. Join the side strips to the side of the blind with flat seams, pressed open. Join the strip to the bottom of the blind in the same way. This should give you a piece of fabric the size of the main piece of fabric used for making an untrimmed blind — and you can continue to make up the blind as described on the previous page.

◁ **Smartly pleated**
The neat, unfussy lines of roman blinds are well suited to modern, minimalist interior design. The blue-grey of the blind, neatly trimmed in clear red is echoed in the window seat, candlestick lamp and chaise longue.

BLINDS AND SHUTTERS

Choose a style which is neat and simple, elegantly swagged or slatted.

Blinds are a versatile way of covering windows. The styles range from the simple clean lines of a plain roller or venetian to the elegant swags of an austrian or festoon blind. Apart from these last two, most blinds have a contemporary feel but they can look at home in many traditional settings, particularly when used in combination with curtains.

Blinds are often the best answer if a window is awkwardly placed or space is limited and many of the simpler styles are cheaper than curtains.

Fabric blinds can be bought ready made or made to measure, or you can make many of the styles yourself using a simple kit following the instructions in this book.

Before you buy or make blinds, you must measure up accurately, using a steel tape measure.

The blinds can be fixed either within a recess or outside. For outside a recess allow an overlap of at least 4.5cm each side. If you are having blinds made to measure, always give the full width and drop dimensions of your finished blind – the manufacturer will make allowances for the fixing brackets.

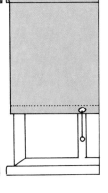
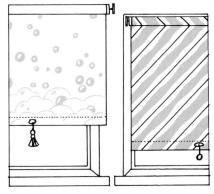
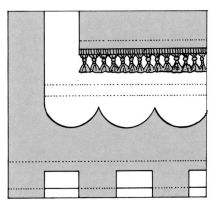

ROLLER BLINDS

Style One of the cheapest of window coverings, roller blinds can be bought ready made, made to measure or as a kit to make up yourself.

In use The fabric rolls round a wooden dowel by means of a spring-loaded mechanism or side pulley and the lower edge is weighted with a lath (thin strip of wood) inserted in a casing. Fabric choice can range from sheer net or voile to medium-weight furnishing fabrics. Waterproof or spongeable fabrics are ideal for bathrooms and kitchens and flame-retardant fabrics are also available.

Watchpoint Bulky weaves or materials with a pile are not suitable.

Border patterns are popular and there is also a wide choice of all-over pictorial prints, many of which are fun for a child's room. Dramatic geometric designs and bold diagonal patterns look particularly effective in a modern setting, while the softer floral or lacy net designs suit more traditional rooms.

The lower edge of a blind can be shaped to suit a more formal style of furnishing and lace, fringing, ribbon and braid add a decorative touch to both home-made or ready-made blinds. Blinds with a spring-loaded mechanism are raised or lowered by a cord which can be finished with the traditional wood acorn, tassel or ring.

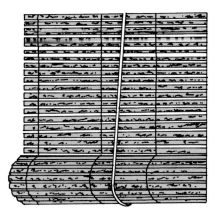
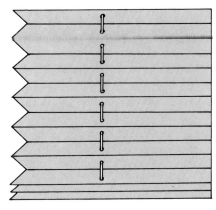

PINOLEUM BLINDS

Style Traditionally made from fine strips of wood woven together with cotton, today they are also made from plastic quills in a range of colours, including white. They filter the light attractively but can be seen through at night.

In use They roll up using a system of cords and pulleys and can be fixed at any level by winding the cord round a wall-fixed cleat.

PLEATEX BLINDS

Style Made from permanently pleated paper or polyester fabric. They are available in a range of attractive colours and sizes.

In use Raise and lower by using cords which pass through holes in the pleats. The fabric blinds can be treated with anti-static that repels dust, or can have a metallic backing to repel sun in summer and keep in warmth in winter.

CANE OR WOOD SLAT BLINDS

Style Cane blinds are made from split bamboo or rattan. Wood slats are strips of wood which are left natural or stained brown or different colours. Light filters through between the wood by day but they provide greater privacy than pinoleum blinds at night.

In use Bulkier than pinoleum blinds, they are constructed and raised and lowered in the same way.

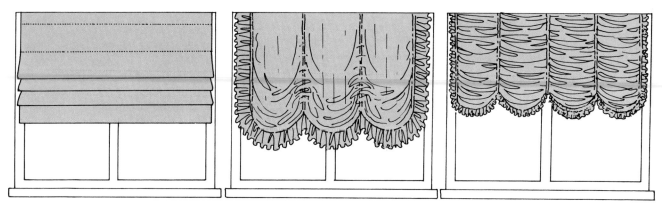

ROMAN BLINDS

Style When let down fully these fabric blinds hang flat like roller blinds; when pulled up they fold into a series of broad horizontal pleats. Plain fabrics or vertical and diagonal stripes look particularly effective.

In use Tape down each side of the blind carries a series of rings through which the cords that raise and lower the blind are threaded.

Watchpoint Lightweight fabrics, sheers or blinds wider than 1.5m need horizontal battens inserted in concealed pockets to keep the folds neat.

AUSTRIAN BLINDS

Style These blinds are raised and lowered in the same way as roman blinds but instead of folds, they gather into deep swags. When fully down they hang like a curtain. They look particularly effective made from silk, voile or moiré which allow the light to filter through; they can be made from furnishing cottons and lined for greater privacy. Add frills to the side and lower edges for a richer, decorative effect.

In use The fabric is gathered on to standard curtain heading tape; the blind can be hung from a pole, curtain track or head rail.

FESTOON BLINDS

Style Unlike austrian blinds, festoon blinds are permanently gathered into ruched swags, even when fully let down. Soft, sheer or lightweight fabrics are most suitable and the lower edge can be shaped or frilled.

In use Vertical ring-bearing tapes are sewn at 23-46cm intervals and the blind is raised in the same way as an austrian blind.

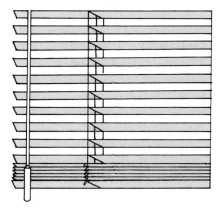

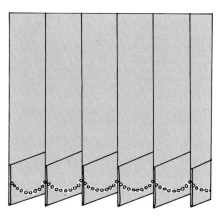

VENETIAN BLINDS

Style Most commonly made from aluminium alloy, these blinds are made to measure and come in a wide range of colours and finishes. They are also available with a mirror finish which gives a highly reflective surface, or perforated, allowing light through even when fully closed.

In use You can control the light and visibility by angling the slats using an acrylic wand or cord. The slats can be 1.5-5cm wide; the narrowest are almost invisible when the blind is lowered and fully open.

WOODEN VENETIAN BLINDS

Style Traditionally made from western red cedar, chosen for its attractive grain, lightness and stability. The wood can be left natural, stained or painted.

In use They operate in exactly the same way as metal blinds but as the 5cm slats are considerably thicker they have a deeper stack when raised.

Watchpoint These blinds work out considerably more expensive than aluminium blinds.

VERTICAL LOUVRE BLINDS

Style These stiffened strips of fabric, often with a textured weave, are made from silk; canvas, both plain or printed; or PVC, plain or perforated. The strips range from 9-13cm wide. They are attached to a track at the top and linked at the bottom, usually by a chain.

In use They can be drawn like curtains and are most often used floor to ceiling over large picture windows or patio doors. They can also be used as room dividers or to fit awkward windows.

Watchpoint Although these have been traditionally used in offices, they can be used equally successfully in the home.

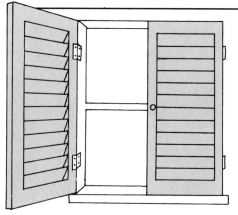

▷ PLANTATION SHUTTERS

Style Made from wood, such as pine and left natural or painted. They can be full length, or divided in half so that they can give light at the top and privacy at the bottom like a café curtain.

In use The panels are hinged to fold back and the louvres on each panel can be opened or closed independently by the central batten.

◁ LOUVRE DOOR SHUTTERS

An inexpensive treatment with a tropical flavour. Choose hinges which will allow the shutters to be opened right back against the wall. They can be solid for total light exclusion or open as normal.

MAKING CUSHIONS

Add extra comfort and a dash of colour to any room with an eye-catching collection of scatter cushions.

Cushions serve both a decorative and practical purpose in a room. Use them to soften the hard lines of modern furniture, to add colour and richness to an austere colour scheme, or as a touch of comfort and luxury.

Basic covers for square, round or rectangular cushions are quick and simple to make. They can either be left plain or you can add a decorative trim, such as piping or a frill, for a professional finish.

Choosing fabric Almost any fabric can be used – from fairly tough furnishing fabric such as heavy brocade or velvet, through cotton and canvas, to lightweight silk and lace. The limiting factor is where the cushion will be used and how much wear it will get. For cushions that will get a lot of use, choose washable fabrics.

Remnant counters are a good source of cheap cushion-sized fabric pieces and you can create a bold effect by mixing colour and pattern. For a co-ordinated look, use fabric left over from bedcovers, curtains or upholstery.

Type of opening The method of opening and its position (a side or back opening) determines the cutting measurements of the cover, so decide what you want to use before cutting out the fabric. If the cover needs regular laundering, use a zip, Velcro or pressstud opening – the cushion pad can be removed and replaced easily. A handsewn opening is simpler to make, but needs to be unpicked and resewn every time the pad is removed.

Always make sure that the opening is large enough to take the cushion pad easily. Ideally, the opening on a straightedged cushion should be about 10cm shorter than the length of the side. For a round cushion, the length of the opening should measure about three-quarters of the diameter of the cushion.

Cushion pads The filling for a cushion must be enclosed in its own inner casing to make a pad that can be removed when the cushion cover needs washing.

Cushion pads can be bought in a range of shapes and sizes. Or you can make your own pad with a filling such as down, feathers, or shredded foam. The amount of filling needed depends on its type and the size of the cushion. A 50cm square cushion, for example, will take about 350g of down, or 900g of feathers, or about 800g of foam.

If the filling is feathers and/or down, use down-proof ticking for the casing. Otherwise calico and lining material are suitable, or you can even use the good areas of old cotton sheets. Make up the casing in the same way as a cushion cover with a hand-sewn opening (see overleaf).

Sewing thread The sewing thread should match the fibre content of your fabric – use polyester thread for synthetics, cotton thread for natural fabrics.

Cushions for comfort
A pile of soft chintz-covered cushions make this window-seat a pretty and comfortable spot. Black piping inserted at the seams pulls the mixture of plain and patterned fabrics together and links up with the smart black-trimmed Roman blinds.

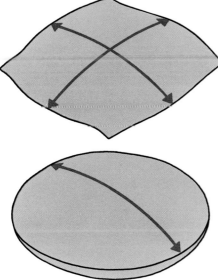

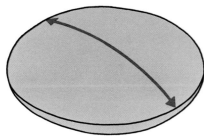

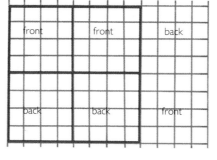

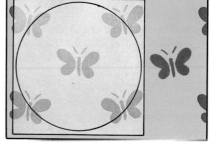

MEASURING UP △

Measure a square or rectangular pad (top) across the width and the length from seam to seam, and add a 3cm seam allowance to both measurements.

Measure a round pad (bottom) across the diameter, and add 3cm.

For a plump-looking cushion do not add a seam allowance – the cover, when sewn up, will then fit snugly.

ESTIMATING FABRIC △

If you're making several covers from the same fabric, plan your cutting layout on squared paper using a suitable scale before you buy it. Mark out an area representing the width of your fabric, then draw in cushion pieces to find the most economical arrangement, and work out the total fabric needed.

CENTRING A BOLD DESIGN △

For the best effect, position a bold design centrally on each cover section. Cut a piece of tracing paper to the size of your square, rectangle or circle and place it over the main design on the fabric as a pattern for cutting out. You may need extra fabric to get the right number of motifs.

SQUARE AND RECTANGULAR COVERS

1 *Mark out and cut fabric*
For a cover with a side opening, mark out and cut two pieces the same size – a front and a back piece. (For a back zip opening you will need two sections for the back piece – see opposite.)

Lay the fabric on a flat surface, and use a ruler and tailor's chalk to draw the cutting lines along the straight grain of the fabric. If the fabric has a pattern, make sure that it runs in the same direction for each piece.

2 *Making a hand-sewn opening* ▷
With right sides of fabric facing, tack round three sides – 1.5cm from the outer edge with a right angle at each corner. (Leave a short side of a rectangular cover untacked.) On the remaining side, tack along 5cm of the seam from each end. Stitch all tacked seams, leaving untacked section open.

At corners, cut seam allowance diagonally, close to stitching to reduce bulk. Remove tacking and neaten raw edges with zigzag stitch or over-cast by hand. Turn cover to right side and insert pad. Tack opening closed, then slipstitch. Remove tacking.

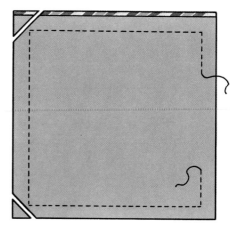

1 *Making a side zip opening* ▷
Place right sides of fabric together. On one side (short side for rectangles) tack along 5cm of the seam from each corner. Stitch, then remove tacking. Press these short seams flat, and press seam allowance of opening to wrong side.

Lay zip (of the same size as the opening) face up. Place open section of seam (with wrong side of fabric to zip) directly over the zip teeth, and tack zip in place. On right side of fabric, stitch down both sides of zip and across the short ends as close to the teeth as possible. Remove tacking.

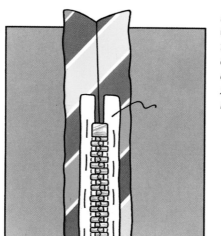

2 *Stitch remaining sides*
With right sides of fabric facing and the zip open, tack and stitch round the other three sides. Remove tacking, clip corners, and neaten raw edges with zigzag stitch or overcast by hand. Turn right side out, and insert pad.

ROUND CUSHION COVERS

The success of a round cover depends on cutting a perfect circle from the fabric, so make a paper pattern first.

For a plump cushion, omit seam allowances from the paper pattern.

Zips are best inserted across the back of round cushions, zips in the side seams may cause puckering.

1 *Draw a paper pattern ▷*

Cut a square of paper slightly larger than the cushion pad and fold it into quarters. Tie string round a pencil and cut this off to half the diameter of the cushion plus 1.5cm for seam allowance.

Lay the folded paper on a board and pin the end of the string to the point of the folded corner. With string taut and pencil held upright, draw a quarter circle on the paper.

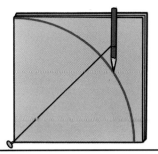

2 *Cut out ▷*

Carefully cut along the pencil line through all four layers of paper. Open out the paper and use as a pattern for cutting out two circles of fabric for a cover. (If you want a zip in the back, you will need a different pattern for the back piece – see below.)

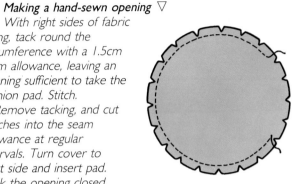

3 *Making a hand-sewn opening ▽*

With right sides of fabric facing, tack round the circumference with a 1.5cm seam allowance, leaving an opening sufficient to take the cushion pad. Stitch.

Remove tacking, and cut notches into the seam allowance at regular intervals. Turn cover to right side and insert pad. Tack the opening closed. Slipstitch. Remove tacking.

1 *Making a side zip opening ▷*

With right sides facing, pin fabric circles together, leaving an opening the length of the zip. Tack seam for 2.5cm either side of the opening, with a 1.5cm allowance. Stitch. Remove tacking, and press short seams flat.

Pin and tack zip into opening, easing fabric slightly to allow for the curve. Stitch. Open zip and place fabric circles together, right sides facing. Tack together, then stitch. Remove tacking, and notch seam allowance (see diagram above). Turn cover right side out and insert pad.

1 *Making a back zip opening*

First use a circular paper pattern to cut one piece of fabric for the front. Then, using a zip length about 10cm shorter than the diameter, mark a straight line across the paper pattern where the zip is to be fitted – either centred or off centre. Cut the paper pattern along this line.

2 *Cut two back pieces ▷*

Place the back patterns on the fabric, adding an extra 1.5cm seam allowance to both straight edges where the zip is to be inserted. Cut out the two sections for the back of the cushion cover.

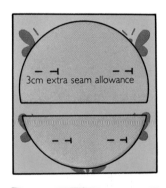

3cm extra seam allowance

3 *Insert the zip ▷*

With right sides of the two back pieces facing and raw edges matching, tack and stitch up to 5cm from both ends of the straight edge. Remove tacking and sew in zip (as for square cover).

Tack together front and back of cover (with right sides facing and zip open). Stitch all round. Remove tacking and notch around the circumference. Turn cover right side out and insert pad.

OTHER OPENING METHODS

In place of a zip you can use a length of press stud tape or Velcro. Make up the cover – for a square or round cushion pad – in the same way as for a hand-sewn side opening. Place tape or Velcro on either side of the opening and slipstitch or machine in place.

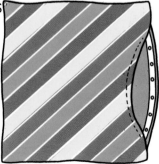

PROFESSIONAL TOUCHES

Cushion covers can be trimmed in a number of ways. For a smart look, add a neat trim to seams using piping cord covered with fabric. Or use a gathered frill, in matching or contrasting fabric, to give a soft and pretty finish.

Both these trimmings are sandwiched between the two cushion pieces and stitched in place with the main cushion cover seams.

PIPING

Piping cord comes in several thicknesses – a thicker cord will stand out more from the seam. It should be used in a continuous strip so add an extra 5cm to the length of cord required for joining up (see below).

Cover with fabric cut on the bias grain, wide enough to enclose the cord plus 2cm for seam allowance. Ready-made bias binding is convenient and comes in several widths and colours.

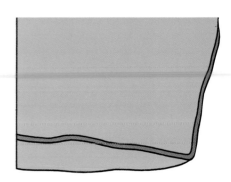

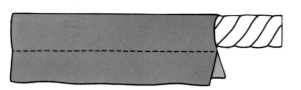

1 *Cover the piping cord* △
Place the cord along the centre of the wrong side of an opened up strip of purchased bias binding. Then fold the bias binding in half over the cord and tack in place. Using a zipper foot, stitch as close to the cord as possible. Remove tacking.

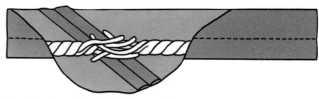

2 *Join lengths of piping cord* △
Join lengths of bias binding using a 5mm flat seam stitched at an angle along the grain of the tape. Then overlap two ends of cord. To make a smooth join, unravel the strands at each end by 2.5cm, and trim each strand to a slightly different length before intertwining them.

3 *Add piping to cushion cover seam* ▷
For best results, use piping on cushions with a back zip opening. Insert zip as described on page 284. With tailor's chalk, mark a 1.5cm seam allowance on right side of either front or back of cushion cover. Position piping along this marked line, with raw edges of piping cord fabric matching raw edges of cushion cover. Tack in place, curving it slightly round corners to avoid sharp angles. Clip seam allowance at corners to reduce bulk.

With right sides facing and zip open, tack front and back of cushion cover together with piping sandwiched in the middle. Using a zipper foot, stitch all round as close to piping as possible. Remove tacking.

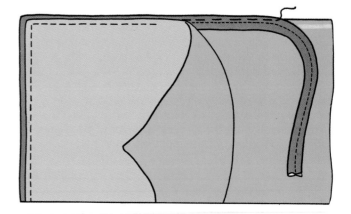

A GATHERED FRILL

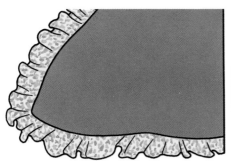

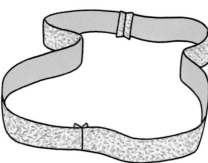

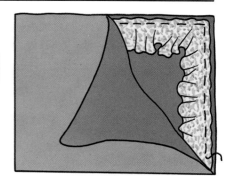

1 *Measure up and cut out*
A narrow frill is most easily made from a double thickness of fabric. Decide the finished width of the frill, add a 1.5cm seam allowance and double this measurement.

To calculate length of frill needed, measure the distance around the outside of your cushion pad. Add a 1.5cm seam allowance (plus 1.5cm for each join necessary to make up the length), and double this measurement.

2 *Prepare the frill* △
With right sides facing, join short ends of fabric with 1.5cm seams to make a continuous frill. Fold fabric in half lengthways, wrong sides facing, and press.

Work two rows of gathering stitches through the layers – 1.5cm and 1cm from the raw edge. For even gathers, work along half the frill length, then cut the threads. Use a new thread for gathering the remaining length.

3 *Add frill to cushion cover* △
Fold one of the cushion cover pieces in half, and mark each end of the fold with tailor's chalk. Open flat again.

Pin frill to the right side of one cushion cover piece, with raw edges matching and each break in the gathering threads on one of the chalk marks. Pull the gathering threads evenly to fit the frill to the edge. Tack and stitch. Then complete as for square or round cushion cover.

SIMPLE GUSSETED CUSHIONS

Make a firm, tailored cushion by adding a generous side gusset to the cover.

This type of cushion has a top and a bottom piece, joined by a strip of fabric called a gusset. The result is a deep, firm cushion with a neat tailored shape.

Gusseted cushions can be square, rectangular or round for use on a plain hard chair, bench or window seat; they're also useful for extra floor seating and make excellent footstools.

Long, firm bolsters are really round cushions with an elongated gusset. Traditionally used at ends of sofas, bolsters make good backrests – particularly when placed along the back of a divan, for example, to support a row of scatter cushions or pillows.

Covers can be left plain or you can emphasize the shape of the cushion with strong piped seams or a decorative gusset: pick out one of the colours in a patterned fabric, or use a toning or contrasting colour to add emphasis to a plain cover. If you want to make a decorative panel insert, make the panelled piece before making up the cover.

Cushion pads A pad or block of solid foam is the best choice for cushions with a gusset as it retains its shape and looks neat. Foam, however, tends to crumble with regular use so you will need an inner cover for the pad. This should be made out of a strong fabric such as pre-shrunk calico, lining material or even old cotton sheets.

Buy foam at least 4cm thick for scatter cushions, deeper for more substantial seating.

Choosing fabric Cushions usually get a lot of wear so choose strong, washable fabrics: furnishing fabrics – such as velvet, corduroy, linen or heavy cotton – are ideal. If the fabric is not pre-shrunk, wash it first to reduce shrinkage.

To work out how much fabric you need for a gusseted cushion, see overleaf. If seams are to be piped, you'll need extra fabric for cutting bias strips or you can use ready-made bias binding.

Types of opening A zip inserted in one side of the cover makes it easy to remove the cushion pad for laundering.

For a square or rectangular cover, the zip should be long enough to extend around each of the two adjoining corners by at least 5cm – this makes it easier to insert and remove the cushion pad. For a round or bolster cover, the zip should measure at least half the circumference of the pad.

If you don't want a zipped opening (or you're making an inner cover), omit instructions given for inserting a zip. Attach the gusset to one cover piece. Then attach the other cover piece: stitch along three sides, and about 5cm in from each corner on the fourth side, leaving a central opening. Insert the cushion pad and neatly slipstitch the opening closed.

Before you begin making up gusseted cushion covers, see the previous chapter for instructions on making basic covers and cushion pads.

Comfortable assets
Cushions with a gusset are ideal for adding comfort to a hard wooden chair, bench or window seat. Here, an attractive piped trim is added to the seams for a more tailored finish on these shaped cushions.

SQUARE AND RECTANGULAR GUSSETED COVERS

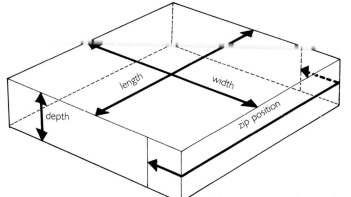

CHECK YOUR NEEDS
- ☐ Fabric
- ☐ Cushion pad
- ☐ Zip
- ☐ Tailor's chalk
- ☐ Ruler
- ☐ Pins
- ☐ Long-bladed scissors for cutting fabric
- ☐ Short-bladed scissors for trimming
- ☐ Sewing machine
- ☐ Sewing thread
- ☐ Needles

For round covers and bolsters:
- ☐ Paper
- ☐ String
- ☐ Pencil
- ☐ Drawing pin
- ☐ Cutting board

Optional:
- ☐ Piping cord
- ☐ Bias binding or fabric strips

1 Measure top and base △
For the top and bottom of the cover, measure the width and length of the top of the pad, and add 3cm to both measurements for seam allowance. Then cut out.

2 Measure the gusset ◁
The gusset is made up of four pieces: one front, two sides, and one back piece which takes the zip.

For the back gusset piece, cut a rectangle measuring the length of the zip plus 3cm seam allowance, by the depth of the pad plus 6cm seam allowance (to allow for zip opening).

For the front and side gussets, measure the length and depth of the remaining cushion sides, allowing 3cm all round for seam allowances. Cut out gusset pieces.

3 Insert zip ▷
Cut the back gusset piece in half along its length. Turn a 1.5cm seam allowance to the wrong side along one edge of each half and press.

Lay back gussets side by side on the table (wrong sides up) with folded sides together and place zip centrally, face down. Pin, tack and stitch the zip in position.

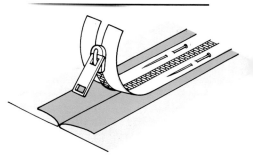

4 Make up the gusset ▷
With right sides facing and taking a 1.5cm seam allowance, pin the ends of the gusset side sections to the front and back sections to form a square or rectangle which fits snugly round the cushion pad.

Tack and stitch. Secure ends of stitching firmly, remove tacking and press seams open.

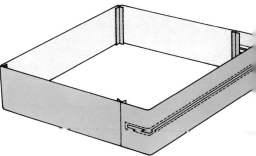

5 Sew to main fabric ▷
With right sides facing and corners matching, pin and tack the gusset to one main piece of cushion cover, then stitch in place with a 1.5cm seam. If you want a piped trim, make up the piping (as shown on page 286) and insert in the seams between gusset and main pieces at this stage – see opposite.

Open the zip, and attach the remaining cover piece in the same way. Press all the seams towards the gusset. Turn the cover through to right side, press and insert cushion pad.

Corner seams
To ensure a neat square finish at corners, stitch up to the corner, then insert the machine needle right into the fabric at this point. Lift the presser foot and pivot the fabric round the needle, turning it to the correct position for stitching down the other side. Replace presser foot and continue stitching.

Finish each corner by clipping into seam allowance, up to the stitching; then snip diagonally across the seam allowance, close to stitching, to eliminate bulk.

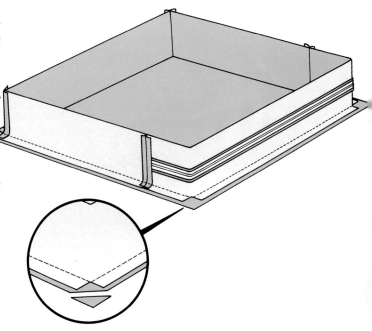

ROUND GUSSETED COVERS

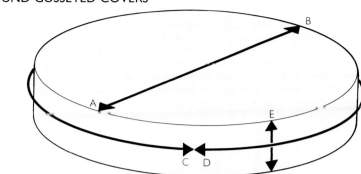

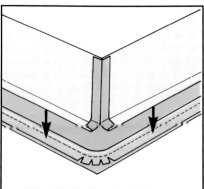

PIPED GUSSETED COVERS

Make up two strips of piping, each the same length as the finished gusset plus an overlap of 2.5cm. With raw edges together, attach piping to both main pieces of cover. Clip into piping seam allowance at corners, then complete the cover.

1 Measure top and base △
For the top and bottom of the cover, measure across the diameter of the cushion pad (A-B) and add 3cm seam allowance.

Make a paper pattern to this size (as for a basic round cushion cover, steps 1-2, page 285) and cut out two circles of fabric.

2 Measure gusset △
For the gusset, measure the circumference (C-D) and depth (E-F) of the cushion pad. Cut one rectangle measuring half the circumference plus 3cm, by the depth plus 3cm.

For the zipped half of the gusset, cut a second rectangle measuring half the circumference plus 3cm, by the depth plus 6cm (to allow for the zip opening).

3 Insert zip
Cut the gusset for the zip in half along its length. Turn under 1.5cm seam allowance along the cut edge of both halves and press.
Lay two halves on the table (wrong sides up) with folded sides together and place zip centrally, face down. Pin and tack in place, and stitch close to the teeth all round.

4 Make up the gusset ▷
With right sides facing and taking a 1.5cm seam, pin the short ends of the two gusset pieces together to form a circle to go round the cushion.
Tack and stitch, leaving 1.5cm unstitched at each end of seams. Secure ends of stitching firmly, then press seams open.

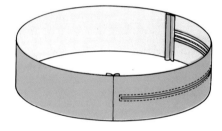

BRIGHT IDEA

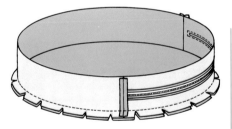

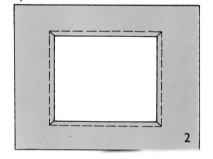

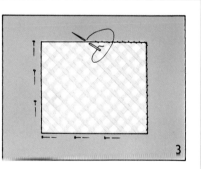

5 Sew to main fabric △
With the zip open and right sides facing, pin, tack and stitch the gusset to one cover piece and then the other.
Remove tacking and notch seam allowances at 2.5cm intervals all round to ease the fabric and give a neat appearance to the seam on the right side. Press seams towards gusset. Turn cover right side out, and insert pad.

Piping
If you want a piped trim, make up piping (as shown on page 286) and attach to each circular cover piece. Then attach gusset, but notch the gusset seam allowances before stitching together.

DECORATIVE PANEL INSERTS
For a pretty patchwork effect, add a panel of contrasting fabric to a cushion cover. Use fabric offcuts, embroidery or lace: for strength, back lace first with a piece of fabric such as silk, satin or tiny cotton print.
Set the panel into the cover piece before making up the cushion cover.

1 Decide the finished size of the panel to be inserted in the cover, then add a 1.5cm seam allowance all round and cut from fabric.

2 Using tailor's chalk, mark out the finished panel on the front of the cover. Then draw another line

1.5cm inside the first for a seam allowance, and cut out a hole along this inner line. Clip into the corners of seam allowance and press seam to wrong side (if the cut-out is round, clip at regular intervals all round the circle).

3 With right sides facing up, pin the panel in position under the hole in the cover. Tack, then slipstitch or topstitch, or use zigzag stitch for a decorative edge.

MAKING BOLSTER CUSHIONS

A bolster is basically a variation of a round gusseted cushion, with the gusset depth extended to the length of the bolster and sewn into a long tube of fabric. This type of cushion is particularly useful on beds and divans.

Zips The zip for a bolster cover is inserted in the side seam of the tube and should measure at least half the circumference of the bolster so that the pad can be put in easily.

1 *Measure and cut ▷*
For the main piece, measure the length (A-B) and the circumference (C-D) of the bolster pad. Add a 3cm seam allowance to both measurements and cut a piece of fabric to these dimensions.

For the end pieces, measure the diameter of the pad (E-F) and add 3cm. Make a paper pattern as for a round cover and cut two circles of fabric.

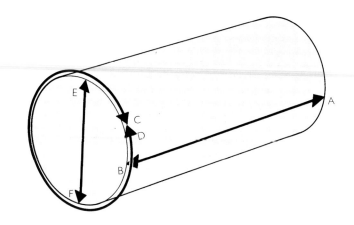

2 *Stitch main piece ▷*
Fold the main piece of fabric in half, with the two edges that are the length of the bolster together and right sides facing.

Pin, tack and stitch along seam allowance from each end, leaving a central opening the length of the zip. Remove tacking; press seam flat, and press seam allowance of opening to wrong side. Pin, tack and stitch zip into opening.

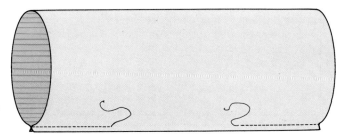

3 *Stitch the ends ▷*
Open the zip. With right sides facing, pin, tack and stitch the two end circles to the main cover piece.

If you want a piped trim, stitch the piping round the ends of the main cover piece before attaching the ends.

Notch round the seam allowances at 2.5cm intervals. Press seams towards the end circles of fabric. Turn cover right side out, press and insert cushion pad.

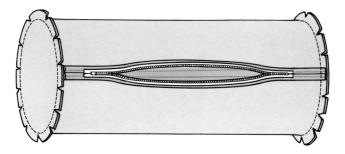

Versatile seating

Fat, padded bolster cushions help to turn this fold-away bed into a comfortable daytime sofa.

CLEVER WAYS WITH CUSHION TRIMS

Cushions add a touch of comfort to any room. Give them added style with one or more of these edging ideas.

A welcoming pile of cushions is a stylish addition to a living room or bedroom. For extra effect, you can give the cushions an individual trim, choosing the finish to suit the atmosphere of the room. For example, frills, lace and ribbon trims add a romantic touch to a bedroom; piping, pleats and a flat trim look smart in a more formal setting.

The variety of styles and shapes for cushions is almost infinite – the effects you achieve will depend on the mixture of fabrics you use as well as the combination of piping, trimming and binding. It is an area where you can really invent your own finishes. They are small and relatively inexpensive to make, and there is no reason why you shouldn't use oddments of fabric.

Contrast piping and double frills are obvious ways of combining different fabrics and colours in one item, but there are several other ways of creating a co-ordinated effect. You can appliqué shapes on to the front of the cushions, or edge a flat cushion trim with zigzag stitch in a contrasting colour. Ribbon bows, or lengths of ribbon top-stitched in place give further scope for decorative finishes.

As well as mixing fabrics, try mixing different shapes when making cushions: square, round, rectangular and even heart-shaped cushions look effective piled at the head of a bed. Once you have learned some of the tricks of the trade, you can go on to design your own shapes – for example, what about a cat-shaped cushion, or a cushion designed to look like a huge sunflower?

Sewing techniques As well as giving you ideas for specific shapes and trims, this chapter deals with some sewing techniques which can be applied in other situations. For example, we show you how to notch the seam allowance on curved seams to get a flat finish, and how to trim away the bulk of fabric from seams (where there is piping and a frill) to achieve a smooth finish.

Always remember when sewing that you should press your work at each stage. This not only keeps the fabric crisp and easy to work, but helps to produce a better finish. Pressing a seam after stitching it, for example, helps to knit the seam together. Don't be tempted to leave pressing until the work is finished – you may not be able to get at all the corners and angles.

CHOOSE YOUR FABRICS

For hard-wearing cushions which will keep their good looks, choose furnishing cottons and linen unions. Slub weaves and raw silks can look particularly effective in a traditional setting. For a more glamorous touch, look at satins and fine silks. You can use dressmaking fabrics if the cushions will not get a lot of wear – but be careful to keep them away from direct sunlight, as dressmaking fabrics fade faster than furnishing fabrics.

Where possible, use remnants of fabric from other furnishings in the room (curtains, bedlinen, tablecloths), so that you achieve a co-ordinated look for a minimum outlay.

If you are adding piping, make your own bias binding where possible, as ready-made binding is usually made from poor-quality cotton.

MEASURING UP

If you have ready-made cushion pads, measure them to find the finished measurement required for the cover. Add 1.5cm seam allowances all round for the front panel of the cushion. Allow an extra 3cm in one direction for inserting a zip in the back panel of the cushion.

If you are making your own cushion pads, you may find it more economical to make the pads to suit the width of the fabric, or the size of the remnants, you are using for the cover. For example, if you are making cushion pads from ticking fabric 90cm wide, by making the cushions 27cm square you will be able to get three cushions from 60cm of fabric, whereas if the cushions

All puffed up
Piles of cushions, with frills and ruching, add importance to the head of a bed. The heart-shaped cushion and ruching have been made up in a lettuce green fabric, giving an overall green look to a fabric which is primarily cream, blue and apricot.

are 30cm square you will need 1m of fabric for the same number of pads.

Frills To calculate the length of a frill, measure the perimeter of the cushion, multiply by 1½ and add 1.5cm for seam allowances where necessary. The width of the frill will depend on the effect you want. The larger the cushion, the wider the frill you will need to achieve a balanced look.

Seam allowances will depend on the finish you choose: a double-thickness frill (where the fabric is folded in half down its length) requires a seam allowance down each long edge of 1.5cm. A bound edge requires a single 1.5cm seam allowance, and a hemmed edge requires 1.5cm down one long edge and a 1cm allowance down the other edge for a 5mm wide double hem.

Pleats For a pleated finish, you will need a strip of fabric three times the length of the perimeter of the cushion (plus 1.5cm seam allowances where necess-ary). The width is calculated in the same way as the width of the frill.

Binding Binding for piping should be cut on the bias, 35mm wide. Binding for trims can be cut to any width, and in most cases (since it does not have to be eased round corners) it can be cut on the straight, which makes cutting easier. Whichever way it is cut, allow a 1cm turning allowance down each long edge, and 1.5cm for joining lengths together where necessary.

CLOSURES FOR CUSHIONS

The various ways of closing the cushion are described earlier in Making Cushions (pages 283-286). In this chapter, we assume that you will set the zip into the back of the cushion – which gives the neatest effect. You will have to adapt the instructions if you choose another form of closure.

CLIPPING AND NOTCHING

These techniques are used on curved seams, to enable the seam to lie flat. Notching is used on external (convex) seams and clipping on internal curves. Thus, on a circular cushion, you have to notch the seam allowance to reduce the bulk once the cover is finished.

1 *Notching convex seams* ▷
Notching involves clipping V-shapes out of the seam allowance of external corners or curves, cutting in as close to the seam as possible without cutting the stitches. The sharper the curve, the more notches you will need. Trimming away the seam allowance will also reduce the bulk, which can look ugly once the cover is finished.

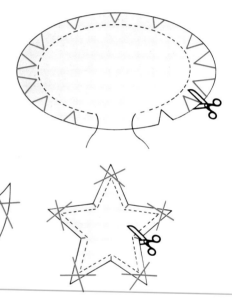

2 *Clipping corners* △
Clipping across corners has the same effect as cutting notches: the bulk of the seam allowance is removed. Corners which are sharper than 90° should have even more of the seam allowance clipped away (see step 3).

3 *Clipping concave curves* △
If you are making a shaped cushion, you may have sharp internal angles or curved seams. The solution is to clip into the seam allowance, clipping as close to the stitching line as you can. Once turned out, the seam allowance will be able to stretch so that the shape is not distorted. On a sharp internal angle, a single clip should be sufficient. On gently curved seams, a series of clips will be needed. The sharper the curve, the closer together they should be made.

GATHERS

You need to gather fabric when making a frill, or adding a ruched insert. It is also a useful technique for easing the fullness at corners when making soft square or rectangular cushions with puffy, round-ed corners. For a double frill, fold in half along length first.

1 *Gathering stitches* ▽
Cut the strip to be gathered 1½ times the length of the seam where it is to be inserted. Fold the ungathered frill into four even sections and mark the fold lines. To gather strips of fabric, make two parallel rows of running stitch, a couple of millimetres apart, within the seam allowance, close to the seam line. It is best to knot the thread at the end, so that you can draw up the gathers from both ends if necessary. Make each stitch about 5mm long. Line up the rows of stitches for crisp gathers, but for a more delicate effect, stagger the stitches.

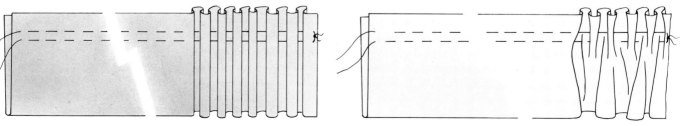

2 *Drawing up fullness* ▷
Once you have made the lines of stitches, draw up the fullness until the length of the frill matches the perimeter of the cushion. This is often easier if the gathering is done in sections. Put a pin in the frill at the end of the row of gathering stitches, and wind the ends of the gathering stitches round it to anchor it. Then move the gathers along the gathering thread until they are evenly distributed. Divide the perimeter of the panel the frill is to be stitched to into four equal sections and mark the edge. Then start pinning the frill to the front panel of the cushion so that the gathers are held in place, and the marks on the frill match the marks on the edge of the panel.

If the frill is to go round a rectangular cushion, you will need to group the gathers together and arrange them so there is extra fullness at the corners.

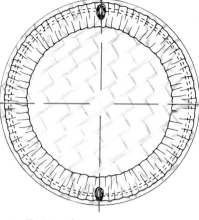

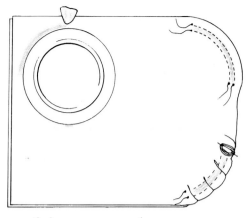

3 *Tack in place*
Once you are happy with the effect of the gathers, tack the frill in place.

It is worth taking quite small, neat stitches so that the gathers cannot be pushed out of place by the foot of the sewing machine when you come to stitch it.

4 *Soft square corners* △
To make a soft, square cushion and avoid spiky corners, mark a curved stitching line at each corner, drawing round a plate, or similar curved shape. Trim away the seam allowance 1.5cm from the marked line. Gather the corners by hand and tack gathers in place. Insert piping into seam to hold gathers firmly and give a neat finish.

RUCHING

This is a variation of gathering, where both edges of the gathered section are stitched (rather than just one edge, as on a frill). You can insert a ruched section into any shaped cushion. Here we give instructions for a circular cushion with ruching round the edge. The measurements given are for a 40cm diameter circular cushion with a 20cm diameter centre surrounded by a 20cm wide ruched panel.

1 *Cut out fabrics*
Cut out fabric for the back panel as usual, cutting two sections which can have a zip inserted between them to form a 43cm diameter panel. For the front panel, cut a circle 23cm in diameter and a panel 192cm by 23cm for the ruched section (the length of the section to be ruched is 1½ times the circumference of the finished cover, plus seam allowance). Cut out binding for piping if necessary (both edges of the ruched area may be piped if wished).

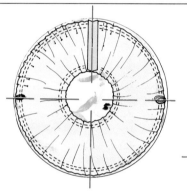

2 *Gather panel to be ruched* △
Join short ends with a flat seam. Mark the panel and the edge of the two circular sections into four equal parts. Make two lines of gathering stitches down each side of the panel to be ruched. Make the stitches even for a more formal effect, or stagger them for a more random effect. Draw up one side to fit round the central circle of fabric, matching marked points and distributing fullness evenly. Pin, tack and stitch in place. Trim (or layer – see below) seam allowance and press towards ruched area.

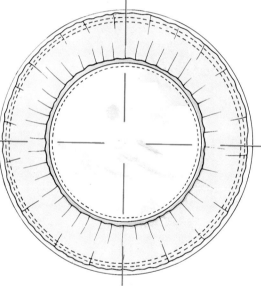

3 *Finish outer seam* △
Draw up the outer gathered edge to match the back panel of the cushion cover. Pin, tack and stitch in place. Notch and trim seam allowances and press before turning right side out and inserting cushion pad.

LAYERING

This technique involves trimming away seam allowances (of cushion cover panels, piping and/or frills) in such a way as to prevent a sharp step showing when the cushion cover is turned right-side out. It is particularly useful when working with bulky fabrics.

1 *Stitch seams*
Cut out fabrics and stitch seams in the usual way, taking 1.5cm seam allowances. Press.

2 *Trim seam allowances* ▷
Trim each seam allowance in turn, trimming more from the piping and/or frill than from the main fabric, so that the seam allowances are all different widths. The narrowest should be about 3mm wide, and each subsequent seam allowance you trim should be 2-3mm longer than the previous one. Press to one side and neaten seam allowances together (with zigzag stitch) before turning right side out and inserting cushion pad.

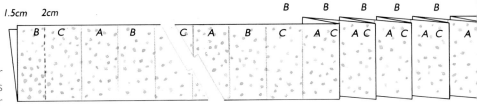

PLEATED FRILLS

A crisply-pleated frill is a smart trim for a rectangular cushion. For a generous finish, allow three times the perimeter of the cushion when making up the trim. Once the pleats are prepared, insert them into the seam as for a frill. Include 1.5cm seam allowances. Where possible, arrange seams so they fall inside the pleats.

1 Knife pleats △
Use a double width of fabric, folded in half down its length, or neaten the edge. Decide on a suitable width for each pleat (2-3cm usually looks good). Leave 1.5cm for seam allowance, then mark the pleating lines. Pleat the strip, so that point A meets point C.

2 Box pleats ▷
For box pleats, prepare the strip and mark it. Follow the diagram to pleat it, folding one point A up to point C and the next back to the same point.

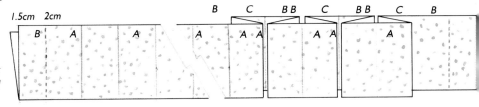

QUICK COVER WITH FLAT TRIM

This cover is easy to make if your sewing machine does satin stitch.

1 Cut out fabric
For the front panel, cut fabric 7cm larger all round than the cushion pad. For the back panel, cut fabric 7cm larger all round, plus 3cm in one direction to allow for zip. Set in zip.

BRIGHT IDEA

Pillowcase-style closure To save the expense of a zip, and the nuisance of hand-sewn openings, make a tuck-in similar to a pillowcase. Cut the front panel as usual. For the back panel, cut two pieces of fabric, one the size of the back plus 1.5cm seam allowance all round. Cut the second panel the same width as the first by 10cm deep. Neaten one edge of the first back panel and one long edge of the second, taking 1cm double hems. Lay the smaller panel on the larger panel, right side of the smaller facing the wrong side of the larger. Tack together, and make up the cushion as though they were a single panel.

▷ *Set and match*
By using fabrics from the same range it is easy to achieve an instantly co-ordinated effect over a wide range of shapes and styles.

2 Stitch seam ▷
Lay the front panel on back panel, wrong sides facing and raw edges matching. Pin and tack panels together, 7cm inside raw edges. Topstitch the panels together, making two rows of stitching for decorative effect.

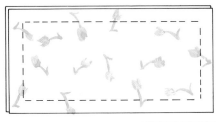

3 Neaten edges ▷
Tack outer edges of flat trim together, 1cm from raw edge. Use a fine satin stitch to join layers of border, then trim away raw edges, cutting as close to the line of satin stitch as you can.

4 Shaped edges ▷
For a more striking effect, after tacking the layers of the trim together, mark scallops or a deep zigzag on the trim with dressmaker's chalk. Stitch with satin stitch as before, following the marked line. Carefully trim away the raw edges.

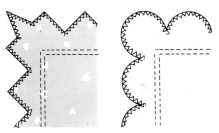

A SIMPLE SLIP-ON LAMPSHADE

Start lampshade making with this
simple slip on shade which
is easy to remove for cleaning.

A slip-on lampshade is the simplest of all shades to make – there is no complicated fitting, no special shaping, and no taping and sewing to the frame. The shade is attached to the frame by a ribboned casing at the top, and held in place with an elasticated casing at the bottom so you can easily slip it off the frame for cleaning.

Choose a frame with a round or oval top and bottom ring. The top ring should be smaller than the bottom ring and the struts must be straight as in an empire or drum, or bowed out as in a tiffany. Do not use frames with a shaped bottom edge.

A shade with a narrow top and a wide bottom throws a pool of light downwards and is ideal for hanging over a dining table, particularly if it is on a rise-and-fall fitting.

Preparing the frame Lampshade frames are available in plain metal or coated with white plastic.

Plain metal frames must be painted, or they will rust and mark the shade. Before painting, remove any rust by rubbing down with sandpaper and file off any rough or sharp spots. Paint the struts and rings with white enamel paint, but do not paint the gimbal (the centre

ring that attaches to the light bulb holder).

Choosing lampshade fabric The thinner and lighter coloured the fabric, the more light will shine through the shade. A thick, dark fabric will only throw the light from the top and bottom of the shade.

Is lining necessary? A lining makes a shade look neater and more professional inside, and also helps to reflect light from inside the shade – a pale colour is the best choice, particularly for a dark fabric shade. A lining will also help to prevent the light bulb from showing through a very thin, light fabric.

Lining does, of course, add extra bulk to the shade fabric. If the top ring of the frame is much smaller than the bottom, as with a large tiffany, this could make it impossible to gather up the fabric tightly enough to fit. In this case, use a lightweight lining such as lawn.

A pool of light
Make up the lampshade in a fabric which matches the soft furnishings in a room. If the fabric is liable to shrink, pre-wash both it and the lining before making up the shade.

CHECK YOUR NEEDS

☐ Lampshade frame
☐ Fabric for shade
☐ Lining fabric (optional)
☐ 4mm ribbon for top casing
☐ 4mm elastic for bottom casing
☐ Frill or beading for bottom edge (optional)

plus:
☐ Safety pin
☐ Scissors
☐ Pins
☐ Needles
☐ Sewing thread

CALCULATING THE AMOUNT OF FABRIC

To calculate the length of fabric needed, measure the frame height, following the curve or slope of the side (A).

Add 5.5cm at the top for the casing (B) – this will form a gathered frill that stands above the ring and hides it.

Then add an allowance for the elasticated casing at the bottom (C). The depth of the bottom casing should not be more than one fifth of the height of the frame, so that heat from the bulb can escape. For example, for a 30cm high frame, you need a 6cm casing. To calculate the casing allowance, double the size of the finished casing and add 5mm.

To calculate the width of fabric needed, measure the circumference (round the outside) of the shade at its largest point and add 2cm for seam allowance.

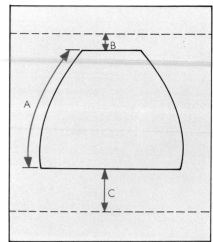

---

1 Cut out fabric
Cut out a piece of fabric to the dimensions required. Cut an identical piece in lining fabric if applicable.

If the circumference of the shade is greater than the width of your fabric, you will need to join two pieces of fabric. Measure half the circumference of the frame and add 2cm for seam allowances, then cut two pieces of fabric to these measurements.

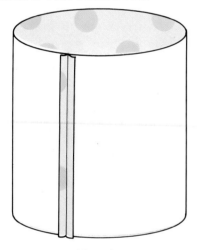

2 Join main fabric △
With right sides facing, join the fabric for the shade with 1cm seams to make a tube. Repeat for the lining fabric.

For unlined shades, neaten the seam edges with a machine zigzag stitch or oversew by hand, then press. Do not neaten seam edges if you are lining the lampshade fabric (see Step 3).

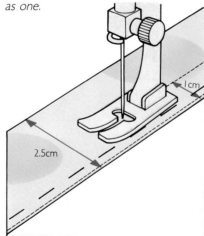

3 Attach lining △
Press fabric and lining seams open, then place wrong sides together and tack round top and bottom edges. From now on, treat the fabric and lining as one.

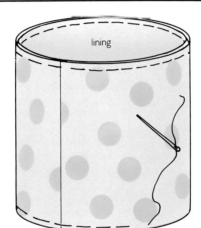

4 Make top casing △
Turn 5mm to wrong side along top edge of fabric and tack. Turn a further 2.5cm to wrong side and tack.

Then sew along lower edge of turn and again 1cm higher up to make a casing for the ribbon. Remove tacking.

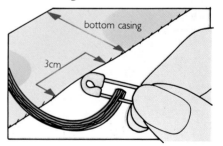

5 Cut a slit in top casing △
With a small pair of pointed scissors, cut a slit on the inside of the top casing through only one layer of fabric (and lining if applicable) just large enough to thread the ribbon through. Overcast edges of slit to neaten.

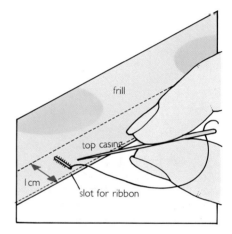

6 Make the bottom casing △
Turn 5mm to wrong side along bottom edge of shade and tack. Then turn the fabric again to the wrong side to the depth of the bottom casing (which you have already calculated) and tack. Slipstitch along the edge of this casing, leaving 3cm open.

Attach a small safety pin to one end of elastic and thread it through the casing. Pin the ends of elastic together to stop them slipping back.

7 **Insert ribbon in top casing**
Measure the top ring circumference, add 20cm, and cut a length of 4mm ribbon to this length. Then thread the ribbon through the top casing in the same way as elastic (see Step 6); pin the ends of ribbon together to secure.

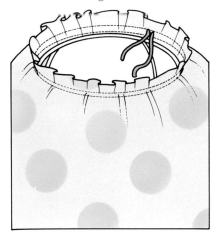

8 **Fit the shade** △
Gently pull the tube of fabric over the frame, aligning at least one seam with a metal strut and the top casing with the top ring of the frame.

Draw up the ribbon in the top casing until the shade fits the ring. Make necessary adjustments so that gathers are even and a small frill stands above them. Knot the two ends of ribbon around the ring to hold the shade.

9 **Adjust the bottom casing**
Unpin the elastic in the bottom casing and pull it up underneath the frame until the fabric is taut. Pin and sew the elastic together securely; cut off any surplus and close the gap in the casing with slipstitch.

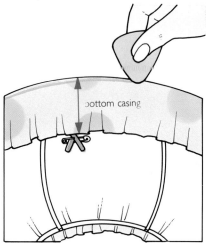

10 **Adding a trim** △
If you are adding a trim (see overleaf), pin the elastic but do not cut off surplus. Mark round the bottom of the frame with a line of tailor's chalk. Untie the ribbon, remove shade from frame and stitch trim in position on marked line.

BRIGHT IDEA

A READY-MADE FINISH

For a shade with a ready-made trim along the bottom edge use broderie anglaise, or a similar fabric, with one pre-shaped edge.

This type of shade is only suitable for a frame that has a bottom that is wider than the top – a tiffany shade or tapered drum, for example. Cut the fabric to the height of the frame, plus top casing allowance, plus the depth of the drop you want to hang below the bottom edge of the frame. For the width, measure the circumference of the bottom edge of the frame and add 2cm for a seam allowance. If you are adding a lining for a fine fabric like broderie anglaise, the depth of the lining should omit the bottom drop allowance: simply add a 5mm turning instead.

Follow the basic instructions for making up and fitting a slip-on shade but do not make a casing at the bottom. Slip the fabric over the frame and pull up the ribbon at the top. The shade will overhang the bottom of the frame, giving a shaped bottom edge.

If the broderie anglaise has slots for threading a ribbon, as shown in the picture, you can use them to hold the shade firmly to the frame.

FINISHES FOR THE BOTTOM EDGE

Although the bottom of the shade can be left plain, a sewn-on trim can look very attractive. A fringe of colourful beads or a frill made from a co-ordinating fabric or lace can add an extra soft and pretty touch.

Adding a patterned beaded fringe ▷

To calculate roughly how many beads you will need, use coloured pencils to mark out a pattern repeat on graph paper. Then count up how many beads of each colour you will need for one pattern repeat and multiply by the number of repeats needed to trim the shade. Add a drop bead for each beaded strand.

Start each strand with a drop bead slotted on a single thread. Then make a double thread by passing the loose end back through the eye of the needle and slot the remaining beads on to it according to the pattern. Neatly sew ends of threads to chalk-marked fold of shade.

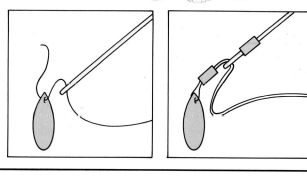

Adding a frill ▷

To calculate fabric for a frill, measure the circumference of the bottom of the frame and cut a piece of fabric or lace 1½ times this length. Neaten both long raw edges of frill with a double hem and join short ends to make a complete circle.

Gather the frill up evenly to fit the bottom of the frame. Remove the elastic in the bottom casing of the shade

and stretch the fabric out. Then topstitch the frill to the shade along the chalk-marked line, taking care not to sew over the 3cm gap left in the casing.

Rethread the elastic and secure, replace fabric on frame, knot top ribbon in place and pull bottom casing elastic up to fit. Sew elastic together, cut off surplus and slipstitch the gap in the casing closed.

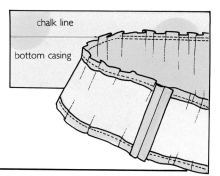

Adding a scalloped edge

For a neat scalloped edge which fits round the frame exactly, first make a pattern by cutting a length of paper the exact measurement of the circumference of the bottom edge of the frame.

Fold the paper in half, then in half again and continue folding until you have reduced the paper to about half the required width of a finished scallop.

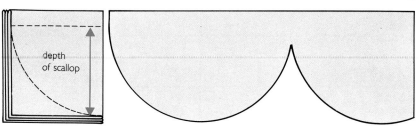

1 Cut a pattern △

Mark the depth of the scallop plus a 5mm seam allowance on to the folded paper and use a compass or a coin to draw a quarter-circle arc to the marked depth. Cut through all the layers of folded paper along this arc. Open up the paper carefully and you will have a

row of even scallops which should fit the frame exactly.

Using the paper pattern, mark scallops on to the fabric by drawing neatly round the scalloped edge with a piece of tailor's chalk.

2 Cut a scalloped edge ◁

Add a 1cm seam allowance at each end of the trim before cutting out the fabric. Neaten the scalloped raw edges with zigzag stitch or blanket stitch and trim away any excess fabric.

Join the ends of the trim with a 1cm seam, press open and trim to match scallops if necessary. Fold the top seam allowance to the wrong side and attach trim to the fabric shade by topstitching along the marked straight edge.

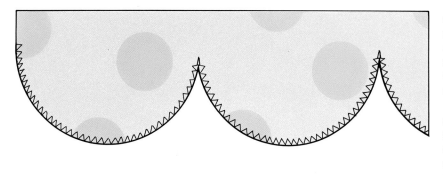

MAKING PLEATED LAMPSHADES

Lighting is an important feature in any room, so make your own shades to match your decorative scheme.

Lighting is one of the main aids to setting the atmosphere of a room, so it is worth paying some attention to the finish of your lampshades. Gently pleated lampshades are the perfect finishing touch in a softly decorated modern room, a cottagey room or a classically styled setting. By choosing fabrics and trimmings to tone or contrast with existing fabrics, you can achieve a well co-ordinated look at minimum cost.

Tailored, tightly stretched, waisted and shaped lampshades require practice and patience to perfect, but gathered or pleated shades with their softer finish are easier to make. The first thing you have to do when making up your own shades is to choose a frame in a shape to suit the style of your room. Then you have to bind the frame with tape, to give you a surface to which you can stitch the fabric you have chosen to cover the frame.

TOOLS AND EQUIPMENT

Lampshade frames Frames come in a wide range of sizes and shapes. This method of pleating the shade can be used to cover any strutted frame with straight or sloping sides. A straight drum-shape is quick and easy to cover. A coolie shade, where the top ring is much smaller then the bottom ring, looks particularly effective because the pleats fan out from the top. Do not use a frame with curved struts at the sides – this style must have straight struts.

Bear in mind that as well as looking at the shape of the frame, you must look at the fixing, to ensure that it will fit your lamp base or ceiling pendant. (Some shades are designed specifically for ceiling pendants.)

Tape is used to cover the lampshade frame so that the pleated fabric can be stitched directly to it. Buy straight cotton tape made specially for the purpose – it is 13mm wide, and you can easily dye it to tone with your fabric.

To find the total length of tape needed, measure all round the top and bottom rings of the shade, and along each strut (but not the struts which hold the shade to the light fitting). Multiply this figure by three.

You will also need pins, needles and sewing thread.

High, wide and handsome
Watered-silk-look fabric set in broad pleats makes a very effective shade for a classic ceramic lamp base. A bias trim in the same fabric adds an extra dimension to the pattern.

CHOOSE AND MEASURE

Choosing fabric Pleated shades should be made from fine fabrics such as chiffon, georgette, crepe, lawn or glazed cotton, that can easily be formed into pleats. Sheer fabric can be used if you back it with a lightweight woven interfacing, or use the fabric double so that the light bulb and frame will not show through.

To calculate the length For a drum-shaped shade, measure the circumference of one ring. Multiply this figure by three and add 10cm. For a coolie shade, measure the circumference of the larger bottom ring. Multiply this figure by 1½ and add 10cm.

If you have to use more than one width of fabric, allow an extra 5cm on each extra piece for joining up.

To calculate the depth measure along one strut and add 5cm.

Lightweight interfacing can be used to back thin fabric so that the frame will not show through. You will need a piece the same size as the fabric for the shade. Alternatively, for fine fabrics, double the length of fabric needed and work with double thickness.

Bias binding is a convenient method of trimming the top and bottom of the shade, or you can make your own bias fabric strips.

If you use bias binding, measure the circumference of the top and bottom rings, and cut a length to each measurement plus 3cm.

If you are making your own binding, cut bias strips (see page 253) 4cm wide and join them to make up lengths to fit the top and bottom rings, allowing 1.5cm for seams where necessary.

TAPING THE FRAME

The top and bottom rings of the frame, and each strut connecting them, must be taped as a base for stitching the fabric shade in place. Do not tape the struts which are for fixing the shade to the lamp base.

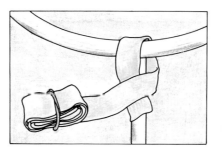

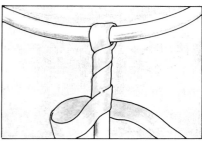

1 Prepare the tape
Measure the struts and, for each except one, cut a piece of tape three times the length. Then wind up the cut tape and secure it with a rubber band, leaving about 20cm loose from the bundle. This will stop it getting twisted as you work.

2 Start taping one strut △
Hold the loose end of tape against the top front of a strut so it hangs down the strut about 5mm. Take the bundle of tape up over the top ring, round behind and across the front to wrap over the loose end.

3 Finish taping the strut △
Work down the strut to the bottom ring, wrapping the tape diagonally so that it overlaps slightly. Make sure that it is wound smoothly and very tightly – if it is loose enough to twist on the metal, start again.

---

4 Secure the tape ▽
At the bottom of the strut, secure the tape by passing it round the bottom ring and back through the loop to make a knot. Pull the knot tight and leave the loose end of tape dangling.
Tape each of the struts except one using this method.

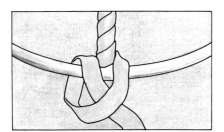

5 Prepare remaining tape
Measure the top and bottom rings, and the last untaped strut. Cut a piece of tape three times this length, and wind it up in a neat bundle, held with an elastic band as before.

6 Tape the top ring ▷
Hold the loose end of the tape against the top ring at the join with the untaped strut. Then wind the tape round to the inside of the ring and back over the ring again to wrap over and secure the loose end.
Then bind the top ring as on the struts, working right round to the untaped strut again.

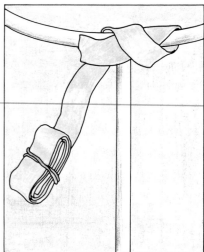

7 Tape the bottom ring ▷
When you reach the untaped strut, wind the tape round it in a figure of eight and then tape down its length. At the bottom of the strut, wind the tape round in a figure of eight and start to work round the bottom ring in the same way as the top.
At each join between bottom ring and strut, trim the dangling surplus tape to leave a 1cm end and work the figure of eight over this end to secure it.
Trim the very end of the tape to 5mm. Turn under and stitch it neatly to the bound ring on the inside.

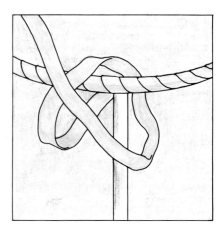

A PLEATED DRUM SHADE
A drum (or nearly drum-shaped) shade is the easiest shape to cover if you are not experienced.

1 Cut out and prepare fabric
The fabric should be three times the distance round the frame, by the depth of the frame, plus a 2.5cm seam allowance all round. For sheer fabrics, cut two layers of fabric, or one of fabric and one of lining, and tack together 3cm from raw edges all round.

Finish the side edges of the fabric, unless they are selvedges, with machine zigzag to prevent fraying. Top and bottom edges are left raw as they are neatened with bias binding.

2 Mark up pleats
Measure the distance between two struts on the top ring and decide on a pleasing number of pleats to fit round this. It is a good idea to check the effect by pleating some of the fabric, as you may find some sizes of pleat suit the fabric better than others.

3 Mark pleat positions ▷
Using tailor's chalk, draw a line to mark a 1.5cm overlap allowance at the end of the fabric (this is tucked into the last pleat to give a neat finish). Then use chalk to mark out the pleat positions along top and bottom edges of fabric. For each pleat, mark its width, then twice its width for the underlap.

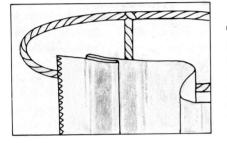

4 Pin to the frame ◁
Leaving the overlap allowance free, make the first pleat. (Keep the fold line straight with the grain of the fabric if it is a straight-sided drum shade.) Pin the pleat to the top ring so that the chalk line lies on a strut and the top edge of the pleat overlaps the ring by 2.5cm.

5 Pin round the frame
Pin the pleats into place around the top of the frame between the first two struts. Then pin round the lower edge of that section keeping the pleats taut, straight and even. Repeat for each section of the frame. If the lower ring is larger, adjust the pleats – see Pleated Coolie Shade (below).

6 Tuck in raw edges ◁
When you get to the point where the fabric meets, lap the last pleat over the raw edge you started with, arranging the fabric so that both the ends are tucked into pleats. Re-pin the first and last pleats if necessary to completely cover the frame.

7 Stitch the fabric ◁
Oversew all round the top of the frame from the outside, making sure each pleat is firmly stitched on to the taped ring and removing pins as you work. Repeat round the bottom ring.

8 Trim seam allowance
Trim off the surplus fabric from above the top ring and below the bottom ring, carefully cutting close to the stitching so that the fabric is flush with the frame. (See separate section overleaf for instructions for trimming the edge of the frame.)

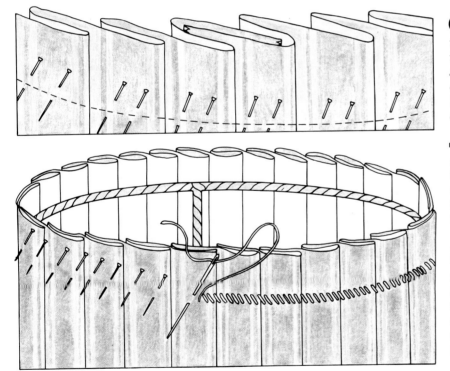

A PLEATED COOLIE SHADE
Working on a coolie shade is slightly different because of the size difference between top and bottom rings.

1 Calculate amount of fabric
To calculate the amount of fabric you need to cover the frame, measure around the bottom ring and multiply this figure by 1½. Measure a strut to give the depth of fabric. Add 2.5cm seam allowance all round and cut out.

2 Calculate the size of the pleats
Divide the length of the fabric by the circumference of the smaller ring to find out how much fullness each pleat must take up. For example, if the larger ring measures 100cm round, and the smaller ring measures 25cm round, each pleat has to take up six times the fullness of the fabric (i.e. the lower ring is 100cm, the fabric is 150cm long, and the pleating round the top of the frame must take up 150/25 = 6).

A good size of pleat in this case would be 5mm, with 2.5cm folded under each pleat. You will then be able to fit 50 pleats (150cm/3cm or 25cm/5mm) round the top of the frame.

The calculations may seem quite tricky, but you can experiment and adjust the size of the pleats and the fullness before the final stitching is done.

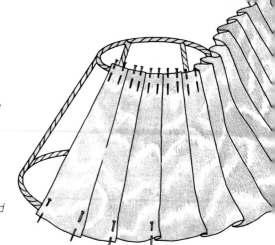

3 *Mark and fold the pleats* ▽
Work along the top edge of the fabric, first marking a 2.5cm seam allowance, then the width of the pleat, alternating with the underlap allowance of the pleat.

Fold up the pleats and pin in place to ensure that your calculations were accurate and the fabric fits neatly round the top.

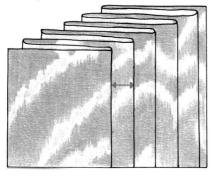

4 *Attach the fabric* ▷
Working on one section of the shade at a time, pin the fabric in place. Pin along the top, from one strut to the next, holding the pleats neatly, then stretch the fabric down in line with the struts and pin the fabric to the lower ring, ensuring the fullness is distributed evenly.

Tuck under seam allowance at the ends of the fabric. Stitch to the rings and trim away seam allowance as for a drum-shaped shade.

TRIMMING THE SHADE

All that remains is to neaten the edges of the shade where you have trimmed the fabric away.

1 *Prepare to trim*
Press 5mm to the wrong side, down each long edge of bias strip (this may be pre-pressed on purchased binding). With wrong sides together, fold the bias binding in half along its length and press.

2 *Attach the trim* ▷
Open out the binding and pin to the shade round upper and lower edges with the right side of the binding facing the right side of the shade. The binding should be positioned so that the raw edge of the binding is close to the raw edge of the lampshade fabric and the first fold line is just below the line of stitches attaching the fabric to the frame. Sew in place using a stab stitch (stab the needle through the binding and the shade fabric, draw the needle through, then stab the needle back through the shade and the binding, taking just a very small stitch each time).

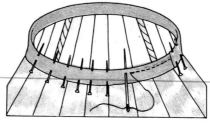

3 *Finish the trim* ▷
Fold the binding over the top of the shade (or the bottom of the shade) and slipstitch it in place stitching just inside the previous row of stitches. Finally neaten the ends: cut one at a 45° angle, turn under and lap over the other one. Secure with small stitches.

Low, soft and charming △
A coolie-shaped shade in a fine, softly pleated fabric makes the perfect partner for a spherical base.

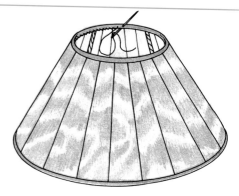

BRIGHT IDEA

Loosely fitted shade For a soft effect, with a minimum of sewing, make a coolie shade which is fitted to the top ring only. Cut the fabric 1½ times the circumference of the lower ring, plus 1.5cm seam allowance, at each end, by the depth of the frame plus a total of 7.5cm seam allowance.

Join the two short edges with a flat seam, right sides together. Hem the lower edge. Bind only the top ring of the lampshade frame, and attach the fabric as described in Step 4 above, round the top of the frame only. Adjust the size of the pleats to take up all the fullness if necessary. The fabric can then be left to fall over the lower ring of the frame.

MAKING YOUR OWN LOOSE COVERS – I

Loose covers for chairs or sofas can give a room a whole new look. Start with simple shapes and clever ideas.

Traditional tailored loose covers are not as difficult to make as you might think. They are pieced and pinned together on the chair itself, rather like dressmaking on a tailor's dummy. This gives you plenty of opportunity to adjust the shape and fit, before you actually stitch the cover.

However, fitted loose covers do involve a fair amount of sewing. Use good quality fabrics, or you may find that having spent days stitching a cover, it wears out after a couple of years. So rather than start with an intricate shape, in this chapter we look at two ideas for simple but stylish loose covers, before

going on to larger pieces of furniture.

If you're not very experienced, it would be a good idea to start by making some gusseted cushions (see Simple Gusseted Cushions). The techniques used to make these uniform shapes are adapted to make full covers. For tied-on styles, try wrapping old pieces of sheeting round the chair or sofa to test the amount of fabric needed before you buy.

FABRICS AND FASTENINGS

Avoid heavy fabrics, as some of the seams will have up to four layers of fabric, plus piping, which may be heavy going on a standard sewing machine. Furnishing cottons and linen unions are usually the most suitable choices – although you can use finer fabrics for occasional furniture which does not get so much wear.

Fastenings Because the covers fit tightly, they may have to have fastenings – usually down one of the back corner seams. These may be hook-and-eye tapes or zips. For the simpler, softer styles in this chapter, use Velcro or fabric ties. Covers are usually tied under the furniture too, with tapes running through casings.

Measuring up Before calculating how much fabric you need, you will have to measure up the chair or sofa. Decide where the seams should go and what type of opening you want to make. Then measure each section of the chair and add 5cm in each direction, taking the maximum measurement where sections have curved seams. You can use the seams on the existing fitted (usually calico) cover as a guide. If the chair or sofa already has a loose cover, you can use this as a pattern.

CHECK YOUR NEEDS
☐ Tape measure
☐ Pencil and paper
☐ Ruler
☐ Dressmaker's chalk
☐ Scissors
☐ Pins and needles
☐ Fabric for cover
☐ Piping cord
☐ Contrast fabric for pleats, piping and ties (optional)
☐ Sewing machine
☐ Thread

Pretty well dressed
This upholstered dining chair is softened with cover, skirt, and contrasting bows in glazed cotton. Adapt the technique for other shapes.

MEASURING UP

The first thing to do is to decide on the positions of the seams and measure up the chair. Here we show how to measure and cut out panels for a dining chair with an upholstered back and seat. The technique can be adapted for other shapes and styles of chair.

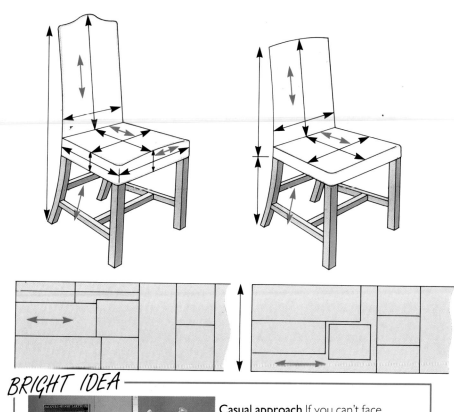

1 *Measuring up ▷*
Measure each section at its maximum height, depth or width, adding 5cm in each direction for seam allowances. In some designs, you will also need to add an allowance for tuck-ins if the cover tucks into a deep crack between back and seat. Allow an extra 15cm along any edge which has to be tucked in.

2 *Plan a cutting layout ▷*
Decide on the fabric you are going to use, and draw up a scale drawing, showing the width of the fabric with two parallel lines. Sketch in the various panels of fabric, ensuring that they lie along the straight grain of the fabric as indicated.

3 *Calculate fabric*
When you are happy with the layout, calculate how much fabric you will need. If you want to pipe any of the seams, work out how much piping and bias-cut fabric for binding you will need.

BRIGHT IDEA

Casual approach If you can't face intricate sewing, cover a chair with the ultimate loose cover: a length of fabric, thrown over the existing cover. Choose a bold pattern for drama or a plain fabric for a more subtle effect. Neaten the edges and tuck the fabric firmly into the angles between the seat, arms and back to anchor it.

SLIPOVER COVER WITH SKIRT

These instructions are for a cover for an upholstered, armless chair, like the one shown on the previous page: they could equally well apply to a hardbacked chair with an upholstered seat. A simple, gathered skirt and bows down each side to tie the cover in place give an informal finish. Measure up and cut out all panels except the skirt.

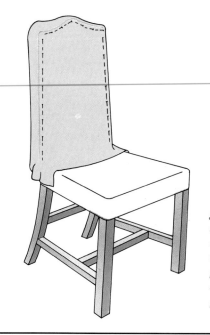

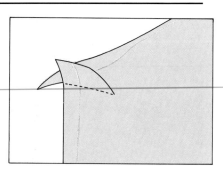

1 *Fit front panel ▷*
Lay the front panel centrally on the back of the chair, pinning it in place with the right side of the fabric facing the chair. Use dressmaker's chalk to mark seamlines. Leave a generous (15cm) seam allowance at the lower edge, where the cover tucks in to the crease between the back and seat of the chair.

2 *Take in fullness △*
At the top corners, if there is not a gusset round the chair back, you may need to take in fullness for a neat fit. Make a small dart, with the point at the front corner of the back of the chair, pinning it so that the stitching line lies along the angle of the corner. Make and pin any other pleats and tucks necessary for a good fit.

3 *Fit the back panel*
Position the back panel on the back of the chair, with the right side of the fabric facing the chair, so that the edges of the panel match the edges of the front panel. Pin the panels together down the sides and across the top, following the chalked seamlines.

4 *Tack and stitch*
Tack the darts and stitch. Press to one side, towards the centre back of the chair. Tack any other pleats and tucks. Pin piping into curved top seam, then tack and stitch seam. Neaten seam allowances together and press towards the back panel.

5 *Seat panel*
Lay the seat panel on the seat, right side facing chair, and mark the seamline round the edge of the chair with chalk.

6 Gusset pieces ▷
Pin seat gusset pieces round sides and front of seat, with right side of fabric facing seat, pinning seamlines at front corners to match front corners of seat panel. Tack and stitch seams at corners of gusset. Press seams open.

7 Position seat section
Re-position seat section and joined gusset pieces round sides and front of seat, right side of gusset facing chair. Pin gusset sections to seat section, ensuring the seamlines match the corners of the seat panel.

8 Check fit ▷
Before stitching gusset to seat, slip the back section over the back of the chair, inside out, and pin lower edge of front panel of back cover to back edge of seat panel. Where the seam at the back of the seat meets the gusset/seat seam, mark the top edge of the gusset (see arrow). Beyond this point, pin the top edge of the gusset to the front panel of the back of the chair.

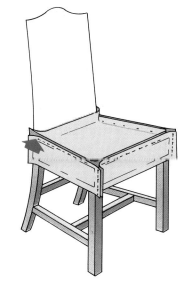
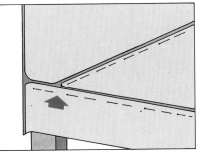

9 Seat seams
When you are happy with the fit, insert piping round top of gusset (allowing sufficient piping to reach to the back edge). Tack and stitch the seam round the top of the gusset, stitching as far as the marked points only (see arrow). Clip seam allowance across corners, trim and press towards gusset. Stitch the piping to the top edge of the gusset from marked point to the back of the seat on each side.

10 Join back section to seat
Fit the sections on the chair again and re-pin the seam along the back of the seat. You may need to trim away some of the 15cm seam allowance at each side of the back seat seam. Pin the seam in a gentle curve, so that there is a tongue to tuck into the angle of the seat. Tack and stitch seam, then neaten seam allowances together. Pin, tack and stitch front panel to top of gusset from marked point to back, clipping into seam allowances. Neaten seam allowances and press towards gusset.

11 Side openings ▷
Slip cover on to chair and fold back seam allowance along marked fold lines down the side openings. Fold back ends of gusset in line with upper part of side openings. Mark points for attaching ties spaced evenly down each side of each opening.

12 Make up ties
For each tie, cut a strip of fabric 7cm by 30cm. Fold in half along length, right sides together, and stitch across one short end and down one long edge, taking 1.5cm seam allowances. Turn right side out.

13 Finish opening edges
Pin ties to front and back panels at each marked point. Pin piping down each opening edge of front panel so that stitching line of piping meets marked fold line. At top of opening, trim piping cord away and fold piping under for a neat finish. Tack and stitch piping in place through seam allowance of front panel, enclosing ends of ties as you stitch. Stitch ties to seam allowance of back panel. Press seam allowances of piping and front panel away from opening, trim and neaten seam allowances together. Press seam allowance of back panel towards opening, so it can be tucked inside front panel. Neaten raw edge.

14 Make up skirt
For the back skirt, measure the width of the lower edge of the back panel from the neatened edge of one seam allowance to the other. Multiply this measurement by 1.5, add 3cm seam allowances, and cut a panel to this measurement by the depth of the skirt, plus 5cm hem allowance and 1.5cm seam allowance. Measure round the lower edge of gusset, round sides and front, from piping down back openings. Multiply by 1.5 and add 3cm seam allowance to find length of skirt section. Cut out panel, joining widths if necessary. Turn under 5mm then 1cm down each side edge of each skirt section and stitch. Run two lines of gathering stitches round top of skirt sections.

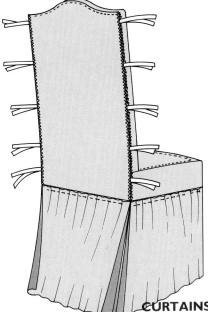

15 Attach skirt ◁
Slip cover over chair, inside out. Draw up skirt sections to fit. Pin skirt panels to lower edge of gusset round sides and front of chair and to lower edge of back panel, distributing fullness evenly. Insert piping into seam before tacking and stitching. Neaten seam allowances together and press towards gusset. With cover in position, mark hemline. Turn up and stitch 1cm round lower edge of hem, then turn up hem along foldline and slipstitch in place.

PLEATED SKIRTS

These covers have inverted pleats in a contrast fabric down the centre of the back and at each front corner of the chair. Piping round the edge of the seat is in the same fabric as the pleats.

1 *Measure up and cut out*
Measure up as before. Cut out panels 5cm larger in each direction, allowing 15cm for the tuck-in at the back of the seat and the bottom of the front panel. For the back panel, add 3cm to the width measurement, to insert the inverted pleat. Prepare piping.

2 *Cut out pleat fabric*
For the centre back pleat, cut a panel the same height as the back panel and 35cm wide. For the corner pleats, cut two panels the same height as the skirt sections, and 35cm wide.

3 *Make up back panel* ▷
Cut the back panel in half down its length. With right sides together and raw edges matching, join each long edge of the pleat fabric to each side of the back panel, taking 1.5cm seams. Press seam and neaten seam allowances together.

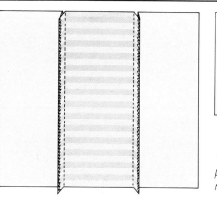

4 *Fold pleat* △
With wrong sides facing, fold pleated section in half so that seam lines match. Tack together down seam lines.

5 *Re-fold inverted pleat* ▷
Open out on a flat surface so that right side of the back panel pieces face down. Press pleat so that it is flat against the back panel with the centre of the pleat matching the seam lines which are tacked together. Tack pleat in place at top edge. Make two lines of tacking

stitches down centre of pleat, close to and on each side of tacked seamline, stitching through to right sides of back panel sections. From right side, stitch pleat in place, topstitching from top of back panel to halfway down the back panel, at approximately seat level.

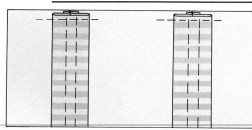

6 *Make up skirt section* ◁
Trim side edges of front skirt so it is 3cm wider than the finished measurement. Join contrast pleat panels and set pleats in place at the corner seams, as for back panel, topstitching the pleat in place for just 15cm down from top edge.

7 *Make up cover*
Pin and tack the remaining seams in the following order, fitting the pieces on the chair as before. Join seat panel to pleated skirt panels at sides and front, inserting piping. Join lower edge of front panel to back of seat panel, shaping the tuck-in allowance to fit down between the front and back sections. Finally, join back panel to rest of seat, down sides and across top edge. Pin and tack before stitching to ensure that the cover will slip on and off easily. If necessary, put a zip or Velcro fastening into one side opening.

8 *Hem and buttons*
Unpick tacking down pleat openings. Fit cover on chair, right side out, and mark hemline. Turn up 1cm all round and stitch, then turn up hem and slipstitch in place. (You will get a neater effect if you unpick the last few centimetres of the pleat seams and stitch the hem of each panel of the skirt separately, then re-stitch seams.) Stitch a button in place on either side of the centre back pleat, to strengthen the seam at the top of the pleat.

◁ *Italian style*
Slick colours and simple lines give these slipover covers with inverted pleats instant pzazz.

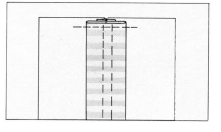

MAKING LOOSE COVERS – 2

From gusseted cushions and slipover covers for upholstered dining chairs it is a simple step to full loose covers.

Loose covers have a great many advantages over tight, permanently fixed covers for upholstered furniture. The first is that they can be washed or dry cleaned regularly, which not only keeps them looking better, but helps them to wear better too. You can have new covers made up when old ones become worn or when you want to change your colour scheme, and you can even go as far as having two sets of covers, to give your room a different look for winter and summer months.

Professionally-made covers are expensive, and there seem to be fewer and fewer local seamstresses who are prepared to make up covers and curtains for a reasonable sum. So if you have simply-shaped chairs and sofas and a little experience of home sewing it is worth making your own.

TRIMS AND FINISHES

Piping Most covers look smarter if the seams are piped: contrast piping gives a crisp finish, but it is probably better to use the same fabric for the cover and the piping if you are not experienced – this will help to disguise wobbly seams and uneven stitching.

Use no. 5 piping cord covered in 3.5cm wide bias-cut binding.

Skirts The lower edge of the cover may be finished simply with a drawstring to pull the edges under the piece of furniture. However, for a smarter finish, a straight skirt with inverted pleats at the corners or a box-pleated skirt may be added. For a softer finish with a country cottage appeal, add a gathered skirt. Complement the finish with scatter cushions trimmed to match.

Closures Traditionally, hook and eye tape was used to hold loose covers tightly closed. This was a closely woven cotton tape in two halves – one with hooks and the other with eyelets or bars to match. Now Velcro is the most popular choice, but you can also use popper tape (similar to hook and eye tape, but with press studs) or zips (choose a medium weight nylon one).

CHOOSE YOUR FABRICS

Tightly-woven furnishing cottons and linen unions are the best choice for loose covers. Look out for fabric which has been treated to resist stains – this is certainly an advantage for the first couple of years of the cover's life. If you want a patterned fabric (which will help to disguise any defects in your sewing and irregularities in the seam lines) try to use all-over patterns, rather than large motifs with borders: these need clever planning and careful positioning to be effective. It is also worth bearing in mind that the larger the pattern is, the more fabric you will need to get accurate positioning of pattern motifs.

SOFAS AND CHAIRS

The general techniques for sofas and chairs are similar. The main difference is that sofas are generally wider than the width of the fabric, so you have to join pieces of fabric to make up some of the panels for the cover. Position a full width of fabric in the *centre* of the sofa (inner and outer back panels, seat and front seat panel) and join small sections to each side to make up the width.

A tight fit
Smart fitted covers show off the simple lines of this sofa. The shape is further emphasized by inserting contrast piping along the main seam lines and round the gusseted cushions.

MEASURING UP

The first thing is to measure up the sofa or chair and decide on seam lines. The tight (usually calico) cover should give you a guide – or follow the existing loose cover if you are replacing it. See overleaf for details of allowances for skirts.

1 Measure at maximum points ▷
Divide the chair or sofa into sections, marking seam lines on the existing cover if necessary. Measure each section at its maximum depth, width or height. Measure up seat and back cushions as for gusseted cushions (see page 288). The red arrows indicate direction of grain, and blue lines indicate seams to be piped.

2 Add seam allowances
To give you plenty of spare fabric, so you can adjust the fit of the cover, add 10cm for seam allowances to each dimension. Along the sides and back of the seat there is generally a crack, into which you tuck the seam of the cover so to anchor it. Allow an extra 15cm along any of the edges of the panels that are going to tuck in (usually the back and lower edge of the inner arm panels, the side and lower edges of the inner back panel and the side and back edges of the seat panel). Allow 20cm all along lower edges of back, outer sides and front of seat for making a casing and drawing the cover tight under the sofa.

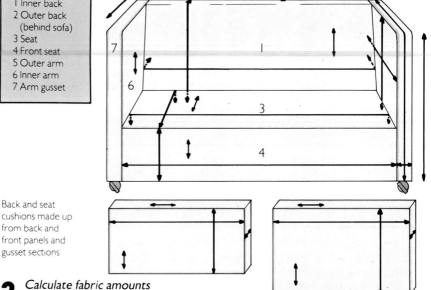

1	Inner back
2	Outer back (behind sofa)
3	Seat
4	Front seat
5	Outer arm
6	Inner arm
7	Arm gusset

Back and seat cushions made up from back and front panels and gusset sections

3 Calculate fabric amounts
On graph paper, make a scale drawing to give you a cutting layout. Start by drawing parallel lines to represent the selvedges of the fabric, and sketch in rectangles to represent the sections of the cover. If the fabric is patterned, mark the repeat along one edge of the diagram, so you can position the panels appropriately. When the layout is right calculate the amount of fabric. Allow extra for bias strips if needed.

4 Measure for closure
Measure the back outside corner of the sofa to give you the length of Velcro or other fastening required.

CHECK YOUR NEEDS
- ☐ Tape measure
- ☐ Pencil and ruler
- ☐ Paper and graph paper
- ☐ Dressmaker's chalk
- ☐ Pins and needles
- ☐ Fabric for cover
- ☐ Piping cord (optional)
- ☐ Contrast fabric for piping (optional)
- ☐ Bias binding
- ☐ Zip, Velcro or hook and eye tape, as necessary
- ☐ Scissors

MAKING THE COVER

Here we give instructions for making a cover in plain fabric (with contrast piping, to make the diagrams easier to follow). The shape is a simple, squared sofa: the seams in the first step are usually unnecessary for a chair. The cover is held firmly under the chair with a casing and drawstring.

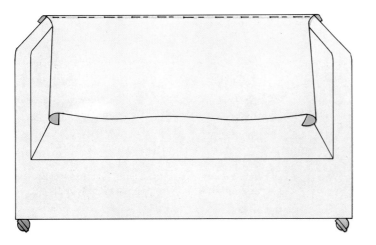

1 Join fabric to make up panels
Cut out fabric, following the cutting layout you sketched when calculating fabric amounts. The inner back, outer back, seat and front seat sections usually need extra seams. Use full widths of fabric for the centre of each of these panels, with pieces joined to each side to make up the width.

2 Make up piping
Cut out 3.5cm wide bias strips, joining lengths as necessary to make up a series of strips to fit round all the seams which are to be piped. Use the strips to cover size 5 piping cord. You will need a fair amount if the sofa or chair has extra cushions – it does help to make it all up before you start.

3 Join back and seat panels ◁
Position the inner and outer back panels on the sofa, wrong side out, pinning each piece to the sofa and marking seam lines with dressmaker's chalk. Pin seam lines to check fit, and take in any fullness with small tucks if the back of the sofa is curved, or with a neat dart if necessary at angular corners. Position the seat panel and front seat panel and pin in the same way, leaving a 15cm tuck-in allowance along the back seat seam. When you are happy with the fit, remove the panels, trim seams to exactly 1.5cm and insert piping where necessary. Tack and stitch seams and neaten seam allowances.

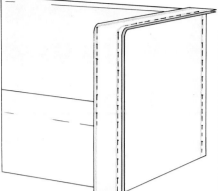
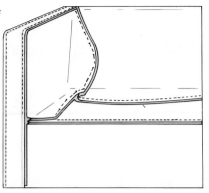
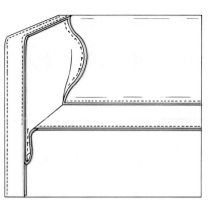

4 *Join arm sections △*
For each arm, pin sections to arms of chair, wrong sides out, and mark seam lines. Position gusset along top of arm and down front of arm. Mark and pin seams as before. Remove arm sections, trim seam allowances, insert piping, tack, stitch seams and neaten seam allowances as before.

5 *Join arms to back of seat △*
Re-position the back and seat section and the arms on the sofa, inside out, and pin seams down the inner back corners. This seam will have to be shaped, with a 15cm tuck-in allowance at the lowest point, tapering to give a neat fit at the top where the inner back panel meets the piping at the top of the inner arm. Pin sides of seat to lower edge of inner arm, with tuck-in allowance. Mark seam lines.

6 *Join front seat to arms △*
With the pieces still in position inside-out on the sofa, tuck the 15cm allowance into the crease down each side of the seat. Pin the front edge of the tuck-in at the side of the seat section to the side edge of the front panel. Pin the remaining side edge of the front panel to the inner edge of the front arm gusset section. Mark seam lines.

7 *Mark back seam lines*
Pin outer back to top arm sections at each side, and pin sides of outer back to outer arms down each corner seam line. Mark seam lines.

8 *Stitch seams*
When you are happy with the fit, remove cover, trim seam allowances accurately, insert piping, and tack (apart from down one back corner where closure is to be inserted). Stitch seams and neaten seam allowances.

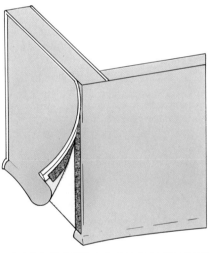

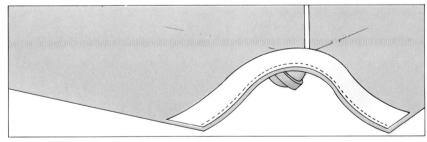

9 *Finish back opening ◁*
Turn under 5mm then 1cm down opening edge of outer back panel. Turn under 5mm down opening edge of outer arm panel. Press under along marked seam line. Pin piping down opening edge of outer arm panel, matching stitching of piping to marked seam line. Tack and stitch in place.
Pin and tack Velcro in place down each opening edge. Topstitch across the top of the opening so that neatened seam allowances are pressed away from back. Alternatively, set zip, hook and eye or popper tape into opening down outer back corner.

10 *Fit round legs ◁*
Fit cover on to sofa, inside out, and trim away fabric for a neat fit round the legs, leaving a 1cm seam allowance. Neaten the raw edge with bias binding, stitching the binding to the raw edge with a 1cm seam, then turning binding and seam allowance to inside and slipstitch folded edge in place.

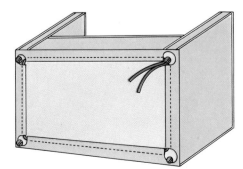

11 *Make casing ◁*
You will now have four flaps, which have to be drawn together to hold the cover in place. Turn under 1cm along each of the four long raw edges, then turn under a further 2cm. Pin, tack and stitch to make a casing. Measure each channel, and cut a length of tape to this length plus about 70cm. Thread tape through each casing in turn, starting from opening corner.

12 *Make up cushion covers*
Make up piped, gusseted cushion covers for any back and seat cushions which form part of the sofa or chair, following instructions in Simple Gusseted Cushions. Position zips in one of the gusset panels (the back panel for the seat cushions and the lower edge panel for the back cushions), so that they cannot be seen when the cushions are in position, and the cushions are therefore reversible.

ADDING A SKIRT

Start by making up the cover: this is measured exactly as for the detailed example, but omitting the 20cm allowance round the lower edge of the front seat, front and outer arms and outer back panels. Make up as far as the end of step 8.

1 Mark skirt seam line ▷
Put the cover on the sofa right side out and mark a line for the top of the skirt. The height of the line will depend on the proportions of the sofa (or chair) but about 15cm is a good depth. Measure round sofa at marked line. Trim cover 2cm below marked line.

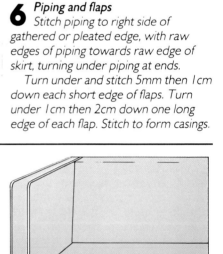

2 Calculate length of skirt
For a pleated skirt, allow three times the measurement round the chair, plus 1.5cm seam allowance at each end. For a gathered skirt, allow 1½ times the measurement, plus seam allowances. For a straight skirt with inverted pleats, add 30cm for each of the four pleats plus seam allowances. Measure from the marked line to the floor and add 3cm for the depth.

3 Cut out fabric for skirt ▷
Cut out strips of fabric to make up the skirt to the appropriate dimensions. Join strips. Where possible position seams inside pleats. For a straight skirt, position seams in the straight front and back sections of the skirt to match up with seam lines down seat front and outer back panels of sofa. Prepare sufficient piping to go all round marked line if required.

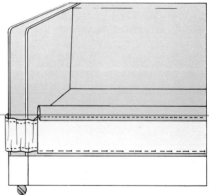

4 Cut out flaps
Measure the length of each lower edge of the sofa and subtract 15cm from each measurement. Measure from the marked line round the cover to 10cm under the sofa. Add 4.5cm. For each lower edge, cut a strip to these measurements to form a flap to go under the sofa to hold it in place.

5 Make up skirt
Turn under 5mm then 1cm down short ends of skirt and along lower raw edge. Gather or pleat skirt, pinning and tacking to hold in place (see page 306 for details of how to make an inverted pleat). At the opening corner, make half the inverted pleat at each end of the skirt.

6 Piping and flaps
Stitch piping to right side of gathered or pleated edge, with raw edges of piping towards raw edge of skirt, turning under piping at ends.
Turn under and stitch 5mm then 1cm down each short edge of flaps. Turn under 1cm then 2cm down one long edge of each flap. Stitch to form casings.

7 Attach skirt and flaps ▷ ▷
Remove cover from sofa. Pin skirt to right side of cover, with raw edge of skirt just inside neatened edge of cover, right sides facing, so that piping is sandwiched between skirt and cover. The stitching line of the piping should match the marked line round the cover. Pin flaps in place so that raw edge of flap matches raw edge of skirt, with right side of flap facing wrong side of skirt. Tack through all layers. Stitch in place and press seam allowances upwards and skirt and flaps

downwards.
Finish the cover by fitting Velcro down the opening edges and making up gusseted cushions as before.

▽ Patterns for camouflage
A fabric with an all-over pattern in soft tones of cream, beige and peach has many advantages: it disguises irregularities in seam lines and helps to mask stains and spills.

BRIGHT IDEA

Extra protection It is a good idea to use remnants of fabric to make arm covers, as the arms get a lot of wear and tear. The seam lines of the protectors should follow the seam lines of the cover. Make up the protectors as large as possible, preferably the same depth as the arm, and the same height as the inner arm, so that they can tuck down beside the seat cushion. To hold the protectors in place, stitch a small hook to each corner and make a hand-sewn bar on the cover for the hook to catch in.

CHAPTER 5

FINISHING TOUCHES

HANGING PICTURES

Pictures need placing with care if they are to look their best and enhance your home.

Most rooms look more welcoming if they contain pictures. These needn't be expensive originals; reproduction prints and posters can be every bit as attractive and effective. But, whether a valuable family heirloom or a 'cheap and cheerful' poster, a picture must be hung where it can be easily seen and enjoyed.

The mistake most often made is to hang pictures too high. As well as being impossible to see without craning your neck, pictures hung too high can make the viewer feel a bit like a dwarf.

Relationships Not only should a picture be hung at the right level, it should also relate to other objects in the room. A picture hung on an otherwise empty wall often seems lost and unconnected, as if it arrived there by accident.

Instead, place a picture above a table, sofa, desk, sideboard, bookcase or fireplace – in fact, any piece of furniture

or architectural detail that will visually 'anchor' it. This is particularly true of small pictures. Large paintings or posters can command a blank wall, but again, few people have pictures big enough to stand on their own.

Positioning You can hang a picture centrally above a piece of furniture, or to one side – whatever looks best. But remember, if all the pictures in a room are hung in the same way – each centred above a piece of furniture, for instance – the effect can be boring. Try hanging one or two off-centre.

Part of a group
This picture is hung quite low and arranged as part of the group of lamp, bowl and vases. For this sort of off-centre arrangement the picture usually looks best hung above a spot about one third along the length of the table below.

▽ **Kitchen lines**
The frame of this picture aligns with
the cupboard top and the tile border.

BRIGHT IDEA

THE RIGHT HEIGHT
The centre of a picture should be no
higher than eye level – halfway
between standing and seating eye
level is the best solution.

△ **Pairing up**
A pair of matched pictures
hung symmetrically over a
sofa creates a formal look.
Note how the space
between the two is the same
as the space between the
bottom of the pictures and
the top of the sofa.

◁ **Connections**
Hanging a large picture fairly
low over a plain sofa makes
good design sense. This is a
painting but some modern
fabrics lend themselves to
being stretched over a
batten framework to make
a large, inexpensive but
effective picture.

GROUPING PICTURES

A group of pictures creates a focal point in a room, but it takes practice to make a pleasing arrangement.

When it comes to grouping pictures, before banging holes in the wall, think about how they relate to one another.

The theme In effect, the group works as a single unit, so ideally the pictures should have something in common. The most obvious example of this is a set of prints; these should all be the same size and have a common theme. A random group of prints can be given harmony by mounting and framing them to match.

Your pictures might have similar colouring – black and white prints for instance – or be all photographs. In this case no further link is necessary.

If the group have a strong subject theme – cats or children perhaps – a variety of media, shapes and frames can be mixed together very successfully.

Even if you can find no link do not despair, arranging your choice within a fairly controlled framework can hold the group together.

Arrangements Measure the amount of wall you have available, then mark out this area on the floor with string or newspaper. Experiment with various groupings to find the most pleasing one. When you are satisfied, very lightly indicate the area of your 'frame' on the wall. Then mark the position of the first picture, usually the largest one, and hang this, follow with the next most important placing and so on (see Bright Idea, overleaf). Check the spacing as you go.

▽ *Artful arrangement*
The charm of this arrangement of flower paintings is in its deceptively casual appearance. The large picture was hung; those either side centred on it; then the last placed with its top centred on the one next to it.

BRIGHT IDEA

Work out arrangement on the floor, marking out the basic guide lines with string or on sheets of newspaper.

Below are a selection of groupings which can be adapted to suit your particular needs.

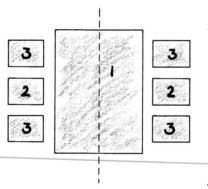

1 Pictures of the same size work best in a square or rectangle. The arrangement depends for its success on the pictures lining up absolutely accurately and all vertical spaces being equal.

2 One large picture and a set of six small ones can be arranged symmetrically. Position the large picture, then a small one centrally on each side. Place the other pictures, equally spaced on either side of them.

3 Rectangular and square pictures of varying sizes can be arranged in two rows. The top row 'hangs' from one horizontal line, the bottom row 'stands' on another. The sides should also be aligned.

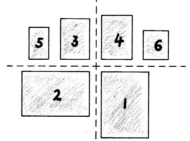

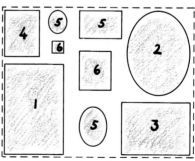

4 Pictures of varying sizes can be grouped with the largest in the middle; the next centrally on one side; then the third and fourth to line with the top and bottom of the second.

5 Group pictures around a cross. Place the largest pictures below the horizontal line balancing them with smaller ones above. Work in sequence as indicated.

6 Position a mixture of shapes within a formal framework. Starting with the largest pictures, fill in the corners; add any which touch the outside edge; then fill in the spaces with the rest.

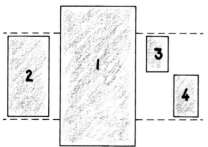

◁ *Modern simplicity*
A selection of posters in similar colourings and with matching frames rest on the same invisible horizontal line; they are equally spaced and centrally placed on the wall. The geometric feel of the arrangement suits the plainness of the room and the horizontal line makes it seem wider.

▷ *In nostalgic mood*
These objects and old photographs grouped over a wash stand have been chosen to complement this turn-of-the century interior. The basis of the design is a horizontal line from which pictures and signs hang. A large oval sepia photograph is placed over the main group and a basket of dried flowers is set below it and off-centre. The latter is balanced by a plant on the wash stand below.

▽ *Quiet prints*
In this arrangement a group of prints on a variety of subjects almost fill one wall of a modern dining room. All have white backgrounds and simple chrome frames. Three of the pictures 'hang' from one horizontal line; the others 'stand' on another. The colours echo those used in the room.

△ Mixed media
When you have a lot of pictures in different styles and media to hang, working within a fairly formal framework gives them unity. Here a variety of prints, sketches and watercolours of people more or less fill a wall. The basis of the arrangement is the bottom line, with the side lines established slightly less strongly. The top is a 'skyline' which gives interest to the design.

▷ Perfect prints
A set of six prints is the most straightforward of all groups to arrange. The classic arrangement is a formal rectangular one made up of two rows of three. They should all be framed and mounted in the same way and be evenly spaced. In this case black-and-white subjects have been mounted and framed in a colour to pick up the dominant one in the room – coral red.

MIRROR IMAGES

Play with reflection – use mirrors in a room to add light and space and to create unusual decorative effects.

Mirrors are more than simply decorative. They can be used deceptively to play with light and space.

If positioned opposite or adjacent to windows, mirrors bring extra light to rooms and are particularly useful in small dark areas. Large areas of mirror can create an illusion of greater space; an entire wall of mirror may double the width or length of a room, while a mirrored recess on either side of a fireplace gives the appearance of a long room with a central fireplace.

Where skirting may interrupt the illusion that a full-length mirror would create, a channel can be installed at floor level behind the carpet to carry the mirror. Alternatively, place some-thing in front of the mirror to disguise the skirting: a plant trough, sofa or side table add interest and also protect people from walking into the glass.

Always make sure that a mirror reflects something of interest – a picture, plant group or view of a garden. Thought should also be given to a mirror's doubling effect. A quarter-circle headboard looks like a semi-circular one when placed adjacent to a mirror. And remember if using a chequerboard tiling pattern by a mirror the effect will be lost unless half tiles are put next to the mirrored wall.

The combination of mirrors and glass can be exciting and works especially well in alcoves where, if ornaments are placed on glass shelves with a mirror behind them, they seem to float. But make sure that both sides of the objects are visually attractive.

△ Double accent
In this cloakroom the mirror plays a decorative as well as practical role. Diagonal lines help to make a room appear wider; in this case the effect of the tiling is accentuated by hanging a mirror in a diagonal position. In such a tiny space a simple colour scheme works best. Here furniture and accessories are picked out in a crisp blue and white.

◁ Illusion of space
A large mirror creates a focal point and gives an illusion of greater space in this small bedroom. Different standpoints reflect different parts of the room and a view of the garden through the window. Notice how a simple bunch of flowers placed against a mirror becomes a sizeable display.

▷ **Two-way image**
At first glance this bathroom appears to lead into a similar room through an opening. In fact, the effect is brought about by running a plainly-edged mirror behind the twin basins. Note the clever positioning of the second poster reflected in the mirror which adds to the illusion.

▽ *Reflected interest*
An ornamental mirror over a table reflects dressers on the other side of a large living room/kitchen and another room through the doorway between them. By adding interest to a plain wall and bringing light to the dark end of the room it could almost be a window.

ARRANGING GLASS

A collection of glass – plain or fancy – deserves attractive display to bring out its sparkle.

The most characteristic aspect of glass is that light passes through it, so make the most of this fact when creating a display.

A selection of vases, with or without flowers, enlivens a windowsill as it catches the light.

Glass on glass gives an almost unreal sense of fragile objects floating on air; even the most mundane things take on a special aura.

Glass- or mirror-topped tables are perfect for this type of display. Choose all one type of object for maximum impact – a collection of drinking glasses, some glass animals or a group of bottles for example.

To make the most of glass at night, you will need to light it well. Lighting from above or below is the best choice. This could take the form of a down-lighter mounted in the ceiling or incor-porated into a built-in display unit.

As glass is transparent, a little light goes a long way. Providing the shelves as well as the displayed objects are glass, a single light is sufficient.

A ceiling-mounted downlighter can be focused to bring a table display to life. Alternatively, an inexpensive, free-standing uplighter is an effective way to light a glass-topped side table but make sure it is positioned so as not to dazzle the occupants of the room.

Finally, remember that glass shows every speck of dirt and must be kept sparkling clean to remain looking good.

▽ *Mirror image*
This arrangement, lit by daylight filtered through a venetian blind, takes advantage of the fact that the curves of the objects distort shapes seen through them. The slats of the blind seem to be bent in a variety of ways. The display gains impact from the mirrored surface.

△ *Alcove arrangement*
A selection of glass arranged on glass shelves is lit from above by a fitting mounted into a bathroom alcove. The top two shelves are filled with clear white and bluish glass bottles, which let light through. Colour and a change of shape are kept for the solid bottom shelf – deep blue vases and goblets.

△ **On the sill**
A variety of vases are given a sense of unity by being grouped together in front of a curtainless window. Flowers in some of the vases help to soften the plainness of the window and to give a degree of privacy. A balance is kept between tall and low arrangements and plant colours are kept to simple yellow, green and white.

◁ **Glowing simplicity**
The stylish simplicity of an arrangement of classical shapes on a marble-topped antique chest complements the modern painting above. A group of large, rounded white shapes are counterbalanced by the small, slim, dark lustre vase. As the white jars are opaque it is possible to hide a very small lamp behind them. This gives the two nearest to the light source a lovely pearly glow. Night lights would give a similar effect but must be placed so as not to be a fire hazard or damage the wall or the glass.

DECORATING WITH RUGS

Whether it's traditional or modern, adding a rug is a quick way to spice up a room scheme.

The spectrum of rugs available ranges from oriental and traditional patterns to zingy modern designs; they do not have to be expensive to be attractive.

The choice Kelims, flat-weave Turkish rugs in geometric designs and rich earth colours, are the least expensive oriental rugs and work well with country house chintzes or with modern stripes and checks. Most often they are made of wool and are extremely hard-wearing and with age the colours actually tend to soften and improve.

There are also very acceptable copies of the more expensive oriental carpets which create the same effect as the real thing. It is well worth looking out for secondhand oriental carpets; these can often be picked up quite cheaply through advertisements in the newspaper or by attending auctions and sales of household effects.

Dhurries, usually in muted pastel colours on a creamy background, are available in wool or cotton and span a range of sizes and prices. Many dhurries, particularly the large wool ones, are fairly formal and work well in a modern, sophisticated pastel coloured room scheme.

At the cheapest end of the market there are all sorts of flat-woven cotton rugs available from chain stores, in a variety of designs and colourways. They are an ideal way to give a room a lift without a big financial commitment.

Colour schemes Rugs have a variety of roles to play in decorating a room. A monochromatic design, for instance, can be given a focus with just one dramatic rug.

One of the devices an interior designer uses to pull the various components of a room scheme together is to choose a rug to echo certain colours and design elements of the fabrics, wallcoverings and furniture. Conversely, you can use a rug as your inspiration and select furnishings to echo its colours and pattern.

On the floor Rugs can be used to 'hold' a seating area together or to split up a multi-activity room. In a long or L-shaped living/dining room, for instance, two matching or sympathizing rugs can be used – one to anchor the seating area and the other to mark off the eating space. A runner might mark a 'passage' between two different parts of a room – perhaps a seating arrangement and a study space.

On the wall Rugs make excellent wall hangings, particularly in smaller rooms where, if used in the conventional way, they would be completely hidden by furniture. You can also throw a rug over a sofa or chair or use a thin, flat-woven

Low line
An abstract design in mostly grey and cream accented with black works well in a simple modern living room where most of the interest is kept low by means of the strong horizontal lines of the table and venetian blind.

The black in the rug is repeated in the painted floor, table and accessories.

one as an unusual bed cover.

Practicalities Choosing a large rug to almost fill a room has a number of advantages over a fitting a carpet. It is always more expensive than you anticipate to carpet over all the odd corners of a room and also involves a certain amount of wastage. A big rug can, therefore, be a rather more economical buy.

In addition, a rug can be turned round to even out the wear and can easily be sent away to be cleaned when necessary.

Instead of replacing a fitted carpet which is worn or stained in the centre, you could put a large rug on top.

With a number of rugs, you can rearrange them around the house and, when you move, you simply roll them up and take them with you.

▷ *Focal point*
A large dhurrie in a geometric design holds the main seating area here and forms the focus of a sophisticated modern scheme.

△ *Wood and wool*
Mellow stripped woodwork, floorboards and furniture set off the texture and warmth of a wool rug with rich oriental colouring.

In this dining room of an older house the effect is to isolate the dining table and chairs on a rug island.

▷ *Seating area*
Rugs work well on top of worn, or inexpensive fitted cord carpet. In this case a design has been chosen to define the seating area and to pull together the colour scheme. The warm rusts and beiges and soft blues of the fabrics and the diamond pattern of the wallpaper are picked up by the rug.

◁ **Textural contrast**
The architectural lines of the furniture and fireplace are counterbalanced by a stylized floral rug with a feel of the thirties. The contrast between the clean-cut shapes and shiny hardness of the furniture, floor and whole room below dado height and the soft, deep pile of the carpet successfully isolates the dining area.

▽ **Country feel**
Plain white walls are the setting for this kitchen/dining room. Stripped wood door and floorboards have been contrasted with streamlined white and red units, red hob, sink and venetian blind.

The multi-coloured cotton rag rug blends the two themes; it picks up the colours of the scheme and echoes the country feel of the pine and the Windsor chair.

◁ **Room divider**

The problem with this sitting room is that doors to the two adjoining areas face each other. Through traffic cuts off a narrow section of the room, rendering it useless.

This disadvantage has been turned to good use by accentuating the passageway effects with a runner. On one side is the seating area and on the other a shallow desk creates a small study space. Extra chairs can be drawn into the conversation circle when necessary.

▽ **Wall hanging**

A richly patterned rug makes a dramatic statement in an otherwise neutral interior. Some oriental rugs are fragile and should not be walked on and, in any case, hanging such a rug on a wall shows the design off to advantage.

Oriental carpets such as this give an opulent feel to a room; if you cannot afford a real one, you can achieve the same effect with a less expensive copy.

BRIGHT IDEA

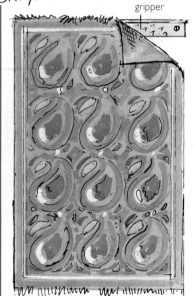

gripper

Hanging a lightweight rug

Screw a piece of carpet gripper strip, very slightly shorter than the rug width, securely to the wall.

Press the rug firmly onto the strip; it will be held in place by the little spikes.

This method is not suitable for fine or large pieces.

THE MAGIC OF PLANTS

Adding greenery brings life, zest and visual interest to a room, whatever its style.

Houseplants are one of the quickest and least expensive ways of bringing life and interest to a room. A splash of green instantly revives a rather tired scheme, and flowering plants provide a lively range of colours.

Placing plants There are few design rules about where to put plants – greenery and flowers look good almost anywhere, as long as they are not in the way of everyday activities.

Treat large floor-level plants as focal points, making full use of your lighting to show them off to best effect. Some plants need less light than others, but normal artificial lighting is no substitute for the natural daylight that all plants need.

Medium-sized plants can be placed on furniture, but there are alternatives – hanging baskets, wall-hung planters, stands or window shelves.

Small plants, such as African violets, need placing with care. They usually look and grow best grouped in a box or on a stand.

The right environment Make sure you match a plant to its growing conditions. Cacti and succulents need plenty of direct sunlight; ferns and palms survive in shade. Cyclamen, azaleas and chrysanthemums don't like the atmospheric dryness and levels of warmth found in the average centrally heated room. It helps to stand them on a saucer filled with gravel and keep it topped up.

Maidenhair ferns are delicate and are unsuitable for draughty windows. Begonias hate gas and won't thrive in a kitchen with a gas appliance, although natural gas is less harmful than coal gas.

Bromeliads such as the urn plant, queen's tears, flaming sword and variegated pineapple plant, and epiphytes such as bird's nest fern and many orchids, thrive in the warm, steamy conditions of a bathroom.

◁ *A splash of green*
Plants bring a fresh, lively look to a bathroom and ferns, ivies, bromeliads and epiphytes thrive in low light levels.

△ *Hang it all*
A china hanging basket filled with variegated ivy, tradescantia and polka-dot plants makes an eye-catching replacement for a disused light fitting and saves valuable shelf space.

You can also buy plastic hanging baskets with drip trays attached. Plant trailers round the edge and uprights in the centre.

▷ **Living highlights**

Plants and flowers help bring the garden indoors and add a human touch to your decorative scheme. The delicate structure of leaves and flowers also helps to soften hard outlines of modern furniture.

Here, the white flowers of these marguerites are perfect for cheering up a shady corner in which a darker plant would go unnoticed. More marguerites repeat the daisy theme in the foreground. With care, and frequent dead heading, they will last a lot longer than cut flowers, as long as they get sufficient sunlight at some time during the day.

◁ **Stepping out**

Greenhouse staging, painted white or dark green, is perfect for displaying groups of small plants indoors.

Alternatively, you could use a small stepladder or disused trolley. To avoid drips, stand plants in saucers or on shallow, gravel-filled plastic trays and keep permanently moist. Choose plants with a variety of shapes and colours and try to include some trailing plants to break up horizontal lines.

▷ **Mutual benefits**

This plant stand containing devil's ivy, spider plant and ivy makes a perfect feature for filling an empty spot in the living room, bedroom or hall. Inexpensive bamboo, wicker and rattan plant stands are widely available, both new and second hand.

◁ **Unusual containers**

Old teapots and jugs can make pretty cache-pots. Fill them with gravel to support plant pots and provide drainage: never plant straight in as the roots become waterlogged.

DECORATING WITH DRIED FLOWERS

Dried flowers have a particular charm and retain their appeal long after fresh blooms have faded.

dry day after the dew has evaporated. Strip off the leaves and tie the flowers into small bunches. Hang them upside down in a cool, shady place out of direct sunlight. The best flowers for drying are the 'everlasting' varieties such as helichrysums and statice. Other non-fleshy flowers, golden rod, achillea, gypsophila, lupin, sea holly, delphinium and hydrangea are also suitable for drying by this method.

Dried flower arrangements can be formal or informal to suit the setting. Baskets of flowers are particularly pleasing in a mellow pine kitchen while brass bowls and china containers of blooms complement dark wood furniture and old oil paintings. A large arrangement of dried seed heads and flowers is one of the most attractive ways to fill an empty fireplace.

There is a wide range of dried flowers available in shops, either loose or in a ready-made arrangement, or you can dry your own. Pick the flowers on a

Baskets of bloom
A selection of dried flowers, seed heads and berries massed together in baskets of varying sizes makes a stunning display. Blooms shown here include statice, hydrangea and helichrysum.

One of the simplest ways to display dried flowers is to group them together in a selection of baskets. Massed gypsophila looks good in a big basket, as do hydrangeas or peonies. Smaller baskets can be filled with more delicate blooms, small seed heads and berries. You can change the display to suit the season. Simple bunches of lavender or dried herbs can be hung from beams or from butcher's hooks hanging from a rail or grid. Discard dried flowers when they begin to lose their colour and start to shed petals.

Dried flower arrangements If you want a formal arrangement, flowers can be pushed into flower-arrangers' foam in the same way as fresh blooms. The foam should be left dry. Look for unusual containers to hold the flowers. Old fashioned china tureens, gravy boats, serving dishes and china candy baskets all make an effective and interesting display. Match the colours of the dried flowers to the colours used in the pattern on the china. If you wish, dried flowers can be mixed with fresh foliage, autumn leaves or berries.

△ An eye for tradition
This formal arrangement of rosebuds, helichrysum, lavender, hydrangeas and achillea complements the dark wood of the Jacobean-style hall table and provides a visual balance for the large brass Bhudda which would otherwise dominate the scene and dwarf the smaller pictures and ornaments.

◁ Floral focal point
An old-fashioned china jardinière topped by a display of dried flowers is a charming and effective way to create a focal point. Here, dried paeonies and hydrangeas echo the colours of the flowers on the pedestal.

◁ *Fireplace display*
An arrangement of dried flowers is a good way to fill an empty fireplace. The flowers can be arranged in a tall vase, a bowl or in a basket, as shown here. A tall, two-tiered basket, overflowing with dried flowers, fills the space in this large, imposing fireplace. One basket or vase of flowers is sufficient for most fireplaces.

◁ *Natural fragrance*
A bowl of pot pourri adds gentle scent and a spot of subtle colour to a room. A glass bowl shows the petals and herbs to best advantage.

MAKING POT POURRI

Bowls of sweetly scented pot pourri are an attractive variation on the dried flower theme. The flowers used in pot pourri depend on what is available. Rose petals are a good base and can be mixed with lavender or camomile flowers, marigold petals, lemon balm, lemon verbena or lemon geranium leaves. Herbs, such as rosemary and thyme can also be used. Thinly pared orange or lemon peel plus a dash of cinnamon, cloves, or nutmeg add originality.

Gathering and drying Collect your flower petals and scented leaves on a dry day after the dew has evaporated. Dry petals and flower heads in a cool, shady place. This will help the flowers to keep their colour. Put a handful of petals in a brown paper bag. Secure the top with an elastic band and leave the bag in a warm, dry place for two to three days. Shake the bag once a day. When petals become papery, they are ready.

Scented leaves and thinly pared orange and lemon rind can be treated in the same way. Leaves are ready when they become crumbly.

Tie lavender and herbs in bunches and hang them upside down to dry. Remove the flowers and leaves when dry and discard stems.

Fragrant oils and orris root are added to pot pourri to enhance the scent. You can buy ready blended oils or make your own mixture. Orris root powder is added to fix the perfume.

Basic pot pourri Place six teacups of rose petals in a large bowl. Add other petals, leaves and herbs of your choice. Sprinkle on four or five drops of oil then three teaspoonsful of orris root powder. Mix well with your hands. Stir daily for a week.

BRIGHT IDEA

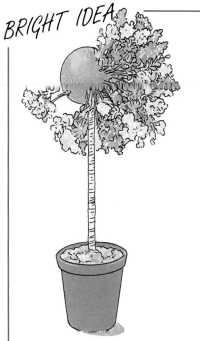

Make a tree Three-quarters-fill a flowerpot with interior filler. Insert a piece of dowelling and leave filler to set. Wind ribbon or raffia around the dowelling 'trunk' and stick a Styrofoam ball on to the top.

Cut the stems of small flowers to about 7.5cm. Push the flowers into the ball to make a well-balanced shape.

△ *Kitchen choice*
Fresh flowers quickly wilt and fade in the kitchen but a dried arrangement will withstand steam and heat. This floral tree is easy to make (see Bright Idea, opposite) and looks effective teamed with country style kitchen units. Dried flowers can be hung in bunches from the ceiling or tucked into cane and basketwork – as shown here around the frame of the mirror.

▷ *Balanced arrangement*
The fireplace in this room has been completely removed and the opening turned into an alcove. The space is too large for a simple flower arrangement so a pair of old scales has been used with a bicycle basket filled with dried flowers on one pan and brass weights on the other. An old school clock balances the display.

DISPLAY CHINA ON SHELVES OR HUNG ON WALLS

Decorative china, whatever its style, deserves showing off and there are several ways of making the most of it.

Any collection of china lends itself well to display. It might be a collection of one type of object – a variety of china eggcups or toast-racks, for example. Or it might be a rich mixture of quite different china objects – perhaps related in shape, colour or style or brought together simply because you like the look of them.

Building up a collection of china can be a lot of fun, too, and it need not be expensive. Junk shops and jumble sales, for example, are good hunting grounds for cheap and cheerful ornaments that can be every bit as effective as antique bone china.

On display China on display generally looks best if it is grouped together, but there's no need to limit the display to china alone. Mixing it with other, quite different things, can provide interesting contrasts of texture and style.

Whatever the display, make sure that you leave enough space so that each piece can be appreciated properly. And remember that the arrangement need not be fixed and static. Moving things round – perhaps even exchanging one or two pieces for different ones – is one of the quickest and least expensive ways of adding a fresh, new look to a room.

Positioning All types of china – from teacups to decorative ornaments – can be placed on almost any sort of ledge, as long as it's not in a vulnerable position. Shelves, open dressers and mantelpieces all fit the bill: glass-fronted cabinets eliminate the need for regular dusting and make ideal showcases for china that is precious.

China plates are, of course, best displayed upright if you are to appreciate their colours and patterns. They make an attractive backdrop to a shelf display, but they can also be hung on walls instead of the usual arrangements of framed pictures.

△ *Wall hanging*
This trio of two wall-hung vases and a painted china plate make a simple and attractive arrangement. The blue and yellow flowers successfully link up three objects with very different shapes and style.

◁ *Shelf display*
This collection of art nouveau china displays a wonderful variety of colour, form and texture.

To prevent plates that are displayed upright from slipping or toppling over, fix a strip of beading to the shelf or cut a shallow groove in the wood.

▷ **Plate arrangement**
Pretty plates – perhaps too old or precious to use – are grouped all over these kitchen walls.

The variations in size and shape make the display more interesting, and the blue-and-white theme is echoed in the matching wall tiles and bright blue wicker chairs.

▽ **Modern lines**
An alcove fitted with built in shelving provides perfect display for china objects of different shapes and sizes. Here, even the floor of the alcove is put to good use – perfect as long a there are no small children in the house!

The delicate colours and textures of this modern collection are elegantly displayed against pale honey-coloured walls to create maximum impact.

△ **Country cottage china**
These bright and cheerful collections of country cottage china are set off by the white-painted shelving against a soft pink background.

Screw cup hooks into shelves for hanging cups and mugs. To display individual plates, use special plate stands such as those on the bottom shelf – available in wood as well as plastic.

△ Kitchen collection

Kitchen china that can be seen and is easily accessible makes a practical and decorative display. Limit shelving to about 20cm deep for easy reach.

◁ Mantelpieces

A mantelpiece is a prime spot for displaying china to advantage: it is an obvious focal point of the room, and the height of the shelf allows each object to be seen easily.

Here, the pretty shelf collection is loosely arranged, in contrast with the bright blue china horses lined up along a moulding of the fire surround.

▷ **Dresser looks**
A china dinner set that is only used on special occasions makes an attractive and almost permanent display on the painted dresser. Do not aim for a completely symmetrical arrangement – the slightly random look as shown here is more attractive.

▽ **1930s style**
A collection of wall-vases from the art deco period make up a personal collage on these walls and there is space to add to it, from time to time.

The theme is continued with the lamp and figure on the table in front.

BRIGHT IDEA

USEFUL ACCESSORIES

Some plates are intended for wall display and have holes in their base so that they can be hung from a picture hook. For hanging ordinary plates, you can buy special plastic-coated wire plate hooks. Wood or wire plate stands are also available for displaying plates safely in an upright position on a shelf or table.

TABLE-TOP COLLECTIONS

An attractive table-top display
of treasured objects can add
the perfect finishing touch to a room.

Whether you are an avid collector or merely like to acquire knick-knacks which take your fancy, displaying them attractively enables you not only to enjoy them yourself but to show them off to others as well! A display need not be made up of valuable collectors' items; simple everyday objects – pebbles from the beach together with unusual rocks, perhaps – can be just as pleasing.

A collection of any sort adds individuality to a room – and one displayed on a table rather than hung on the wall is more flexible since you can easily alter the layout or replace some of the items as the fancy takes you.

Arranging the display Although there is no blueprint to success, the best advice is to approach the display as an artist might approach a still-life composition. Scale and proportion are all important. If there is a mixture of sizes, try to balance the large and the small, the tall and the short.

It's often easier to achieve a pleasing display if the objects are linked in some way – by subject, colour, texture or even size. But there is nothing to prevent you from creating a stunning display of items linked by no more than the fact that you like them!

The great blessing of a table-top collection is that if you aren't completely satisfied, you can simply start all over again. Try and try again – until you are completely satisfied with the end result.

A charming miscellany
This idiosyncratic assortment of objects is safely positioned against a wall. A richly-coloured floor-length tablecloth with a matching over-cloth draws attention to the arrangement.

CHOOSING THE TABLE

Above all else, the table should be stable and placed where it won't be bumped into by even the most careless members of the family.

The dimensions of the table should reflect the size of the things to be displayed. A few tiny objects may get lost on a large and imposing table top – conversely, large things may overcrowd a delicate side table. In practice, the only way of finding out whether your choice works is to try it out. A set of tiny thimbles arranged to one side of the top of a large chest of drawers may work well – while the same items seem to disappear if they are more spread out. The smaller the objects, the closer the grouping needs to be so that each piece gains strength from its companion.

▷ *Glass with a brass trim*
Arranging these ceramic ornaments into groups with similar colouring and shape gives a pleasing order to this collection of small objects. Tall candlesticks together with the gilt-framed painting and brass shelf edging frame the collection.

◁ *Peach and leaf green*
Leaves, flowers and budgerigars are the theme of this unusual table-top display. The collection of china with a nature theme is complemented by pot plants and cut flowers.

▽ *A formal note*
Polished wood is the perfect setting for this symmetrical arrangement of china boxes and figurines. The trellis wallpaper is an appropriate backdrop for the flowering jasmine.

TABLE SETTINGS

The table arrangement sets the scene for a meal – whether it is a simple bread and cheese lunch or a formal dinner.

It's not necessary to have a vast stock of different china and glass, although, if you can afford it, an everyday plus a 'best' set will give you greater scope. If not, stick to something simple. All-white china or a classic shape in white or cream with just a line of colour around the edge will give scope for a variety of looks. Use plain glasses and add a cloth in a primary colour and checked napkins for an informal lunch, pastel linen and delicate flowers for a summery supper or lace and candles as a setting for dinner.

Table decorations play an important part in creating the style of the setting – fruit, flowers, candles and so on can be chosen to suit the seasons as well as the occasion. Keep central arrangements low or your guests will have trouble talking through it! If you are not using the whole table, you can place the arrangement at one end, if there is sufficient space.

Flowers and fruit

A pastel setting is built around flower-strewn china. The theme is expanded with a frosted fruit and silk flower table centre. The cloth is four quarter circles of fabric in flower shades with ribbon covering joins.

FROSTING FRUIT

It is a simple matter to give fresh fruit a festive sparkle.

To create frosted highlights, brush egg white lightly on to the fruit where required. Then sprinkle with granulated sugar.

For all-over frosting on stemmed fruit, hold the fruit by its stem and dip into the egg white. Turn in granulated sugar to cover, then gently shake off the excess.

▷ *Against the wall*
As the table is pushed against it, the wall here almost becomes part of the setting. Tableware and napkins in an all-over printed design echo the wallpaper's pattern and muted colour. They are set off by tones of plain pink – chairs, cloth and candles.

◁ *Soft elegance*
A setting in pale pink and cream creates a romantic mood and picks up the colouring of trellis wallpaper and painted bamboo furniture. A lace cloth softens the plain one below and candles give a flattering soft light. The arrangement of garden flowers is low enough to allow conversation.

▽ *Versatile white china*
A sophisticated setting where the food is as carefully arranged as the table. The dramatic flower arrangement is the sole indulgence in an almost severe scheme. As it fills the empty sixth place it does not block the diners' view across the table.

A totally different, rustic mood could be created in this plain room by using the same china on a blue and white checked cloth with red cutlery.

DRESSING THE TABLE

Tablecloths can play an important role in linking the various elements of a room into a harmonious scheme.

A carefully-chosen cloth need not only be used to create a well-dressed dinner table by acting as a background for attractive china and glass. It can also play a much more important and permanent role in a room's decoration.

A floor-length cloth on a round display table, for example, can be designed to pick up patterns and colourings used elsewhere in the room, perhaps with a top cloth in an accent colour or a co-ordinating design.

In a rather severe modern dining room with venetian blinds at the window and a large central table, a plain long cloth will provide a softening touch. Square side tables, similarly treated, could serve the same purpose.

The fabric can be used to link differing styles of furniture; a modern, monochrome treatment of a traditional bird or flower design, made up into a simple square or rectangular cloth, helps harmonize modern chairs and antique occasional pieces

If you are thinking of re-upholstering your furniture or putting up new curtains but are not quite sure about your choice of fabric, you could make a tablecloth from a couple of metres just to see how well the colour and pattern fit into the room. This is a safer bet than buying metres and metres of fabric only to find you've made a mistake.

Tablecloths can also add a real finishing touch to a room scheme when they are used to cover unsightly second-hand tables or cheap, unfinished chipboard display tables.

▽ *Lace topping*
The cloths here – a traditionally patterned lace fabric over a plain cotton – pick up the themes of this room. The undercloth is in the warm, sunny yellow of the walls; the top one complements the lace of the curtains. The fresh green of the shutters, which is picked up in the painted furniture, counterpoints the scheme.

△ *Blue and white style*
The way fabric has been used in this rather stark scheme adds a softening touch without detracting from the stylish appeal of the room. The floor-length tablecloth in a sophisticated geometric batik pattern complements the table's rectangular shape and tones with the fabric used to cover the screen.

◁ *Perfect balance*
In this room, with its strong scheme of blue and white, the table has a floor-length cloth in a pattern to match the wallpaper. To balance the strong design, the pattern elsewhere in the room is reduced to a minimum – even the pictures on the wall are in simple, dark tones. The design of the wallpaper and tablecloth fabric has been highlighted by topping the floor-length cloth with another cloth which matches the brightest blue in the design, while the table stands on a rug of the darkest shade.

▽ **Theme of flowers**
The round table with its double layer of cloths is an integral part of this summery room. The undercloth tones with the colouring of the curtain fabric, while the top cloth picks up the colour of the wall; its applique edge echoes the flowery theme of the other fabrics. The whole arrangement creates interest in an otherwise empty corner.

▽ **The perfect link**
Classic furniture from different periods is linked by the choice and style of tablecovering. The undercloth and matching curtains in a stylized floral pattern complement the side table and armoire while the simple blue and white colourway suits the pure lines of the Bauhaus chairs. The top cloth creates a simple backdrop for the table setting.

DECORATIVE BEDHEADS

Transform a basic divan by making a new bedhead or enhance an old wooden bed.

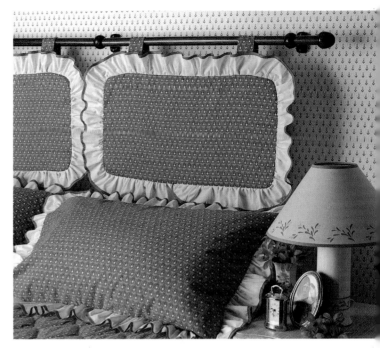

A bedhead makes a dramatic focal point in the bedroom. Some are purely decorative, while others serve a practical purpose as well. Reading or breakfasting in bed is much pleasanter if you have something comfortable to lean on, and a bedhead will also stop pillows from slipping down behind the bed.

There's quite a variety to choose from – including headboards covered in fabric and a hand-decorated wooden bedhead – and all are relatively easy to make.

For greatest comfort, make a bedhead that is padded with wadding or foam and cover it with fabric to match or co-ordinate with the rest of the room.

It's a good idea to choose fabric in a colour that won't show head marks too quickly and that can be sponged clean, or sprayed with a fabric protector such as Scotchgard. A loose cover – slip-over or throwover – is always a practical choice since it can be removed easily for regular washing. Make sure you use a washable Terylene wadding, available in several different thicknesses, to add padding if required.

△ **Cushioned to comfort**
It is easy to hang comfortable cushions with fabric loops from a curtain pole fixed to the wall above head height for sitting up in bed.

Here, a decorative frill with piped trim adds a professional finish.

▽ **Quilted comfort**
A pretty patchwork quilt folded over a pole is one of the simplest ways of making a bedhead. It is padded for comfort and held in place by Velcro strips sewn to the back edges.

▷ **Simple backing**

An eye-catching floral print transforms a humble divan.

The bedhead is made from a piece of chipboard screwed to two wooden battens which are fixed to the divan base. Cover the front and edges of the chipboard with a piece of thin Terylene wadding, and staple or tack it to the back of the board. Then smooth the fabric over the padding and secure with staples or tacks.

▽ **Slip-over cover**

You can give a new look to a plain headboard with a removable, washable cover.

Make the cover on the tea-cosy principle, with plain fabric for the back and padded or quilted fabric on the front. This pretty quilted bedspread is edged with striped fabric for definition.

◁ Lacy touch

Antique cotton lace, draped high above a wooden bedhead, is a decorative touch that suits this pretty Victorian room. The swags are crowned with a posy of dried flowers and spread along the picture rail.

▽ Bed curtains

These drapes give the graceful effect of a four poster without its bulk.

To make your own, mount a semi-circular chipboard shelf (24mm thick) on the wall with a metal shelf bracket and cover the underside with fabric. Make two curtains from lightweight fabric, gather and fix to edge of shelf with tacks. Cover tacks with braid. Hang the sheer curtain from a curtain pole fixed to the wall.

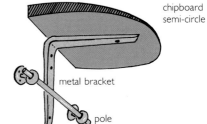

chipboard semi-circle

metal bracket

pole

△ **Buttoned up**
A deep-buttoned fabric headboard is soft and luxurious. If upholstering your own, choose a simple shape with gentle curves that is easy to cover.

▽ **Shelf space**
One way to build a bedhead over an old fireplace – the stepped shelving doubles as a bedside table with space for ornaments and flowers.

△ **Victorian charm**
Flowers and ribbons transform this wooden headboard, and it's easy to achieve the same effect. Buy paper cut-outs made specially for decoupage or cut out suitable designs from a piece of wallpaper. Glue them down, then apply two or three protective coats of clear polyurethane varnish.

PERFECT PATCHWORK

Used as a bedcover, a hanging, for cushions or accessories, cheerful patchwork adds life and colour.

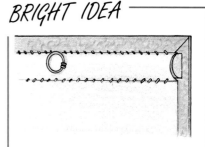
HANGING A QUILT
Cut a 25mm by 6mm batten slightly shorter than the width of the quilt. Using 50mm wide tape, stitch a casing close to the top of the quilt and insert the batten. Sew two curtain rings to the casing 300mm from each end and one in the centre, and hang from picture hooks.

Cheerful, colourful patchwork adds a comforting country air to any room in the house. Use it in the traditional way as a bedcover, or branch out with patchwork cushions, tablecloths, hangings and accessories.

If you are lucky enough to own an original hand-made quilt, the best way to display it is on the wall. Position the quilt where it can be admired, facing seating or a bed. If the quilt is old and valuable, keep it out of direct sunlight as this fades the fabric. A modern quilt, which can stand up to wear and tear, can be thrown over a shabby sofa or chair for an instant facelift. Alternatively, use a piece of ready-quilted fabric.

There is no need to limit yourself to just one big piece of patchwork in a room. Add instant colour and life with a scattering of patchwork cushions – make them yourself in colours to complement your room scheme using a patchwork pieces kit. Skilled sewers can make patchwork lampshades, add a patchwork edging or centrepiece to a tablecloth or stitch placemats to complement china. A patchwork border or edging is also a clever way to lengthen or widen curtains.

Mix and match
You can mix and match patchwork successfully, providing that all the pieces are in similar colours. The quilt on the wall is made in a design called Dresden Plate.

◁ *On display*
If you are lucky enough to own a beautiful original quilt like this wall-hung American pieced design, it can become the centrepoint of a room scheme. The crisp blue and white colouring is complemented by plain soft and dark blue quilts on the bed, and by a paler blue and pink check design on the chaise longue. More patchwork, this time in strong blue-black and white covers the bedside table. The secret of this successful room scheme is the use of one colour in several shades to unify the mixture of patchwork patterns and shapes.

▷ *Patchwork in paint*
The central cross motif of this simple pale green and rose pink quilt is used again and again in this pretty bedroom. The bed headboard, chest and walls are painted in palest pink, then stencilled with the motif, using a template copied from the quilt. The central wheel motif made up in fabric to match the quilt becomes an attractive framed picture. Simple pink and green quilted cushions complete the scheme.

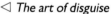

◁ *The art of disguise*
Upholstered seating which is dull, past its best or in a fabric you hate can be given a new lease of life with patchwork. No sewing skills are needed – just drape the quilt over the sofa or chair for an instant facelift. Patchwork in pale, summery colours gives formal seating the right relaxed comfortable look for this cool, plant-filled garden room. The simple padded rag rug reflects the patchwork theme.

BAYS AND BOWS

A curved or angled window adds interest to the outside of a house and can be made into a charming internal feature.

Bay and bow windows can give the effect of living in a goldfish bowl, particularly when the room faces a busy street. It is, therefore, necessary to find a way of giving privacy without blocking out too much light. Curved and angled windows present technical difficulties when deciding how to hang curtains.

Curtains may be hung around the bay to sill or ground length, depending on the style of the room – long curtains being more formal than short ones. If you have a radiator or built-in seat under the window you are limited to short curtains or blinds. Fortunately, there are enough different styles of blind to make windows look tailored, pretty, or grand.

Until recently the only way to hang curtains around a curved or square window was to use flexible track. In some instances the rail incorporates a valance rail to take a frill, giving a softened look. Alternatively, the curtains can be given an attractive heading such as pencil or pinch pleating and hung from a plain track.

It is now possible to buy two different sorts of pole to use in a bay. The first has 'elbows' to join lengths of pole to make up the shape. The second is a system where a continuous brass pole, incorporating a cording action, is bent to suit a particular window.

△ *Maximum light*
A wide square bay has plain white venetian blinds across the front and side windows to filter the sunlight. Only the top portion of the main window is covered; the lower part has glass shelves to add interest.

▽ *Pattern repeat*
Simple, light roller blinds provide shade and privacy, while still allowing light to filter through.

◁ **Breakfast corner**
The bay-shaped window alcove of a basement room has been made into a cosy seating area with built in seating following the curve. To avoid covering too much of the small window an austrian blind was chosen. Dress curtains in matching fabric cover the shutters.

▽ **Frill detail**
To give importance to a bay and to add interest to curtains hung from ordinary curved track, a swagged pelmet has been fitted across the whole area. The bound edge of the frill picks up the theme of the frills on the chairs.

△ **Lowering the line**
Roman blinds plus matching
full-length curtains have an
elegant tailored look which
suits these long sashes. The
partially-lowered blinds,
together with the wide
border either side of an
unusually high picture rail,
visually reduce the height of
this tall room.

▷ **Continuous rail**
A brass rail is decorative
enough to use without
valance or pelmet. This one
is specially shaped to fit the
bay. Four curtains in the
brightest shade of yellow
picked from the upholstery
fabric are looped back at
each end of the bay and at its
corners. The curtains are
generous enough to draw
but roller blinds make it
unnecessary to do so.

△ **Light perfection**
Sheer festoon blinds complement this airy room scheme.

▷ **Room without a view**
Removable panels of painted trellis completely cover these windows and hide an unattractive outlook.

BRIGHT IDEA

MOCK BLIND

You can cover up a window permanently while still allowing it to be easily opened.

You could choose a lightly patterned fabric and stick it to the glass. Alternatively, paint a simple design on to the window with stained-glass paint or cover it with self-adhesive vinyl which looks like stained glass.

PLUG-IN LIGHTING

Plug-in table and standard lamps can be positioned just where needed to create interesting and attractive effects.

There's nothing quite so attractive as a room lit by the warm, comfortable glow of table, standard, or floor lamps.

Positioned on low sofa tables, on shelves, a chest, or a sideboard, a table lamp can be used to illuminate a collection, brighten a dark corner, or provide a pool of light for reading. Table lamps come in all shapes, sizes and styles, so it is easy to find something to suit your room. Lamps which beam light downwards and sideways (usually fitted with a wide-based shade) are useful if you want to light a table top or a corner. Vase-shaped uplighters wash light over the wall and ceiling, an attractive way to show off a painting or an interesting architectural feature.

Tall standard lamps look best in a corner or behind a chair. A lamp with a traditional shade, or a shade which covers the top of the bulb, beams down, giving a comfortable pool of light just right for reading. Modern standard lamps are starkly stylish, adding interest to a simple, high-tech look room. Many of these lamps are uplighters and should be positioned so that light washes a wall or the ceiling.

Floor-standing spotlamps look best hidden behind a display of plants so that light shines through the foliage, throwing delicate leaf shadows on ceilings and walls.

Before you buy lamps, look carefully at socket positions. You may need to have extra outlets installed for lamps to be positioned where you want them. Trailing cable is dangerous and tucking cable underneath a carpet or rug can cause a fire.

Always have new sockets installed by a professional electrician.

A pool of light
A table lamp with conical shade beams light down, adding instant interest and comfort to a corner. This type of light is the ideal way to illuminate a collection of small boxes, plates or figures arranged on a table, or on a display cabinet as shown here.

◁ **Hidden assets**
A chrome floor-mounted uplighter placed below a pair of glass tables adds life and interest to an otherwise dull corner. This type of light can be used to beam through large plants.

△ **Lights fantastic**
Standard lamps combined with recessed ceiling lighting are perfect for this sophisticated room. Floor-standing reading lamps can be angled to suit people using the sofa.

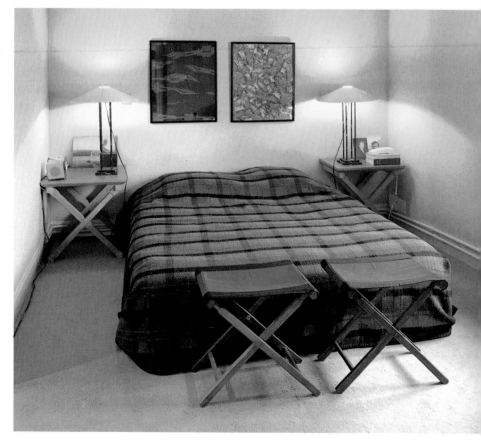

▷ **And so to bed . . .**
The perfect bedside lamp beams light over just half of the bed, so that one partner can read while the other sleeps. Lamps should be tall enough so that the light falls in exactly the right position for reading but not so that the beam hits the reader in the eye.

These two stylish examples are exactly right and tall enough for the shade to be safely out of the way of books and other bedside clutter.

DISPLAY LIGHTING
Successful display lighting is surprisingly easy to achieve.

With forethought and planning, display lighting can be simple to install. First decide *what* you want to display, and *where* it is to be positioned. Utilize recesses on either side of a fireplace and tables in the corner of a room. Use walls for small collectables as well as pictures and prints. Don't let displays interfere with main traffic areas, focus interest on wasted spaces instead. Vary levels of illumination and concentrate light over small areas to add drama.

With clever lighting, displays of sentimental junk can become important, precious objects appear to their best advantage, and textures and colours can be emphasized. Different effects are achieved by altering the position of the light source in relation to the object on display, and the type of light used.

Backlighting throws objects into semi-silhouette. while glass appears to glow.

Display lighting can be concealed or be part of the display itself. Shelves are usually lit with a tungsten filament or fluorescent tube hidden behind a baffle. A recessed downlighter concealed behind a fascia at the top of a run of shelves will provide a more defined beam of light. Sophisticated low voltage cabinet lights are available from specialist shops but remember to leave room for the transformer. Table-top displays are often grouped around a lamp, which can either be in sympathy or act as an accent to the display.

Lighting for valuable pictures and old fabrics should not cause fading or discoloration and plants should not be subjected to excessive heat.

△ *Concealed lighting*
Concealed tungsten strips light the collection of crockery and the work surface, punctuating the run of kitchen units. The pale paint finish helps reflect the light.

▽ *Illuminated corner*
The table display is backlit and thrown into semi-silhouette by the lamp, while the translucent shade emits a warm glow over the two prints and casts light up towards the ceiling.

△ *Multiple light sources*
An eyeball downlighter is directed on to the wall, the plant is backlit by an uplighter and the sofa table displays are grouped around simple ceramic lamps.

◁ *Traditional picture lights*
The most foolproof and efficient way of illuminating paintings eliminates glare and shadows caused by frames.

▽ *Tungsten halogen task lighting*
Localized, intense light and strong shadows emphasize the sculptural qualities of the display.

WINTER FIREPLACES

In winter, a fireplace with the fire lit makes the perfect welcoming focal point for a room.

The fireplace and its surrounding area plays a large part in creating the mood of the room. Take your cue from the fireplace itself when deciding how to treat the wall, mantelpiece and hearth.

A classic marble surround calls for a formal treatment: an imposing fire-basket, with brass fender, fire dogs and implements on the same grand scale. Above it the same formal mood should prevail: a regular grouping of pictures, all of one type, or a large gilt mirror, with a symmetrical arrangement of objects on the mantelpiece itself. On the other hand, a cottagey brick fire-place is complemented by a willow log basket and rustic iron implements. The same informality affects the choice of pictures and objects.

Ancient and modern
A well-lit formal group of a modern painting and ethnic objects contrasts with an Edwardian fireplace.

△ Informal brick
An interesting collection of cottagey pictures and bric-a-brac adds seemingly casual charm to this arched rustic brick fireplace.

▷ Classic elegance
A club fender and an elegant mirror reflecting candle lamps make a formal arrangement to suit this classic hearth.

▽ Modern simplicity
Combine a black cast iron stove with sleek, unobtrusive tiling, modern pictures and streamlined furniture for a touch of Scandinavian simplicity.

BROKEN COLOUR PAINT FINISHES

With a broken colour paint finish, you can add texture and colour to make a room quite unique.

Different paint techniques can be used to create a wonderful variety of textured effects, and they offer an exciting alternative to plain, painted walls or wallpaper.

On the practical side, the soft effect of broken colour is often more flattering to a room than an expanse of solid colour and most finishes will help to disguise rough plaster walls and minor blemishes on woodwork. Dirt marks tend to show up less too.

Broken colour techniques This chapter looks at some of the effects you can create by sponging, ragging and rag-rolling with different colours.

Sponging is easy because you simply dab on one or more colours to create a pretty mottled finish, and the overall colour effect is built up gradually.

Ragging and rag-rolling use bunched up rags to break up and lift off wet paint, producing a loose overall pattern rather like crushed velvet. This is simple to do but you have to work fast to treat the paint before it dries: when covering a large area such as a wall it helps if there are two of you working together.

Paints to work with Sponging is easiest with water-based emulsion paints. However, you can use oil-based eggshell paint for a crisper, stronger-coloured

Pale and interesting

Ragging makes such a definite pattern that you can achieve striking effects with quite muted colours. Here, this ragged finish – using a pale shade of blue over a white base – creates a visually interesting but relaxing background for a pretty bedroom.

The flat blue fabric for curtains and bedding emphasizes the soft, broken colour on the walls.

mottle, while a tinted oil glaze will give soft, translucent prints.

For ragging and rag-rolling, it's best to use an oil glaze. This is slow drying so that you have plenty of time to work on the finish, and it holds a pattern of rag prints distinctly.

As far as the base coat goes, the general rule is to use oil-based eggshell paint under glaze or eggshell; emulsion under top coats of emulsion.

Materials For sponging, a natural sea sponge produces a soft, irregular mottled effect, while a synthetic one gives a crisp, even finish. You can also sponge on paint with a crumpled cloth for a simple ragged effect. For ragging and rag-rolling, you need a good supply of lint-free rags.

It is a good idea to experiment with different colour combinations and to practise the techniques on spare board or card pre-painted with your base coat until you get the right effect.

▷ *A bold finish*
Ragging, along with rag-rolling, is one of the most dramatic finishes when used with bold combinations of colour. Here a pale mushroom background is ragged with a deep rose pink, and light touches of white and grey are sponged on top using a rag, to give an overall pattern of soft crumpled velvet.

The rose pink colour is repeated below the dado.

◁ *Water colours*
A cool turquoise rag-rolled finish works well with bright white tiles and, combined with mirrors, helps to give this small bathroom a feeling of space.

Rag-rolling involves movement so it's best confined to large, straightforward surfaces such as walls; smaller areas – these window frames, for example – can be 'sponged' with a rag to match.

▷ *Blue-on-white*
This mixture of deep blue sponged on to white looks fresh and sharp. The bath panel is also carefully sponged for a smart co-ordinated look.

Sponging with one colour looks best if it's fairly regular, so spend a little time going over patches of thick colour to even out the effect.

◁ *Bright all over*
Here a clever mix of warm, earthy colours, with cool splashes of blue-grey for contrast, is sponged over walls and ceiling: the result is strong and vivid but not overpowering.

Sponging in two or more colours works best with the lighter colour sponged last: remember to space your first prints so that there's room to fill in the other colours.´

△ **Stoney look**
Walls and skirting are lightly sponged in two shades of soft coffee-brown emulsion over a cream base, imitating the mottled appearance of a polished pebble.

The overall effect is cool and uncompetitive.

BRIGHT IDEA

LEAF PATTERN

This plain wooden tray is sponged with a decorative swirl of leaves, with a few touches of gold felt pen added.

To get the same effect, apply primer to bare wood, then two or three coats of emulsion or eggshell paint: rub down between coats using fine wet-and-dry paper with soap and water to prevent scratches.

Cut a simple shape from foam sponge with a sharp craft knife and a pair of scissors. Apply the decorative layer of paint, then a coat or two of clear varnish to protect it.

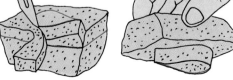

PAINTED WOODWORK

Imaginative use of colour on architectural details can transform a plain room into something special.

There is no rule which says you must paint woodwork white, or strip it, or colour it to merge with the walls.

In a room whose walls, window frames and doors are in the same neutral colour, you could paint the skirting board a clear contrasting colour. This will define the line between floor and walls.

You can enliven plain, flat walls by adding mouldings so as to create panels. Use a heavy moulding and drag the walls and woodwork in the same colours to give a grand 18th-century feel. For a more modest effect, use simple beading instead; paint walls a flat pale colour and beading and skirting to contrast.

On a stepped cornice you could use more than one colour; choose colours on the same side of the colour wheel – say blue and green, or apricot and peach. A dragged or washed finish gives a more subtle effect than a solid colour.

Built-in furniture – cupboards, dressers, radiator covers – can be given greater importance with paint. Give a radiator housing the look of marble or stone or make a dresser more interesting by painting it in contrasting colours.

▽ **In the grand manner**
A plain room has been given a grand look by dividing the walls into panels with beading. Pastel blue paint has been unevenly dragged over a creamy base coat. The wet top coat has then been wiped off raised surfaces.

△ **Simply effective**
A simple way to give smooth walls a modern panelled effect is to stick on pre-cut and mitred mouldings. Bright coral paint picks up the colour of the woodwork and contrasts well with the flat-painted creamy walls.

△ Paint effect

An imposing cornice is given definition
and impact by using two colours – blue and
green. A contrasting raspberry picture
rail adds further interest to cream walls.
The top coat is washed on to cornice and rail
and the walls are rag rolled; these broken
finishes give a softer effect than solid colour.

▽ Stone finish

A built-in unit to house a radiator is given the
appearance of golden marble with ginger
paint dabbed on with a rag over a pale yellow
base coat. Maple-framed pictures above echo
the colouring of the finish. This treatment
would be equally effective on a plainer housing
with a brass mesh front, or simple shelf.

△ Built-in dresser

Paint in strongly-contrasting colours makes a
pleasant alternative to stripped wood for a dresser.
The door frames are in the same green as the
skirting and trolley and pick up the wallpaper
colour. The architrave and panel beading are
in bright corally red. Door panels and chair in a
much paler green stop the effect being too heavy.

PLAIN AND SIMPLE PAINTED FURNITURE

A coat of paint gives old or worn furniture an instant facelift and adds a dash of inspiration to any room scheme.

Secondhand wooden furniture is a sensible, economical choice if your budget is limited or if you have small children. Wooden furniture in good condition looks attractive if it is simply cleaned and polished. Scratched, stained or discoloured pieces can be given a new lease of life with a simple coat of paint. Choose a colour to either complement existing decoration, add a bright splash of accent or provide a contrast.

A painted dining table and chairs work particularly well in a kitchen or family dining room. In such a setting you have scope for imaginative and cheerful colour treatments. You could pick up four bright shades from a blind and use one for each of a set of dining chairs. Or, perhaps, paint the seat, uprights, rails and back struts of each chair in different combinations of all four colours.

In a child's room you could paint each drawer of a white chest in a different colour – blue for socks, red for sweaters and so on – as a fun way to encourage tidiness.

If the room is for an adult, adopt a more sophisticated approach using subtle colours. A utilitarian cupboard can be given a more elegant look by adding fake panels using moulding. Paint the moulding in a contrasting or complementary colour. Moulding can also be added to the doors of bedside tables.

Paint will give your furniture a protective surface which copes well with knocks and spills. When the surface becomes damaged, or you grow tired of the colour, it is a simple matter to repaint the piece.

Party pieces

Ordinary cane seats pick up colours from fabrics and wallcovering in this pastel-coloured dining room. For a tea party the theme is carried even further with beribboned balloons and gaily-wrapped parcels.

▷ **Attracting attention**
Brightly-painted chairs are the focal point of this kitchen/dining room. Four colours – red, blue, yellow and green – have been used in different combinations on each one.

▽ **Panel effect**
This old chest-of-drawers has been painted in one of the colours used to spatter the walls. The chest has been given a coat of eggshell paint in a soft spring green, then 'panels' have been added using a white outline. Knobs are painted to match.

BRIGHT IDEA

Painted lines A plain drawer or door can be given a panel effect with a contrasting painted line.

Draw in the rectangular shape using a soft pencil. Now curve the corners. Make a template for the curve and position it in one corner of the rectangle and hold it in place on the straight edges using masking tape. Using a small brush, paint carefully round the curved edge up to the pencilled line. Repeat with other corners.

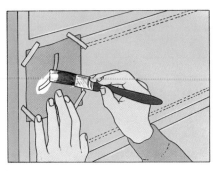

When totally dry, mask off either side of the pencil lines, leaving a small space between of about 2mm.

Paint over the line, leave to dry and remove masking tape. When quite dry remove tape.

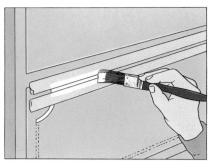

WAYS WITH OLD CHAIRS

Dining chairs which have seen better days can easily be given a new lease of life.

Dining chairs dating from the Victorian period and after are in plentiful supply at junk shops and auctions so prices are usually low. Provided that the chairs are free from woodworm and that the frame is in reasonable condition, they can easily be given a brand new look. Look for chairs with interesting moulding and carving as this allows you to pick out details in a contrasting or complementary colour.

When choosing chairs with upholstered seats, look for examples where the seat is intact. A sagging seat needs re-upholstering which is quite a tricky job.

Begin by checking the frame. If the joints of a chair have worked loose, they should be knocked apart and cleaned, then re-glued and clamped until the glue has set.

The next step is to strip the chair of old varnish. You can do this with paint stripper or try a mixture of meths and thinners applied with fine wire wool. This is just as effective as paint stripper and not as unpleasant to use. Wash the chair frame after stripping to neutralize the stripper, sand lightly, then apply a coat of primer. This is essential otherwise the top coat will not cling. You can paint the chairs using satin or high gloss paint, or eggshell – which is an oil-based paint with a matt finish. Acrylic paint (sold in tubes at art shops) is also suitable and is very easy to apply. Tinted or natural wood stains allow the grain of the timber to show through but are only worth applying if the wood is in good condition, as the stain will not hide imperfections.

Choose the fabric for covering chair seats first, then choose the colours for the frame. These can be either contrasting or complementary.

To paint a chair with a drop in seat, lift the seat out of the chair frame. To re-cover the seats of the three plain chairs, stretch fabric of your choice tightly over the old seat, mitring at the corners for a neat fit. Tack or staple to the underside and return the seat to the chair.

To stencil a chair as pictured, overleaf, rub white emulsion paint into the wood using a cloth. When it is dry, apply a very pale green matt vinyl emulsion. Use a dry brush and apply the emulsion sparingly so that you get a patchy, faded-wood effect. You will need to wipe the brush from time to time to keep it clean.

Use stencil crayons to pattern the chair – a simple design, such as the leaves on the chair overleaf, works best. Apply pattern at random and vary the intensity of colour. Leave the stencilling to dry for two days, then seal with at least two coats of clear polyurethane varnish.

◁ *The plain chair*
Strip, sand and prime the chair. Paint it in just one colour, using eggshell paint which gives a matt finish, or pick out details on the legs and back in another shade, as shown. Cover the seat in a complementary or contrasting fabric.

▽ *The original chairs*
The chairs were selected from this junk shop line-up. Similar models can be found at very low cost. Make sure that frames are free from woodworm and that the seats are intact.

△ **Two shades for success**
Strip, sand and prime the chairs. As this chair has plain paintwork, scratches and imperfections may show up, so fill them with white interior filler. Sand smooth. Paint the main part of the chair in a satin gloss paint to match your chosen fabric and the fancy centre section in a contrasting or complementary colour. Re-cover the seat as described on the previous page.

▷ **Stencil style**
Stencilling looks attractive and is easy if you use stencil crayons. The chair must be stripped and sanded first, then given a base coat of emulsion before stencilling.

△ **The covered chair**
A tailored cover turned this imitation leather 1950s-style chair into an elegant piece of furniture. You can make the cover in plain, even-weave linen or use a furnishing fabric to co-ordinate with curtains or other upholstery. The cover can be removed for cleaning. If using a patterned fabric, be sure to allow enough fabric for the pattern to match at sides.

DESIGNING WITH STENCILS

Add a stencilled border or motif
to walls or furniture to
give a room an individual touch.

Stencilling is an ancient technique which was taken from Europe to America by the early settlers and it has become part of that nation's folk art.

As wallpaper became more popular so stencilling declined, but recently there has been a revival of interest and there is a wide range of ready-made stencils. You can also make your own designs, getting ideas from wallpaper books.

Characterless rooms with bare expanses of wall can be made interesting with stencilled panels or you can use stencils for decoration in much the same way as a wallpaper border – at cornice level or immediately above the skirting.

A stencilled border at picture or dado rail level is a clever way to break up the walls of a high-ceilinged room – it will make the ceiling appear lower. You can also emphasize the good features of a room – perhaps by outlining an attractive arch or stencilling a swag above a pretty window.

▽ *Picking up a motif*
Some motifs call for an informal treatment. Here butterflies from the pattern of the fabric are rearranged in flights. Try out the positions of random groupings on a large sheet of newspaper before you start to stencil the wall.

Above are two motifs for you to trace and enlarge; the paint has been smudged sparingly for a subtle effect.

△ Dresser surround

A stencilled garland of flowers and fruit outlines a dresser and picks up the colours of the china on the shelves. Three ready-made stencil patterns combine to make up the top 'bar', corner 'knot' and pendant.

◁ Climbing roses

A trellis with climbing roses is stencilled over the arch to link this hall and stairway. The motif is taken from the fabric of the tablecloth and lampshade.

▽ Decorative door panels

These bedroom walls and cupboards are painted cream and a border design of a spray of flowers runs round the cornice and cupboard doors. The edges of the doors are finished in beading which frames the stencils.

WALLPAPER BORDERS

Whether walls are painted or papered, you can add a wallpaper border for interest and distinction.

Wallpaper borders provide tremendous scope for decorating. A splash of pattern adds eye-catching interest to plain walls, while a patterned border can be combined with patterned wallpaper to create a well-finished effect.

Visual trickery Borders are particularly useful for dividing up a lot of blank wall space, and are a good solution if you need to alter the proportions of a room visually.

They can be run along the top edge of a wall as a substitute for a cornice – or used instead of a picture rail or dado. If a ceiling is very high, position a border at picture-rail height and decorate the wall above the same as the ceiling. And a border can be used as a divider to give a neat edge between different finishes and colours.

You can mix and match borders too – use one at cornice level and a second at dado-rail height, for example. To make it easy, many borders are available in co-ordinated ranges which include wallpapers and sometimes fabrics.

Choosing a border There are wide borders and narrow ones, in geometric and floral patterns as well as plain colours. You can even make your own border from a wallpaper with a striped design; cut strips using a straight edge and sharp scissors or a craft knife.

▷ **Baby ducks**
This bold motif matches the paper in colour and tone but works on a larger scale. Strips of hearts, trimmed from the edge of the border, are used to outline the tiled area and panelled cupboards.

▽ **Rose border**
A pretty printed border gives this low-sloping room definition, and adds a splash of pattern to plain, painted walls. The same pattern is used on the bedlinen and for the curtain tiebacks.

△ Dividing line

Part of a beautifully co-ordinated range of paper and fabric, this blue-and-yellow border at picture rail height links the two contrasting wallpapers. Depending on the height of your walls, a picture rail should be between 30 and 45cm below the ceiling. Pin a strip in place to check the position visually.

Note how the cornice has been picked out in blue to add definition to the decorations.

△ Flowered edge

These trailing flowers make an attractive feature of the doorway. Continued along the dado rail, the border plays up the dividing line between different finishes – sprigged wallpaper above, plain pink paint below.

◁ Panel games

A wallpaper border, used to create a decorative panel, cleverly focuses attention on a picture in a large space. Or use the border itself as a frame round a picture or mirror by placing it close to the edge.

You can also divide up a large wall with a series of bordered panels.

CLEVER DIVISION WITH DADOS

Dividing walls with a dado rail reduces height and allows you to mix colour and pattern.

Originally called a chair rail (because it prevented the backs of chairs from banging against the wall and damaging decoration) a dado rail is a length of ornamental wood, plaster or plastic which is fixed across walls to divide the height.

The area between the dado rail and the skirting board is called the dado. In the 18th and 19th centuries, this space was usually covered with a hard wearing material, such as wood panelling or a heavily embossed wallcovering. In the 50s and early 60s, it was fashionable to remove dado rails, leaving blank areas of wall.

These days, dado rails are back in favour and are an ideal starting point for a scheme which involves the use of plain and pattern together, two colours, or

for dividing a large and a small pattern, From a purely practical point of view, a dado rail is ideal for dividing the wall in an area where the bottom half of the wall is subject to knocks as all you need to do is redecorate the lower half as needed.

You'll also find a dado rail a useful, easy way to lower the height of a high-ceilinged room. Paint or wallpaper the area below the dado in a dark colour and the area above light. Dado rails can be bought from DIY stores.

A wallpaper border can be used to give a rail effect. Choose a border from a co-ordinated collection and mixing colour and pattern becomes simple, or use the border to divide a paint effect, such as marbling or sponging, from plain paintwork above.

ADDING A DADO RAIL

Rail height The usual height for a dado rail is 90cm from the floor – about one third of the measurement from the floor to the picture rail in a high ceilinged room. If the room is very high, add a picture rail about 30cm below ceiling level. In a room with a ceiling of average height, the rail should be positioned about one third of the way up the wall.

Visual effect A dado rail does not always work well in a modern, low-ceilinged room, so try the effect by running a piece of tape or wide ribbon across the wall before you go to the expense of buying rails.

▽ *Divide and rule*
The use of both dado rail and cornice in this dining room means that warm, sunny yellow can be mixed effectively with paler primrose and plain white to divide the wall space visually and add interest. Imagine this same room with plain, one-colour walls and ceiling and you can see why the dado rail is so useful and effective.

△ In traditional style

This Edwardian hallway shows a dado rail used in the traditional way, with heavily embossed wallcovering below, painted in hard-wearing gloss paint, and a more delicate, patterned design above. White paint links the dado rail with the other woodwork and reflects light from the front door.

The wine-coloured wallcovering and leafy green plants complement the colours used in the stained glass door panel. When a dado rail is used in a hallway, it is usually carried on up the staircase and first floor landing and the same decorative treatment is used.

◁ Mix and match

Using a dado rail allows you to use two designs from a co-ordinated collection on one wall. Here both a dado rail and a border divide an abstract and a floral pattern, both taken from the same collection. The border is used above the dado, along the top of the wall and around the under-stairs alcove, drawing attention to the stronger line of the wood rail.

When using co-ordinated collections, use the strongest pattern below the dado rail and match it to curtains, cushions and other accessories. Here, wallcovering has been used on the central panels of the small cupboard doors – a clever touch which completes the scheme.

▷ Low level interest

This elegant room illustrates the original purpose of dado or chair rails, which was to keep the back of the sofa from touching the wall. The dusty pink colour used beneath the dado rail and the rug in front provide a 'frame' for the patterned sofa.

If you have furniture covered in patterned fabric, always keep the area below the dado plain to avoid a space restricting jumble of colour at floor level. A striped border used above the dado rail echoes the colours used in the fabric and wallcovering.

▽ Linking schemes

A border of butterflies and flowers in cool blue-green and white is used as a 'dado rail' to link this bedroom and landing. Plain blue is used below the border on the landing to complement the pretty small print wallcovering used in the bedroom beyond. The same colour is used on the skirting, window frame and other woodwork to reinforce the link between the two rooms.

BRIGHT IDEA

Divide with tiles A row of border tiles used just under halfway up the wall lowers the ceiling and makes a tall, chilly bathroom seem smaller and warmer. There are many tile collections featuring a patterned tile, matching border tile and plain one for use above.

If the walls are already tiled, it may be possible to remove the centre row and add co-ordinating border tiles. Alternatively, remove the bottom half of the tiles and re-tile with patterned tiles and a border, or simply cover the old tiles with new. Ridge the adhesive to make them cling sufficiently.

▷ **Back to the wood**
If you are stripping doors, window frames and other woodwork, strip the dado rail to match or fit a new rail and stain it to the same shade as the rest of the wood. Stripped wood looks best with country-style patterned wallcovering. Here, a floral stripe is used below the dado rail with a larger version of the same flowers above. The curtains are in matching fabric.

▽ **Make a bold statement**
Although this dramatic black-and-white striped wallcovering would look effective used alone, the addition of a plain black dado rail to match the table, floor tiles and other woodwork adds impact. Bright, scarlet anthuriums bring a splash of warmth to the room.

▽ **Mixing old and new**
This old polished chest seems an unlikely partner for modern metal framed pictures and a stylish lamp, yet the scheme works well. The secret of success is the dado rail which adds a touch of tradition and divides the picture frames from the mellow wood.

WAYS WITH WALL TILES

Tiles are hard-wearing, practical and come in many different shapes, colours and designs.

Ceramic tiles are the perfect choice for kitchen and bathroom walls. They won't peel away from the wall or discolour – no matter how steamy the room – and come in colours and shapes to suit all styles of kitchen unit and bathroom sanitaryware.

Major tile manufacturers offer excellent co-ordinated ranges so that you can successfully mix and match a border, a main body pattern and a patterned inset.

Borders and patterned tiles can be used to create panels of pattern in a wall of plain tiling. Make a rectangle of border tiles and fill the centre with pattern. Many tile ranges feature murals, a picture made up of six, eight, ten, twelve, or more tiles which can be used to add colour and interest to a large plain wall.

There's no need to stick to tiles that match. A collection of Victorian tiles makes a glorious jumble of pattern and colour. If you haven't enough to fill the wall, space them out with plains in complementary colours.

DIAGONAL TILING

Wall tiles look effective fixed diagonally, especially if you use alternate stripes of colour, or graduated colours, starting with pale and working up to dark (or vice versa).

Start in a corner, using a set square to find the first true diagonal. Mark the wall into diagonal stripes the width of the tiles you plan to use. Centre a tile on the true diagonal line, then fill in the space below and at either side with cut tiles. Continue until the wall is covered.

Something old...
Colourful Victorian and Edwardian tiles make a stunning surround and splashback in this unusually-shaped bathroom. Note how dark, fairly plain tiles have been used to make a mock skirting board around the bottom of the bath.

MAKE YOUR OWN MOSAIC

Old tiles need not be in good condition to be of interest. Broken pieces can be used to make a colourful tile mosaic. Tile the wall in the normal way, but leave a section bare (how big depends on how many broken pieces you have). Spread tile cement thickly on the bare section, then arrange the broken pieces of tile in a decorative mosaic.

△ **Formal but fun**

Tiles with an informal pattern, such as these cheerful cherries, can be arranged in a formal chessboard pattern with complementary plain tiles to add a touch of style to a splashback or a worktop. Alternatively, arrange the patterned tiles in a row to make a border with the plains below.

▷ **On the border**

Patterned tiles can be used with plains or with complementary patterns below them to create an interesting border effect. Choose a tile with a pattern towards the top, or look for a tile range which features a custom-designed border tile. These are available in both modern and classic styles.

378

△ In the picture

Unusual picture tiles, like the charming animals, birds and desert scene featured above, are expensive so mix them with budget-priced plain tiles for a clever effect at a sensible price. Here matching plain tiles are used on the worktop and the walls for a smart, practical effect.

▷ 3D drama

Three-dimensional profile tiles make a dramatic frame for a mirror – and can be used to make a mock dado rail half way up a large wall of plain tiling. You can achieve the same effect with trompe l'oeil border tiles.

◁ Plain and simple

Brick-shaped tiles are unusual and effective, especially if you add an interesting geometric design in a contrasting colour, as shown here. Colour could also be added in stripes or squares, depending on the wall size.

△ **Tiling with a difference**
Plain tiles fixed diagonally are more interesting on a large area than conventional tiling, especially if you add a patterned inset.

▽ **Clever deception**
This striped tile design is cleverly patterned so that the tiles look as if they have been fixed to the wall in diagonal lines.

FIXING DIAGONAL TILES

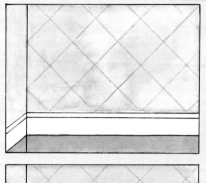

1. Find the true diagonal and mark the wall into stripes.

2. Centre the first tile on the true diagonal.

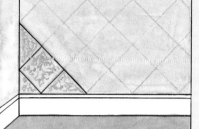

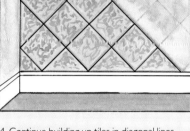

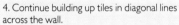

3. Fill in below and at the sides with tiles cut as necessary.

4. Continue building up tiles in diagonal lines across the wall.

INDEX

ACKNOWLEDGEMENTS

Photographic credits

Front cover (t) Robert Harding Picture Library (cl) Marks and Spencer plc, (cr,bl)) IPC Magazines/Robert Harding Syndication, (br) Crown Wallcoverings, 1 IPC Magazines/Robert Harding Syndication, 2 IKEA, 4 Wood brothers ltd, 5 IPC Magazines/Robert Harding Syndication, 6 Tintawn Carpets, 7 Coloroll, 8 Arthur Sanderson and Sons Ltd, 9 Jerry Tubby/Eaglemoss, 11 Sara Taylor/Eaglemoss, 12 Syndication International/Ideal Home, 14(t) National Magazine Co/David Brittain, 14(b) Texas Homecare, 16 Camera Press/IMS, 17 Arthur Sanderson and Sons Ltd, 18 Designers Guild, 19 & 20 John Suett/Eaglemoss, 21 Dulux, 23 Coloroll, 25 Next Interior, 26 Dulux, 33 Simon Butcher/Eaglemoss, 34 National Magazine Co/David Brittain, 35 PWA International, 36 Next Interior, 37 Arthur Sanderson and Sons Ltd, 39 Dulux, 40(t) Syndication International/Ideal Home, 40(b) PWA International, 41(t) EWA/Michael Dunne, 41(b) Habitat, 42(t) Cover Plus from Woolworth, 42(b) PWA International, 43(t) Cover Plus from Woolworth, 43(b) National Magazine Co/David Brittain, 44 John Suett/Eaglemoss, 44 EWA/Michael Dunne, 46(t) Dulux, 46(b) Syndication International/Homes and Gardens, 47 Arthur Sanderson and Sons Ltd, 48(t) Syndication International/Ideal Home, 48(b) Crown Paints, 50 Crown Paints, 51 Habitat, 53 Hazel Digby/Eaglemoss, 54-5 Next Interior, 57 Osborne and Little, 58 Dulux, 59(t) Cover Plus from Woolworth, 59(b) Dulux, 60(t) PWA International, 60(b) EWA/Spike Powell, 61(t) Jerry Tubby/Eaglemoss, 61(b) Michael Boys, 63 Casa Viva, 64 & 65 EWA/Clive Helm, 66(t) EWA/Michael Nicholson, 66(b) Habitat, 67 Dulux, 68(t) Ken Kirkwood, 68(tr) EWA/Spike Powell, 68(b) EWA/Clive Helm, 69 Paper Moon Ltd, 72 EWA/Michael Dunne, 73(t) Arthur Sanderson and Sons Ltd, 73(b) EWA/Michael Dunne, 74 Habitat, 75 EWA/Michael Dunne, 76 Swish Products Ltd, 78 Dorma, 79 National Magazine Co/Jan Baldwin, 80 Syndication International/Woman and Home, 81 Crown Wallcoverings, 83(t) EWA/Di Lewis, 83(b) Crown Wallcoverings, 84(t) EWA/Spike Powell, 84(b) Vymura International, 85 EWA/Michael Dunne, 86 & 87 Sara Taylor/Eaglemoss, 88 National Magazine Co/David Brittain, 89 Camera Press, 90 Schreiber, 91 Arthur Sanderson and Sons Ltd, 92(t) Coloroll, 92(b) Interior Selection, 93(t) Interior Selection, 93(b) Collier Campbell, 94(t) EWA/Di Lewis, 94(b) Jerry Tubby/Eaglemoss, 95(t) Brian Yates, 95(b) The Picture Library, 97 Bill McLaughlin, 98 EWA/Spike Powell, 99 Sara Taylor/Eaglemoss, 100 Arthur Sanderson and Sons, 101 Sara Taylor/Eaglemoss, 102 EWA/Michael Nicholson, 103(t) Maison Marie Claire/Duronsay/Pfeufter, 103(b) EWA/Michael Dunne, 104(t) Next Interior, 104(b) Photon/John Hollinshead, 105 Simon Butcher/Eaglemoss, 106(t) Dulux Paints, 106(b) National Magazine Company/David Brittain, 107 Habitat, 108 Perrings, 109(t) Dulux, 109(b) EWA/Jerry Tubby, 110 The Original Bathroom Company, 111 Kuhlman Own Brand Kitchens, 112-3 National Magazine Company/David Brittain, 113(t) Crown Paints, 113(b) EWA/Spike Powell, 114 & 115(t) EWA/Michael Dunne, 116 & 117 Sara Taylor/Eaglemoss, 118(t) Dulux, 118(b) Sara Taylor/Eaglemoss, 119(t) Habitat, 119(b) Curtain Net Advisory Bureau, 120 Sanderson, 121(t) EWA/Michael Dunne, 121(b) Bill McLaughlin, 122 & 123 Sara Taylor/Eaglemoss, 124(t) EWA, 124(b) Syndication International, 125(t) Dulux Paints, 125(b) EWA, 126(t) Dulux Paints, 126(b) Camera Press, 127(t) Sue Stowell, 127(b) & 128 Sara Taylor/Eaglemoss, 129 Chris Stephens/Eaglemoss, 130(t) Smallbone of Devizes, 130(bl) Jalag/Peter Adams, 130-1 & 131(t) Syndication International, 131(b) Crown Paints, 132 Jerry Tubby/Eaglemoss, 133(t) Next Interior, 133(b) PWA International, 134 Mark Westwood/Eaglemoss, 135 Sara Taylor/Eaglemoss, 136(t) Crown Paints, 136(b) Dulux Paints, 137(t) EWA/Tom Leighton, 139 Sara Taylor/Eaglemoss, 140 Crown Paints, 140-1 Dulux Paints, 141(t) Next Interior, 141(b) Syndication International, 142(t) Interior Selection, 142(b) Sara Taylor/Eaglemoss, 143(t) Bill McLaughlin, 143(b) Next Interior, 144 Sara Taylor/Eaglemoss, 145 Hazel Digby/Eaglemoss, 146(t) Maison Marie Claire/Chabaneix/Peuch, 146(b) Jean-Paul Bonhommet, 147(t) Brian Yates Interiors, 147(b) PWA International, 148(t) Textra, 148(b) Hazel Digby/Eaglemoss, 149(tl) EWA/Michael Dunne, 149(tr) Smallbone of Devizes, 149(b) PWA International, 150 Hazel Digby/Eaglemoss, 151 Sara Taylor/Eaglemoss, 152(t) Syndication International, 152(b) Houses and Interiors, 153(t) National Magazine Company/David Brittain, 154(b) Bo Appeltoft, 154(t) Pallu and Lake, 154(b) Arthur Sanderson and Sons, 155 Syndication International, 156 PWA International, 157 Di Lewis/Eaglemoss, 158(t) Ken Kirkwood, 158(b) Richard Paul, 159(t) Arthur Sanderson and Sons, 159(br) Syndication International, 160 PWA International, 161(t) Syndication International, 161(b) Hygena, 163 Luxaflex Blinds, 164 Habitat, 165 Next Interior, 166(tl) Next Interior, 166(tr) Schreiber, 166(b) Armitage Shanks, 166(br) Cover Plus from Woolworth, 167(t) National Magazine Co/David Montgomery, 167(b) Next Interior, 168 William Douglas/Eaglemoss, 169 Bruce Hemming/Eaglemoss, 170 Simon Butcher/Eaglemoss, 171 Syndication International, 172-3 Habitat, 172(b) Dulux, 173(tr) Allmilmo, 173(b) Syndication International, 174 William Douglas/Eaglemoss, 175, 176 Steve Tanner/Eaglemoss, 177 Jaycee Furniture Ltd, 178(t) National Magazine Co/David Brittain, 178(bl) PWA International, 178(br) C.P.Hart, 179(t) National Magazine Co/Dennis Stone, 179(b) Marks and Spencer plc, 180(t) Coloroll, 180(b) Dulux paints, 181 EWA/Michael Dunne, 182(t) EWA/Spike Powell, 182(b) Pipe Dreams, 183(t) EWA/Michael Dunne, 183(b) EWA/Clive Helm, 184 EWA/Michael Dunne, 185, 186 Steve Tanner/Eaglemoss, 187 Coles and Sons, 188(t) Designers Guild, 188(b) EWA/Michael Dunne, 189(tl) Arthur Sanderson and Sons, 189(tr) Next Interior, 189(b) Arthur Sanderson and Sons, 190 Arthur Sanderson and Sons, 191, 192

Steve Tanner/Eaglemoss, 193 Jalag, 194(t) Dulux paints, 194(bl) EWA/Michael Nicholson, 194(br) EWA/Spike Powell, 195(t) Arthur Sanderson and Sons, 195(b) Camera Press, 196 William Douglas/Eaglemoss, 197 EWA/Andreas von Einsiedel, 198(t) Syndication International, 198(b) EWA, 199(tl) Hamilton Weston Wallpapers, 199(tr) EWA/Jerry Tubby, 199(b) EWA/Michael Dunne, 200 EWA, 201, 202 Di Lewis/Faglemoss, 202 PWA International, 202(t) Osborne and Little, 202(b) Moben Kitchens, 203(t) Syndication International, 203(c) National Magazine Co/Spike Powell, 203(b) Dorma, 204 Dorma, 207, 208 Nelson Hargreaves/Eaglemoss, 209 PWA International, 210(t) Crown Wallcoverings, 210(b) EWA/Neil Lorimer, 211(t) Arthur Sanderson and Sons, 212 Crown Wallcoverings, 213, 214, Steve Tanner/Eaglemoss, 215 Syndication International, 216(tl) Cristal Tiles, 216(tr) Crown Paints, 216(b) EWA/Spike Powell, 217(t) Arcaid/Richard Bryant, 217(b) Magnet and Southern, 218 EWA/Spike Powell, 219, 220 Di Lewis/Eaglemoss, 221 Kingfisher Wallcoverings by Nairn, 222 Next Interior, 223 National Magazine Company/David Allen, 225 Curtain Net Advisory Bureau, 227 Arthur Sanderson and Sons, 14 Jan Baldwin/Eaglemoss, 231 & 234 Curtain Net Advisory Bureau, 235 Harrison Drape, 238 Jan Baldwin/Eaglemoss, 239 Arthur Sanderson and Sons, 242 Jerry Tubby/Eaglemoss, 243 Syndication International, 246 The Picture Library, 247 Swish, 250 Textra, 251 Rufflette, 255 EWA, 257 Curtain Net Advisory Bureau, 258 Crown Wallcoverings, 269 Sunway Blinds, 272 Michael Boys, 273 Habitat, 275 Arthur Sanderson and Sons, 277 EWA/Michael Nicholson, 279 Curtain Net Advisory Bureau, 280 EWA/Michael Dunne, 283 Designers Guild, 287 Sara Taylor/Eaglemoss, 290 Dorma, 291 EWA/Jerry Tubby, 292 Jerry Tubby/Eaglemoss, 295, 297, 299, 302 Jan Baldwin/Eaglemoss, 303 & 304 Syndication International, 306 PWA International, 307 & 310 Tulleys of Chelsea, 311 Today Interiors, 312 Coloroll, 313 Next Interior, 314(tr) National Magazine Company/David Brittain, 314(tl) National Magazine Company/Hugh Palmer, 314(b) Camera Press, 315 Maison Marie Claire/Scotto/Belmont, 316 National Magazine Company/David Brittain, 317(t) Syndication International, 317(b) National Magazine Company/David Brittain, 318(t) Jalag, 318(b) EWA/Michael Dunne, 319(l) Syndication International/Freda Parker, 319(r) Crown Paints, 320(l) EWA/Michael Crockett, 320(r) EWA/Michael Nicholson, 321(t) Crown Paints, 19(b) EWA, 321(t) Jean-Paul Bonhommet, 322(b) Richard Paul, 323 Maison Marie Claire/Hussenot/Penon, 324(t) Camera Press, 324(m) Syndication International, 324(b) National Magazine Company/John Cook, 325(t) Maison Marie Claire/Patau/Bayle, 325(b) National Magazine Company/Jan Baldwin, 326(t) EWA/Spike Powell, 326(b) Jalag/Berndt/Moller, 327(l) Syndication International, 327(r) Sara Taylor/Eaglemoss, 328(t) Dulux Paints, 328(m) Maison Marie Claire/Patau/Postic, 328(bl) Insight/Linda Burgess, 328(br) Sara Taylor/Eaglemoss, 329 National Magazine Company/Jan Baldwin, 330(t) EWA/Michael Crockett, 330(b) Maison Marie Claire/Primois/Belmont, 331(t) PWA International, 331(b) Freda Parker/Eaglemoss, 32(t) National Magazine Company/Jan Baldwin, 332(b) Syndication International, 333(l) EWA/Neil Lorimer, 333(r) Crown Paints, 334(t) EWA/Spike Powell, 334(bl) Mr Tomkinsons Carpets, 334(br) EWA/Tom Leighton, 335(t) EWA/Tom Leighton, 335(b) Victor Watts/Over 21, 336(t) Smallbone of Devizes, 336(b) EWA/Clive Helm, 337 Maison Marie Claire/Patau/Bayle, 338(t) EWA/Michael Dunne, 338(bl) EWA/David Cripps, 338(br) The Picture Library, 339 PWA International, 340(t) EWA/Spike Powell, 340(m) Freda Parker/Eaglemoss, 340(b) Jalag/Uhlrich Ruhde, 341(t) Maison Marie Claire/Chabaneix/Pench, 341(b) Crown Paints, 342(t & bl) Richard Paul, 342(br) National Magazine Company/John Cook, 343(t) Marks and Spencer plc, 343(b) PWA International, 344 Camera Press, 345(t) PWA International, 345(b) EWA/Michael Crockett, 346(t) Marks and Spencer plc, 346(bl) Coloroll, 346(br) PWA International, 347 EWA/Tom Leighton, 348(t) EWA/Michael Dunne, 348(m) Dulux, 348(b) Jean-Paul Bonhommet, 349(t) Faber Blinds, 349(b) EWA/Michael Nicholson, 350 EWA/Michael Dunne, 351(t) Interior Selection, 351(b) Antiference, 352(t) Sunway Blinds, 352(bl) Crown Paints, 352(br) EWA/Tim Street-Porter, 353 David Hicks/John Spragg, 354(t) David Hicks, 354(bl) Freda Parker/Eaglemoss, 354(br) Jean-Paul Bonhommet, 354(t) The Original Kitchen Company, 355(b) Bo Appeltoft, 356(tl) Guy Bouchet, 356(tr) Osram GEC, 356(b) Guy Bouchet, 357 EWA/Michael Dunne, 358(tl) Freda Parker/Eaglemoss, 358(tr) Charles Hammond, 358(b) National Magazine Company/John Cook, 359 Faber Blinds, 360(b) PWA International, 360-1 EWA, 361(t) EWA/Tim Street-Porter, 361(b) PWA International, 362(t) Dulux, 362(b) Chris Stephens/Eaglemoss, 363(t) Crown Paints, 363(b) Cover Plus from Woolworth, 364(l) Arcaid/Richard Bryant, 364(r) EWA/Michael Dunne, 364(bl) EWA/Michael Dunne, 365 Coloroll, 366(t) Camera Press, 366(b) Syndication International, 367-8 National Magazine Company/Max Roberts, 369 EWA/Michael Dunne, 370(l) Syndication International, 370(r) EWA/Michael Nicholson, 371(t) Nursery Window, 371(b) EWA/Spike Powell, 372(l) Arthur Sanderson and Sons, 372(r) Perrings, 372(b) Kingfisher Wallcoverings, 373 Crown Paints, 374(t) EWA/David Lloyd, 374(b) House of Mayfair, 375(t) Sinclair Nelson Designs, 375(b) Brian Yates Interiors, 376(t) House of Mayfair, 376(b) EWA/Andreas von Einseidl, 376(br) Arthur Sanderson and Sons, 377 Richard Paul, 378(tl) Tilemart, 378(tr) EWA/Michael Dunne, 378(b) EWA/Jerry Tubby, 379(tl) Tilemart, 379(b) Guy Bouchet, 380(t) EWA/Rodney Hyett, 380 Cristal Tiles, back cover (t) IPC Magazines/Robert Harding Syndication, (cl,cr) Harris Stencils, (b) Abode Picture Library.

Illustrators

David Ashby (Garden Studios), Craig Austin (Garden Studios), Lindsay Blow, Terence Evans, John Hutchinson, Kevin Jones Associates, Coral Mula, Fraser Newman, Stan North, Adam Willis.